D0640773

OTHER VOLUMES IN THIS SERIES:

SIR EDWARD ELGAR

THOMAS HARDY

JELLICOE

LORD KELVIN

LORD ROBERTS

F 508 *L. Caswall Smith*

J. M. BARRIE
(1921)

J. M. BARRIE

BY

W. A. DARLINGTON

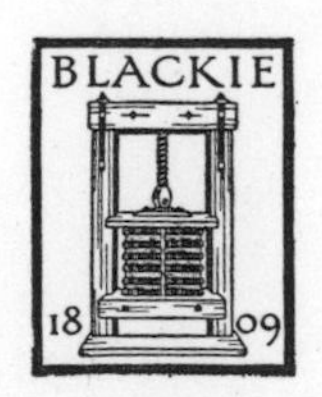

BLACKIE & SON LIMITED
LONDON AND GLASGOW
1938

BLACKIE & SON LIMITED
50 Old Bailey, London
17 Stanhope Street, Glasgow
BLACKIE & SON (INDIA) LIMITED
Warwick House, Fort Street, Bombay
BLACKIE & SON (CANADA) LIMITED
Toronto

First published 1938

Printed in Great Britain by Blackie & Son, Ltd., Glasgow

PREFACE

WHEN I was first invited to contribute a Life of Barrie to this series, the idea at once pleased and disturbed me. There was almost nobody among the authors of my time about whom I would more gladly write; but how could I presume to do so, since I had never known Barrie, and many people without that handicap were available? I told the publishers something of my doubts, and they answered that if I would do what I had previously, in another series, done for Sheridan, they would be well satisfied. This, though encouraging, did not solve my difficulty. It was obviously not possible for me to do anything in the least like what I had done for Sheridan. Sheridan, when I wrote about him, had been dead for more than a hundred years, all those who had known him were dead too, and all private information concerning him had become public property. To go over the evidence, and from it to find out what kind of man Sheridan must have been, was not only a fascinating task but a safe one. Nobody could impugn my right to speak.

It was very different with Barrie. Since I could not write of him with intimate personal knowledge, and since it would obviously not be to the interest of his literary executors (who would no doubt be appointing some one of his many friends, before long, to write a big, full biography) to give me access to any of the new material in their possession, was there anything left which gave me a special right to speak of him at all? Of one thing I was quite determined, that lacking some such special right I must not undertake the task, because a short life of Barrie written after his death, and containing nothing but a re-hash of what had been written about him during his life, was foredoomed to be a dull piece of hack-work. In order to settle this question in my own mind, I began to read some of the books about Barrie that were already in existence, and soon afterwards I wrote to Messrs. Blackie accepting their invitation. I had found a gap on the Barrie bookshelf which I might hope to fill as well as another.

Barrie was a theatre man. He was a literary man of great powers also; but in spite of a hankering after novel-writing that persisted to the end of his life, he let the theatre become his chief means of expression, and he used it with a certainty and a delicate skill that have never been surpassed. Yet I found to my astonishment that not one of the men who have written accounts of his life, whether their prime object was to tell his story or to "place" him as an artist, has had any inside knowledge or experience of the theatre at all. None of the writers in question seems to think that this can matter. Most of them, having dealt with Barrie the novelist, go on quite confidently to measure Barrie the dramatist with the same yardstick, and never dream that the implement is now useless.

My claim to speak, therefore, is that I am, alike by inclination and training, a theatre man. I believe that the theatre is the only place where plays can really be judged; and that if they are to be judged from the printed page at all, the only man who should make the attempt is the man with "a theatre in his head"—the man, that is, whose methods of judgment have been learnt in the theatre, and who can call the peculiar theatrical imagination to his aid. All published plays, therefore, are a snare to the purely literary critic, and Barrie's are particularly dangerous to him because of the form in which they are printed. Barrie, like all other good theatre men, meant his plays to be acted, not read, and for many years would not have them published—though one got into an " acting edition " because he had lost control of the copyright. And when at last he did publish them, he did so in a new form designed to please his own literary sense. He elaborated his stage-directions so much that the plays could be read almost like pieces of continuous prose. Indeed, in one edition of *Alice Sit-by-the-Fire*, he actually did print half of the first act as continuous prose, with the dialogue inserted, like conversations in a novel, between inverted commas.

The theatre-trained man, when he reads a play, ignores the stage-directions as much as he can. They are little use to him. All he wants of them is a bald description of the scene, and some sort of indication what the characters look like. Having got that, he reads the dialogue only, and the performance in the " theatre in his head " promptly begins. The man with the purely literary approach to a play, on the other hand, adores stage-directions, because they are the nearest thing in this form of composition to the descriptive passages which he is used to in novels. And when he comes across stage-directions as full and as enchantingly written as Barrie's, he lets them mount to his brain like wine.

Since I must give chapter and verse for this assertion, let me take an example from the work of a man whose ability I respect and whose book I enjoyed. Mr. Thomas

Moult, after having written about Barrie's novels in a most discerning and illuminative way, goes to pieces when he comes to the plays and says things which I can only account for by suggesting that he is maddened by over-indulgence in the heady brew. In pointing out the beauties of *Mary Rose*, for instance, he quotes a long passage from the end of the second act, where Mary Rose vanishes. Exactly two-thirds of that quotation (yes, I have counted the words) is stage-direction, including a description, exquisitely done, of how the fairy call comes and how Mary Rose receives it. The theatre man, who thinks of stage-directions simply as instructions in the light of which the producer, the designer, the composer and the actors can go about their share of the play, regards all this fine writing as pure waste. What is more, he knows that in this passage as published Barrie is not giving instructions at all, but is describing, seven or eight years after the event, the effect actually made by this scene in the theatre. At the time when the play was written he did not even know what those effects would be, as I shall show in a moment. Therefore, though Mr. Moult's quotation from the stage-directions can legitimately be put forward as evidence of Barrie's *literary* skill, it can prove nothing one way or the other about his ability as a dramatist. Only the few lines of dialogue at the end of the quoted passage can do that.

Barrie's actual stage-directions, as they appeared in the original manuscripts of his plays, were intended not for the delectation of readers but for use in the theatre. They were full, but they were precise and practical, and I have the word of Charles La Trobe, who has been stage-manager at the Haymarket Theatre for many years and was in charge of *Mary Rose*, that they were "extremely easy to work from". He showed me the original typed copy of *Mary Rose* which is preserved at the Haymarket, and so I am able to give the exact words in which Barrie originally expressed his idea how Mary Rose's disappearance should be carried out. Here they are:

The island has begun to "call" to Mary Rose. The sound . . . is soon like a great storm of waves and screaming winds, whose effects may possibly be best got musically but perhaps best by stage mechanism.

That is Barrie the dramatist speaking. The one who captured Mr. Moult's fancy was Barrie the literary man. In the event, the effect *was* got musically. Norman O'Neill was the composer, and he had the idea of adding atmosphere by making human voices call Mary Rose's name through wild music.

Barrie did not like this at first. His suggestion was that there should be some kind of metallic clang, and that Mary Rose should vanish in mid-stage. Holman Clark, the producer, was an adept at this kind of magical effect; but ingenious mechanical tricks, when experimented with at rehearsal, seemed out of place in such a play, and it was the author himself who saw that the best way after all was the simplest, of making Mary Rose walk off the stage as if drawn by some unseen, irresistible force. Barrie's objection to the music still remained, however, and Holman Clark spent the better part of a morning in the orchestra pit making strange unearthly noises without hitting on one which seemed suitable. Meanwhile, O'Neill had written his music, and Barrie was persuaded to listen to it. As soon as he heard it he liked it, and when he came to rewrite his play for publication he described its effect in detail; and so something which Mr. Moult selects as being specially praiseworthy in Barrie's dramatic work turns out not to be Barrie's work at all, but merely his description of O'Neill's work.

The theatre man, of course, does not care whose work it is. It makes no difference to the play whether the stage-directions are in the author's limpid English or have been written in at rehearsal by one of the producer's underlings. One of the stage-directions in the prompt copy of *The Boy David* actually reads as follows:

(SAUL) BRACES HIMSELF THEN THROW JAVELIN INTO TENT, HARPSTOP, SAUL FULL OF REMORSE GOES R. AND SITS DAVID STEALS OUT OF TENT AND GOES UP NEARLY OFF, SEES SAUL DOWNCAST, RETURNS AND STARTS PLAYING HARP, SAUL EVENTUALLY REALIZES ITS DAVID LOOKS AT HIM HE LOOKS UP, AND HEAVES SIGH OF RELEIF.

Barrie neither worded, punctuated nor spelt that entry, which was made when the original javelin scene proved incomprehensible at the Edinburgh first night and had to be altered. The alterations were doubtless made by Barrie himself, but they were entered in the book by anybody who happened to be holding it at the time. Although the result is little better than illiterate jargon, it serves its purpose of setting out the movements of the actors in the new version of the scene; and as the new version was much more effective than the original one, I am sure that the lack of grace in the stage-direction would not trouble the mind of Barrie the practical dramatist. Another stage-direction from the prompt book of *The Boy David* which never got into print contained Barrie's original suggestions for the staging of the death of Goliath. He wanted this event to happen on the stage, so that the audience should see the giant fall. This was attempted at Edinburgh, but proved ineffective, and so in London Goliath died "off". The prompt book preserves both versions of this—the first one blue-pencilled, but still legible—and the original direction reads:

We see Goliath in all his dreadfulness. . . . The proposal is to get this effect—if it can be got—by having his figure out of perspective, helped by stage-craft beyond the capacity of the author. If this idea has to be reluctantly abandoned Goliath should be a genuine giant built up to seem higher than he is, and if this is followed it is not necessary that he should be the person who really speaks the few words that come from his mouth.

Again, the practical dramatist speaks. And indeed, in the published version of *The Boy David*, he speaks for all to hear. Barrie died before he could rewrite this play for publication, and so for the only time some of his genuine stage-directions did at last find their way into print.

This matter of stage-directions is in itself a small one, but it does show how wide is the difference in outlook between those who write about the theatre from the inside and those who come to it from without; and difference in outlook leads inevitably to difference in judgment. Mr. Moult, for instance, dismisses *The Twelve-Pound Look* as "an anecdote", adding with an air of faint surprise that "many people have taken it seriously"; and then goes on to give half a page of panegyric to *The Will.* Well, that may seem a sensible judgment to a man who sits at a desk examining the two plays in cold print, with no " theatre in his head " to help him, but it is not a judgment with which many theatre men will concur. Among theatre people it is a fairly general opinion, and most certainly it is mine, that while *The Will* is an excellent piece of craftsmanship, *The Twelve-Pound Look* is the best one-act play that Barrie ever wrote. As to its being an anecdote, even at his desk Mr. Moult ought to have observed that the two plays have exactly the same theme—namely, the emptiness of a merely material success; but he would have to go to the theatre to find out that, before an audience, the warm humanity of *The Twelve-Pound Look* makes it much the more impressive statement of that theme.

I must not carry this argument farther, or it will seem to have a polemical tone which is very far from my purpose. I make no apology, however, for stating my case thus fully, for I have always found that the purely literary critic is very reluctant to admit that his method of approach to the theatre invalidates his judgment. Barrie was a literary man in his study, a theatre man on the stage, and the difference between the two was always very clear in his mind. Therefore, when a big authoritative "Life" comes to be written, it should be done by some writer with a claim to be listened to with equal respect in the world of books and in the theatre world. But till that big book appears, I hope that there may perhaps be room for a little book written, as I am bound to write it, chiefly from the theatre's point of view.

There is a formidable list of people to whom I owe acknowledgments. To Barrie's literary executors, Lady Cynthia Asquith and Mr. Peter Davies, I am grateful for permission to quote from Barrie's writings, published and unpublished, and for the benevolent attitude they have adopted during the writing of the book. Sir John Hammerton has earned gratitude from all writers about Barrie, for his big book *Barrie: The Story of a Genius*, not only contains a vast store of facts but also shows where to look for more. In passing, however, I feel that I ought to warn future searchers after truth that this book, written by an exceedingly busy journalist, bears signs of hasty proof-reading; there are occasional inaccuracies of names and dates, usually so obvious that they must be slips of the pen rather than genuine mistakes. But Sir John has avoided the worst mistake into which writers on Barrie have tended to fall, that of copying another's blunders. He has gone to original sources for his facts, and so has done admirable pioneer work for all who come after. Besides this general tribute I must give him my personal thanks for help, advice and the run of his Barrie library, all placed most generously at my disposal.

To Miss Irene Vanbrugh I am under a special obligation, both for letting me ransack her clear and detailed memory, and for lending me her treasured copy of *Ibsen's Ghost*. To Sir Seymour Hicks my debt is almost as great, for putting his memory and his scrap-book at my service. Mr. Golding Bright, who lent me the prompt book of *The Boy David*; the management of the Haymarket Theatre, who let me have their prompt copies of *A Kiss for Cinderella* and the revival of *Quality Street*, and the original typescript of *Mary Rose*; Mr. T. C. Irving, who allowed me to use Barrie's schoolboy letters to his brother, which were first published by Mr. E. V. Lucas in the *Sunday Times*; Mr. Harold Forrester of Edinburgh, who not only gave me access to those letters but made with his own hand accurate copies of them for me to keep; all these go to swell the tale. As for that walking encyclopædia of stage lore, Mr. John Parker, a man whose accuracy of mind is positively frightening, I do not know what I should have done without him. He seems not only to know his own vast tome, *Who's Who in the Theatre*, by heart, but also to be able, at any moment of the day or night, to provide from memory a commentary on its entries. He has given me much information, and to him must go the credit for the rediscovery of Barrie's theatre articles in *Time*; for he drew my attention to a reference to them in Walter Sichel's autobiography. Also, he has corrected the proofs of this book, which is, humanly speaking, a guarantee of its accuracy as to dates.

I have not found it necessary to quote substantially from Barrie's novels or plays; indeed, I have avoided doing so of set purpose, because this is a short book, and once one begins quoting Barrie it is almost impossible to stop. For the occasional sentences that I have used I make acknowledgment to the publishers, Messrs. Hodder and Stoughton; and I am indebted to Messrs. Duckworth for permission to quote from *Dogs and Men*.

One more note. There are two stock threadbare adjectives which Barrie once asked a gathering of critics not to use of his work. I have not used them here. Except in this sentence, " whimsical " does not appear; and if " elusive " has crept in anywhere, that is only because it has eluded me.

CONTENTS

ILLUSTRATIONS

Chapter I

LEGEND

WHEN James Matthew Barrie died on 19th June, 1937, full of age and honours, he had led the life of a hermit for nearly thirty years. In his quiet flat high up in the now vanished Adelphi Terrace in London, overlooking the Thames Embankment, he saw few people, and his public appearances were so rare that each was treated by the newspapers as a nine days' wonder. Even in private, among his friends, he was apt on occasion to withdraw into himself. At such times he would sit wrapped in a sad silence out of which nothing could tempt him.

That a man so famous and so solitary should become a figure of legend even in his lifetime was inevitable. In these days, any man of mark who is detected in the act of trying to keep himself to himself is considered to be acting in a manner prejudicial to good order and the public interest. If no intimate details of his life are known, Rumour will invent some for him. If such details are known, Rumour will embroider them. Only by sacrificing his privacy can such a man hope to be known for what he is; generally he prefers to acquiesce in his own legend.

Barrie did more than acquiesce in the legend concerning himself. He outdid Rumour at her own game. In his youth he kept silence about himself, or at least, entered the confessional only in disguise, as the Little Minister or the schoolmaster of Glen Quharity; but in his later years, when he had added public speaking to the arts in which he excelled, he became communicative, and sometimes added to the legend characteristic touches much more picturesque than any that Rumour had been able to invent, but even less reliable.

I make this point at the outset, for it is fundamental. Anybody who proposes to write (or, for that matter, to read) a biography of Barrie must have it always in mind. The chief source of information about Barrie is Barrie himself. In *Margaret Ogilvy*, in *The Greenwood Hat*, and in many of his speeches he has given us a wealth of autobiographical detail, always set forth with supreme craftsmanship and bearing the stamp of truth. But its truth is the truth of the artist, not of the historian. Barrie wrote about himself as he wrote about a character in a play or book, selecting, rejecting and inventing what material he needed to make his creation lively and life-like. He must not be relied on for exact dates, or for accuracy concerning the places where things happened or the order in which they happened. Again and again, in *Margaret Ogilvy* or in the speeches, he telescopes into one sentence of continuous narrative events which in fact were separated by many miles and many months.

The clearest and most detailed example that I have found of Barrie's way of mixing fact and fancy in his autobiographical passages is the story of the fascinating widow. This lady made her first appearance (in her bereaved state, that is) on 5th March, 1935, at the luncheon given by *The Daily Telegraph* to the committee which was to organize Marie Tempest's jubilee matinée at Drury Lane. Barrie proposed the toast of Miss Tempest in what proved to be his last public speech. Delivered in his customary manner, without inflection of voice or expression of face, with the speaker's eye fixed for much of the time on the ceiling, this speech was an enchanting farewell performance. He began by explaining to the company that he had once done Miss Tempest a great wrong, and that although she did not even know of the incident, he was now going to take a long-sought opportunity to confess and apologize.

"Know then," he went on, "that in ancient times, when I was a boy and Miss Tempest was still unborn, I played in school theatricals and had the part of a captivating widow in a picture hat to which my long tresses were secured with glue. . . . The years rolled on and when I came to London I naturally went to see Miss Tempest, the young actress they were already all talking of. Conceive my shock when I found her playing *my part*! . . . I said to all who would listen that I thought Miss Tempest quite good, but that she seemed to me to lack some of my womanly touches."

It is not probable that many people who heard this anecdote believed that the widow had ever existed except in the speaker's imagination. But some might have remembered that before her widowhood she had appeared in an earlier speech, and had then been played by a different actress. This was at Dumfries on 11th December, 1924, when Barrie was presented with the freedom of the borough. He had been at school there, and his speech—one of the finest he ever made—was packed full of intimate personal reminiscence, in which occurred the following:

My first play was very properly written for the Dumfries Academy Dramatic Society, on whose boards I also made my only appearances as an actor. That was due to the histrionic enthusiasm of an Academy boy, certainly the best amateur actor I have ever seen, who I am glad to know is here to-day, and who blushes so easily—at least he blushed easily a century or two ago—that I shall cleverly conceal his identity under the name of Wedd. . . . Our Wedd was truly great in low comedy, but not so convincing as a young lady with her hair attached to her hat, the sort of part for which he usually cast me. . . .

. . . I think I did greatest credit to our admired Wedd on one occasion when the curtain rose on my husband and me about to partake of breakfast, and in his stage-fright my husband pulled the table-cover and its contents to the floor. How would a superb actress have risen to that emergency? I have asked some of them—Sarah Bernhardt and others—and none of them conceived anything equal to what that Adèle did. (Adèle was my name, I was taken from the French; but the unworthy youth who played my husband *would* call me Addle, to my annoyance.) I went behind him, and putting my arms round his neck—yet not forgetting even in that supreme moment to be wary about my hair and hat—I said, " You clumsy darling!" The house rose—I don't mean they went out. Several of them cheered, led on by Wedd who, when not actually on the stage himself, was always somewhere in hiding, leading the applause. Thus was a great comedienne lost to the world. The next time I saw that play was in London, with Miss Irene Vanbrugh in my part. You can guess I was critical, and she was nervous. I told her I thought her good, but that she was lacking in some of my womanly touches.

On first encountering those two passages I was inclined—as, I think, the reader will also be—to reject the Tempest-Bernhardt-Vanbrugh references altogether as mere Barrie-isms, and to be very sceptical about the remainder of the story. But when, for the purposes of this book, I began to read what was known of Barrie's youth, I was astonished to find that the main facts were precisely as he gave them in the Dumfries speech. In 1876, Barrie was honorary secretary of an Amateur Dramatic Club founded at Dumfries Academy by Wellwood Anderson, son of a local bookseller, and original of " Wedd ". In March, 1878, the Club produced a triple bill, which included *The Weavers*, described on the programme as " Mr. J. L. Toole's favourite comic drama in one act ". Barrie had the part of a young wife in this play, and her name was Adèle.

There is no record of any play called *The Weavers* having been produced at Toole's or any other London theatre. This has discouraged biographers from making any attempt to identify this play, and has led two or three writers to make the entirely unfounded assertion that Barrie wrote it himself. In actual fact, it was *The Spitalfields Weaver*, a farce by T. Haines Bayly, an old piece dating from 1838, which Toole was fond of reviving. When he took it out on tour, however, he sometimes changed its title to *The Weavers* on the ground that Spitalfields meant nothing to playgoers who did not know London. Like most English plays of its time, it *was* (as Barrie says) an adaptation from a French original. Toole gave it a run at his own theatre beginning on 25th January, 1890, at which time Barrie was living in London and could well have seen it. And a programme of this production yields two more striking pieces of evidence in proof of Barrie's accuracy. One is that the name of the heroine is spelt not " Adèle " but " Adelle "—a clumsy Anglicization (assuming that it is not a misprint) which may have been a justification for the youth who pronounced it " Addle ". The other is that the part was played by Irene Vanbrugh. Furthermore, Miss Vanbrugh appeared, under Toole's management, in the two first plays of Barrie's ever to be produced on the London stage, *Ibsen's Ghost* and *Walker, London*; and when I asked her whether Barrie did in fact make the remark to her about his " womanly touches ", she answered most positively that he did indeed, she believed after a rehearsal of the latter play, and that it was a standing joke between them for years.

All this goes to establish what I believe to be the truth, that though Barrie sometimes took an impish delight in decorating or even fantasticating his own portrait, he never falsified it. There are many points of detail in the Dumfries speech which are pure invention—for instance, the statement that he wrote his first play in order to get away from female parts; the facts being that the play in question was written before he had acted any parts at all, male or female, and that his appearance as Adèle (or Adelle) took place a year and a quarter later. But we have seen that the tale is true in all its main essentials. What, then, are we to think about those parts of the story which cannot now be corroborated or denied? Are we to believe, for instance, that the " clumsy darling " incident happened, or to dismiss it as a happy invention? For myself, I am inclined to believe it, if only because Barrie repeats it in *The Greenwood Hat*, the book in which, because it was written originally for private circulation among his friends and not for the public eye, he seems at last to be aiming at unadorned autobiography. But I realize, all the same, that in the case of Barrie we can lay down no comforting hard-and-fast rule such as Lewis Carroll's Bellman made for himself, that what he tells you three times is true. Each unsupported statement must be examined on its merits, and be believed or not accordingly. We should do well, also, to keep before us Barrie's own confession that in writing *The Greenwood Hat* he abandoned the idea of giving the book a subtitle *Memories and Fancies*, " not being always sure, despite the best intentions, where the memories became fancies and the fancies memories ".

This account of the life of Barrie, then, lies before us like a pleasant but treacherous water-meadow which author and reader must cross in company. To the casual eye it may seem all solid earth, but we know better. We know that it will prove to have places where the earth will sink suddenly under our feet; but so long as we remember to distrust those spots where the grass seems greenest and most inviting, I have hopes that we may arrive at the other side together and in fairly good order.

Chapter II

EARLY YEARS

KIRRIEMUIR in Forfarshire is a small place of fewer than 4000 inhabitants and was smaller still when Barrie was born there on 7th May, 1860. Five miles east by south of it is Forfar, the county town. Five miles due south is Glamis Castle, which was known to the world at large chiefly for its ghosts until it gave a Queen to the British throne.

The town stands in beautiful country at the foot of the Grampians. It has some historic and antiquarian interest, and the much prized right to call itself a "regality"; but it is not in itself specially notable. The opposite view has been strongly expressed by partisans, for the Scot, like the American, is apt to rhapsodize about his "home town". But only natives will dissent with any passion from the general opinion that Kirriemuir's best claim to fame is the fact that the ninth child of a poor weaver living in the Tenements on the Brechin Road became a great writer, and described his birthplace in his books.

Ten children in all were born to David Barrie and his wife—known even to her family by her maiden name of Margaret Ogilvy, in accordance with an old Scots custom. Of these ten, three were boys. Two of the girls died in infancy nine years before James was

BARRIE'S BIRTHPLACE, KIRRIEMUIR

born. Of the other five, only Jane Ann Adamson Barrie, the third of the family, enters much into her youngest brother's story. But James's brothers—the one directly, the other in the most roundabout of ways—shaped his career. Alexander, the eldest, was senior to James by eighteen years and looked after his education. David, the second brother, was killed on the eve of his fourteenth birthday. James was seven at the time, and his feeling for his mother, already profound, was deepened by the sight of her unassuageable grief until it became the great passion of his life and the acknowledged inspiration of all the best of his work as a novelist.

David Barrie, the father, was a little better off than most of the weaving community, and his house in the Tenements was a good one by their standards. But the most that a hand-loom weaver could earn in a week was little more than a pound, and the house, though better than the ordinary weaver's two-roomed cottage (in the Scots phrase, a but-and-ben) had only four small low rooms.

Money went much farther in those days than it will now, but the achievement of David and Margaret Barrie in bringing up a large family in such conditions with a high standard of self-respect was something on the heroic scale. David does not figure largely in his son's writings, though he is always spoken of with respect when he does appear; but it is clear that he was a man of great force of character. He had little education himself as a young man, but he had a great veneration for learning. Not only did he determine that his sons should somehow have the advantages that he had himself missed, no matter what sacrifice that might entail upon himself; he also contrived, in such spare time as he could get, to acquire for himself a considerable culture.

He had his reward. His son Alexander, a man of similar temper to his own, went to Aberdeen University and had a brilliant scholastic career. And David himself, when he was fifty-six and his young son James was still only a child of ten, was able to adapt himself so well to the new conditions brought in by the introduction of the power-loom that instead of being compelled, like many other hand-loom weavers, to yield up his position as bread-winner to his daughters, he found himself appointed to a position in the counting-house. His days of grinding economy were behind him for ever. Until that time came, however, David divided his time between his loom and his books, and may perhaps have seemed a withdrawn and formidable figure to a sensitive little boy.

David Barrie was a pillar of the South Free Church, and here the family worshipped. Margaret Ogilvy had been born into another Communion, the Auld Lichts, who were the strictest and poorest sect of all those into which the Presbyterian Church of Scotland had split after the Secession of 1733, and the keenest heresy-hunters. Margaret left them on her marriage, and it was entirely by hearsay from her that James got his knowledge of them. It is odd to reflect that he never in his life set foot in the Auld Licht Kirk in which his Little Minister preached and round which the lives of so many of his characters revolved.

Not much is known in detail of James's earliest years. James Robb, two years his junior, was one of his chief friends among the village boys, and the friendship between them endured all their lives; but though Robb was ready to speak about their joint exploits as children, he put nothing on record that was thrilling or unexpected. Barrie was no infant prodigy. He played the usual games, got into the customary forms of mischief, and did not strike either his contemporaries or his family as being in any way remarkable. He was not even particularly small for his age at this time; nor had he developed the shyness that became characteristic later.

At the age of six or so he went to a school kept by two maiden ladies, daughters of a retired minister, Mr. Adam. This was obviously the original of the Hanky School in *Sentimental Tommy*, which was so called because at prayers the children were required to use their handkerchiefs as praying-mats. The rule was made in the interest not of the pupils' comfort but the preceptresses' carpet—though it must be a moot point whether a small boy's handkerchief is less likely than his knees to harm a precious fabric. This school did not pretend to offer very much in the way of teaching, and James did not stay there long. He went on to the South Free Church School, and there began his serious education. But as it turned out, his time here also was short. In 1867, Alexander Barrie, who since his graduation had been running a private school at Bothwell in Lanarkshire with the aid of his eldest sister Mary, was appointed classical master at Glasgow Academy. He was now in a position, by taking his little brother under his wing, both to direct the boy's studies and to help the family finances. Accordingly, James Barrie was entered in the school roll of Glasgow Academy on 19th August, 1868.

To leave home at the age of eight must have been a

wrench for him, for already his feeling for his mother had gone beyond the unthinking acceptance of early childhood. In the book that he wrote about her after her death, he tells, in a passage that has the print of sincerity in every line, how he first came to realize her, when he was six years old. To be precise, his age was six years and eight months on 29th January, 1867, when the news came that young David Barrie, who was at his brother Alexander's school at Bothwell, had fallen on the ice and had badly hurt his head. A second telegram, which reached the parents when they were waiting at the station for the train that was to take them to David's side, told them that the boy was dead. Perhaps he was Margaret's special pride among her children. At all events the shock of the news went near to killing her; and when she recovered from the long illness which followed upon it, she was no longer the woman she had been, but frailer and more frightened of the things that life could do to her. So it was that James first remembered her as a woman with a soft face and timid lips, and knew only from hearsay that there had been a time when her face was not so soft and her lips not timid at all.

This long illness determined the lives of two of Margaret Ogilvy's children. Her daughter Jane Ann, then a girl of not quite twenty, dedicated herself to her mother's service from that time, and never left her until, three days before Margaret's death, she died herself; and James, though necessity took him often from his mother's side, was in his own way even more deeply dedicated. It was Jane Ann who, coming from her mother's room with her face full of anxiety, told James to go in and say to Margaret that she still had another son. The little boy paused inside the door, frightened by the darkness and the silence. He heard a listless voice say, "Is that you?" and, thinking she meant David, he said in a little lonely voice, "No, it's no him, it's just me." The wisest doctor in the world could have devised no better way of making her forget for a moment her own unhappiness. He heard a cry and, though it was too dark to see, he knew that she was holding out her arms to him.

From that moment he set himself to coax his mother back to her customary cheerfulness, and his efforts had about them a childish pathos that often left her between laughter and tears. If he saw anybody in the village do something that made others laugh, he ran to her room and did it before her. He kept a record of her laughs on a piece of paper, and a great moment came when, at the instigation of the doctor, he showed her the paper and told her what the strokes on it meant. She laughed twice then, once at his explanation and again when he entered a stroke for the first one. Slowly she got better, but ill or well she was from that time onwards his inspiration and his ideal. Going away to school only intensified his feeling, by making him more sharply aware of it.

Little is known of his Glasgow life. It lasted less than three years, and came to a natural end when Alexander Barrie resigned his mastership there. The Academy records show that James won a prize in his class and a prize for religious knowledge, and give a bare account of his attendances, but there is not one line in all his own writings which can be related to his Glasgow school life. It must, however, have been from Glasgow, during a school holiday, that he paid the momentous visit recorded in *Margaret Ogilvy* when, at the age of eight or nine, he had his first taste of a way of living more spacious than his own. The relative he was visiting kept a servant, who was therefore to be James's servant also while he was a guest in the house. His relative met him at the station, a sister greeted him at the house door, but he chafed at every delay dictated by good manners, so eager was he to go into the kitchen and make sure that the servant really was there. Everything goes to show that this relative was Margaret Ogilvy's brother, David Ogilvy, a divine of some eminence (he was made a D.D. of Aberdeen on his retirement in 1896). He had a manse at Motherwell, near Glasgow; and the sister of the story was either Mary, the eldest, or perhaps Sara, now a girl of fifteen, who afterwards became her uncle's adopted daughter and was his housekeeper for many years.

Not long after this the Barries' own lives achieved a greater spaciousness. In 1870, David Barrie was at last rewarded for his years of patient self-education, and was given the post of factory clerk in Laird's Linen Works at Forfar. In May of that year the family removed from the cottage in the Tenements to another in the county town which, though it too had no more than four rooms, was altogether a grander affair. James was at home for this adventure, and made the journey perched on the cart that took the furniture. Margaret Ogilvy was not well enough to take any active part in the removal. She stayed with her lame neighbour, Bell Lunan (Mrs. Addison) for three weeks, and did not go to Forfar till her family had settled in.

For a year after this move James stayed on at Glasgow Academy, which is a fairly clear indication that his brother Alexander wanted to continue to keep an eye on him. But Alexander resigned his mastership at the Academy in June, 1871, and became an assistant inspector of schools connected with the Free Church of Scotland, probably with the prospect of getting a government inspectorship as soon as the new Education Act took effect. He still made Glasgow his headquarters, but his work took him about the country, and he was no longer able to look after his young brother. Accordingly, James went home and entered Forfar Academy. Exact dates are lacking here; but there is in existence a school photograph, taken at Forfar in the summer of 1871, which shows James and eighteen other boys grouped demurely in front of two top-hatted and ferociously hairy masters.

It is probable that James was sent to Forfar Academy merely as a temporary measure, till Alexander should have settled his own future. However that may be, he was not to stay there even so long as that. His father, who had proved a great success at his office job, was now given the appointment of confidential clerk at the Gairie Linen Works, the new firm which was bringing the power-loom to Kirriemuir, at Whitsuntide, 1872. Early in that year, therefore, the Barrie family went back to its native town, not to a cottage any more but to the upper part of an imposing new villa named Strathview.

It is not very important that we should know exactly how much schooling James Barrie got during this period, or where he got it. What is important, in the light of his later development, is that from the time he left Glasgow Academy till he joined his brother again at Dumfries he was living at home. This was a space of two years, at what he has himself described as the most impressionable age of a boy's life, and the most vivid to look back on. During these two years his imagination was alive, alert and creative; and it had abundant material on which to thrive, for he was hearing from his mother the innumerable stories she had to tell of the Kirriemuir of her youth, out of which he later made his best novels. During these two years, also, he and she began to read together books borrowed from the library at a penny for three days, or bought by patient saving. He went about in a world of romance, out of which not even the fisherman's intentness on his prey could tempt him. He was now, as always, the keenest of anglers; but he lost trout because his mind was wandering when they nibbled. Boys who were his friends at the Forfar school remembered in after life how on their walks he would hold them entranced with stories told at enormous length and embroidered with minute detail.

Also, if we are to trust his own statement that it was in a garret that he first tasted blood, it must have been towards the end of these two years that he conceived the idea of putting down his stories on paper, for not until it moved into Strathview had the Barrie family possessed a garret that was habitable. To this apartment James retired to write tales of high and impossible adventure, into which no character was admitted whose counterpart he knew in real life. His heroine was borrowed from a series of magazine stories which had particularly caught his fancy. She was a seller of water-cress, and was all the more romantic in his eyes because he did not know what water-cress was. Later on, when he came to write in good earnest, he had learnt enough to substitute the men of his own world for the knights on black chargers in these tales of wonder; but the water-cress lady kept her hold on his imagination. It took him years to get her out of his system, if indeed he ever did. But from the time he encountered her his mind was made up as to his future calling. Literature was his game.

Chapter III

SCHOOL AND COLLEGE

THIS first adventure into the literary life was brought to an end by the operation of the Education Act, under which in 1873 Alexander Barrie was appointed Her Majesty's Inspector of Schools for the Dumfries district, and took a house in that town with his sister Mary to look after him. Here, when the new school year began in the autumn, James joined him and was entered at Dumfries Academy, where he was to stay for five years.

The reason Barrie himself gave for writing no more stories at this time was that he went to a school where cricket and football were more esteemed. He might with equal truth have said that he had come to an age when cricket and football were more esteemed by him. All the evidence—and there is a good deal of it, one way and another—goes to show that during those important years of development he had little of the difficulty in joining in the life of a community which was increasingly his characteristic in after years, and that he lived a normal schoolboy's full and care-free life. He himself said, long after, that those five years at Dumfries were probably the happiest of his life.

This was perhaps due to a lucky accident. Like most shy people, Barrie responded easily to genuine friendliness in others. It was his great good fortune, therefore, to make a life-long friend on his very first day at Dumfries Academy. This was a boy called Stuart Gordon, who came up to him in the playground, and, after a short, impromptu and mutually satisfactory examination in the works of Fenimore Cooper, told him he liked his cut, and enrolled him a member of his pirate crew. Gordon, whose father was Sheriff Clerk, lived in a house with a large garden on the banks of the Nith; and in this garden the pirate crew, night by night, enacted " a sort of Odyssey that was long afterwards to become the play of *Peter Pan*". Barrie's own accounts of this meeting differ in detail, as usual, but they agree in substance, and they show how he escaped the danger that overhangs a shy boy at a strange school, of failing to find kindred spirits and so being driven in upon himself.

So it came about quite naturally that, apart from the cricket and football, he was too busy living his stories to have time to write them. His chief recorded connexion with letters at this time is the fact that he kept the pirates' log-book. Later on, when he had outgrown piracy, he reached the age where self-consciousness deepens and self-criticism begins. At this age it is the habit of the schoolboy author-in-embryo to slake his passion for playing with words by taking what seems to other boys an unnatural interest in his set compositions in school and his letters to his friends out of it. If he " writes " at this stage, he does it in secret. Here Barrie's development was along completely normal lines, as is shown by a packet of his letters to a friend which has come to light. The friend, Peter Irving, had just left Dumfries Academy and gone into a lawyer's office in Edinburgh; and in the first letter Barrie, aged fifteen, announces his progress from one Latin book to another with a clever boy's slightly ponderous humour:

> Balbus is no longer—he fell down from one of those eternal walls and broke his back (at last) Caius has fled from the city for good and all, Cæsar and Phæthon have retired into private life, Pyramus has got thirty days for stealing a gold watch (I'm afraid he was a bad lot) and Thisbe has committed suicide (hanged herself with the garden rake).
>
> Virgil and Sallust rule triumphant now . . .

After more of this, he goes on in a more ordinary style to record the splendid fun he had had in the holidays, and to recount the average number of fish he had caught. And in a postscript marked " Private " he adds a typical bit of schoolboy scandal: " Dunbar *is* going it with the girls this year out walks nearly every night with them especially Minnie Jocelyn. You are not to mention I told you this to any one *here*." But throughout this earliest extant specimen of Barrie's writing, as in all that follow, is the sense that he enjoys writing for its own sake. The craftsman is already at work polishing his set of tools, though he has no idea yet what use he is going to make of them. It is no surprise to learn from a letter in the following year that he has had highest marks in the English Literature paper, or from one written a year later still that he expects to get an essay prize. In fact, there is talent in every one of these letters, though not a single premonitory spark of genius. What is more, the letters show him joining in every sort of activity in school and out. He takes part in the discussions of the debating society, but likes best of all " the monthly meetings for recitations, readings, &c. I gave one thing at one of them, 'The Stuttering Minister's Speech', which rather took." He is reading Ballantyne and Jules Verne. He is going to see *As You Like It* and Sanger's Circus. He and a boy called C. Wilson walk to Carlisle and get a paragraph in the paper under the heading "Plucky Pedestrians". He goes to Kirriemuir for the holidays (staying at Pathhead Farm—the original of T'nowhead in the Thrums books—evidently because now that his home was with his brother at Dumfries, there was no bed for him at Strathview), and is uncertain whether the better way of spending a Saturday is to fish in a burn depleted by drought, or watch Kirriemuir play Dundee at cricket.

These are remarkable letters because, and only because, they would not have been remarkable if they had been written by Dunbar, or C. Wilson, or any of the other boys mentioned in them. And they explain how it came about that when one of those boys, Wellwood Anderson, started an Amateur Dramatic Club, Barrie was not only one of the first members to be enrolled, but entered with zest into the preparations for the first public performance. In one of the letters (undated—but it must have been written in the autumn term of 1876) he says: "You really must excuse me, but I have never been so busy since I came here." The reason is "rehersals", at which "we have good fun". The play is *Paul Pry*, in which W. Anderson is playing the name-part, and has bought a wig for 13*s*. 4*d*. Barrie has invested 13*d*. in whiskers, and paid the "enormous sum of 2*s*. 6*d*", for an engine-driver's hat. The public performance is looming near, for the first dress rehearsal is to be held that very night, and Barrie hopes to be able to enclose a programme before he shuts his envelope.

That programme, if Peter Irving ever got it, would show that the entertainment in prospect was a triple bill, in which the first play was to be Clement Scott's *Off the Line*—for which, no doubt, the engine-driver required his half-crown hat, and perhaps also thirteen pennyworth of whisker. It would also give Peter Irving two interesting pieces of information not included in the letter. One was that in *Paul Pry*, the last play of the three, Barrie was to get into skirts and play Phœbe.[1] The other was that the middle play was to be *Bandelero the Bandit*, Barrie's own first effort as a dramatist. Nearly fifty years later, Barrie volunteered some amusing but entirely untrustworthy information concerning this composition, in which, he said, he himself played a part compounded of all his favourite characters in fiction, entailing so many changes of clothes that he was hardly ever on the stage.

He was now an author confessed, and though he did not attempt the dramatic form again while he was at school, he tried his hand at both prose and verse, in a manuscript magazine called *The Clown* which Wellwood Anderson brought out. To this he contributed *Reckolections of a Skoolmaster, Edited by James Barrie, M.A., A.S.S., LL.D.*, which ran through four numbers. Also, in secret, he wrote—or, to be quite precise, has several times said that he wrote, for here no corroboration is possible—a vast novel called *A Child of Nature*, full of cynicism and impassioned love-scenes. He sent it to a publisher, who thought it was the work of a clever lady and offered to publish it for £100. Meanwhile, tradition says, the young author actually got his first taste of

[1] Dumfries Academy was a mixed school, but no doubt it was unthinkable in 1876 that the girls should act with the boys.

print by reporting his school cricket matches for the local papers.

It was in the second year of the Dramatic Society, and Barrie's last at school, that the famous performance of *The Weavers* was given. This too was part of a triple bill, one of the other plays being *The Shufflerig Party*, in which Barrie played the Rev. Heavycloud Weatherdull; and it is worth recording that in this part he sent his audience into fits of laughter by that same solemnity which was later his great asset as a public speaker. The date of this event, the last of his school career of which we have any exact knowledge, was March, 1878.

In one of the Peter Irving letters, written from Pathhead, Kirriemuir, in the summer holiday of 1876, Barrie says that he *thinks* he will be going back to Dumfries for another year at school, and that if he does he will have to work hard as he is likely to go on to "Aberdeen College", which had been his brother Alexander's University. In actual fact, as we have seen, he went back for two more years. Why the idea of Aberdeen was given up and Edinburgh substituted is not known, but a reason can be suggested. We know from *Margaret Ogilvy* that Barrie's expressed intention of becoming a writer was received by his parents at first with amused indulgence, which deepened into alarm as time went on and his purpose held. We know that his mother gave up with reluctance her dream of seeing her youngest son a minister or a professor, and that her sympathy with and pride in his writing was a thing of slow growth. It is possible, therefore, that in this letter's uncertainty whether he is going back to school even for another year, and in the subsequent change of plans concerning

College, we have echoes of the family arguments which must have been going on at this time concerning Barrie's future.

It can be only a guess, but it is a guess that fits the facts, that Barrie's own idea was to leave school in 1876 and begin fitting himself at once for a writing career; that his family, fighting a rearguard action to save what could be saved of their own plans, managed to persuade him to go to College and take his degree; and that he then decided to go to Edinburgh in order to study English Literature under David Masson. This guess is supported by a remark made by Barrie himself in *An Edinburgh Eleven*, written six years after his graduation: "Though a man might, to my mind, be better employed than in going to College, it is his own fault if he does not strike on someone there who sends his life off at a new angle." He goes on to say that in his case the someone was Masson.

If this was in fact the idea, it was amply justified by events. Professor Masson was a fine man and a great teacher, and his influence on his pupils was profound. It is difficult to believe that those four years could really have been "better employed", even though it may have seemed to the twenty-eight-year-old Barrie, looking back, that it had been a great waste to have spent half his life as an intellectual adult in grinding economy and hard work for a degree which was never to be any practical use to him. He spent those four years in constant and leisured contact with a man who not merely wrote well himself but was the cause of good writing in others. And Barrie—the young Barrie—needed guidance. He had great facility, which might have been fatal to him if it had got out of hand. As

Stevenson saw, there was a journalist at Barrie's elbow even when he did begin his career. Without Masson's influence that journalist might have taken charge so completely that the deeper Barrie, of whom we confidently use the word " genius ", might have been hard put to it to contend with him.

So far as the chronicling of plain facts is concerned, there is little to say of Barrie's University career. He made no personal mark at Edinburgh as he had at Dumfries. He did not shine particularly as a scholar, though he always did well in his English Literature papers, and excited Masson's personal interest.

In *An Edinburgh Eleven* he has sketched in the background against which his life was lived at this period. These character-studies of the outstanding figures of his University give us glimpse after glimpse of the students' conditions, which formed a combination of plain living and high thinking unknown in English college life. He tells of students so poor that they played Box and Cox in their lodgings, one reading while the other slept, so as to avoid paying for two beds. He tells of students who died under the strain of semi-starvation and overwork. He shows us the gaiety of youth rising superior to hardship, he tells us of " rags " and the battle of wits eternally waged between professor and pupil. But of himself and the part he played in these matters he says hardly a word. These were the years which turned him from boy to man, but only by inference and guesswork can we trace that development.

Yet when the inferences all lead clearly in the same direction, the guesswork can be done with confidence. One marked change that these years brought to Barrie was the growth in him of that acute shyness which was characteristic for the rest of his life. By the end of 1880, this had taken such a hold of him that when his sister Isabella married Dr. Murray in the Christmas vacation of that year, and a wedding-party was given at Strathview, James could not at first be induced to appear at all. At last he yielded to great pressure and came in long enough to recite, with intense dramatic fervour, *The Dream of Eugene Aram*—a delightful period touch, this. As soon as the performance was over, without speaking a word to anybody, he departed and was no more seen.

If a happy schoolboy, at ease among his fellows, can be so quickly transformed into a violently self-conscious young man, he must have been subjected to some very powerful influence. What was this influence? No easy theory will do, such as the one hitherto found sufficient, that Barrie has been working hard at College and so has formed, all of a sudden, the habits of a recluse. For one thing, there is no evidence that he worked particularly hard for his degree; for another, the effect is out of all proportion to the cause.

A much stronger, simpler and more satisfying reason for the change in him can be suggested. At school, where he had his assured position as a senior and prominent member of the community, and where he was surrounded by boys and girls of all sizes and ages, the fact that as time went on he grew no bigger would be taken for granted both by the boys and the girls. In fact, the only proof on record how the girls in the Academy regarded him is his own story that they held a plebiscite to decide which boy in the school had the sweetest smile, and that he headed the poll. But when he left, and joined a community of adult strangers, his small size must at once have made him conspicuous in a way that rankled, and was to go on rankling, in his mind for many years to come. All at once he became aware that he was, to use his own words, " as thin as a pencil but not so long ".

This phrase comes in *The Greenwood Hat*, where Barrie is describing his twenty-seven-year-old self, "James Anon", on the way from Scotland to St. Pancras to deliver his assault on London. He follows it with another illuminating sentence: " Ladies have decided that he is of no account, and he already knows this and has private anguish thereanent." Later in the same book he elaborates this description: " In short Mr. Anon, that man of secret sorrows, found it useless to love, because, after one look at the length and breadth of him, none would listen." And the best proof that this sensitiveness about his lack of inches had already begun while he was at College is to be found in *An Edinburgh Eleven*, in the character-sketch of the great Professor of Greek, John Stuart Blackie. Out of his enormous class of students the Professor would ask a small number to breakfast, choosing his guests apparently at haphazard, since they were distinguished neither scholastically nor socially. It was Barrie who saw that the only thing the Professor's choices had in common was the possession of some physical peculiarity which had happened to strike his notice.[1]

As for the development of Barrie's writing at this time, that can be judged only by its results in after

[1] A sentence which may be significant in this connexion occurs in the speech made by Barrie in 1930, when he was made Chancellor of his old University. Referring to the lack, in his day, of such things as hostels and unions for students, and the social atmosphere they give, he said: " The absence of them maimed some of us for life."

years. He wrote nothing at the University which has survived. On the other hand, it was during these years that he learnt to write. He learnt, as most other authors have had to learn, by that weary system of trial and error which at the beginning consists almost entirely of error. Essays on " deeply uninteresting subjects ", a volume on the older satirists, a story about Mary, Queen of Scots—all these were projected or begun. By this time, we must suppose, his mother had come round completely to the idea that he must be an author, so that he no longer needed to conceal his ambitions for fear of hurting her. About this time it must have been that he had a conversation with her that was to prove strangely prophetic. He had discovered somewhere a dictum that a novelist who knows himself and one woman really well is better equipped for his labours than most. He talked this over with his mother, who remarked that he already had half the necessary qualification, as he knew himself; and then they laughed together over the ludicrous notion that as she was the only woman he knew well, he must make her his heroine.

So he groped his way forward, writing nothing that anybody wanted to print except some dramatic criticisms for *The Evening Courant*. These can have brought him in little money and less fame, but they were immensely valuable to him all the same. Not only did they give him useful practice in journalism; they enabled him to go more regularly to the theatre than his pocket would have allowed, and to indulge his love for and increase his knowledge of the stage. His interest in the theatre was always a practical thing. Even as a schoolboy visiting the little theatre in Dumfries, he always tried to get a seat at the side so as to rid himself of stage illusion and watch what was going on in the wings; and later in life, while he seldom went to see a play, he was always interested in rehearsals. This preoccupation with the process of manufacture rather than the finished article is most significant.

He took his degree on 21st April, 1882, but he returned to Edinburgh after the summer vacation to look about him for work, and to use the University Library for his book on the satirists, which was to begin with Skelton and Tom Nash, and which actually was half-written before its author found something of more immediate importance to do. The unfinished manuscript lay about for years as a dusty memento of a venture into the academic side of literature for which he had no real bent, and which he was never to repeat.

It is easy enough to see why he started out on it. The worship of erudition for its own sake, a common Scots characteristic which his father and elder brother possessed in more than common measure; his four years' sojourn in scholastic surroundings and his personal admiration for Masson—all these were influences strong enough to impose upon him a sense that his passion to write ought not to make him waste his scholarship. All about him were people who believed that in the domain of letters it was better to know things than to do things—people who would have seen nothing odd in the shocked exclamation of a maiden lady whom he told, about this time, that he was to be an author. She flung up her hands and said: "And you an M.A.!"

In fact, education had now done all it could for him, and it was high time for him to migrate to another world, where it mattered nothing to anybody whether he was an M.A. or not. Some such reflection must have passed through the mind of John Morley, who, having the young aspirant presented to him, asked what sort of things he proposed to write. Barrie mentioned three subjects, *The History of Universities*, *A Life of William Cobbett*, and (of course) *The Early British Satirists*. Morley " decided that the young man was too grave a character to make a living out of literature ". It was a very natural decision, and we have good cause to be thankful that it was a wrong one.

Chapter IV

JOURNALISM

IF Barrie's family had been reconciled with difficulty to the idea of his writing for a living, they made amends now. His mother was already quite won over, and was sharing with mingled pride and trepidation his most ambitious plans. And his sister Jane Ann actually gave him his start. She found an advertisement in a paper, and suggested that her young brother should answer it. He did so, backing his application with a testimonial from Masson, and was promptly engaged as leader-writer on *The Nottingham Journal.* The salary was £3 a week, which he and the rest of the family thought an enormous sum; and, what was more, it was to begin at once. In the midst of his joyful preparations for his journey, however, it suddenly occurred to him that leaders were things that he had always skipped, and that consequently he knew neither how they were written nor what they were about. He need not have been disturbed, if he had only known. His intensive practice in writing essays on deeply uninteresting subjects was just the training he needed for the task (indeed, when asked to send a specimen of his work he submitted a treatise on *King Lear*). However, this was a discovery he had yet to make for himself, and meanwhile he collected all the newspapers in the house—from the linings of boxes, from under the carpet, from down the chimney—and sat down to learn his job.

Once in Nottingham, where he arrived early in January, 1883, and over his first strangeness — of which we get a full account in Rob Angus's arrival at Silchester in *When a Man's Single*—he settled down quickly into the collar. What he had wanted was a chance to work, and now he had it in full measure. He was expected to write twelve columns a week. Besides his daily leaders, which were never less than a column in length and might run to two or more, he contributed a weekly article and a weekly column of random notes to the paper, and filled up the required measure with book reviews. Such practice was exactly what he needed. To write all day and every day, with the knowledge that what he wrote was going to be printed and published whether it was good or bad, was an admirable tonic after his experience as a free-lance, trying his luck with contributions that were all misfits. All through his time at Nottingham, which he afterwards used to speak of as a year, but was in fact nearly two, he kept up this enormous output.

The Nottingham Journal was a casually run paper, and, though its circulation did not enable it to aim at a very exalted standard, it prided itself on having a literary flavour. This was very fortunate for Barrie, for it enabled him to write of subjects familiar to him. The line that separates the aspiring amateur writer from the professional is often very fine indeed. A man may find that he has crossed that line unconsciously almost overnight; and once the professional certainty of touch has come to him, he finds that many of his amateurish efforts, which editors have scorned, only need rewriting in the light of his new knowledge to be acceptable.

This now happened to Barrie. One of his earliest signed contributions to his paper (he used the pen-name " Hippomenes " as his signature) was *The Complete Playgoer*, a satire in dramatic form which appeared in three parts. Hammerton, who ran this to earth in the files of the paper, describes it as " quite the crudest and most amateurish thing " that Barrie printed. Yet it may have had some success locally; for when, in the summer of 1883, the *Journal* published a serial story called *Vagabond Students* in its weekly supplements, the advertisements proclaimed that it was by the author of *The Complete Playgoer*. The first of these compositions was published almost immediately after Barrie's arrival in Nottingham; the second deals with the adventures of some students of " a Northern University " during the Long Vacation. It is therefore not so much a guess as a certainty that Barrie brought both these manuscripts with him in his box when he came South.

Others of his weekly signed articles show signs of having been conceived in the academic rather than the journalistic atmosphere. An essay on *Lear's Fool*, for example, is exactly the kind of thing that might be suggested by some casual remark of Masson's in the lecture-room, but has an air of unexpectedness in the columns of a small provincial daily paper. It must have given him a feeling of satisfaction to know that the days of his apprenticeship had not been entirely without practical use. Meanwhile, he was getting the majority of his subjects from the world about him, and developing the true journalist's knack of being able to turn out a readable article on anything or nothing. He had at all times a prodigious capacity for hard work and this enabled him to keep up with his task; but never can three pounds a week have been much more thoroughly earned in the history of newspapers. He also put into the paper a comedietta called *Caught Napping*.[1]

His industry was not appreciated, however. H. G. Hibbert, who afterwards made a name in London as a writer of gossip about the stage, was sub-editor of *The Nottingham Journal* at the time, and has given an account of the paper and Barrie's connexion with it. Actually, the *Journal* was being allowed to die by its two owners, who had inherited it from their father without inheriting his enthusiasm. (It was amalgamated with *The Nottingham Express* in 1887.) There was no editor, and Hibbert, made responsible at the age of twenty for the make-up of the paper, found himself entirely at the mercy of the real autocrat of the office, the foreman printer—the original of Penny in *When a Man's Single*. This man divided all " copy " into two categories. There was news, and there was " tripe ". News had to go in; " tripe "—which included everything that Barrie contributed—had to take its chance. According to Hibbert, Barrie took his work with great seriousness and suffered horribly under this treatment.

Hibbert's home was in Nottingham, and his mother befriended Barrie. His account, though it is too floridly written to be trustworthy in small detail, and though it shows the gossip's desire to tell a good story rather than the historian's determination to get at the truth, is really the only responsible first-hand evidence of Barrie's

[1] This is almost certainly the play mentioned in Hibbert's *Fifty Years of a Londoner's Life* as having been written for Minnie Palmer, although the title is there given conjecturally as *Polly's Dilemma*. A copy of *Caught Napping* came recently into the market and agrees with Hibbert's description in several striking details.

life in Nottingham that we have, and it must be given due consideration. According to him, Barrie had an immense sense of his importance, due not to vanity but a natural feeling of superiority to his surroundings. He was shy, and painfully sensitive; yet—a touch that matches exactly with the account of his behaviour at his sister's wedding—he rather fancied himself as an actor, and on the slightest provocation would give an imitation of Irving as Romeo and Modjeska as Juliet. He had an exquisite delicacy with regard to women. He drank nothing. He made no friends, and was morbidly unhappy all his time on the *Journal*.

This may be an absolutely true record. It is easily possible that among the easy-going, rather raffish group of young men who staffed the three local newspapers Barrie may have felt too strange and miserable to look for a congenial spirit. Yet one of those young men was Barrie's life-long friend, T. L. Gilmour, who appears as Gilray in *My Lady Nicotine* and under his own name in *The Greenwood Hat*. He was on the *Journal* with Barrie, and since three years or so later they were to share lodgings in London, it seems reasonable to suppose that their friendship may have begun now.

One thing is certain, however. Happy or unhappy, standoffish or shy, proud or humble, Barrie never regarded Nottingham as anything but a place where he could sharpen his weapons for the assault on London. As soon as practice enabled him to turn out his weekly twelve columns without completely exhausting his energy and his stock of subjects, he began to spend his spare time writing articles intended for any London paper that would take them. Frederick Greenwood of *The St. James's Gazette* showed an interest in his work, but his first acceptance came from another editor when, on 9th August, 1884, W. T. Stead of *The Pall Mall Gazette* printed an article of his called *The Manufacture of Penny Numbers: By a Manufacturer.* It came just in time to give him encouragement, for a few months later his engagement with *The Nottingham Journal* was terminated, and he went back to Scotland to become once more, and to remain, a free-lance. It has usually been assumed that Barrie resigned his post in order to go up to London and try his luck, but this can now be conclusively shown to be wrong. Hibbert, who was on the spot, has no doubt that Barrie was "sacked", though he is vague about the reason, suggesting at one moment that Barrie was considered to be writing above the heads of the local readers, at another that he chose a tactless moment to ask for a rise in pay, and at yet another that he was a victim of the proprietors' decision to do without a leader-writer in future, and to buy their editorial opinions from an agency at three-and-six a column. In corroboration of Hibbert's belief is the attested fact that at some time while he was at Nottingham Barrie applied, unsuccessfully, for a vacant assistant-editorship on *The Liverpool Daily Post.* In the absence of exact dates, it is a permissible guess that he applied as soon as he knew that he was not to stay with *The Nottingham Journal.*

At any rate, sacked or not, he left Nottingham in the autumn of 1884, and made no move towards London until the following spring. Hammerton, who was editor of *The Nottingham Express* ten years later, long after it had swallowed the *Journal*, made a thorough search of the files of the old paper, and gives 27th October as the last date on which Barrie contributed to it. Almost immediately afterwards, on 8th November, a very lively article appeared in F. W. Robinson's weekly, *Home Chimes*, signed J. M. Barrie and entitled *A Night in a Provincial Newspaper Office*. This was the first contribution bearing his name that ever appeared in a London paper, and its appearance must have been an epoch-making event for him. Probably it meant much more to him at the time than the anonymous publication, nine days later, of a contribution to *The St. James's Gazette*; but to the older Barrie, looking back on this exciting time, it was clear that the second article was in truth the epoch-making event. It was called *An Auld Licht Community*, and it represents Barrie's earliest realization—which came to him, in his own phrase, as unlooked for as a telegram—that there might be something worth writing about in his native place.

Where and when this idea, which was to carry him to fame and fortune, actually came to him is a puzzle which we can solve only conjecturally. Barrie himself confuses the issue hopelessly, for in *Margaret Ogilvy*, writing with the idea of simplifying this part of his life into a few sentences, he makes two irreconcilable statements. One is that it was nearly eighteen months after beginning his leader-writing that he had his inspiration. The other is that he sent his mother a copy of the paper containing *An Auld Licht Community* a few days afterwards. If the first statement is true, Barrie thought of the article in Nottingham somewhere about July, and either he or Greenwood was very slow with it. If the second, he thought of it after he had got back to Scotland, wrote it at white-heat, and did indeed, as he says, see it in print in a few days. The second version of this story seems to me so much the more likely that I reject that "nearly eighteen months" with no misgiving at all; Barrie is never so misleading as when he is being vaguely particular about dates, though he is usually to be trusted when he gives a date precisely. It may be objected that if he was back in Scotland he would not have needed to *send* the article to his mother, since he could show it to her. The answer to that is that on leaving Nottingham he probably went not to Kirriemuir but to Dumfries, to his brother's house, which was still his home. Certainly it was from Dumfries that he left for London in the following March.

The odd thing is that when Barrie sent off his first Auld Licht article he thought that he had exhausted the subject, and next tried Greenwood with something different. Greenwood rejected it, but softened the blow with the remark: "I liked that Scotch thing—any more of those?" Almost immediately, of course, some more of those Scotch things were forthcoming. Meanwhile, *Home Chimes* had taken a couple of short stories, and Barrie began to wonder whether the moment for going boldly to London had not arrived. He had a little money in hand, saved from his Nottingham salary, and he was confident of his ability to live, if need be, on a pound a week. Some time in March he wrote to Greenwood, asking him for advice on the point, and promising to abide by his decision. Greenwood advised him to stay where he was for the present, and within a week Barrie packed the stout wooden box which had seen his uncle, his brother and himself through their University careers, and took train for St. Pancras on the night of 28th March, 1885.

He describes his arrival at the end of that journey next morning as the romance of his life. Here he was at last in London, the city he knew almost by heart from the maps he had pored over with his mother when they discussed his future, always with an uneasy look at the green patch marking Hyde Park, where unsuccessful authors from the country were understood [1] to pass their nights shivering on the seats. But not only that. As he dragged his big box to the left-luggage office his eye fell on a placard of *The St. James's Gazette*. It read, "The Rooks Begin to Build," which was the title of an article Barrie had posted from Dumfries a few days before. It was an omen. London had welcomed him, and he went off with a high heart to find a room near the Museum, in which he intended to do much reading—and which he was destined never to enter for that purpose—and to buy a top hat in which to approach Greenwood. This hat was religiously used for its appointed purpose and for no other, except to give a name, forty-five years later, to its owner's last book.

Before noon on that day, he says, he sat down at his desk (which had "the size and methods of a concertina") to begin four years of the most ferocious hard work that ever a free-lance writer went through. His own estimate is that he wrote something over eight hundred articles in that time, of which one hundred and forty were accepted in the first two years. He mentions casually two 20,000-word stories, also, which brought him three guineas apiece. He went through a lean time to begin with, for after his initial success with the Rooks, he wrote fourteen rejected articles before finding acceptance with one called *Better Dead*, but he was never in any danger of occupying one of those dreaded seats in the Park. And by the time two years

[1] Erroneously, of course. Nobody passes the night in Hyde Park.

were up he must have been within sight of that ambition, so high that the young man who arrived at St. Pancras hardly dared formulate it even to himself, of some day earning a pound a day. Greenwood and Robinson of *Home Chimes* continued to take a good deal of his work, and outside London he soon found a ready market in *The Edinburgh Evening Dispatch*. He got his connexion with this paper through Alexander Riach, its London correspondent, who was also on the staff of *The Daily Telegraph* and had become one of Barrie's earliest and best personal friends. When Riach was made editor and went back to Edinburgh, Barrie's contributions to his paper became regular and frequent.

Just after the first two years in London were up, two things happened which made 1887 a memorable year for Barrie. Robertson Nicoll, who had founded *The British Weekly* in the previous year, saw an article of his in *The Edinburgh Evening Dispatch* and invited him to become one of his own contributors; and Barrie published his first book, *Better Dead*, which came out in November, 1887, though it is dated 1888 on the title-page. These two events, in themselves unconnected, have a considerable joint significance. They mark very definitely the end of one period in Barrie's development as a writer and the beginning of another.

The point is this. Barrie's claim to greatness as a writer lies in an ability, peculiar to himself, to mix satire, sentiment and humour. Only at the times when the three elements mix in exactly true proportion can he do his truest and finest work. In all his early writings the most characteristic of these three elements, sentiment, is rigorously excluded. He knew how strong it was in him, and he distrusted his ability to control it. In that character-sketch of his young self in *The Greenwood Hat* from which I have already quoted is the pregnant statement that James Anon " hates sentiment as a slave may hate his master ". Against this tyrant his best protection was satire, and therefore in these early years the more satirical he was the safer he felt. This, I suggest, is the reason, which in after life he failed to discover for himself, why the coldest, emptiest and most completely unfeeling of all his satirical ideas should have appealed to him as being worth expanding into a book. *Better Dead* is a very small volume, published at a shilling. It begins in Scotland—not at Thrums, but at Wheens—with a chapter in which Barrie carefully makes fun of everything that is nearest to his heart. Then it brings the hero to London, and involves him in the doings of a society for murdering any citizen who has come under its notice as having made himself a public nuisance. The book is written in short, jerky, snip-snap sentences as unlike Barrie's later style as can be imagined. Satire is there in abundance, humour in plenty. Sentiment is not so much absent as outlawed. And the whole is a negligible little book, which was published at the author's expense and lost him £25. It was the first and last time that he ever wrote, in book or play, of Scottish scenes and characters without that warm feeling which came later to be the hall-mark of all his best work.

His attempt to keep sentiment at bay was unconsciously helped by London editors, who did not share Greenwood's liking for " those Scotch things ", or feared the effect of dialect upon their readers. In writing for them, accordingly, he dealt with day-to-day matters about which he had no deep feelings, and could adopt a cheerfully flippant tone. Also, though he had gathered together the best of his descriptive articles and anecdotes about the Auld Lichts in the hope that he might find a publisher for them, nobody would have them even as a gift. Robertson Nicoll altered all this. As the editor of a weekly which combined the interests of literature and nonconformist religion, he drew a very large proportion of his public from Scotland and the North, so that he was ready to let Barrie write of and for his own people. And as the adviser to a great publishing house, he was ready to take up the despised bundle of articles and see that a book was made of them. The results were that Barrie, without dropping his connexion with Greenwood or Riach, was able to create an entirely new literary personality in Gavin Ogilvy of *The British Weekly*; and that in April, 1888, *Auld Licht Idylls* was published, was greeted with a chorus of praise by English and Scottish reviewers alike, and settled down to be a success with the public. It was dedicated—and it might well be—to Greenwood.

Admirable though the book is, it is still the work of a man afraid of himself, for there is little sentiment in *Auld Licht Idylls*. The only sketch in it which appeals to the sense of pity is the description of Cree Queery and Mysy Drolly his mother. It is written in a dry detached manner, suitable to the middle-aged school-master who is supposed to be the narrator; and its quality lies in descriptive power and humorous observation. There is much understanding of the Auld Lichts, those grim and difficult people, but not a line of flattery. It is no wonder that Margaret Ogilvy, instead of showing the book proudly in Kirriemuir as the author pictured her, hid it close. This is the first book of which Thrums is the scene, and Barrie indicates by this name that he is referring not to the whole town, but to that small part of it where the weaving community dwelt. " Thrums " is a weaver's word, meaning the fringe of threads left on a loom when the web is taken off. Later on, when Barrie went on from description to invention, he used the name to mean the whole town, though even so he took his humbler characters from the corner of it that he knew best.

With the introduction of Thrums to the bookshelves, Barrie ceased to be simply a journalist. He still wrote for the papers, it is true. Indeed, he wrote for them more prolifically than ever. But he wrote with the knowledge that the manufacture of lively squibs about shoes and ships and sealing-wax was not to be his life's work.

Chapter V

THE FIRST NOVELS

ONCE Robertson Nicoll had appeared on the scene, Barrie's career went swiftly forward. Even before *Auld Licht Idylls* was through the press, its author had taken advantage of his newly-won security of tenure on *The British Weekly* to write his first long connected story—if we except his three-guinea pot-boilers—and to publish it serially in that paper. This story was *When a Man's Single.* It is an imperfect but delightful piece of work, and its very faults give it added interest. Except for its love-story, it is very largely autobiographical. The career of Rob Angus, the gigantic literary saw-miller of Thrums (who has a casual mention in *Auld Licht Idylls*, by the way), follows almost exactly the career of his creator. Rob gets a post as leader-writer on a provincial paper, *The Silchester Mirror*, whose likeness to *The Nottingham Journal* is striking and complete. From there he goes to London as a free-lance, and after a period of loneliness and disappointment finds friends among his own kind and a livelihood. Finally, he achieves success.

Most of the faults and some of the virtues of *When a Man's Single* are due to the method of its composition. Robertson Nicoll must have accepted the story on the strength of the opening Thrums chapters and Barrie's outline of the rest of the story, for publication actually began when only three chapters had been written, and very soon the author was only a chapter ahead. In such circumstances, it is fairly easy for an author who is also a journalist of experience to make sure of delivering his "copy" by the appointed time; but it is impossible for him to give any kind of guarantee as to quality. *When a Man's Single* bears many traces of hasty writing and ramshackle construction. It suffers often from the fact that its author could not cast back and alter his earlier chapters, since those chapters were already in the hands of his readers when the later ones were being written. But the very fact that it had to be written swiftly and urgently has given it a liveliness and a sense of youthful vitality which might have been lost with too careful revision.

The artistic importance of the book consists in the Thrums chapters, for here we get the first glimpse of the real Barrie, not simply a clever journalist with a gift of humour but a great writer. Here at last he has the courage to let his soft heart rather than his hard head guide the hand that holds his pen. The account of little Davy Dundas trotting so purposefully to her death is not very well designed. Not only has it little or nothing to do with the story that is to follow, but it does not even explain with any clearness how the child died. Nevertheless, here for the first time we have the authentic tone of that Barrie who at his best could wring our hearts as could no other writer of his time. Nobody of judgment who read those chapters could doubt the quality of the man who wrote them, or that the subsequent story tacked on to them so arbitrarily was the work of somebody perhaps more expert but much less significant.

To the biographer, however, the chief immediate interest of the book lies in the story of Rob Angus after he has left Scotland. The Silchester chapters, which are still read with special admiration for their clear and humorous observation of journalistic life by every journalist who comes across them, also show us the difficulties of a youth, at once crude and sensitive, in the process of having his corners rubbed off. The London chapters must be read in double harness, so to speak, with *The Greenwood Hat* if we are to realize how freely the author has drawn upon personal experience for his detail.

This was natural—indeed, it was almost inevitable. It was the essence of the story that Rob Angus must love and marry a woman far above him in social position. Once committed to the creation of Mary Abinger, Barrie had to supply her with a background; and so few glimpses had he had by that time of the world inhabited by the Mary Abingers that he was compelled to put into the picture almost everything that he had seen. For instance, his friend Gilmour and he had hired a house-boat at Tagg's Island in the Thames, where he had stayed for a month or more having his first taste of the gay life; so to Tagg's Island all his characters must go, whether they wanted to or not, since if they decided on any other resort their creator would not be able to provide for their entertainment. Rob's emotions on his first sight of Fleet Street, his gradual absorption into the easy, friendly bachelor life of the men of his own craft, his assimilation of a new code of manners, all may be taken as being equally true of Barrie. Alexander Riach of the *Telegraph* appears in the story thinly disguised as John Rorrison of the *Wire*, and it is probable that Barrie got his passport to Bohemia from Riach in much the same way as Rob got it from Rorrison.[1] The small boy who brings the school captain home for the holidays appears both in Rob Angus's story and in Barrie's autobiography, and so does the cow which, in those comparatively sylvan days, inhabited Tagg's Island.

Another fact, implicit in *When a Man's Single* but explicitly stated in *The Greenwood Hat*, is that Barrie's widening knowledge of the world still included no knowledge of women. During his own interlude at Tagg's Island, Barrie had written a series of articles in the *St. James's* describing the place, its life and its inhabitants; and in the evenings he would sit in a little inn (he " was on the verge of beer " by this time) listening to the youths from other house-boats—swash-bucklers in white flannels—discussing these articles, and speculating who could have written them. " As for the real author, no one ever suspected him; even on such a little island Mr. Anon failed to impress. As for knowing a pretty girl when he saw one nobody conceived it of the object in the corner. It was equally inconceivable to the ladies of the island." That this was bitter to him there is no doubt, for elsewhere he confesses that Anon's deepest ambition, deeper than his Rothschildian dream of earning a pound a day, deeper even than his desire to reach some little niche in literature, is a longing to be a favourite of the ladies. " If they would dislike him or fear him it would be something, but it is crushing to be just harmless." And so

[1] " Sandy " Riach makes another, less dignified, appearance in the last chapter of the book, where Barrie entrusts the circulation of the news of Rob's marriage round Thrums to " Sandersy Riach, *telegraph boy* ".

he pictures himself wandering forlornly on the island with no companion but the cow, looking on at the bright butterfly life about him but unable to take part in it. He is like a child at a confectioner's window; and if we are inclined to wonder if the picture is a true one, there is Mary Abinger to prove it, a figure as sweet and as unreal as any on the lids of the confectioner's boxes. She is a boy's dream of womanhood, not a woman. She is, in fact, the little water-cress seller, gone up in the world and with the thinnest imaginable veneer of sophistication. And the men in the book, who in themselves are real enough, are touched with Mary's unreality whenever they come near her or speak of her.

When a Man's Single was published in book form in October, 1888, and was followed two months later by *An Edinburgh Eleven.* This was a slim volume, also reprinted from *The British Weekly*, embodying a series of character-sketches of notable people to do with Edinburgh, and more particularly its University, which Barrie had contributed from time to time. Naturally, this book's appeal was chiefly local; but so lively were the portraits and so quick the humour that informed them that they can still give pleasure to readers who have never heard of most of the originals. Three books in a year sounds prodigious; but a journalist as industrious as Barrie, once he finds a publisher, can very soon see his name repeating itself on title-pages. Only seven months more went by before he saw it again, this time on the book which was to carry him to real success, *A Window in Thrums.*

This book is hardly less casual in construction than *Auld Licht Idylls*, to which it is a companion-piece. Once again the dominie of Glen Quharity is the nar-

THE "WINDOW IN THRUMS"

rator, and once again he is used to string together a series of chapters many of which have already been printed as separate articles. There is no connected story in the earlier part of the book; and when the last five chapters begin to knit themselves together to that close which Barrie's publishers found unbearably sad, but which moved both Stevenson and Robertson Nicoll to the deepest admiration, it becomes clear that the book can have been planned beforehand hardly at all, but was left to take shape as it went along. But that matters nothing. Here at last is Barrie writing at full power. He is treating of what he knows, and his fear of letting himself go has left him. He is in control of himself, and knows it, and can search his heart in confidence. Also, most important of all, his mother has at last become his heroine. Jess McQumpha, the lame woman of the Window, gets her outward characteristics from the Barries' neighbour, Bell Lunan. In herself, however, she is drawn direct from Margaret Ogilvy; and her daughter Leeby is drawn from Margaret's daughter Jane Ann. Here at last are women who are human beings, not simply projections of a youthful ideal. Jess is allowed faults which would have blotted a Mary Abinger out of existence; but because she is a real woman and a fine one, her faults show only as the natural complement of her qualities. They increase our understanding of her without losing our sympathy. For instance, in the chapter called *A Tale of a Glove*, Jess's possessive maternity drives her to a petty exhibition of jealousy such as no moralist could approve. No little seller of water-cress could behave so, and survive; but Stevenson's comment is, "A great page . . . and as true as death and judgment."

Barrie's practice as a journalist was always to get his subjects from his own life or that of those about him. Consequently, once his connexion with *The British Weekly* enabled him to write regularly on Scottish subjects, the years of compulsory exile in London were ended. His pen could be busy wherever he was, and from the time of his emancipation he divided his life between London and Kirriemuir. Strathview was now the property of Dr. Ogilvy, who had bought it to retire to when the time came, and the whole house (instead of the upper part they had first occupied) was rented from him by the Barries, so that there was room for the author both to live and to work there. At what precise date he was able to make the place his home again is not certain. The implication in *Margaret Ogilvy* is that he could be with his mother again for half the year even before *Auld Licht Idylls* became a book. At any rate, we can safely assume that most, if not all, of *A Window in Thrums* was written in Scotland. One absolutely precise date can be given. Barrie's growing importance, and his established success, made it possible for Greenwood to propose him, some time in 1889, for membership of the Garrick Club. One of the most delightful chapters in *Margaret Ogilvy* describes her inability to take this great event with proper seriousness, or to think of it as anything but a low scheme whereby a set of barefaced scoundrels (the committee) proposed to cheat her foolish son out of large sums of his hard-earned money. The date of Barrie's election to the club was January, 1890, George Meredith being one of his strongest backers; and the obvious deduction is that he had been spending a good deal of time in Kirriemuir before this.

A side-light on his movements at this time is thrown by his contributions to *Time*, a monthly magazine edited by Walter Sichel. In May, 1888, Sichel published a story of Barrie's called *My Neighbour*, in which the erratic Richard Abinger of *When a Man's Single* appeared again, now married but far from settled down. This was followed in the Christmas number by a wild burlesque in the manner of *Better Dead*; and then, with the new year, came a series of articles of quite extraordinary interest. These appeared monthly throughout 1889 under the title " What the Pit Says ". They were in the nature of dramatic criticism, but the author obviously had a free hand whether he dealt with plays, players or his neighbours in the audience, and whether he went to a first night or dropped in on a play casually during its run.

These articles, which have too long lain buried and forgotten, were written rather as entertainment than as serious criticism, and very entertaining they are; but their particular importance is that they illustrate better than any other of Barrie's writings how well he knew and understood the theatre before ever he came to write for it. His opinions on the plays he saw are firm and downright, and invariably have a basis in sound sense. In fact, he has that air of authority without dogmatism which no man can achieve unless he knows what he is talking about. For example, here is a sentence which few people would have had the vision to write in 1889 about one of the spectacular productions of Shakespeare then fashionable: " I do not know that elaborate stage furniture has not taken the poetry out of Shakespearian comedy, which mocks at realism."

The evidence given by these articles as to Barrie's

way of life is simply that the first seven are written about London productions; while of the last five one certainly and two more in all probability deal with performances seen in Scotland. The December article, which brings the series as well as the year to a close, is an account of Mrs. Langtry on tour with a production of *As You Like It* which she did not bring to the St. James's until February, 1890. This, and a general article on the music-hall which precedes it, could have been written at Strathview as easily as in London.

The year 1889, then, marks the end of Barrie's journalism. He evidently felt this himself, for in *The Greenwood Hat* he gives four years as the duration of the career of that " spare and diligent crumb ", James Anon. He had now a name. He had a club. He had a banking account, and he no longer put on formal garb in order to visit editors. In short, he could afford to be an author; and the publication in the spring of 1890 of his last book of collected articles, *My Lady Nicotine*, signalized the end of one phase just as the appearance in October, 1891, of *The Little Minister*, the first novel that Barrie had ever been able to plan and carry out at leisure, celebrated the beginning of another.

The autobiographical stuff in *My Lady Nicotine* is purely incidental. Indeed, the most interesting thing about this book from our point of view is the odd light that it sheds on its author's literary method. The papers that make it up are not in any way related to one another, but they are given a sort of unity because they are supposed to be written by a seasoned smoker, and they refer largely to the devotion of himself and his friends to a certain brand of tobacco. Seven years later an enterprising firm of tobacco merchants, finding

Elliott & Fry, Ltd.

J. M. Barrie in 1891

that their particular blend had been supplied to Barrie, got him to write a testimonial identifying it with the "Arcadia Mixture" of the book, and this advertisement greatly helped them in piling up an enormous fortune. The ironical point about the story, however, is that Barrie, when he wrote the articles, hardly smoked at all. He was doing what he so often did in his journalistic writings, assuming a character. Later on, perhaps by auto-suggestion, perhaps by sheer pressure of public opinion, he became the heavy smoker that he had pretended to be.

This trick of assuming a character is worth examining, for although Barrie said that his pen was clogged when he wrote in his own person, the truth is not quite so simple as that. It depended whether he was writing as a journalist or an artist. As journalist, when—as I have already suggested—he had to make almost a conscious effort to keep the strongest thing in his nature at bay, he must have found it very helpful to assume the character of an Indian bridge-builder, a dog, a young woman in love, or whatever it was. But when he wrote as an artist—that is, when he allowed his feelings to be engaged—he wrote straight out of his own heart, and it mattered nothing to him whether the feelings he described were presented as his own or as another's Better proof cannot be given of this than that the best piece of sustained prose-writing he was ever to achieve, *Margaret Ogilvy*, was written in the first person and with himself as a character only second in importance to its subject.

Meanwhile, in *The Little Minister*, he brought off a masterly compromise, for he drew the three chief characters in that happiest of romances one from each of his three models. Gavin Dishart, the minister, is drawn from Barrie himself, not merely in his thoughts but in his appearance. He has Barrie's own sensitiveness about his lack of inches, here turned to much better literary use than when it had appeared disguised as Rob Angus's gigantic size and strength. Margaret Dishart, the minister's mother, is avowedly Margaret Ogilvy. And Babbie, the enchanting gipsy heroine, is the little seller of water-cress grown at last to the fullest stature of which she is capable. She is more real than Mary Abinger, because more humour has gone to her conception, and more skill—also more leisure—to the elaboration of her portrait. But she is still not a human being, or anything much more than a boy's dream. Whether Barrie knew that is not clear; but it is not to be doubted that his artist's instinct felt it. When his publishers had suggested an alteration to the "unbearably sad" ending of *A Window in Thrums*, Barrie had refused even to consider it, and said that he would never again have had any respect for himself if he had consented to bring Jess's son back in time to see her before she died. No such blow to his self-respect was threatened when he brought *The Little Minister* to a happy ending far less probable than the one his publishers had suggested for *A Window in Thrums*. After all, Jess's son might have come home in time without straining probability at all; but that Babbie, with her gipsy blood and her aristocratic upbringing, should settle down happily in the Auld Licht Manse in Thrums, to bear the Little Minister's children and keep house for him on less than a hundred a year, is an idea not to be entertained outside a fairy-tale.

CHAPTER VI

APPROACH TO THE THEATRE

BARRIE was never the kind of man to whom the life of a club could appeal. In later years he belonged to many, but entered them seldom, and in his writings he professed not to know what went on inside them. But in the first pride of his election to the Garrick—and perhaps in apprehension of what his mother might say if he allowed the subscription she so heartily begrudged to run to waste—he conquered his shyness. This shaped his future career. He made friends with Irving; and Irving told him he must write for the theatre—drove him (so Barrie says) to write his first three plays, and found him managers for them. Barrie was not unwilling. As we have seen, he had always been fascinated by the theatre.

It was not Irving, however, who " drove " him to his first attempt on the professional stage but H. B. Marriott Watson, a colleague of Barrie's on the *St. James's*, who figures as " Marriott " in *My Lady Nicotine*. Marriott Watson was one of W. E. Henley's young men, a promising novelist, and he had an idea for a play about Richard Savage, the eighteenth-century poet. He suggested that Barrie should collaborate with him in this, and Barrie consented. Henley, who had his eye on Barrie as a coming man, wrote a prologue to the piece, which was given a trial matinée (at the authors' expense) at the Criterion Theatre on 16th April, 1891. The company was quite a strong one, the name-part being played by Bernard Gould, who later abandoned a promising stage career, turned cartoonist, and achieved fame as Bernard Partridge of *Punch*; and Cyril Maude had a smaller part. The story, however, was neither historically accurate nor theatrically plausible, and the play fell flat. The best that criticism could find to say of it was that it showed some promise of better work to be expected from its authors in the future. The stubbornly cheerful article which Barrie wrote after this failure is in *The Greenwood Hat*, and in it he suggests that perhaps the play had done some good after all, if only by inducing the Ibsenite and the anti-Ibsenite critics to agree about something.

This reference to the controversy then raging in intellectual London may easily have been the germ of the idea which was to start Barrie off, six weeks later, on his real career as a dramatist. At any rate the gay one-act burlesque, *Ibsen's Ghost*, which was produced by J. L. Toole at his own theatre on 30th May of the same year, must have been dashed off quickly since Ibsen's *Hedda Gabler*, which it parodies, was not produced at the Vaudeville till 20th April. It is in fact no more than a brilliant journalistic comment on the Ibsen cult of the time, put into dialogue form. Barrie showed it to Irving, who took it to his great friend Toole and insisted that he must produce it. Toole knew nothing whatever of Ibsen and little more of Barrie, but he took Irving's word for it and put the play on.

Barrie never published *Ibsen's Ghost*. The "prompt" copy got lost, and no other was available. Forty years later, however, having a curiosity to see what his first play had been like and how he had dared to make game of the dramatist he had always known to be the greatest of his age, he applied to the Lord Chamberlain on the chance that the licensed copy was still lying in his office; and it was. Having scraped the text clean of Toole's "improvements", Barrie had copies made privately for half a dozen friends, with a preface consisting of a lively and very characteristic account of its production. He says there—and Irene Vanbrugh, who had her first original part in this play as a girl of nineteen, confirms—that Toole never from first to last had any idea what the play meant. Toole himself, in a remarkable make-up, played Ibsen. He "wandered through the thing", says Barrie, "searching vainly for what it might be about, which, cunning one that he was, proved to be the best way of playing it". The play had the same effect as *Richard Savage*—though for a happier reason—of uniting the critics, for its satire, though pointed, was not barbed. For so short a play it created a remarkable stir, and Barrie relates in his preface to *Peter Pan* that at the first performance a man in the pit found it so funny that he went into hysterics and had to be removed. Irene Vanbrugh made a personal success with extraordinarily close parodies of both Marion Lea and Elizabeth Robins, who were then acting Thea and Hedda in the Ibsen play at the Vaudeville. And Tesman was played by George Shelton, afterwards famous as Smee in *Peter Pan*.

And so, modestly and humbly, Barrie entered the theatre. All through the rehearsals of *Ibsen's Ghost* he sat quiet, and let Toole do with the play almost whatever he liked. Partly this was because he had fallen under the spell of the man who had been his favourite comedian when he was at school, and whom he now found " a figure so lovable that, had he not already been, Dickens would have invented him ". Partly it was because he was moving as a stranger in a new world whose ways were different from those of the world outside, and must be learned.

That he learned them with characteristic thoroughness, the rest of his working life was to prove. Opinions differ very widely on Barrie's stature as an artist, but nobody who knows the theatre has ever attempted to deny his quality as a craftsman. His stage technique, within its own limits, is practically flawless—and because of the theatre's mechanical difficulties, technique matters relatively far more in play-writing than in any other form of literary composition—yet it was his habit later on in life to deny that he had any stage technique at all. In a preface to a collected edition of Harold Chapin's plays, for instance, he declares that in order to know what to say he has had to buy a book about how to write plays, and has retired abashed before the author's knowledge and the difficulty of the subject. And in *The Greenwood Hat* he picks up this point again, and adds " I never knew (and I don't know now) how plays are written, nor gave stage-craft any conscious thought ". Since from this point onwards we are to watch how Barrie's work shifted more and more away from the study and on to the stage, it is important to decide at once just how far we can believe in his picture of himself as a man who, in the theatre, went right not deliberately but by instinct or accident.

To an extent, I am sure the picture is a true one. The faculty which makes the dramatist, without which no man on earth can ever become a dramatist, is an ability to make division of himself while he is writing —to become two people, one an author who is putting a play down on paper, the other a detached observer sitting at an imaginary performance of the play upon an imaginary stage. A novelist needs no such faculty; he can be at the same moment writer and reader in his own undivided person. But unless a dramatist, while writing, can clearly see and hear how the events he is imagining will look and sound, *and how an audience will react to them*, when they are produced on the stage, he is wasting time and effort. Because they have lacked this faculty, many accomplished novelists have seen their plays fail on the stage—Henry James, George Moore, Joseph Conrad and others equally famous; and indeed, about the time when Barrie began to try his hand in the theatre, it had come to be an accepted canon of criticism that no novelist could write a play. Now, to Barrie, this ability to split his personality was natural. He used it not merely in writing plays but in ordinary life. He himself said so plainly in his rectorial address at St. Andrews in 1922, when he told his audience about his second self, " M'Connachie ". With the wayward M'Connachie to hold the pen and the practical Barrie to watch the performance, it is perhaps not very surprising that the plays came right, or that the dramatist did not recognize his method as " stage technique ". Yet in the very act of disclaiming the possession of technique, he shows that he was always aware of the necessity for the writer of plays to be his own audience. " My own plan," he says, " was simply to make everything clear to myself in the hope that this would clear a way for the spectator."

But if we admit that Barrie's clear vision and surefootedness in the theatre were partly the unconscious gift of temperament, he is not to be believed when he implies that he had never given any thought to the problems of theatrical craftsmanship. The criticisms he wrote for *Time* were full of constructive ideas, and many of the other articles he wrote during his years as a free-lance journalist had the stage for subject. One in particular, contributed in 1889 to *The Scots Observer*, showed that he had thought hard enough to be able to rise superior to the prejudices of the time. The article was called "The Coming Dramatist", and its concluding paragraph deserves quotation in full:

> One would think that there are novelists with us who could write plays that would be literary as well as effective. Some of them have tried and failed, but obviously because they did not set about it in the proper way. Plays and novels require quite different construction; but the story-writer who is dramatic could become sufficiently theatrical by serving a short apprenticeship to the stage. There are such prizes to pluck for those that can stand on tiptoe, that the absence of an outstanding dramatist is as surprising as it is disappointing.

These are not the words of a man who does not know how plays are written. The tone is much more like that of a general surveying a stretch of country over which he hopes to have a chance to make a successful attack, although his predecessors have failed. So far as we know Barrie did not meditate such an attack at the time when this article was published; but it is plain that if the campaign was ever to take place, its strategy was already determined. And it is interesting to notice that when the time came everything went exactly according to plan.

With Irving to urge him on, Barrie now set himself to write a full-length play for Toole. He was not unwilling, but he has confessed that he did at first tread this new walk of literature rather contemptuously—as did most writers of eminence at that time. He did not trouble to think out a new idea for his play, but went back to *When a Man's Single* and found what he wanted there. He took the chapters of the book which tell how the impressive baronet whom Mary Abinger's father has been entertaining in his country house turns out to be a barber masquerading as a gentleman, and of them he made his story. The " untheatrical " novelist, having got so far, would probably have gone on to transfer the characters of his book to the stage. Barrie, knowing that " plays and novels require quite different construction ", took the bolder, more original and infinitely more sensible course of beginning again from the beginning. He took the Tagg's Island houseboat, which had already done him such good service, and made it his setting. He invented an entirely new set of characters. And the result was a farcical comedy called *Walker, London*, which to the casual eye had almost no relation at all to the novel from which it came.

It was produced at Toole's Theatre on 25th February, 1892. Toole played Jasper Phipps, the barber with social aspirations, and the part suited him exactly. Irene Vanbrugh had the part of an erudite young woman from Girton—an elaboration from a character who makes a brief appearance in the description of a students' party in *An Edinburgh Eleven*—and George Shelton was once more in the company. Seymour Hicks, another actor whose career was to be much bound up with Barrie's, played a lively young medical student, having got the part by telling Toole that Barrie thought him just the man for it, and Barrie that Toole did. The most difficult part to cast was the heroine—who had to combine youth, beauty and charm with an ability to flirt. Jerome K. Jerome, consulted on the point, recommended Mary Ansell, a young girl who had done well on tour in a play of his own, had made a success at a special matinée, and was now playing with Charles Wyndham at the Criterion. Barrie met Miss Ansell and conceived a great admiration for her; and whenever Toole, who notoriously hated spending money on his productions and was already appalled at the prospective cost of the practicable house-boat, suggested other less expensive actresses, Barrie simply said: "Mary Ansell gets the par-rt." And so in the end it was. She not only got the part, but played it (according to Clement Scott) "with infinite spirit and refinement", and before long it was clear, to the ladies of the company at all events, that the author was in love with his *ingenue*.

The play was a great success, running for 511 performances. It moved Clement Scott to hail Barrie as a new Robertson, and Scott was an infallible judge of what was effective in the theatre. For all that, it can only rank as a good piece of journeyman's work. Nobody has ever taken the risk of trying to revive it, and Barrie would have prevented its publication if he could.[1] Yet its value to him was great, for it enabled him to serve more than an apprenticeship to the stage. *Ibsen's Ghost* had taught him much, and when *Walker, London* went into rehearsal he was no longer content to let

[1] Barrie sold the play to Toole outright, and therefore lost control of it. It has been published in an "acting edition" only.

Toole have a free hand. As in the question of Mary Ansell's engagement, so in other matters he now knew clearly what he wanted, and in his own quiet way he saw that he got it.

With a play running steadily, and a novel going through edition after edition—not to mention that his earlier books were still selling—Barrie could now have afforded to stop and look about him. First, however, he settled down to write, no doubt at Irving's invitation, a play with a part for Irving himself. This was *The Professor's Love Story*. It was completed by September, and though Irving, when he read the play, did not like the part for himself, he is said to have suggested that it might suit John Hare. Hare—if the story told by Alexander Woollcott, the American critic, is true—tried to read the play but was defeated and enraged by Barrie's illegible handwriting. Thereupon Barrie wrote out a fairer copy and sent it to E. S. Willard, who accepted it. If Barrie did this, he must have been very quick about it, for Willard, who had returned from America in June, 1892, and went back there some time in September, certainly did accept the play [1] and take it back with him, producing it in New York just before Christmas.

Barrie was therefore by no means idle, even though London saw no new work of his for more than a year after the production of *Walker, London*. But compared with the ferocious labour of his years as a free-lance journalist, his life was that of a gentleman of leisure. He was by this time very much at home in his exciting new world, he knew all literary London, and found it

[1] It is said that Willard bought the play outright for £50, and that Barrie bought it back later.

at times both easy and pleasant to come out of his shell. His life-long interest in cricket, for instance, had led him to form a private team. He and his two close friends, Gilmour and Marriott Watson, out one day for a walk at Shere, stopped to watch the village team perform; and Barrie, encouraged by the elderly appearance of the players, decided to challenge them. The fixture was made, and a distinguished eleven was collected which included, among others, Bernard Partridge and two African explorers—explorers always had a fascination for Barrie. On the way down in the train the question of a name for the club was discussed, and Barrie, who had by this time discovered that however impressive his eleven might be in the great world, it was not likely to shine on the cricket-field, asked one of the explorers the African for "Heaven help us". The answer was "Allahakbar", so the club became the Allahakbars till they changed their title, in their captain's honour, to the Allahakbarries. In this inaugural match they made eleven runs, and were overwhelmed.[1]

By now, the days when James Anon had had to fall

[1] In later years, the Allahakbarries became a famous institution, with several matches annually against villages and at country houses, and a special occasion each summer when they played Broadway in Worcestershire, where Mary Anderson was the presiding genius. She understood nothing of the game, but was always fiercely partisan and, Barrie alleges, had a "powerful way" of taking the Allahakbarries' top scorer for a walk round the field and persuading him to play for her side in the second innings. Barrie himself was not much of a cricketer, and seldom made any runs to speak of. He knew the game thoroughly, however, and was not negligible as a bowler. Conan Doyle, perhaps the best cricketer who ever played for the Allahakbarries until they made a glorious last appearance at Kirriemuir in 1930 with Macartney and Mailey, of the Australian team, in their number, says of him:

> Barrie was no novice. He bowled an insidious left-hand good-length ball coming from leg which was always likely to get a wicket.

back on the Tagg's Island cow for feminine society were very far behind. Barrie was a celebrity, and could never again have private anguish because women thought him of no account. He did not cease, no doubt, to suffer pangs at the suspicion that their interest was for the author rather than the man, for the belief that they considered him " harmless " was to continue to rankle all his life. But he was no longer abashed by them, nor apt to treat them as beings of a different and mysterious order. He was, for instance, on terms of delightfully easy friendship with Irene Vanbrugh and her three sisters, in spite of the fact that two of the four were leading London actresses—creatures such as would surely have sent the diffident Anon scudding to his cow for protection. More than that, he was by now the declared suitor of another leading London actress, and though he had not yet persuaded Mary Ansell to be engaged to him, he had hopes that she would consent.

Towards the end of 1892 his health, which had hitherto been excellent, began to trouble him. There is a reference to this in a letter from Stevenson, written in December, trying to persuade him to go out to Vailima. (The two men were friends now, though they had never met and were destined never to meet.) But early in 1893 he was well enough to undertake a very curious commission. The rift between Gilbert and Sullivan which had appeared during the run of *The Gondoliers*—that is, some time in 1890 or at the beginning of 1891—was still in existence. Their next joint work, *Utopia, Limited* (produced in October, 1893), was consequently not yet even contemplated, and D'Oyly Carte, in great difficulty with the task of keeping the policy of the Savoy Theatre going until the two touchy collaborators should consent to be reconciled, asked Barrie to write him a libretto. Why Carte hit on Barrie is not clear, unless we assume that this is the third of the plays for which Irving found Barrie a manager. That Barrie should have agreed to try his hand is not so surprising. Ever since he had begun writing as a small boy, he had had a fondness for dropping into verse, and a certain blindness to the fact that his verse was not very good. This blindness now allowed him to try quite gaily to fill Gilbert's shoes, though he had not Gilbert's sense of rhythm, his mastery of rhyme, his ability to make verse move as freely as prose, nor even his knowledge that the lyrics of a comic opera should advance the play's action, not hold it up. Barrie constructed *Jane Annie, or The Good Conduct Prize*—named, it need hardly be said, after his sister—in the traditional two acts, and had written the first act and planned the second, when his health again failed. In order to get the opera finished he called in Conan Doyle—already famous as the creator of Sherlock Holmes, and one of the stalwarts of the Allahakbarries, but not a happy choice as a lyric-writer. Doyle promised to help, but when he examined the work, as he says himself, his heart sank. He could not conceive what had made Barrie accept the commission, and he completed the " book " purely from friendship, and with no hope of success. *Jane Annie* came to the Savoy on 13th May, 1893, and left it again only a few days later. The critics found little to praise but one of the settings, which was a golf green in the grounds of a girls' school. One of them complained that writing *about* schoolgirls had made the authors write *for* schoolgirls.

Another failure, though not an important one, followed this. On 3rd June, a one-act adaptation from

Vanity Fair, called *Becky Sharp*, was produced at Terry's Theatre as part of a quintuple bill. Barrie was said to have reproduced Thackeray's words without capturing his spirit. The experience was useful to him if it taught him that this kind of stage adaptation from other men's books is seldom worth a good dramatist's while; and he certainly never attempted anything of the sort again.

The breakdown in his health which had interfered with the writing of *Jane Annie* proved to be the forerunner of a series of bouts of illness. Mary Ansell left the cast of *Walker, London* before the end of the play's run, and went North to help nurse him through one of these. He was well enough in the winter to take the chair at a Burns dinner at Greenock, for a lively description of the occasion was published by Henley in *The Scots Observer*. This anonymous article made fun of Barrie's appearance, his manners and his oratory, and it caused great offence among his admirers, who rushed to his defence. Henley was delighted (for the article was in fact Barrie's own), and even when it was insinuated that he had written it himself for mean and unworthy motives, would not let the joke be " given away ". Not long afterwards, however, Barrie fell ill again, this time much more seriously. Mary Ansell, to whom by this time he was engaged, nursed him through a sharp attack of pneumonia. And on 9th July, 1894, when he was convalescent but not yet strong enough to face a church ceremony, they were married privately at Strathview.

Meanwhile, Willard had at last returned from America and had given *The Professor's Love Story* its first London performance at the Comedy Theatre on 25th June; and the news that his play was settling down to a successful run must have seemed to the author a very timely and appropriate wedding present. It was not such a good piece of craftsmanship as *Walker, London*, for its story had a fundamental flaw—the idea that an absent-minded man of science could fall in love with his pretty secretary and, on being told what was the matter with him, could first ask: " But who is the woman?" and then take flight to Scotland to escape the unknown siren, *taking the secretary with him*. Crude incredibility of this kind is no doubt what Barrie has in mind when he confesses that he did not at first treat the theatre with proper respect; and the final judgment on the play's quality is that the author did not publish it. Still, Willard's acting as Professor Goodwillie and some excellent incidental comic writing carried the play on for a run of 144 performances; and it has been several times revived.

CHAPTER VII

MARGARET OGILVY

THE romance that hangs about islands had always had a special appeal to Barrie. Islands were always cropping up in the stories he wove and the games he played as a boy, and when he was a man they still held him under their spell. There is an island in *The Admirable Crichton*, one in *Peter Pan*, and one in *Mary Rose*. And so, when repeated invitations came from Robert Louis Stevenson that Barrie should visit him in his home in the South Seas, he had always promised himself that some day he would set out on the long journey and meet the man whose works he admired and whose friendship he valued so much. Now that success was assured, he could command both time and money for the journey. But one thing still held him back. Margaret Ogilvy was now an old woman, and it was her fear, unspoken yet not hidden from the son who knew her so well, that if he went far away she might die without seeing him again. While she lived, therefore, he could not go; and in the outcome he never went at all, for on 3rd December, 1894, Stevenson himself died suddenly and unexpectedly. Yet, by the irony of fate, Barrie might almost as well have gone to the South Seas after all, for when Margaret Ogilvy did come to die soon after, he was too far away to reach her.

He was making one of his rare trips abroad, having

gone with his wife to Switzerland to shake off the last effects of his illness. A fortnight had gone by, and he had just had a reassuring letter about his mother's health from his sister Jane Ann, when a telegram arrived to say that she, Jane Ann, was dead. He started for home at once, but it was three days' journey. In London he learnt that his mother still did not know of her favourite daughter's death, and that the family was waiting for him to tell her. But he was too late by twelve hours to see her alive. She died on 3rd September, 1895, within three days of her seventy-sixth birthday; and Jane Ann, who was forty-eight, on 31st August. Barrie had for long been preparing himself for his mother's death, but Jane Ann's was a dreadful shock. She was the most reserved of all that reserved family, and her devotion to her mother was so absolute that no member of the household even suspected that she was gravely and incurably ill, if indeed she knew it herself. But by dying so, she solved a problem that otherwise might have proved insoluble—whether she could have made any kind of a life for herself now that her mother was dead. After his first grief was over, Barrie saw this, and was thankful that she had been spared "the long littleness" of such living.

We have seen already how deep was the influence that Margaret Ogilvy had over her son; it is time now to try to estimate its value. Consciously as his mother, unconsciously as his source of inspiration, she moulded his life and his work. From the time he was a small boy he idealized and all but worshipped her. She was the centre of his universe, it was to her that his work was dedicated, at her feet that he laid his early successes. And he served her so faithfully that when she died he

Margaret Ogilvy

A photograph of Barrie's mother taken at Glasgow about 1871

was able to say, simply and unhesitatingly, that he looked back through the years and could not see the smallest thing left undone that he could have done for her since he was a boy. Such devotion as this, which in speaking of his sister he calls the fierce joy of loving too much, can be a destructive as well as a creative force. It takes a strong personality to inspire such feeling, and needs a strong character to keep it under control. Because Margaret Ogilvy was a woman of fine temper who used her power wisely, her son's devotion to her and his devotion to his art were never in opposition. He was able to turn the two streams into the same channel, and they flowed with double strength. Yet because, with all her qualities, she was a limited woman, some of her limitations had the profoundest effect upon Barrie both as a writer and as a man.

For example, she had been compelled by her mother's death to be a housekeeper to her father and a mother to her little brother from the age of eight. She undertook the task with a gay gallantry that was always characteristic of her, but except for occasional outbreaks, she had to say good-bye to her childhood, and she had to snatch her playtime, as she snatched her scanty education, in the intervals between household tasks. The tales of how she had had to grow up so much too soon worked powerfully on her small son's imagination, and he tells how it was the horror of his boyhood that he too must some day give up the games. Something of this horror remained with him all his life; and if it gave him, as an artist, the inspiration for *Peter Pan*, it deprived him, as a man, of the ability or the desire to look squarely at life.

For another example, perhaps more important still,

Margaret Ogilvy handed on to her son her feelings about sex-relationships. She was married to David Barrie for more than half a century. She bore him ten children, and she was at all times a dutiful and faithful wife to him. Yet it is overwhelmingly clear to anybody who reads her story that all her deepest feelings were for her children. Her husband hardly comes into the tale at all. He is mentioned casually here and there, and once there is a direct reference to him as " a most loving as he was always a well-loved husband ", a man Barrie is very proud to be able to call his father. But the passage reads like a testimonial, and is obviously one of respect rather than of warm affection. Father and daughter, mother and son—these are the relationships between the sexes which meant most to Margaret Ogilvy. The one hero of her life was her own father. The one undying sorrow of her life was for her dead boy. One feels that if David Barrie the elder had died in his son's stead she would have mourned him sincerely, but that time would have healed that hurt before very long. She was fond of reading books of exploration, and when she read in her newspaper of the triumphant return of the leader of some expedition, her comment would be that his mother must be a proud woman. That the explorer might have a wife never occurred to her, or was an irrelevance.

As with the mother, so with the son. In all Barrie's writings there is hardly to be remembered a scene between husband and wife that goes beneath the surface, while the many scenes between mothers and sons and the exquisitely written father and daughter scene in *Dear Brutus* are all deeply and truly felt. John Shand in *What Every Woman Knows* never ceases to stray from Maggie Wylie's side until she makes it clear that she is more mother to him than wife. Grizel with Sentimental Tommy has the same attitude. She wants Tommy to be a husband to her, but only so that she can be a mother to him. And when Mary Rose returns from her other world, she has hardly more than a puzzled regret when she finds her young husband grown middle-aged and grey. All her thoughts are for her baby son; when she finds that he too is lost to her, she dies and becomes a ghost and haunts the house till he comes back. All these characters act as they do because of Barrie's knowledge that his mother would have acted so in the same situations. When he has her for his model he is certain of himself and her. Outside that intense but narrow experience he cannot attempt the profundities, for he has no other model that he can draw " in the round ".

Still it is not given to many artists to know even one sitter as he knew his. Critics have referred to Barrie's life of his mother as an " idealized " biography, and in the sense that it is a labour of love and not a detached study the book can be so described. But if the suggestion is that he touched up the portrait, turning an ordinary human being into an impossible angel, then it must be denied at once. His feeling for his mother was true and genuine; he loved her for her faults as much as for her virtues. Therefore he had no need to pretend. He drew her, faults and limitations and all, knowing that when he had shown her to others as he saw her himself, the faults and limitations would not be the least of her attractions. She had her vanities, her snobberies, her obstinacies; she could be, on occasion, a very tiresome old lady indeed. She was a possessive mother, who accepted her daughter's life-long devotion and her son's adoration without a qualm. True, she never took them for granted; she was too perceptive for that. But she never reflected that by dominating the lives of these two of her children she was compelling them to look backwards instead of forwards. Also, if the episode of the glove in *A Window in Thrums* has as much basis in real life as the rest of the book, she could be blindly jealous.

Yet such faults only serve to set off her virtues. With them all, she was a fine character and a great personality. Kirriemuir did not recognize this—Hammerton quotes remarks by her neighbours which show that they could see no special reason why she should have a book written about her—but then Kirriemuir is a town which wants to be loved for itself alone, and has always been puzzled by Barrie's fame and resentful of the public's interest in "Thrums". It is true enough that Margaret Ogilvy's special quality might never have been recognized outside her own home if her son had not become a great writer, but that is equally true of many remarkable women whose names are honoured in history as the chief influence in the making of men of genius. Conan Doyle, meeting her in 1893, when she was near the end of her life, was instantly impressed. And indeed, the mixture of courage, humour, tenderness and intelligence that was hers, together with her power of concentration, would have made her a person of mark in any walk of life.

Just before her last illness Barrie finished *Sentimental Tommy*, in which Grizel, the most real and most lovable of all his heroines, appears as the little girl in a magenta frock and a pinafore that his mother used to be. He never read her any of that book; by the time it was finished she was no longer capable of the effort to follow a story. To him this was, he says in *Margaret Ogilvy*, as if his book must go out cold into the world, but I wonder whether perhaps it was not as well that she could not take it in. Robertson Nicoll refused to have it said that the figure of Sentimental Tommy was drawn from Barrie himself, but his attitude cannot be justified now. The confessions which Barrie makes in *The Greenwood Hat* concerning himself agree too exactly with his description of Tommy Sandys to allow much doubt that Tommy is a projection of those traits in his own character which he most feared and disliked. For example, one of Tommy's most outrageous exploits in sentimentality was to change his own clothes for another boy's "mourning blacks", and to sit sorrowing for some dead stranger while the owner of the clothes took a short holiday from grief; and on the opening page of *The Greenwood Hat* Barrie tells this story of himself. Tommy, in fact, plays Hyde to Barrie's Jekyll, and I feel that the mother who knew him so well would have seen this and have been hurt by the bitterness of some of the self-criticism.

Sentimental Tommy was not published till a year later, no doubt because from January, 1896, till November of that year *Scribner's Magazine* was running it as a serial in America. By the time it appeared in book form Barrie had written *Margaret Ogilvy*; both books were published that autumn. The novel was welcomed by that large body of opinion which was looking to Barrie as one of the chief hopes of English letters, and distrusted profoundly his adventures in the theatre. This new book was by no means a perfect novel, but it represented a growth in power and grasp, and was taken as a promise that the author had no intention of letting the stage interfere with his best work. *Margaret Ogilvy*, on the other hand, had a very mixed reception. For some, it was incomparably the finest thing he had yet done; to say that it was a literary masterpiece was only to state the least of its qualities—it was the most beautiful tribute ever paid by a son to the memory of his dead mother. For others, in Scotland particularly, it was simply a violation of privacy. J. H. Millar, then a critic of standing in Scotland, described the book as "an exercise compared with which the labours of the resurrectionist are praiseworthy, and which many men (I believe) had rather lose their right hand than set themselves to attempt". To those who think, as I do, that *Margaret Ogilvy* is a book such as a man might well give his right hand to achieve, a book that deserves to live and do honour to its subject and its writer when most of the writings of our time are forgotten, it seems incredible that such a judgment can seriously have been pronounced. Yet there are still people who share Millar's prejudice, and even outdo his violence. Only recently, an applicant for some information or other concerning Barrie was met with a blank refusal of help from the official to whom he had written, on the ground that even Barnum, the showman, had never sunk so low as to exhibit his mother's bones with tears to the populace. Such a view is sentimentality run mad. There is no logic in it, nor any sense of proportion. If Barrie had been a painter, and his portrait of his mother had been done in oils instead of ink, this kind of detractor would never have raised a whisper.

Meanwhile, after his two books had gone to press and before they were published, Barrie set off with Robertson Nicoll for New York. He had now a following in America as enthusiastic as the one at home. There was business concerning copyrights to be done and the suggestion of a dramatization of *The Little Minister* to be looked into; and these inducements, together with the excitement of travelling so far from home for the first time in his life, were strong enough to make him face the fact that America required its lions to roar in public as frequently and as loudly as possible. Fortunately, perhaps, for Barrie's peace of mind, he found that he was not the chief lion of Scotland in America that season. " Ian Maclaren "—in ordinary life, the Reverend John Watson—was there on a triumphant lecture-tour. His book, *Beside the Bonnie Brier-Bush*, was the most popular of all the Kailyard School of fiction which had come into existence after the success of *A Window in Thrums*. It had swept the United States; and Watson, who was a man of great charm, with all the social graces that Barrie lacked, had made himself as popular as his book. While the full glare of the limelight fell on the lesser writer, Barrie's shrinking figure contrived to pass comparatively unnoticed in the shadows.

All the same, this American visit proved to be the turning-point of Barrie's career. The suggestion that *The Little Minister* might be turned into a play had come from Charles Frohman, soon to be the greatest theatre-manager of his time, who had in mind an actress for the part of the heroine—Maude Adams, at that time playing in *Rosemary*. Frohman and Barrie met, found that they were kindred spirits, and made friends; and so was formed the association which was to make Barrie a serious dramatist. He always insisted afterwards that just as he had been first urged into the theatre by Irving (and in a smaller degree by George Meredith), so he was kept there, rather against his will, by Frohman. Even in his last book we still find him maintaining that novels were more his line. There are various accounts, which cannot now be reconciled with one another, of how Frohman persuaded Barrie to make the adaptation he wanted, and after it was made to strengthen the part of Babbie so that he could use it for his purpose of making Maude Adams a star. Setting aside picturesque but unreliable detail, we have two solid facts—that Barrie went to see *Rosemary* at Frohman's invitation on the night of his arrival in New York, and that the dramatic version of *The Little Minister* was given its first production at the Empire Theatre there on 27th September, 1897, under Frohman's management and with Maude Adams as Babbie. The London production followed little more than a month later, on 6th November at the Haymarket, but here no strengthening was needed for Babbie. She was charmingly played by Winifred Emery, but the star part, if there was one, belonged to Cyril Maude as the Little Minister himself.

In making this adaptation Barrie showed more clearly than before how well he understood that novels and plays need quite different treatment. When he took part of the plot of *When a Man's Single* to make *Walker, London*, there was no ostensible connexion between the two compositions, and consequently no temptation to try to transfer to the stage scenes that had been successful with novel-readers. In *The Little Minister* he was attempting that task in which so many have failed, of telling over again in one medium a story already familiar in another. To succeed in such an enterprise a man needs craftsmanship and the courage of his convictions. Barrie had both. He did not try to transfer his novel to the stage—he began again from the beginning, telling the story in a new form and making drastic changes where theatrical effect made it advisable. He did not attempt, for instance, to explain the very complicated relationship between Lord Rintoul and Babbie the gipsy as it stands in the book; he knew that it would waste stage time to small dramatic purpose. He boldly simplified the story, changing his heroine's red gipsy blood to a more usual blue, making her Lady Babbie and Lord Rintoul's daughter, turning the little water-cress seller, in fact, into a princess in disguise. Literary critics have girded at this and other changes in the story, complaining that they debase *The Little Minister* as a play to a level far below that of the novel. There are two answers to these critics. One is that nobody but a very sanguine optimist expects an adaptation from one medium to another to be on the same artistic plane as the original. The other is that they do not know the theatre.

Chapter VIII

TOMMY AND GRIZEL

WE have seen that Barrie was a romantic about women. This is a condition of mind natural enough to a boy, but the man who does not outgrow it lays up for himself a store of trouble. He has little hope of making a success of marriage, because when he falls in love he loves not the real woman but his own imagined version of her. He commonly ignores the virtues and qualities that she has, and endows her with a new set that he would like her to have. If the woman is very much in love with him, or has a profound feeling for him of any kind—admiration for his work, for instance—she will unconsciously (or even consciously) mould herself to his ideas, and become outwardly the woman he wants her to be. So long as she is content with life on such terms, the marriage will seem an ideally happy one. But when her feeling for her husband, whatever it is, has lost its first heat, the wife wants, like all the unhappy heiresses in the stories, to be loved for herself alone. She needs a real relationship between man and woman, based on a thorough knowledge of one another's characters; and this is a thing which, except by a miracle, she will never get from a romanticist.

It would be mere impertinence on my part, writing so soon after Barrie's death and with the little information that is available, to attempt to make any detailed statements about the course of Barrie's married life with Mary Ansell. But the main facts are known to all—that they lived together without disharmony for nearly fifteen years, and that Mrs. Barrie then fell very deeply in love with another man, a young novelist called Gilbert Cannan, and left her husband, who divorced her in 1909; and no outline of Barrie's character or estimate of his artistic quality can have value if it fails to take these events into account. I have myself no doubt at all that the Barries' marriage did follow some such course as that of the hypothetical case described above. My chief authority for this is Mary Ansell herself, who in her book, *Dogs and Men*, published in 1924, goes very near to saying so. She is writing of her love for animals, and the passage reads:

> Their candour, their surprising confidence, disarms me. . . . I, too, become helplessly myself. They never withhold themselves from me as men withhold themselves. When the dogs loved me, they did it without forethought or afterthought, because they couldn't help it. But men didn't love me unless they wanted to; unless I fitted in with their idea of me. The dogs didn't have an idea of me. They just loved me—me—me—with passion and warmth, without thinking about it.

She goes on to say that she has only known what it was to love clever men, whose reserves were impregnable; and that she loved her dogs because they could never be clever in that way. "They could never be complicated as the men were complicated."

That is clear enough, but if corroboration is wanted I go to Barrie himself for it. He has not spoken directly of his marriage in any of his autobiographical writings, but in *Tommy and Grizel*, which appeared in 1900 and was the last and very much the finest and most mature of his Thrums books, there are many passages which I can only interpret as being intended to analyse and account for those very reserves and complications in himself to which Mary Ansell refers. In this book Tommy Sandys and Grizel are adults, but only she has "grown up". He is still Sentimental Tommy. The theme of the book is their love for one another; but while Grizel's love for Tommy is deep and true, the love of a woman for the man she hopes to marry (though, being drawn from Margaret Ogilvy, she will certainly "mother" him too much when she has got him), Tommy's love for Grizel is a boy's love, gusty and uncertain. The obstacle between them is Tommy's sister Elspeth, a sweet, backboneless creature whose dependence on her brother is absolute. But when Elspeth transfers her dependence from Tommy to the young Thrums doctor, and Grizel turns confidently to her lover for an answer to her own joy, that their time of waiting is over, she reads in his eyes only terror. He has been deceiving himself and her. He is afraid of marriage, afraid of reality, and—since she is an utterly real person—afraid of her.

All through this book the feeling strengthens that Tommy is Barrie's Mr. Hyde. The story heels gradually over towards tragedy—not Tommy's tragedy, for he is far below tragic stature, but Grizel's tragedy that the life of a woman so fine should be wrecked by her devotion to a man so unworthy. Tommy is by now a famous author—his great work, by a fine touch of irony, is all about women—but Grizel cares nothing at all for his fame or his book. Her one care is that he should grow up, and become real. It is as though Barrie were saying to himself, as the figure of Tommy dwindles and dwindles to his miserable death: "This is what *you* might become if you failed to be honest with yourself—if you let sentimentality, that 'leering distorted thing',[1] get the mastery over you." At the end of the book he comes very near to open confession that Tommy is himself, when in his own person he addresses the reader: "Have you discovered that I was really pitying the boy who was so fond of games that he could not with years become a man, telling nothing that was not true, but doing it with unnecessary scorn in the hope that I might goad you into saying, 'Come, come, you are too hard on him.'"

One is tempted also to wonder whether Grizel's haunting fear of something evil in her nature, that might at any moment break out and thwart her passionate desire to be good, is perhaps another transmutation of Barrie's fear of his sentimental side. Obviously, however, we cannot hope here to disentangle autobiographical fact from artistic embroidery. All that we can say with any certainty is that in the character of Tommy autobiographical fact is a main ingredient, and that Barrie seems to have known clearly enough the complications of his own nature. Also, Tommy is not the only one of Barrie's characters who realizes in the shadow of the altar that he is a born bachelor. Dick Abinger, or, to give him his pen-name, "Noble Simms", in *When a Man's Single*, goes through the same experience. It is therefore justifiable, I think, to suggest that Barrie had always had a suspicion that he might be temperamentally unfitted for married life, and that by the time

[1] *Tommy and Grizel*, p. 264.

he wrote *Tommy and Grizel* he knew it for a fact. This is, and must remain, a guess; but it agrees with the impressions of those of Barrie's old friends to whom I have mentioned it. One of them said flatly: "He should not have married, and he knew it. That is why he became friends again with his wife after she left him."[1]

Though *Tommy and Grizel* represents Barrie's high water mark as a novelist, it is, like all his novels, uneven—almost one might say lopsided. It was Barrie's way as a journalist (a way which he passed on to Tommy Sandys as a writer) to work most easily "in character". Tommy tells Grizel that some must write from their own character, but that it is to him a chariot that won't budge. "I have to assume a character, and then away we go." Barrie in *The Greenwood Hat* says that James Anon nearly always, except in his early articles, liked to assume a character, and that it was done to avoid identifying himself with any views. That is all very well for journalism, where the views expressed by the assumed character are those of the writer, and the character is a mere cloak for self-consciousness. In imaginative writing, where the character to be assumed is one altogether different from his own, Barrie finds transmigration into another body very difficult indeed. In *Tommy and Grizel* the two chief characters are brilliantly alive, because Barrie has created them out of the depths of his nature, and his knowledge of himself and his mother. But when he tries to draw Alice, Lady Pippinworth, the cold, heartless huntress of men who is Tommy's bad angel, he fails almost completely. Never for an instant does he show that sympathy which a

[1] In Barrie's will appears the entry: "To my dear Mary Cannon [sic], with my affectionate regards, £1000 and an annuity of £600."

writer must feel even for those of his characters of whom he profoundly disapproves. She is nothing but a lay figure with a rather ridiculously sinister expression. And Elspeth, Tommy's sister, is another lay figure with an expression of set sweetness.

Because Barrie, even at the age of forty, still suffered from this inability to bring fully to life any character that he saw objectively, I am convinced that those of his admirers who bitterly deplored his increasing pre-occupation with the theatre were wrong. The lack of form in his novels was not simply a question of faulty technique, which he might be expected to improve with practice; it corresponded to the curious mixture of deeps and shallows in his nature. When he had form imposed upon him by the rigid necessities of the theatre, he became instantly a craftsman of the highest order. In Harley Granville-Barker's phrase, his Pegasus went better in harness. Also, in the theatre the disproportionate contrast between deeps and shallows was not so clearly visible. Lady Pippinworth in the novel was nothing but an author's puppet. But if she had been put into a play, and had been worked upon at rehearsal by an actress of quality, a producer of vision and the author himself, she might have been given, if not life itself, at least the semblance of life. For example, Lady Sybil Tenterden[1] in *What Every Woman Knows* is a character in the Pippinworth class. She is not a real woman—but she is an actable part.

Barrie was to become a more completely equipped artist in the theatre than he could ever have been

[1] Her name was originally Lazenby, but was changed in the published play to avoid confusion with the Lasenby family in *The Admirable Crichton*.

outside it, and therefore an almost forgotten event which took place just before the publication of *Tommy and Grizel* is a very important landmark in his career. This was the production of his play, *The Wedding Guest*, at the Garrick Theatre on 27th September, 1900. To the astonishment of all theatrical London, this proved to be no gentle comedy but a tensely serious affair in which an artist on the point of marriage finds himself confronted by a discarded mistress, mother of his child. The critics, having recovered from their initial surprise, detected signs of the Ibsen influence, and fell to joyously. William Archer, as Prime Ibsenite, welcomed Barrie into the fold as " our new dramatist ". Clement Scott was now no longer on *The Daily Telegraph* to lead the opposing forces, but his successor assumed his mantle for the occasion. The play, in which H. B. Irving and Violet Vanbrugh played the leading parts, ran well for two months and then collapsed. Barrie never attempted anything in this manner again, and was no doubt wise to refrain; the importance of *The Wedding Guest* to us lies not in any intrinsic merit that it may have had, but in the proof it gives that its author had now dropped his " rather contemptuous " attitude to the theatre. All his plays, till now, had been in the nature of highly successful pot-boilers; and he showed what he thought of them himself by not allowing them, in spite of their success, to appear in print.

No artist of any kind enjoys being adversely criticized, for his work is so much a part of him that he cannot help being hurt when it is roughly handled. Some artists are so sensitive under criticism that they cannot help imputing malice, or at the best stupidity, to the critic. Others, stronger of fibre, wait till their feeling of injury has abated and then examine what criticism has had to say in the hope that they may find something to profit by. This was Barrie's way, as he says himself; and so we may imagine him retiring to his little study at 133 Gloucester Road and deciding, in the light of the reception of *The Wedding Guest* by critics and general public alike, that his intention to take the theatre more seriously did not mean that he must write more serious plays, but simply that he must give the theatre the best of himself. He had started off boldly, but in the wrong direction. He must take a step back and begin again.

He had done with Thrums as a setting; but he must still rely on Thrums as a source of inspiration, if only because his youthful memories were so much the most vivid. Casting back among these memories, or perhaps searching his last novel for dramatic material, he remembered the two Misses Adam and their genteel little school in Kirriemuir. He had already turned them to good use in the *Tommy* books, setting them in the blue and white room which in real life belonged to his married sister Isabella, and inventing a broken romance for one of them. Now he saw in that broken romance a delicate little comedy, to be set no longer in the Thrums of his boyhood, but in the England of Jane Austen and the Napoleonic wars—but still in the blue and white room. And so, taking his favourite stroll in Kensington Gardens (where about this time he made friends with a family of small boys, sons of Gerald du Maurier's beautiful sister, Sylvia Llewelyn Davies), he thought out *Quality Street*, the first of the series of plays which put to silence those who were still saying that Barrie had no true vocation for the theatre.

It is not a big play; but in it we see, for the first time, the artist (who knows what he wants to say) and the craftsman (who knows how to say it) working together in complete accord and with complete success. For the first time, also, Barrie is telling in the theatre a story which could not be so well expressed in any other medium. The central incident of *Quality Street* is the masquerade of Phœbe Throssel as her imaginary niece, Livvy. The thirty-year-old schoolmistress, worn out with years of drudgery, flings off her cap and shakes out her ringlets in a defiant gesture to show that her youth is not lost but only in hiding—and is, to all appearance, a girl again. Such a story might be difficult to make plausible in a novel, where the reader may decline to take the author's word for it that Phœbe can carry off the imposture. The playgoer has never a doubt, because the imposture is carried out before his eyes.

The very fragility of its plot makes this play an achievement all the more remarkable. It depends for momentum not upon a tale that moves forward of its own weight, but simply upon its author's skill in keeping it going. Nothing in Barrie's whole range of writing is much more remarkable than the dramatic inventiveness with which he contrives, particularly in the last act, to make threads of gossamer take the strain of dramatic tension without snapping. Nowhere has he achieved a more perfect blend of humour and sentiment, or shown a lighter and surer touch. That this was no happy accident can be proved—supposing proof to be needed—by two letters sent by Barrie to Seymour Hicks during the London run of the play. Hicks was playing the dashing Valentine Brown, and Frohman had told Barrie that their leading actor was indulging his incorrigible habit of "gagging". Barrie went in to see, but Hicks—as he confessed with the half-mischievous, half-guilty grin of a naughty boy when he showed me the letters—got wind of the author's presence and took out his "improvements". In the first of the letters, therefore, dated 22nd November, 1902, Barrie writes that he does not understand Frohman's message, and that he is cabling to him "Quality Street is played exactly as we rehearsed it". But a little later, Barrie slipped in again to see the play, and this time the naughty boy was caught. Barrie writes on 24th February, 1903:

I find that a good deal both in words and business has crept into the latter part of the 4th act of "Quality Street" that was not in it when produced. . . . My feeling is that in this part of the play (and not in any other, for I think you better than ever in the serious parts) we have got out of the spirit of the piece and what I meant for comedy has become farce.

I am anxious for Frohman to see the production at its best and I wish you would have a rehearsal of this scene only of the last act and cut out all words and business that were not in the piece as I left it. If you would like me to come down and go over it with you I shall do so with pleasure. You see in a play of this kind if the delicacy goes the strong [1] thing is gone.

Quality Street was produced in New York on 11th November, 1901, with Maude Adams as Phœbe; but for some reason Frohman waited nearly a year before bringing it to London. It came to the Vaudeville Theatre on 17th September, 1902, and it ran for 459 performances, Ellaline Terriss playing Phœbe to her

[1] This word is an indecipherable whorl in the original. "Strong" is the only guess I can find which fits both the shape of the whorl and the meaning of the sentence.

husband's Valentine. Even Archer could not lament the loss of his proselyte in the face of this enchanting romance; and only six weeks later that most solid and sound of critics had reason to hope that after all "our new dramatist" might be able to find his own way to do more important work, for on 4th November, 1902, *The Admirable Crichton* was staged at the Duke of York's Theatre. H. B. Irving played Bill Crichton, the perfect butler who, wrecked on a desert island with the rest of the survivors from the yacht of his master the Earl of Loam, becomes in two years, by natural selection, the ruler of the island. The other castaways, aristocrats though they have been in ordinary life, are proud to be his subjects; and the haughty Lady Mary—played by Barrie's old friend, Irene Vanbrugh—is overwhelmed by the honour he does her when he chooses her for his consort. But they are rescued, and automatically butler and lady go back to their former stations.

The play caused a sensation, by reason not so much of its dramatic merits as of its implied social criticism. People discussed its subversive ideas with enormous solemnity. Archer questioned whether Barrie had the slightest idea of the immensity of the attack which he had delivered on the existing system—and in this he was no doubt right, for it is most unlikely that Barrie had intended to deliver any attack at all. H. M. Walbrook, looking back after the war, came to the conclusion that the dramatic critics of the time had taken the comedy much too seriously, since the aristocrats of the play are figures of farce rather than comedy. My own view is that the social criticism in the play was purely accidental. Conan Doyle claims a modest share in the conception of *The Admirable Crichton*, saying that he once suggested to Barrie, when they were out for a walk, that there might be a good story in the idea of master and man cast away on a desert island, when the man, being better able to cope with the situation, would become master. That this was the main point of the play to Barrie is proved by his remark in *The Greenwood Hat* that he wrote the third act of this play before writing acts one and two; and this also shows that the characters were invented to fit the dramatic situation, not to point an argument. In other words, the aristocrats were shown as fools or weaklings because the story required fools and weaklings, and not because Barrie thought that aristocrats were necessarily either foolish or weak. If the Lady Mary of the third act is to be both a trim young Amazon who can outrun a buck and kill it with a home-made bow and arrow, and a deft parlour-maid who serves a meal to Crichton with the devotion of an acolyte serving a shrine, then the more languid, the more dependent on and contemptuous of her servants is the Lady Mary of the first act, the more effective will be the contrast in the theatre.

The accident that this story touched a sensitive spot in the social consciousness of the time has spoilt the play's chance of survival. Although *The Admirable Crichton* ranks among the very best of Barrie's plays, it has " dated " as the others have not. Barrie himself seems later on to have regretted that this idea had not come to him after instead of before the war, for in 1920 he wrote a new last act for the play in which Crichton no longer accepted meekly the return to his old subservient position. But such afterthoughts rarely succeed. *The Admirable Crichton* had too much artistic integrity in its original form to bear being tinkered with. It had a theme that was universal, but its treatment turned it into a piece of social satire, which is perhaps the most ephemeral of all kinds of writing.

Chapter IX

PETER PAN

SOME time in 1902 the Barries migrated from the south to the north side of Kensington Gardens, their new house being Leinster Corner, overlooking the Park at Lancaster Gate. Barrie's friendship with the Davies children was now firmly established, and he brought to his games with them a child's zest and a man's breadth of imagination. He had a genius for games, as his wife tells us in her book. His romps with Porthos, the big St. Bernard, which were enjoyed equally by both participants and did not cease till both were exhausted, often made a shambles of the little Gloucester Road house, and one of the reasons given for leaving it was that Porthos needed more room. Barrie's games with the small boys were more elaborate, and the rarest of all his printed works is the single surviving copy of *The Boy Castaways of Black Lake Island*, " published by J. M. Barrie in the Gloucester Road, 1901 ". This describes itself as " a record of the terrible adventures of three brothers in the summer of 1901, faithfully set forth by No. 3 " [1]; and it is an embroidery on the games of pirates and red Indians which Barrie and his youthful gang played at Barrie's country house, Black Lake Cottage, near Farnham.

Meanwhile, in Kensington Gardens themselves, an-

[1] No. 3, now Peter Davies, the publisher, was about four at the time.

other saga was coming into being. References to this can be found in the dedication "To the Five" which Barrie wrote to the play *Peter Pan*, when at last it was published in 1928, but at the time all that Barrie allowed the public to know of it was part of *The Little White Bird*, which came out in November, 1902, and set the staider critics sadly by the ears because it was called a novel and turned out to be nothing of the sort. It was more completely lacking in form than any other book even of his. Some of its chapters were separate pieces, previously published, and now dragged in to make part of a rambling tale into which they fitted with some unease; it wandered out of the real world into fairyland and back in the most disconcerting way, without warning, explanation, or apology. One thing, however, was certain. By whatever label it was described, this curious composition was utterly charming. The critics gave up the attempt to classify, and went on to praise. And thus Barrie took formal possession of that half-world which lies on the borders between realism and fantasy, and of which he has been the undisputed king ever since.

To the general body of readers, *The Little White Bird* is chiefly known as the book which gave Peter Pan for the first time to the world. Peter walks into the middle of the book without warning, becomes its chief inhabitant for five chapters, and departs as unceremoniously as he came, and he represents Barrie's first attempt to give a local habitation and a name to the great game of make-believe which he and the Davies children played together. But the book is of more interest than that to the theatre-lover, for in it is to be found the original idea, not only of *Peter Pan*, but of every long play that Barrie was ever to write into which enters the fantastic element. The ball scene in *A Kiss for Cinderella*, for example, is to be found here, already worked out in one or two of its details, in the chapter called "The Pleasantest Club in London", where Irene, the little Cockney nursemaid, tells the child David the story of Cinderella with herself as its unconscious heroine. The main idea of *Dear Brutus* is to be found in one of the maxims of old Solomon Caw, who rules the Island in the Serpentine: "In this world there are no second chances." And in the chapter called "A Night-Piece" is a passage about the ghosts of dead young mothers, who come back into the world to find out how their children fare. This is a clear foreshadowing of *Mary Rose*. Indeed, the scene in which Mary Rose meets her son grown up, and will not own him because he is no longer the child she knew, is already set down in full.

To the biographer, *The Little White Bird* is full of significance. The book has nothing in it of the kind of personal reminiscence that went to the making of *Sentimental Tommy*, though it is true that Porthos, the St. Bernard, is introduced under his own name and with his own peculiar habits (especially a fondness for mechanical toys). On the other hand, one cannot read far in it without beginning to realize that Porthos's imaginary master, Captain W., is drawn pretty closely to the measure of Porthos's real master. The description of this lonely bachelor, his sorrow for the love he has lost and his yearning for fatherhood, is charged with a profound and poignant emotion such as Barrie only achieved when his own feelings were deeply engaged. In some passages the sense of thwarted paternity is strong enough to make the book embarrassing to read.

The success of *The Little White Bird* was the crowning event of a very full year for Barrie, and as both *Quality Street* and *The Admirable Crichton* continued to run merrily throughout the spring and summer of 1903, it was perhaps not surprising that he produced no work of major importance in that year. He was not idle, however, for in September, just after *The Admirable Crichton* had been taken off at last, he staged at Wyndham's a curious gastronomical morality-play called *Little Mary*. This was little more than a casual comment on the habit of the English upper class of eating too much. Its heroine was an Irish girl, who cured the "best people" of most of their ills by putting them on a regime prescribed by a mysterious oracle whom she called Little Mary. The revelation which came at the end of the play, that this being was in fact the stomach, was a most successful theatrical surprise on the first night, but it was thought that once the joke was known people would not trouble to see the play. On the contrary, it ran for 208 performances at Wyndham's, and added a phrase to the language. For years afterwards we were accustomed to refer to our stomachs as our little maries, though most of us would have been hard put to it to explain whence the expression came, or why it meant what it did mean. The play was never published, nor is it ever likely to be revived except as a curiosity.

Barrie had a collaborator in *Little Mary*. One day at the Davies' house he gave "No. 2", who was about ten at the time, a large package of sweets, and the boy's mother warned him that if he ate them all at once he would be sick in the morning. "Not in the morning, mummy—to-night," was the answer; and Barrie embodied the line in his play, drawing up a delightful burlesque of a legal agreement in which J. M. Barrie (to be hereafter called the aforesaid) undertook to pay John Ll. Davies (to be hereafter called the abovementioned) the sum of one halfpenny per diem during the run of the play of which he was part author. The date of this document is 6th December, 1903, by which time *Little Mary* had already been running some weeks, so perhaps at its first production the play may have been Barrie's unaided work [1].

After this, nothing more from Barrie's pen appeared in the London theatre for over a year. *The Admirable Crichton* was produced in New York, with William Gillette in the name part. *Quality Street* ran its course. *Little Mary* disappeared, and with it No. 2's independent income. Then, some time in the autumn of 1904, Charles Frohman began to stop his friends in the street and tell them of a wonderful new play that Barrie had just given him, an extraordinary affair about a being called Peter Pan, who was half a very ordinary boy and half a fairy. Barrie himself had no great hope that the play would have much appeal to the public, but his own affection for it was so great that he must put it to the test. As a practical man of the theatre he saw that it would be immensely expensive to produce, and to make up to Frohman for the loss he would have to face, he had written another play called *Alice Sit-by-the-Fire*, which was almost certain to succeed since it was in

[1] This incident had a counterpart long afterwards. In his last years Barrie was a frequent visitor at Glamis Castle. Princess Margaret Rose entertained him to tea there on her third birthday, and showed him one of her presents which had specially pleased her. Barrie said, " Is that really yours ?" and the little girl answered, " It is yours and mine." The spontaneous tact of this so delighted Barrie that he used it in *The Boy David*, which he was writing at the time.

his usual vein and had a good part for Ellen Terry.

Frohman's faith in Barrie was by this time so great that he had promised to put on both plays without reading either, and with the author's warning sounding in his ears he must have sat down to the manuscript of *Peter Pan* with some trepidation. But from the moment he read it he fell in love with the play, and it became a labour of love with him to see that Barrie's ideas should be carried out as fully as lavish expenditure and theatrical ingenuity could contrive. All kinds of mechanical effects were necessary. Four of the characters had to fly—not merely swing to and fro at the end of wires, as fairy ballets were accustomed to do in pantomimes, but fly about a room, perch on a mantelpiece, and depart by a window. We have grown so used to these things now that we take them for granted, forgetting that when they were first attempted they were portentous novelties. Frohman took difficulties in his stride, and never lost confidence. Rehearsals went forward with the company pledged to secrecy, and in the atmosphere of hope mingled with doubt that is the special characteristic of the stage; but theatre people are always suspicious of anything new, and doubt must have predominated. Barrie tells of a depressed-looking man who would appear from time to time out of the shadows carrying a pot of paint or a mug of tea, sigh like a reproachful ghost in the author's ear that the gallery boys would never stand it, and vanish. But when the play was produced at the Duke of York's on 27th December, 1904, the gallery boys were captivated like everybody else. There was an immense chorus of praise, and Frohman, back in America by this time and anxiously waiting for news, had the proudest moment of his life.

" It was alway yet the trick of our English nation, if they have a good thing, to make it too common." Shakespeare knew his England, and if he had lived later would have found America no less given to the same fault. *Peter Pan* was and is a masterpiece, but its admirers on both sides of the Atlantic have done it the great disservice of making it a cult. That is, they have claimed too much for it, and so have brought into existence by natural reaction a body of opinion predisposed to give it less than its due. A very eminent critic told me once that he never hears Peter Pan's cry, " I don't want to go to school and learn solemn things . . . I want always to be a little boy and have fun," without a shudder of disgust. Well, it is true enough that the sentiment is not a very exalted one, and true again (this, of course, is what the critic in question meant) that Peter's words reflect Barrie's own reluctance, when he became a man, to put away childish things. But a critic who feels scorn or disgust for this reluctance is failing in the first duty of criticism, which is to meet the artist on his own ground. He is blaming Barrie for not being St. Paul, when St. Paul was the last person on earth that Barrie would have wished to be. The fact that Barrie was always looking back with longing to " the dear dead days that were so much the best ", and that he could say with sincerity that nothing that happens after we are twelve matters very much, prevented him from finding happiness and peace of mind; but it made him as an artist. Now, with his powers at their fullest maturity, with his memory of his own youth, vivid as it already was, made more vivid still by his friendship with " The Five ", he was able to pour into the composition of *Peter Pan* the quintessence of all that lay deepest in himself. It is thus that great plays are written; and *Peter Pan*, even though it looks backwards rather than forwards, is a great play.

Barrie says he has no recollection of writing it, and the statement is so fantastically unlikely that one is inclined to believe it. In one sense, he had been writing it all his life. The little boy of seven, who with James Robb staged an entertainment in a tiny Kirriemuir wash-house that was the original of Wendy's house; the young schoolboy whose chief horror it was that some day he would have to give up his games, and could not see how it was to be done; the older schoolboy who played a sort of pirate Odyssey in a garden at Dumfries—all these were already collaborating in the work. Tommy Sandys, in *Tommy and Grizel*, has an idea for a fantasy about a boy who would not grow up. Peter Pan himself appears, as we have seen, in *The Little White Bird*, but here he has not much in common with the hero of the play, for he is a naked baby of a week old; a part which no star actress would care to play. It was in Barrie's games with " The Five ", in Kensington Gardens and on the Black Lake, that the threads began to be drawn together, and this gives just enough justification for his explanation that he obtained the Peter Pan of the play by rubbing all five of them violently together. It is a pretty figure of speech in the best Barrie manner, but it does not disturb our knowledge that Peter is Barrie himself, and that Wendy, like Grizel as a girl, was drawn from Margaret Ogilvy.

Wendy had no part in the Black Lake saga, but Porthos had; and so Porthos is the real original of the dog Nana in the play. His sex had to be changed, however, and in the end his breed was altered too; for by

Donald McLeish

THE PETER PAN STATUE IN KENSINGTON GARDENS, LONDON

Designed by Sir George Frampton, R.A.

the time the play was ready for the stage Porthos was dead, and a Newfoundland, Luath, had succeeded him; and it was Luath's coat that was copied for Nana.

Nina Boucicault acted Peter on that memorable first night, and those who saw her will not have it that she has been surpassed by any of the lengthening list of actresses who have played the part since. She did not play it very often, however, for after 145 performances Frohman took the play off, having decided to treat it as a Christmas entertainment, with revivals each year so long as the public should remain faithful; and at the first revival, in 1905, she was succeeded by Cecilia Loftus. Meanwhile, on 6th November, 1905, Maude Adams had appeared as Peter in New York. Here Frohman allowed the play to run its full course, and Miss Adams's success swept the country. The play became an institution in two worlds, and is still an institution here. For more than thirty years it has been revived every Christmas, in its original scenery and with no more than a few incidental changes. No other play in the history of the theatre has had to stand such a test, for most " classics " have the advantage of fresh interpretation to prevent their traditions from growing musty. Yet, stained and staled as it now is, *Peter Pan* still shines like a fine jewel in a tarnished setting. That mixture of humour and sentiment which was the best of Barrie's magic is untouched—and perhaps untouchable—by time. Here and there, when the mixture has failed to fuse, we have touches of mawkishness, or obvious stage tricks such as the popular but nauseous appeal to the audience to clap its hands if it believes in fairies. This incident was not in the play originally, and the appeal seems to have been made for the first time by Maude Adams in New York. It is possible, therefore, that Barrie was not primarily responsible for it, though he has since assumed responsibility by including it in the published version of the play. However, such lapses into sentimentality are very few, and do not affect the structure of the play or spoil its fabric.

How strong that structure is, and how liberally shot with gold the fabric, time has shown. Barrie speaks, in his dedication, of a score of acts that had to be left out when he came to give the Peter Pan saga to the public in "the thin form of a play"; and that is the impression one gets from *Peter Pan*, of material so abundant and so ready to the author's hand that he was embarrassed to know what to leave out rather than what to put in. His omissions are, in fact, masterly. Writing as a child for children, he takes the child's privilege of skipping awkward explanations. Yet so sure is his step in this borderland country of his that we never question his most surprising statements—we accept the dog nurse, and Hook's Charles the Second clothes, and Smee's sewing machine as calmly as we accept the more usual appurtenances of fairyland. And so complete is his hold over any audience that is ready and able to give him a child's sympathy, that the narrative tension of the tale never slackens even when—as in the Mermaid's Lagoon, which is a detachable act, written in after the play was first produced, and often omitted since—the narrative itself stops dead. Was ever subtle burlesque better blended with genuine excitement than in the scene on Hook's ship? But indeed, Captain Hook ranks as one of the great comic creations of our time. Like Pistol, he is a villain above life size, who has brought grandiloquence to a fine art; but he is a better stage figure than Pistol, who often eludes the actor.

When *Peter Pan* ended its original run, it was succeeded at the Duke of York's by *Alice Sit-by-the-Fire*, on 5th April, 1905. Barrie and Frohman could afford to smile now at the idea that the profits on this play had been relied on to pay for the losses on the bigger venture, and the smile must have grown a little ironic when the new play proved hardly able to do more than pay for itself. It was a rather thin little comedy, which contained the promised good part for Ellen Terry and very little else. There was some gentle satire at the expense of conventional comedies of the day, with their mechanical seduction scenes; there was some gentler satire still at the propensity of adolescent youth to regard these plays as an exact mirror of life; there was Ellen Terry as a wise and humorous mother, guiding her young but cocksure daughter through a ridiculous adventure without letting her find out that from first to last she had been making a fool of herself. With the proverbial Terry charm superimposed upon the Barrie charm, this little play had every chance. But it lacked strength to run for more than 115 performances, which by the standards of actress and author was something far short of success. The play was a short one, and the evening's entertainment was filled out by the production of a fantasy in one act, *Pantaloon*, whose interest lies less in its own merits than in the fact that it was Barrie's first attempt, since he had become an experienced dramatist, in the shorter form of which he was soon to prove himself a master.

Chapter X

SHORT PLAYS

TO the end of his life Barrie was what Stevenson had once called him, " a very Scotty Scot "; but little by little the centre of his existence was shifting south, and one by one the ties that bound him to his native place were snapping. David Barrie, his father, had died in June, 1902, at the good old age of eighty-eight. He might have lived many years more, but he was knocked down while crossing a road, and, though not badly hurt, did not long survive the shock to his system. In November of the following year Sara, Barrie's only surviving unmarried sister, died very suddenly, leaving her uncle, David Ogilvy, in sole possession of Strathview and bereft of his devoted housekeeper. And on 25th August, 1904, he too died. The house now became the property of Alexander, Barrie's elder brother, who retired to it in 1907, when his long service as Inspector of Schools came to an end. The fact that he was now a visitor in his old home is oddly reflected in Barrie's writing. In his earlier plays Scotland, if it appeared at all, was always the country in which the characters lived (as in *The Little Minister*) or to which they went (as in *The Professor's Love Story*). Now it became the country from which they migrated, or to which they paid a short visit.

What Every Woman Knows was his next big play;

indeed, it was his next play of any kind except for a very damp political squib called *Josephine*, produced at the Comedy on 5th April, 1906, and *Punch*, an unsuccessful skit on Bernard Shaw, which served it as curtain-raiser. The two chief characters in *What Every Woman Knows* are both Scots, and the first two acts of the play pass in Scotland. But the whole force of the action comes from the fact that these two, John Shand and Maggie Wylie, his wife, go South to conquer England, and that John finds, to his great surprise, that without the humble and despised Maggie he cannot make his conquest. This comedy ranks, perhaps, just below Barrie's very best, but it is an endearing piece of work which lingers gratefully in the memory. Chiefly this is due to the character of Maggie Wylie, the wise Scotswoman who knows so much better than anybody else exactly how dependent upon her is the husband who thinks himself the sole architect of his own fortunes. Maggie is Margaret Ogilvy once again, but with an individuality of her own as well. John and Maggie were played by two of the triumphant *Peter Pan* cast. Gerald du Maurier, who had been not only Mr. Darling but a magnificently comic Hook as well, again showed, as a Scots railway porter, that his range was not as limited as some people liked to pretend; and Hilda Trevelyan won all hearts with a Maggie who, quite rightly, was her Wendy grown up and speaking with a Scottish accent.

The transition from middle-class Scotland to upper-class England in this play is done with a realistic certainty new in Barrie's work. It is true, as I have said already, that Lady Sybil Tenterden has too much about her of Sentimental Tommy's Lady Pippinworth; but the Comtesse de la Brière, the frivolous, shrewd Frenchwoman who sees what Maggie Wylie is up to and is no more content than Puck in *A Midsummer-Night's Dream* to let well alone, is quite another story. She is the best character belonging to his new world that Barrie has yet drawn, and her value to the play is not easy to overestimate. *What Every Woman Knows* was produced at the Duke of York's on 3rd September, 1908, and had a run of 384 performances. The New York production followed on 23rd December with Maude Adams as Maggie, and that, too, had an enormous success. But this triumphal progress of a play about a marriage that began badly but ended well must have seemed to Barrie an ironic twist of circumstance a few months later. The play was still running, when, in July, 1909, he found that his wife had a lover, and that she wanted him to divorce her. The news came as a complete surprise and a terrible shock, and he did everything that he could to persuade her to stay with him. She, however, recognizing with a directness characteristic of her that all was over between them, refused either to let him forgive her or to agree to a separation, and on 13th October, 1909, he brought an action and obtained a divorce.

The break-up of his marriage dealt Barrie a blow from which he never fully recovered, and for the time being it brought down his private world in ruins. In his work from this time onwards there was apt to be a note of disillusion and sense of failure; the cheerful, boyish optimism of his earlier romances was gone. Barrie himself, conscious of the change, made a characteristic joke about it in *The Greenwood Hat*, accounting for it by the attack of writer's cramp which compelled him, a few years after this,[1] to write with his left hand instead of his right (no great hardship, as he was naturally left-handed). Worse than this, he seemed to have lost the zest for writing, and to be unable to face the effort of planning anything on a big scale. For six or seven years he produced nothing but one-act plays, some of which may have been in his desk already at the time of his divorce. The only long play which he completed during this time was not merely a failure but, as I shall show when the time comes, was an ill-advised attempt to expand a one-act play already in existence.

There is a point about the order of Barrie's one-act plays which is worth noticing. When he collected the best of his plays into one volume in 1928, he first printed the full-length compositions in the order in which they had been written and produced, except for *Peter Pan*, which had to come at the beginning because it had before it the long dedication "To the Five", which now served as preface to the book. After the long plays come the short ones, but they do not stand at all in order of production. Barrie has arranged them like this: *Pantaloon*, *Half an Hour*, *Seven Women*, *Old Friends*, *Rosalind*, *The Will*, *The Twelve-Pound Look*, four war plays, and *Shall We Join the Ladies?* This order is roughly chronological, for the first seven were written before the war, the next four in the war years, and the last one after the war. The thought came to me that it might be *exactly* chronological, the order being that in which Barrie had *written* the plays. For a time I took this seriously as a theory, but I finally gave it up when an examination of the war plays in the volume proved

[1] According to his own account, after the writing of *The Old Lady Shows Her Medals*.

that they are *not* arranged in order of composition. These four plays are *The New Word*, *A Well-Remembered Voice*, *Barbara's Wedding*, and *The Old Lady Shows Her Medals*, in that order. It is an attested fact that *The Old Lady Shows Her Medals* was first produced in April, 1917; and in *A Well-Remembered Voice* there is a reference to meat-tickets, which did not come into use till the beginning of 1918. This seems to me conclusive.

One thing, however, did become clear while I was investigating this point. Barrie had a way of burying his one-act plays as a dog buries bones, and only dug them up when he happened to want one, and could remember where it was. When he wrote a full-length play, he always found a manager, generally Frohman, standing at his elbow while he finished it, ready to snap it up before the ink was dry. Not even his least characteristic writings in that form "hung fire". It was different with short plays. Even when it was by Barrie, a one-act play could never be certain of immediate production because the demand for such pieces was not great. The steady retreat of the dinner-hour later and later into the evening had shortened the theatre programmes. In mid-Victorian days playgoers would have felt defrauded if they had been offered an evening's entertainment consisting of one play only, but in the late Edwardian times of which I am now writing one play a night had already come to be the rule, staged at an hour to suit the late diners. Now and then, when a play was shorter than usual, managers would remember the old tradition and put on a "curtain-raiser". But when Barrie began to write his one-act plays even the "curtain-raiser" was beginning to drop out of fashion.

It is not very surprising, therefore, if Barrie allowed

his one-act plays to accumulate in his desk. He wrote them on impulse, while an idea was hot in his mind, and without worrying his head about chances of production. Also, he was vague and casual about them to a degree. There is a story, for instance, that when Frohman started a repertory theatre scheme at the Duke of York's in 1910, and had Granville-Barker as one of his right-hand men, Barker wanted some one-act plays for a triple bill and asked Barrie if he had anything of the sort. Barrie thought he had one somewhere, written six months before, probably in a drawer of his desk. Barker rummaged, and found *The Twelve-Pound Look*. This tale is related by Frohman's biographers, and probably, like many stories in their interesting but unreliable book, is true in essence but inaccurate in detail. For one thing, Barrie's contribution to the triple bill was not one play, but two, *Old Friends* being the other. The story, therefore, cannot be accepted as it stands.

The Twelve-Pound Look was Barrie's first production after the divorce proceedings, and I do not think it needs a stretch of imagination to suggest that it is a transmutation into story form of his own feelings at the time. Just as in *Tommy and Grizel* he made the worst of himself into a sentimentalist, so now he made the worst of himself into Sir Harry Sims, the man successful in every worldly respect and yet a failure in his private life. The play was produced at the Duke of York's on 1st March, 1910, and from the first it had a very great success. Besides *Old Friends*, it had as companion in the triple bill a dramatic dialogue by George Meredith, *The Sentimentalists*, which the critics agreed would have been a charming piece of work to read. We may suspect that Barrie influenced the choice of this fragment (for it was no more) as a tribute to his old and much-admired friend, who had died nearly a year before; but Meredith was no dramatist. *Old Friends* had no great merit, though Barrie had enough affection for it to publish it. It is a very ordinary little piece, with the hereditary craving for drink as a theme. After this run was over, these two pieces went on to the shelf; but *The Twelve-Pound Look* refused to be forgotten. It was revived in the following year at the Little Theatre, and soon afterwards it gave its author a new and very unexpected experience.

The managers of the great systems of music-halls, which in those unmechanical days were the chief popular houses of entertainment, had discovered that their audiences liked seeing famous stage actors and actresses in good short plays. Irene Vanbrugh had an offer to "go on the halls" which Dion Boucicault, her husband and producer, who had staged several of Barrie's plays for him, thought that she ought to accept. The play she wanted for this purpose was *The Twelve-Pound Look*; but Barrie had a prejudice against music-halls, thinking that his work was unlikely to appeal to big popular audiences, and he refused to let her do the play.[1] Miss Vanbrugh pleaded so hard, however, that at last, as a gesture of friendship to the actress, he allowed himself to be persuaded. Much to his astonishment, he found on visiting the London Hippodrome that the play went even better before its new public than in the regular theatre. His prejudice vanished. Indeed, he confessed

[1] A curious coincidence may be noted here. In an article on the music-hall contributed to *Time* in 1889 (referred to on p. 52) Barrie pronounced this form of entertainment "mostly stupid and vulgar". But he went on to say that its tone was improving, and added that the rate of progress "would be increased if the proprietors were allowed to produce stage-plays, as of course they ought to be".

that he actually preferred the music-hall audience, with its direct, hearty expression of its opinions, to the politer but less responsive, and therefore less inspiring, audience of the theatre. After that, Miss Vanbrugh had a triumphal progress with *The Twelve-Pound Look*, and Barrie found a new outlet for his ideas. In September, 1913, *Half an Hour* was given its first stage production at the Hippodrome, Miss Vanbrugh playing the heroine, and a topical skit on the censorship, *The Dramatists Get What They Want*, was contributed to the revue, *Hullo, Ragtime*, at the same theatre a month later.

Meanwhile, in 1911, Barrie had gone back to his former love with the publication of *Peter and Wendy*, which was the story of the play *Peter Pan* retold in the form of a novel. Once again he showed his firm determination to keep the two forms of composition apart. The book followed the main lines of the play, it is true, but it was a novel in conception and execution. If anybody could pick it up and read it now without having heard of the play, he would find nothing of the theatre sticking to it. This Peter Pan of the Neverland is not quite the original Peter of Kensington Gardens, but neither is he the Peter Pan whom Pauline Chase was now impersonating each year at the Duke of York's Theatre. Indeed, the differences between book and play disconcerted the many sentimentalists who had by this time lost all sense of proportion, regarded the play as a kind of holy writ, and visited it in much the same frame of mind as if its performance were a religious ritual. These worshippers were presented, in the next year, with an appropriately sentimental idol for their adoration in the shape of Frampton's pretty-pretty statue of Peter Pan, which was set up in Kensington Gardens.

Rosalind was Barrie's only new production in 1912. It is a charming trifle, with something in it of *Quality Street*, for it tells how a young man, very much in love with an actress, goes on a walking tour and finds (as he thinks) the actress's mother, revelling in middle-aged comfort. In reality it is the actress herself, taking a rest from the necessity to be gay and young. Barrie's flair for stage effect has never been better shown than at the end of this play. A telegram recalls the actress to London to play Rosalind, and she changes herself almost before our eyes (to-day, I suppose, she would do it actually before our eyes) from middle-aged frump to brilliant young dazzler. *Rosalind* was part of yet another triple bill at the Duke of York's, and in spite of the fact that the other two plays were the work of Shaw and Pinero, it outlasted them both, and gave Irene Vanbrugh a chance that no actress of her ability could possibly have missed.

The next year brought yet another mark of success; on 14th June, Barrie was made a baronet. It is said that he had been offered a knighthood in 1909, but had refused it on account of his impending divorce. It must have been with a sense of tragic irony that he, to whom the parental relation had always meant so much more than any other, now accepted a hereditary title which nobody would inherit. Perhaps something of this feeling was behind the remark he made at the private and informal dinner which some of his friends gave to celebrate the event: "When I began writing novels, people said they were not real novels. When I began writing plays, folk said they were not real plays. I expect men are going about now saying I am not a real baronet." Perhaps it is to this feeling that we must

L. Caswall Smith

J. M. Barrie
(1913)

relate the bitterness of *The Will*, which was produced about ten weeks later, on 4th September, at the Duke of York's.

The critics were impressed by *The Will*, as indeed they had cause to be; and their praise was all the more emphatic because the chief event of the same evening, Barrie's first new long play for five years, was a dismal failure. This was a comedy called *The Adored One*, which has the strangest and most chequered history of any play that Barrie wrote. It has not been published, but its first act is practically identical with the one-act play, *Seven Women*, which is in the collected edition of the plays. A naval officer, arriving at a house where he is to dine, finds that his hostess has asked him half an hour too early. His host, before disappearing apologetically to get dressed, enumerates the women who are expected to dinner—there are among them, for instance, a woman with no sense of humour, one with almost too much, a coquette, a devoted mother, and a murderess. After the host goes upstairs, Leonora arrives, and the sailor whiles away the time in trying to discover which of the various women she is, only to find in the end that she is herself all seven, including the murderess. Thus far *Seven Women*; and thus far Barrie had a delighted audience for *The Adored One*. But then it turned out, in the long play, that the lady really *was* a murderess. She had pushed a man out of a railway-carriage because he had insisted on keeping the window open, when her little girl had a cold. The play went on to a trial scene in the Gilbert and Sullivan manner, in which Leonora won the hearts of the jury and was acquitted against all the evidence. There was no indication that this was intended for burlesque, and the curtain fell, for the first and last time in Barrie's career, to the sound of hisses. For once, he had failed to make his fantasy fuse with his realism.

Barrie deferred to criticism he found just, as was his way, and went quickly to work to remodel the play. It was now made clear that Leonora was not really a murderess, and that the trial scene was only a dream. It was too late, however; the damage was done. Not even Mrs. Patrick Campbell's acting as Leonora had been able to prevent the word from going round that the play was a bad one, and the revision was too late to save it. But Barrie had his consolation. On 5th January, 1914, the new version of the play was produced in New York as *The Legend of Leonora*, with Maude Adams in the name-part, and had a success. The New York critics accused the London public of lack of humour for having rejected the play, which, in all the circumstances, was not quite fair to London. And in the end, London had the chance to show that it was not blind to the quality of the best part of the play, for when Irene Vanbrugh appeared four years later in *Seven Women*, she had almost as great a success with Leonora as with Rosalind. *Seven Women* gives us the strongest proof that exists of Barrie's bone-burying propensity with his short plays. It has been generally assumed, because its first production came so long after that of *The Adored One*, that what Barrie had here done was to take the one undeniably effective act of his despised long play and round it off to make a new " one-acter ". Irene Vanbrugh is my authority for saying that the process really worked the other way round. To her knowledge, the one-act version of the story is the original. The other two acts were tacked on, with a good deal less than

Barrie's usual skill, when a demand rose for a new long play.

The next new production in 1913 was *Half an Hour*. This went into a variety programme at the Hippodrome on 29th September, not four weeks after *The Adored One* had had its stormy reception; and it too, though it met nothing but praise, promptly became the subject of controversy. It was a highly concentrated play of tense, swift action, timed to occupy just half an hour in playing (the rule in music-halls was that no play might last longer). Irene Vanbrugh took the part of Lady Lilian Garson, a wife who leaves her brute of a husband in order to go to Egypt with her lover. He, going out to look for a cab, is run over in the street and killed; a doctor who happens to be passing breaks the news to Lady Lilian. She, in desperation, and not knowing what else to do, goes back to her house, contrives to dress in time for dinner and destroy the evidence of her flight—and finds that the doctor of the previous scene is a guest at her table. After the first performance of this piece, an indignant playgoer wrote to *The Times* complaining of the deleterious influence which writing for the music-halls was likely to have on dramatists of Barrie's standing, since a fine idea for a three-act play had here been sacrificed to the need for speed and sensation. Albert de Courville, then manager of the Hippodrome, answered the objector neatly and completely by saying that the play had not been specially written for that or any other variety theatre, that Frohman himself had told Barrie that the plot was good enough for a long play and it was a pity to waste it, and that it was by Barrie's own determination that the play had been kept to the shorter length.

If, as I still feel may have been the case, Barrie had a vague chronological order in his mind when he arranged his one-act plays for publication, we have here a possible reason why he put *Half an Hour* so surprisingly early in the order. May he not have written it many years before, and then have felt, as Frohman and *The Times* letter-writer clearly felt, that the plot was too good to waste on a one-act play? May he not have kept it by him with the idea of turning it into a big play some day; and then, when it came to the point, have felt too weary to make the effort? This is, admittedly, a guess; but not, I hope, a wild one.

Chapter XI

THE WAR YEARS

AT the outbreak of the war Barrie, in common with the rest of his countrymen, was faced by the necessity of adjusting himself to a world turned suddenly upside down. Like the nation in general, he began with an outburst of indignation at the invasion of Belgium, and then settled to the long business of keeping a stout heart and making the best of things. *Der Tag*, produced at the Coliseum on 21st December, 1914, was the one direct comment upon the war that he made in the theatre. It was a fine *pièce d'occasion*. It had some of the faults inherent in all art that is made to serve a political purpose, but it put into dignified language the cause for which the Allies were fighting, and was memorably acted by Norman McKinnel as the Kaiser and Irene Vanbrugh as the Spirit of Culture. Then Barrie, never very happy in the world of affairs, went back to his characteristic vein. War-time England, with its alternation of gaiety and sadness, was akin to something in his own nature. He was to do some of his best work during those years.

He led off badly, however. Gaby Deslys, a French music-hall performer with good looks but no conspicuous talent except for the wearing of clothes which contrived to be at the same time voluminous and scanty, was then a favourite with London audiences. Barrie, for some odd reason, conceived a great admiration for her and wrote a revue, called *Rosy Rapture, or the Pride of the Beauty Chorus*, specially designed for her. Frohman put it on at the Duke of York's on 22nd March, 1915, and it failed completely. It was a curious trait in Barrie's character that he never could bring himself to admit that he had no ability for devising this kind of entertainment. *Rosy Rapture* went the way of *Jane Annie, Josephine* and *Punch*, and in the reverberations of its fall people hardly noticed that a piece of work in Barrie's most characteristic style, a short play called *The New Word*, had been dragged down with it. H. M. Walbrook paints an ironic picture of Mlle Deslys, at the end of this melancholy affair, bowing among masses of floral tributes and blowing kisses to a bored and resentful audience, anxious only to escape. This brought to an inauspicious close the partnership between manager and author which had meant so much not only to Barrie but to the theatre in two countries. The *Lusitania* was torpedoed a few weeks later, on 7th May, 1915, and Charles Frohman went down in her.

The New Word was the first of the short war-time plays which Barrie has preserved. Unlike the plays which were written in the stable conditions of peace time, each of these war plays contains internal evidence which tells us the approximate date at which it was written. We should be able to tell, even if we did not know that it was produced in March, 1915, that *The New Word* was written early in the war. The new word itself, which is "second-lieutenant", would show that. Also, the young subaltern who is showing himself off to his parents in his new uniform still wears a sword; and his mother still has a hope that the fighting will all be over before he has time to finish his training. The play is only a trifle, based on the idea, always a favourite of Barrie's, of the embarrassment which attacks two grown-up male relatives when for any reason they have to confess their liking for one another. This habit of undemonstrativeness is not, perhaps, carried to the same lengths in England as in Barrie's native country, and one may doubt whether an average English lawyer and his son would be quite so suspicious of one another as the two in *The New Word.* All the same, the little play has a germ of truth, and its mixture of sentiment and humour proves that Barrie had found his own special touch again.

While we are on this subject of father and son, perhaps it will be well to consider, out of its place, Barrie's other, and much more serious, play on the same subject. *A Well-Remembered Voice,* written and produced in 1918, shows us a married couple whose son has been killed at the Front, and it is written with that absolute command of an unforced pathos which comes to Barrie only when he is writing out of his own experience. Though he had no son of his own, he had stood in the relation of a father to " The Five " ever since the tragic and untimely death of both their parents, and had sent them all to Eton; and George, the eldest of them, was killed at the Front while *The New Word* and *Rosy Rapture* were in rehearsal. It is no wonder, therefore, that *A Well-Remembered Voice* is full of personal touches, and that for once in Barrie's writings there is an admission that the feeling between father and son can be deeper and truer even than that between a son and his mother. The mother in this play is utterly desolated by her son's death. She wears deep mourning, she cannot bear to read the papers, she spends her time at futile séances in which she imagines herself to be in touch with her son's spirit. Her husband, on the other hand, is " carrying on " much as usual, and it is generally felt that this, added to his unsympathetic attitude to the spiritualism, is an additional cross for his noble wife to bear.

Then, one evening, the boy's spirit returns. He may only appear to one of his parents, and he has chosen his father because he now knows that his mother is not the one who misses him most. Father and son (the son, by the way, is nothing but a voice to the audience, though to his father he is not only a visible but a palpable presence) have a conversation whose poignant quality is its matter-of-fact friendliness, its Eton gossip, its fishing technicalities, its story of how Dick's dog has eaten the cook's meat-tickets, all the familiar touches of the life about him which Barrie, at his best, always used to such heart-breaking effect. Dick knows now that death is a little thing; and in the light of that knowledge his father learns for the moment to believe it too. When he prepared this play for publication, Barrie followed his usual custom of illuminating his text with literary additions, and he began with an account of what the mother and son had been to one another in life; how she had tried hard, or fairly hard, to conceal her husband's deficiencies from Dick (but Dick knew); how all the lovely things which happened in that house had been between her and Dick, with the father gently but firmly shut out. Is there here, perhaps, a belated realization that old David Barrie, sitting with his Bible in the corner at Strathview, may have felt himself shut out from all the lovely things that were between Margaret Ogilvy and her son and daughter?

After *The New Word* nothing of any significance came from Barrie for the rest of 1915. *The Fatal Typist*, described by Walbrook as " one of the author's practical jokes " was given a performance at a matinée in aid of the Australian wounded in November at His Majesty's, and has not been heard of since. But on 16th March, 1916, *A Kiss for Cinderella* was produced at Wyndham's, and proved that Barrie was at last getting back to his true form. This was the first full-length play he had written for eight years (I do not count *The Adored One*, for reasons already given). Though not one of his best, it was as characteristic as any. Once again he showed his unique talent for blending reality—even the unpromising reality of war-time—with fantasy; and while the merging of the one world into the other is not done with quite the uncanny skill shown in *Peter Pan*, *Dear Brutus* or *Mary Rose*, it was done quite well enough to please the war-time audiences, half soldiers on leave who were not disposed to be minutely critical. It ran for 156 performances.

The weakness of the play is in its first two acts, as a recent attempt to revive it has proved. They lay no solid foundation, and the pathetic little drudge, Miss Thing, who mothers unwanted babies and runs an establishment called " The Penny Friend ", where for a penny she will shave you, or doctor you, or tailor you, or comfort you, is never allowed to have two feet on the ground. Consequently, we hardly know in which of Barrie's two worlds we are supposed to be, and the dream scene, where his little heroine turns into Cinderella at her ball, with her policeman friend as the Prince, loses some of its effect. The last act, where Cinderella is in a quite definitely real hospital, recovering from a genuinely dangerous illness, and her slow-witted but " romantical " policeman is clearly and certainly in love with her, is the best of them all. It is never Barrie's artistry that is at fault in this play, but only his craftsmanship.

" Cinderella " in this play is the little Cockney nurse Irene out of *The Little White Bird*, as we have seen already; but her habit of " mothering " babies in cradles made out of packing-cases she gets from Moira in *Little Mary*, and her mixture of practical good sense with imagination from all the succession of Barrie heroines back through Grizel to Margaret Ogilvy. She gave Hilda Trevelyan an opportunity to show herself at her most enchanting, and the scenes between her and Gerald du Maurier as the Policeman, especially the love-scene at the end, were the old authentic blend of sentiment and humour. Barrie was himself again, and those of his admirers who believed that his best work might be still to come were given new reason to hope. Another practical joke, *Shakespeare's Legacy*, followed a month later, and then, after a year's gap, *The Old Lady Shows Her Medals*.

This, longer by nearly half than the other short pieces, is full of the true Barrie magic. One is inclined to ask, perhaps, in the opening scene, whether Barrie really knew much about the intimate talk of London charwomen, for he never quite spoke the vernacular of his " beloved solitary London " like a native. But when the brawny rough Black Watch private, all agog with suspicion that a liberty has been taken with him, faces the meek old lady who is longing to " mother " him but knows that she must be very cunning if she is to be given the chance, then a real breath of Scotland[1] comes to a dingy London basement, and the author knows every inflection of voice, every twist of thought of them both. The craftsmanship, also, is delicate and sure. This play is good to read, but far better to see, for with the unforced skill of which he was becoming more and more a master, Barrie saw to it that the most expressive moments of the play are conveyed in action rather than words. I do not refer here only to the last scene of all, in which Mrs. Dowey, after Kenneth is killed, looks through her few relics of him before setting out with mop and pail for her day's work, but to such moments as the one, early in the play, where we first realize that the "son" of whom she has been bragging is, in fact, a stranger, and that he is about to arrive and demand an explanation. The part of Mrs. Dowey was given to Jean Cadell, a practically unknown actress whom Barrie had seen when she played in a revival of *The Little Minister* in 1914; and she made her name in it. In the same bill with *The Old Lady Shows Her Medals* at the New Theatre was *Seven Women*, staged at last in its original form with Irene Vanbrugh as Leonora.

Six months more went by, and then, at Wyndham's Theatre on 17th October, 1917, *Dear Brutus* was produced. This, to my mind the best of all Barrie's comedies, is also the most astringent; but it seemed to a war-weary world to be almost a frolic. The critics saw only its gay humour, its delicate fancy and exquisitely-handled sentiment, and the fact that it was in no sense whatever a war play. Nobody seemed to see till later that it was, as Barrie himself described it many years

[1] Barrie has told us that in writing *The Old Lady* he was thinking of his Edinburgh landlady, Mrs. Edwards.

later, an uncomfortable play such as he could only have written with his left hand. The germ of this play had been in his mind ever since he gave old Solomon Caw of Kensington Gardens the maxim " In this world there are no second chances "; but now, in a more disillusioned mood, he amended the maxim to read, " If there were second chances in this world, few of us would take them ". The message of the play is as uncomfortable as it well can be. Eight people go out into Lob's magic wood at the end of the first act to seek a second chance; only one is a better being in the wood than out of it—and he the only one who did not whine about his luck before he went. If we are underlings it is our own fault; but only the exceptional people can rise to be anything better.

Yet this bitter warning not to expect too much of ourselves leaves us, in the theatre, full of an uplifting hope. Not only its first audiences felt this; it is the actual effect of the play. Patrick Chalmers, in *The Barrie Inspiration*, refers to it as a play " of sheer romantic refreshment and of optimism which sent an audience out into the dark streets again, happy, grateful and reassured ". And I must confess that I myself, writing in 1921, included it without misgiving in a list of plays which had the quality of " sunshine ", and was startled when somebody asked me why. The paradox is not difficult to explain, however. There are two good reasons why an audience seeing *Dear Brutus* in the theatre swallows the pill and tastes only the jam. One is that people listening to a story have a primitive tendency to concentrate their interest on the fate of the hero and heroine, and to be quite callous about the misfortunes of minor characters. The hero and heroine of *Dear Brutus* are Will and Alice Dearth. They are the two exceptional people of the play, who are capable of learning by their adventures in the wood. Dearth regains his self-confidence; Alice learns that she is better off as she is than she would have been if she had married the other man; she knows now that she has dragged Dearth down, not he her, and she has courage to face that knowledge. There is a hint that they will come together, and that the dream-daughter Margaret will no longer be a might-have-been. That is the first reason, and the second is perhaps only the same one in a different dress. It is that we are all, to ourselves, the heroes and heroines of our own little dramas; we all have a conviction that if there is a chance for exceptional people then there is hope for us.

How *Dear Brutus* stands in relation to the rest of Barrie's plays as an artistic achievement is a question which I would rather keep for consideration at the end of this book, when all the plays have been discussed. But here is the place to discuss the perfection to which Barrie had now brought his craftsmanship, for no better example is to be found than the opening act of *Dear Brutus*. It is the object of art to conceal artifice, and because hardly anything that seems natural in the theatre really is so, the dramatist has more to conceal than most artists. The problems which Barrie set himself in *Dear Brutus* were not easy ones. He had not, for instance, the comparatively simple task of establishing an atmosphere of fantasy at once, as he had done in *Peter Pan* by raising the curtain on a nursery with a dog-kennel in it and the entry of Michael on the back of Nana loudly refusing to be bathed. Since this was to be a serious comedy about real people, he had first to establish a world of normal reality and then, almost at once, to superimpose upon it a world of fantasy which the audience must accept without question. Till this was done, the real business of the play could not begin, therefore it must be done as quickly as possible; yet at the same time the foundation of the individual character-drawing must be laid. Before the revelation came at the end of the act, that for anybody who went into the magic wood there would be a second chance, it must be shown clearly what each one of the eight characters hoped to find there. In fact, Barrie had fifty minutes or so in which to make a mass of explanations, none of them simple, some of them—Lob's identity with Puck, for instance—frankly incredible, and to make them sound as though they were not explanations at all.

How brilliantly he set about his task the first few pages of the play bear witness. Nothing could be more normal and ordinary than the scene on which the curtain rises. The five ladies of a country house-party have just left the dining-room, where the men are sitting over the port, and one man—husband of the dark discontented woman who seems to be taking the lead—is likely to do the decanter more than justice. Something is afoot, but something quite normal, for it has to do with a telegram which the discontented one is writing out. The butler comes in with coffee, is accused of stealing rings, confesses, and is given the alternative of going to prison or of explaining to the assembly what is the mysterious thing they all have in common, on account of which Lob has asked them all to his house on Midsummer Eve. And so, barely five minutes after the beginning of the play, the knowledge that these are ordinary people about to undergo some extraordinary adventure is already present in the minds of the audience. A dramatist of less skill might easily have taken twice as long to explain half as much, and have achieved no sense of action whatever.

It is to be noticed, also, with what ease and skill Barrie induces us to suspend our disbelief in the idea of the magic wood. First of all we hear of it from the butler, who dare only hint at what he suspects, but obviously believes in the wood and is terrified of it. Therefore, when the men come in and begin to discuss it in detail, but flippantly and without belief, we already know more than they do. Their incredulity destroys ours. We *know* there is such a wood, just as Lob and Matey the butler know it, and we suspect that the incredulous ones will be wandering in it before very long. The wood established in our minds, it only remains for the author to present it to our eyes. There is, however, a practical difficulty here. Since it is Midsummer Eve, and warm enough for the company to go wandering about the country-side in search of adventure, the windows looking on to Lob's garden are wide open, and the curtains drawn back. If the garden is to be changed into a wood, the dramatist knows that he must get those curtains drawn so that the scene-shifters may do their work; yet if he draws them without a good excuse, the audience may suspect his purpose, and so the dramatic effect will be spoilt when, later, Dearth throws back the curtain and shows that the trees have crept right up to the house in the eerie moonlight. The only way to close the curtains without attracting undue attention is to make the act of closing them part of the play, and this is done with a most deceptive cunning.

Mabel Purdie, about to enter from the garden, sees her husband, the philanderer, kissing Joanna Trout. She draws back, but they have heard her; so she comes in, and with a word of ironic apology, draws the curtains so that the other guests may not see what she has seen. I have shown that it was Barrie's little way to pretend that he did not know how plays were written. Did he not, indeed?

Dear Brutus ran for 365 performances, almost till the end of the war, and a great part of its success was due to the scene between Dearth and his daughter Margaret in the wood. Nothing that Barrie wrote for the stage in all his long career was more touching than this scene. The broken-down artist who in the first act had got himself drunk in order to keep his self-distaste at bay was now seen as a clear-eyed, contented man, no great shakes as a painter perhaps, but happy in his work and happier still in his love for Margaret. The relation between parent and child was here given complete expression. Margaret and her father had an understanding so perfect and yet so human, and both of them under its influence radiated such a delight in life, that our knowledge that they were creatures of a dream which must break up about them if Dearth approached the house again was almost too poignant to be borne. The acting of Gerald du Maurier and Faith Celli in this scene was unforgettable, and only five years went by before they acted the same parts in a revival of the play which ran at the same theatre for another 258 performances. It was always one of Barrie's chief virtues in the theatre that he gave his actors chances to show themselves at their best, but in this scene he surpassed himself.

A Well-Remembered Voice was produced at Wyndham's on 28th June, 1918, and this completes the tale of Barrie's war-time plays. Some time during 1917 or 1918, however, he must have written *Barbara's Wedding.* This was " buried " for many years, and Hammerton gives the date of its composition as 1915. There is proof, however, in the text of the play itself that it could not have been written before the middle of 1917 at the earliest; for Barbara's marriage is to Captain Dering, who at the outbreak of the war had been the Colonel's gardener, and it is nearly three years since Billy, the Colonel's grandson whom Barbara had expected to marry, was killed in action. This little piece is skilfully planned and written, and if it had been produced at the time of its composition would have had its appeal. But by August, 1927, when Robert Loraine produced it at the Savoy, its sentiment seemed a trifle over-sweet.

Chapter XII

MARY ROSE AND AFTER

THE war ended, the lights of London were lit again, and the sweep of the Thames with its seven bridges could once more be admired by night as well as by day from Barrie's high window in Adelphi Terrace House. After its first outburst of relief, the country settled down in a grim frame of mind to the business of adjusting itself to a new set of conditions. The plays and books of the time reflected the general mood, and the world seemed to be full of morbid young cynics drowning their sorrows. Anybody who at that time remembered that laughter was a thing that could be done on the right side of the face, or that it was possible to be sad without being suicidal, was doubly welcome. Barrie, who knew more about depression and bitterness than the young cynics were ever likely to learn, now earned our gratitude twice over—first, in 1919, for sponsoring *The Young Visiters*; and then, in 1920, for having written *Mary Rose*.

About *The Young Visiters* there still hangs a faint air of mystery, owing to the absolute conviction of some people, even now, that Barrie was himself its author. Patrick Chalmers, the latest commentator at the moment when I write this sentence, has not a doubt on the subject, saying that the connoisseur in Barrie can come to no other conclusion. For all that, I believe that the book is what it purports to be, a story written by Daisy Ashford as a child of nine. The publishers' guarantee that it is so, which Mr. Chalmers airily dismisses, seems to me to have a certain weight, and Barrie's own solemn asseveration is in a tone which he does not employ when he is " just saying things ". On the other hand, he was never one to spoil a joke for a ha'porth of truth, and I have no doubt he touched Miss Ashford's manuscript up, just as he touched up some of his own old writings when he republished them in *The Greenwood Hat*. I have always suspected that the moment when Mr. Salteena " ate the egg which Ethel had so kindly laid for him " was a little too good to be true. Be that as it may, it was Barrie's prestige, and Barrie's preface, that gave the book its send-off and made it the happiest literary joke of the year. Later on it was turned into a play by two ladies, and had a run of over 100 performances at the Court Theatre. During its run two Barrie plays were put on—*The Truth about the Russian Dancers*, a minor piece designed to show Tamara Karsavina's skill, and produced at the Coliseum; and *Mary Rose*.

Mary Rose was produced at the Haymarket on 22nd April, 1920. It proved to be the last of Barrie's great successes in the theatre, and one of his best plays—to many people, I suppose, it is his best. It ran for 399 performances, and it gave to yet another fine actress, Fay Compton, one of her most memorable parts. Yet to me this play, though certainly a gem, is a gem with a fatal flaw in it. It is easier, though, to say that the flaw exists than to explain with certainty where it lies. The dramatic critic's approach to a play differs from the literary critic's approach to a book in no way more widely than in this, that he does not think about a play until it is over. As Desmond MacCarthy once put it in an illuminating phrase, he lets the play wash over him, and then examines the markings in the sand; and sometimes, though the markings may be clear enough, he finds it difficult to say what has caused them. Every time *Mary Rose* has washed over me I have found the same markings in my own little strip of sand, and they indicate that I have not responded emotionally to the appeal of the story. Why? I think it is because Barrie has weighted the scales too heavily against his heroine. He is not content with the old simple tale of the human being who, having been rapt away into another and more beautiful world, returns to the world of men but is no longer able to find peace or happiness in it. He adds to it another idea of his own, which is not at all simple—the one already mentioned which occurs in *The Little White Bird*, that the only ghosts are the ghosts of young mothers searching for their babies, and hating them when they find them grown up. That is an idea in Barrie's most sentimental vein, and it blends very badly with the older story.

In James Hogg's *Kilmeny*, which may have put *Mary Rose* into Barrie's mind, the girl who is carried away into the " land of thought " returns to earth because of her love for her native land, and goes back again because she is now too good and pure for this world. The thought is simple and clear, that after a taste of Paradise no earthly things can have value. But Barrie's addition is neither simple nor clear. What order of heavenly being can this be, which heaps misery on misery for Mary Rose, and keeps her spirit earth-bound in frantic search long after she has forgotten even what she is searching for? There is some suggestion that she is being punished because in Paradise (or wherever she had gone) she pined too bitterly for her baby. It seems a punishment unworthy of Paradise. One reflects that the glorious beings of the Land of Thought would not have treated Kilmeny so, and is forced to the conclusion that the real reason for Mary Rose's sufferings is that an experienced dramatist has let his knowledge of theatrical effect carry him away. Barrie has, for once, piled on the agony too lavishly. But even so, *Mary Rose* remains one of the best of his plays, and one of the best plays of our time. The workmanship throughout is almost perfect, and even if the scene between the ghost of Mary Rose and her grown-up son Harry is faulty in conception, the skill with which it is accomplished, and kept on the right side of mawkishness, is masterly.

Mary Rose is another of Barrie's characters who do not grow up. She, like Sentimental Tommy, like Peter Pan, most of all like Barrie himself, clings desperately to her childhood. Mrs. Morland warns Simon that ever since her first disappearance on the island, Mary Rose has been curiously young for her age. Mary Rose herself is scared of marriage chiefly because she fears Simon may not let her play once she is his wife; and even when she is a ghost, she sometimes gives up her weary search for a little and plays by herself—and guiltily asks Harry not to " tell ". On the island, though she is a wife of four years' standing and her son is nearly three, Simon treats her, and she behaves, like a little girl pretending to be a married lady. And in the ghost scene, she talks like a bewildered child.

Barrie was sixty when *Mary Rose* was produced, but

as he was to live to be seventy-seven and to retain his faculties bright and clear to the end, he was by no means an old man. Some other reason must be found for the fact that after this he wrote no more plays for more than a dozen years. Perhaps the narrowness of his range accounts for it—he had now told all the tales that had been clamouring in his mind for expression, and though he had by no means " written himself out ", he must now rely on some stimulus outside himself to set his pen moving. Certainly he had such a stimulus for the only new dramatic composition of his that was seen in the theatre between *Mary Rose* and *The Boy David*. One of the Davies brothers, who collectively and individually took upon themselves the right of frank filial criticism of Barrie's work, challenged him to write a " thriller ". Barrie's response was *Shall We Join the Ladies?*

There has been much speculation about this little work, which appears in the published version as " the first act of an unfinished play ". Any statement made by Barrie about himself is received by his commentators with a scepticism that is almost automatic. It has been held by some that Barrie, for some strange elfin reason, wrote his disembodied act without any intention of carrying the story on. This, of course, is nonsense. It has been more widely, and more credibly, maintained that Barrie wrote the first act and then saw that he had made too brilliant a start, and would not be able to avoid slackening the dramatic tension in the remaining acts. He therefore abandoned the play. This theory makes sense, but I cannot believe it to be the true explanation. It is a fact that it is extremely difficult to live up to a very exciting first act, but it is absurd to suggest that Barrie was not capable of doing it. In writing a " thriller " it is practically obligatory for an author to do what Barrie did with *The Admirable Crichton* —that is, to begin at or near the end, and work backwards. The first object of this kind of play is to lay false trails; and a man cannot lay false trails until he knows very certainly where the true trail leads.

It is not to be thought that Barrie, the best theatrical craftsman of his day, would have made so amateurish a blunder as to begin writing before he knew what the solution of his puzzle was to be, or without arranging a dramatic surprise for his concluding scene, or without having it very clear in his mind how the mystification of the audience was to be carried on in the second act. The existing act is the best proof of this, for it is a classic example of the art of dramatic preparation. Almost every line in it is carefully calculated to lead up to something in the next act. One of the twelve people sitting round Sam Smith's dinner-table poisoned Sam Smith's brother in Monte Carlo. At first it seems that none of them can have done it, but as the act proceeds it becomes clear that every one of them has something to hide. By the end of the act, all twelve are possible suspects, yet so far there is no real evidence against any individual. The act performs perfectly its proper functions, of arousing excitement in the story and interest in the characters, and of making a challenge to the detective instinct; but to say that it rouses anticipation to a pitch which no conceivable subsequent acts could satisfy is to overstate the case.

I have been confidently told, on authority that should be excellent, that Barrie's real reason for abandoning the play was very simple. Michael Llewelyn Davies,

No. 4 of " The Five ", now a boy of twenty up at Oxford, was drowned while bathing in a dangerous part of the Thames near Sandford Pool on 19th May, 1921. Barrie was struck to the heart; and the suggestion is that after this he could no longer bear to go on with the play. This sounds to me a better reason than the other, and it may well be the true one. Against it is the fact that Barrie had already given permission, before the boy's death, for the production of the unfinished work. It was actually in rehearsal at the time, with a glittering " all-star " cast, for the opening of the theatre of the Royal Academy of Dramatic Art on 26th May. If Barrie had intended to go on with his play, it is easy to believe that its tragic associations may have made it impossible for him. But if he had intended to go on with it, why did he allow it to be staged in its unfinished condition? Perhaps the answer lies in the fact that the performance was to be a private one on a special occasion, and that the cast was one of the strongest that have ever appeared on a single stage at one moment. Be that as it may, the fragment caught the public interest, and was performed again at a charity matinée at the Palace. After that, Barrie having persisted in his intention not to finish the play, it was put into the regular bill at the St. Martin's on 8th March, 1922, as a curtain-raiser to Galsworthy's *Loyalties* and was acted there 407 times.

Not for many years after this was Barrie to meet any outside influence strong enough to set him writing another play. He was now acknowledged to stand at the very head of his profession, and the official recognition of this in the New Year honours list of 1922, when he was given the Order of Merit, met with general approval.

Only Meredith and Hardy among imaginative writers had so far held this most coveted distinction, and Barrie must have been proud to be given a place beside two men whom he knew as friends and profoundly admired as artists. The award came appropriately in time to mark what would naturally be called his retirement, but for the odd fact that it proved to be much more like an emergency from retirement. For a dozen years he had lived the life of a recluse, seeing only his personal friends; and although, like other quiet figures of history, he wielded an enormous influence because his hermitage became the resort of great men of all professions (and it would have much surprised James Anon, who had no interest in affairs, to see how often his successor consorted with eminent politicians), he had steadily refused to appear from behind the scenes. Not once during those years did he consent to speak before an audience—not even the small and indulgent audience that an after-dinner speaker has to face.

Even before his retirement to the Adelphi he had been a reluctant speaker. He had never addressed a big public audience; but even so each occasion, however trivial in itself, was an ordeal to him, involving great care in composition and unhappiness in anticipation. His method was to write his speeches out in full and get them by heart, and a most successful method it proved in practice. Once he was on his feet, his characteristic grimness about not being beaten came to his aid, and his inimitable technique (learnt at school) as a wooden-faced humorist carried him triumphantly through; but he always paid for his success afterwards with an acute nervous reaction. He might have persisted in his absolute refusal to face any more such ordeals, but that, early in 1922, circumstances were too strong for him. St. Andrews University invited him to be its Rector. The post was too honourable and too much to Barrie's mind to be refused, and its acceptance involved the delivery of an address in public to an audience larger and more critical than he had ever yet faced.

He accepted, and went to work on his address with the care and the artistry which he would have brought to the writing of a new play. And on 3rd May, he delivered a speech on Courage which reverberated round the world, and ranked—and still ranks—with his best achievements. How little he trusted his powers as an orator on such a grand scale may be seen from the text of the speech itself. He apologized for his vocal shortcomings, he assumed that many of his audience would not hear what he said and assured them that they were the lucky ones, and he told them that this was his first public speech and was to be his last. But by the time his long address was over, he had destroyed all chance that he would be allowed to make these words good, and perhaps had destroyed his own self-distrust. The text of this speech, which was plainly too good to be lost, was afterwards published as a book; and in that form it later received a tribute which, for its happy ignorance no less than its obvious sincerity, must have appealed mightily to Barrie. In 1926, an American film journal invited various stars to write about their favourite books, and one world-famous lady, now forgotten, said that she had derived much inspiration from a little pamphlet called *Courage*, which was " a printing of an address given by a little-known English Episcopalian rector ".

Topical

J. M. BARRIE AND DAME ELLEN TERRY

At St. Andrews, on the occasion of his Rectorial Address, 3rd May, 1922

Barrie never again delivered a speech quite on this heroic scale. But St. Andrews had deprived him, if not of his reluctance to speak, at any rate of his excuse for not speaking, and for the future he was less difficult to persuade. Most of his big speeches were made on official occasions, as, for example, when he received the Freedom of Dumfries in 1924, of Jedburgh in 1928, or of Kirriemuir in 1930, or when, also in 1930, he was made Chancellor of his own old university. Sometimes, however, he could now be tempted to speak simply to oblige one of his friends. In 1922, at A. B. Walkley's invitation, he spoke at the dinner of the Critics' Circle; and the first sentence of his speech, directed dispassionately at the ceiling, was the one word, " Scum!" Two years later, at Wallasey, he addressed the girls of a school of which his niece Lilian, Alexander Barrie's daughter, was headmistress. Later still, in 1928, he allowed Stanley Baldwin, with whom he was on terms of warm friendship, to persuade him to speak to the Worcester Association.

Whatever the occasion, these speeches were listened to, and subsequently read, with the utmost eagerness. They were invariably witty and charming, but sometimes now they began to have a new quality—they were reminiscent. It was as though Barrie had found in his public speeches a new medium in which he might do in fact what he had done so often in fiction, live over again some of the best moments of his life. Indeed, it is very nearly true to say that Barrie spent the years 1922 to 1930 in writing his autobiography, not in the usual way, for Barrie never did anything in the usual way, but in instalments. Everything new that came from his pen between these years was full of memories

—not the speeches only, but the preface to *Peter Pan*, and *The Greenwood Hat* (of which the private edition was printed in 1930). Between them they amount to a far better autobiography than most men have the wit to write.

During much of this period of reminiscence, Barrie was steadily engaged on another retrospective task—the rewriting of his plays for publication, to which reference has already been made. Nothing that he did was more characteristic of him than this. His conviction that plays were intended for the stage, and therefore should not be put before the reading public, he shared with many other good theatre men, Shakespeare and Sheridan at their head. His method of overcoming the difficulty was all his own. To all intents and purposes, Barrie invented a new literary form when he prepared his plays for the press. The narrative passages which have taken the place of stage-directions are sometimes exquisite, but in some cases they have the regrettable effect of making the play seem less good than it actually is. This is particularly so in the introduction to *Dear Brutus*, where the description of Darkness and Light as the two chief characters of the play, and the elaborate passage about the moonshine and the flowers, is in Barrie's worst sentimental vein. Nowhere in the play itself does he descend to this level, except in the short scene where Lob comforts some flowers that he has knocked out of their bowl; the falsity of which is apparent, since if Lob had really felt like this about his flowers he would not have allowed them to be picked.

Another occasional occupation of Barrie's during these years was to write an "amateur" play for his friends. How many such compositions may exist I do not know, but I have read one, an elaborate affair called *The Stanway Ghost.* This was written to be acted by Lord Wemyss and his grand-children at his house, Stanway in Worcestershire, at Christmas 1926. The plot had more than a touch of *Dear Brutus* about it, for the " ghost " of the title was a great wheel which appeared outside a window, as Lob's wood did. Through this each of the grand-children had to pass, and emerged as a grown-up.

In such tasks Barrie occupied his diminishing working hours until, in 1931, he had an opportunity to make a single and most impressive return to Fleet Street. He wrote a story for *The Times*, which was published as a special supplement to the Christmas Eve number of that year. No doubt it was his mood of reminiscence that made him go back to the Scotland of a bygone day for the setting of *Farewell, Miss Julie Logan.* This exquisite fantasy, the last prose tale he was ever to write, is too short to be called a novel; but it is long enough to show him still supreme in his own domain, which lies between the world of fact and the world of fancy, and is good neighbour to both.

Chapter XIII

THE LAST CHAPTER

TWO more years went quietly by, during which it seemed that Barrie's work was done. After September, 1931, when he unveiled a statue of his old friend Thomas Hardy in Dorchester, he made no public appearances of any great moment. Nothing was less likely than that any stimulus could be found strong enough to make him take up his pen again to write a new full-length play. But in December, 1933, Elisabeth Bergner, an actress who had left Germany on account of the rising anti-Jewish feeling in that country, made her first appearance on the London stage as a pathetic little waif in *Escape Me Never*. She became the talk of the town; Barrie paid one of his infrequent visits to the theatre to see her, and conceived an instant and profound admiration for her acting. Early in 1934, the rumour went round that he was writing a play for her, and by August of that year the play was finished and C. B. Cochran had agreed to present it.

It was easy to understand why Barrie had felt an artistic affinity with this actress, for her stage personality was exactly in tune with his own creations. She would have made an ideal Peter Pan, and people began to wonder whether something of the same kind was being provided for her. As in the case of *Peter Pan*, Barrie insisted on the strictest secrecy about the subject of his play. For a year the secret was kept, but when preparations began to be made for production public curiosity became impassioned, and driblets of information leaked out. By August, 1935, all that was known was that Barrie had written " a play without a heroine ". Then came a postponement owing to the illness of the actress, and this meant the end of Barrie's cherished scheme of springing a surprise. Somebody knew that the play was on a Biblical subject, somebody else that Bergner was to play a boy. At last, in October, 1935, it was announced that the play dealt with King David, and that the title would be either *The Two Farmers* or *The Two Shepherds*.

The date of production was now fixed for February, 1936, and a little later came an announcement that the play would be called *The Boy David*—a title which Barrie had had in his mind all along, but had suppressed as it would have given away the secret. Rehearsals had actually begun, when the actress fell ill again. Barrie was now nearly seventy-six, and his health was failing; it began to look as though Fate meant to rob him of his desire to see this last play of his (which, it was said, he considered to be his best) in action on the stage. Indeed, by the time rehearsals began again in the autumn he was not strong enough to appear at all of them. But on 21st November, 1936, the play was given its first performance at Edinburgh; and Barrie, though too ill to be present, was not too ill to get to work on his text in the light of criticisms that were made, and to make important alterations before the play came to London.

I have compared three different versions of this play —the original typescript, still untitled; the prompt book (which, as it contains the alterations put in between the Edinburgh and the London productions, is almost two versions in itself); and the final printed text. In the main, the play remains the same throughout, but in the three scenes where Barrie gave his stage collaborators difficult problems to solve, there are constant alterations. These three scenes are the death of Goliath, Saul's attempt to kill David with his javelin, and David's vision of the future. In the first version Barrie wanted Goliath to be not the giant of the Bible, but a big man who could have a real running fight with David. Later, he changed his mind and asked for a giant, which proved ineffective on the Edinburgh stage; so that in the final version, acted and published, Goliath remained " off ".

The javelin scene was more complicated. The order of events as originally written was that Saul and David were inside Goliath's tent, David playing the harp; that Saul flung his javelin, transfixing David and pinning him to the tent side; that Saul then rushed outside and told Samuel that he had " slain the Son of Jesse "; that Samuel prayed to God, who miraculously restored David to life; and that David then resumed his harp-playing as if nothing had happened. The scene was acted like this at Edinburgh, but all that the people in the audience were allowed to see was the head of Saul's javelin as it came through the tent wall; they therefore had no idea at all that David was supposed to have been killed and miraculously restored. The only interpretation they could put on the scene was that Saul, having flung his javelin, left the tent without seeing that it had missed its mark; and that David must now be sitting in the tent reflecting that he had had a very narrow escape, and that to die would have been an awfully big adventure. Barrie saw that he had asked too much of his producer and his audience, and rewrote the scene leaving out Samuel altogether. As it was seen in London, and now stands in the published version, the close of this scene is one of the most moving in the play, and is a proof that to his life's end Barrie remained a practical man of the theatre, who never hesitated to cut and alter his work to fit the theatre's needs. In the same way the vision scene was cut and rewritten to fit the actors' needs, but in this scene the "cuts" have been restored in the published text.

At last, after its many vicissitudes, *The Boy David* was brought to London and produced at His Majesty's Theatre on 14th December, 1936. Cochran was as lavish as Frohman had been over *Peter Pan*, and public interest made the occasion the chief theatrical event of the year. The play was acknowledged to have in it all Barrie's old certainty of touch; yet it ran only for seven weeks, and had fewer performances than any play of his since he first entered the theatre, except for the out-and-out failures such as *Josephine* or *Rosy Rapture*. Barrie was bitterly grieved. Granville-Barker, in his preface to the published version of the play, says of him that up to the point when illness kept him from rehearsals, Barrie "had given of his best, and—secretly diffident as he could be about his work, and scrupulously, even harshly, critical—he thought it good, and that all promised well. He made no open complaint about the result; that was not his way. But the grief struck the deeper."

So far as workmanship was concerned, Barrie not

merely thought that *The Boy David* was good; he was a master of his craft, and he *knew* it was good. Granville-Barker's detailed analysis of the skill with which the dialogue is fashioned and the characters brought out is fascinating to follow, but it tells nothing that is new even to those—of whom I am one—who consider that *The Boy David* has no claim to rank with Barrie's best plays. It is not the detail of this piece that is at fault, but the design. To put the thing bluntly, either there is nothing wrong with *The Boy David* or it is all wrong. If it is wrong, it is wrong for the very reason which, to Barrie's mind,[1] made it triumphantly right—namely, that the part of David was written for Bergner and fitted her exactly. The theme of the play is a fine one; it is the old, tragic tale how the great man's pride makes him take credit to himself for a power that comes from God. This pride is full-blown in Saul, in David we see it only in the bud. It brings Saul down, and will do the same for David if he forgets to be humble in the day of his greatness. In the hero of such a tale, virility is the first quality that is needed. Barrie knew this well enough, for Saul has it in full measure, and in the visions of the future, when the boy David sees himself as a grown man, the virility of the older David is insisted on. How, then, can the hero of the tale be acted by a woman? How can he be turned into a wistful, sexless creature, own brother to Peter Pan, without allowing the tale to dwindle? The case against *The Boy David* is not that Barrie handled a big theme badly, but that he handled it perfectly in a small way.

[1] This is proved by Barrie's will, in which he left £2000 to Elisabeth Bergner " for the best performance ever given in any play of mine ".

Never was a writer held in greater affection by his public than Barrie, and the proof was to be found in the general regret when his last play proved not to be a success. Even those critics who did not like it would have done so for his sake, if they could. It was not fitting that his career should end on a note of failure, even so honourable a failure as this. In spite of his way of brooding apart in his eyrie, people felt about him not as an aloof genius, but as a friend with whom they had in the past spent many happy hours, and with whom they now sympathized in his disappointment. Short of going to the theatre to see his play, they would have done anything in their power to comfort him in his distress, so potent was the magic of his personality, the disarming humour and pervasive charm of his writing.

But charm, and the hold that it has upon the popular imagination, is a dangerous element in the make-up of an artist who has a claim to greatness. It is so often used by second-rate artists to cover up their lack of solid qualities that we run the risk of thinking that if a man has charm he can have nothing else. As regards Barrie the danger is very great, more particularly in judging his work for the theatre, because its apparent ease and lightness often obscure its strength. The appeal of the theatre is to the emotions of an audience, not to its intellect, and therefore there is a perpetual temptation to a dramatist to get easy effects by writing sentimentally. In Barrie's case the temptation must have been specially strong, for the sentimental side of his own nature was always ready to pour out and sweep him away if he opened the sluice-gates. He needed constant watchfulness and an iron restraint if he was to guard himself against this besetting fault, all the more so because the great majority of theatre-goers, sentimentalists themselves, were delighted when he yielded to it.

The final test of sentimentality—that is, of false emotion—in the theatre is repetition. There are fashions in mawkishness, and what brings tears from one generation often induces nausea in the next. No plays that have been written in our time have been subjected to that test more ruthlessly than Barrie's, and the astonishing thing is not how badly but how well they come through the ordeal. *Peter Pan* is, of course, the greatest example of this; it has been put to the proof unceasingly, and most of it is pure gold.

During the years while Barrie was writing, the theatre went through great changes, and the art of playwriting began to take itself seriously again after losing its self-respect for a period. In the history of that revival, it is easy to forget or take for granted the part that Barrie played—still more easy owing to his own way of taking hard work honestly done for granted in himself. He headed no movements, enunciated no theories, founded no school. Nevertheless, his part is a great one, for he brought to the theatre something of which it stood badly in need; an absolutely original mind. For a time, as he has said himself, he worked for the theatre with some contempt, as was the fashion among writers of the time, and wrote plays to the same pattern as everybody else. But when he learnt to respect the theatre, he soon began to make demands on it. He soon began to go outside the rigidly naturalistic convention which was the only one that playgoers then knew, and to try for effects which others had not dared to attempt. Granville-Barker has pointed out with his usual clarity of thought and word the new demands that Barrie made upon the mechanics of the theatre, but even these were not so bold as the demands he made upon the imagination of his audiences. The plays that he wrote now were his own; good or bad, they were the work of J. M. Barrie, and nobody else in the world could have written them. His range was narrow, and he could not stray far outside it without disaster; but within that range he was a very great dramatist.

Will his work live? That question time alone can answer; all that we can say now is that his best work is as worthy of the attention of posterity as anything that has been written in English in his day. *Peter Pan* has already proved itself to contain imperishable elements. Other plays have kept their place in the theatrical repertory for many years and then vanished into oblivion; but no play in history, unless it was destined to become a classic, has maintaincd a constant hold on the public imagination right through a period in which both the mechanics of the theatre and the canons of popular taste underwent a revolution. *Peter Pan* is a portent. So long as it retains its copyright it belongs to a children's hospital, and this fact, combined with its undiminished appeal to the youngest generation of playgoers, will doubtless keep it alive for some time yet. Once the present series of annual revivals ceases, however, and the complicated settings and machinery are broken up and dispersed, the difficulty and expense of reproducing the play may tend to keep it on the shelf.

Of the other plays, *Dear Brutus* seems to me to have much the clearest claim on the interest of generations to come. Its theme is universal, and nothing in the telling of the story ties it to its own time, as the social satire in *The Admirable Crichton* or the political stuff in

What Every Woman Knows tie those two plays. And though two essays in pure narrative, *Mary Rose* and *Quality Street*, have a freshness not likely to decay with the operation of time, they have not the vigour which makes for survival. *Dear Brutus* has that vigour. Also, there is nothing in it that can puzzle posterity; and except for an odd passage here and there, easily to be cut or amended, there is nothing in it of sentimentality.

When James Barrie, as a young boy in Kirriemuir, first confessed his intention of becoming an author, his only support came from an old tailor in the town, who quoted, with an earnestness that the boy never forgot, Cowley's lines:

> What can I do to be for ever known
> And make the age to come my own?

Myriads of writers have set out to answer that question as best they could. Not many have been able to answer it more honourably than the man who, after a long life, could point to *Peter Pan*, *Dear Brutus* and *Margaret Ogilvy*.

The breakdown in Barrie's health which had prevented him from putting the final touches to *The Boy David* at Edinburgh proved to be premonitory of the end. He was able to go to rehearsals in London, but was not in the theatre on the first night. Soon afterwards he fell ill again, and spent his seventy-seventh birthday in bed. Early in June he was well enough to dine at the Garrick Club with Lord Horder, his doctor, but a few days later he developed pneumonia and was taken to a nursing-home, where he died on 19th June, 1937. He was buried at Kirriemuir five days later.

So passed from the scene one of the most romantic

and pathetic figures of our time. He had achieved almost every honour and success that James Anon could have coveted for him and he left one of the largest fortunes [1] ever made by a writer. By all material standards he was to be accounted the luckiest of men, but in his moods of despair he knew that the things he himself thought best worth having in life had never been his. And yet, if all were known, perhaps he wrote his own best epitaph when he said: "Those who bring happiness to others cannot keep it from themselves."

[1] £173,467.

M&A INTEGRATION

M&A INTEGRATION

A Framework for Executives and Managers

David M. Schweiger

McGraw-Hill

New York Chicago San Francisco Lisbon London Madrid
Mexico City Milan New Delhi San Juan Seoul
Singapore Sydney Toronto

Library of Congress Cataloging-in-Publication Data

Schweiger, David M.
M&A integration: a framework for executives and managers / David M. Schweiger.
p. cm.
ISBN 0-07-138303-4
1. Consolidation and merger of corporations. 2. Personnel management. 3. Human capital. 4. Management. I. Title: Mergers and acquisitions integration. II. Title.

HD2746.5.S39 2002
658.1'6—dc21 2001044892

1 2 3 4 5 6 7 8 9 0 DOC/DOC 0 9 8 7 6 5 4 3 2

ISBN 0-07-138303-4

This book was set in Palatino. It was composed in Hightstown, N.J.

Printed and bound by R. R. Donnelley & Sons Company.

This book is printed on recycled, acid-free paper containing a minimum of 50% recycled, de-inked fiber.

To:
Dianne, for the love and support,
Andrew and Evan, for giving my life meaning,
Mom and Dad, for the foundation and love, and
Bonnie and Zoe for the comic relief.

Without all of you, this and many other things
would not have been possible.

CONTENTS

PREFACE

The fact that you have picked up this book and are reading this preface suggests one of several things:

1. You are curious about the integration of mergers and acquisitions (M&As) and how the integration process impacts value creation.
2. You are getting ready to undertake your first merger or acquisition and want to make sure the integration is handled properly.
3. You have made one or several acquisitions in the past and are looking to improve how you handle the next one.

Regardless of the reason, you have just joined the growing rank of people who have come to understand the importance of integration to the success of M&As.

During the last 20 years I have conducted research on how integration impacts value creation. As a result of what has been learned, I have been able to help a number of companies develop and improve their integration process. When I first began working in the M&A arena, it was quite difficult to get the attention of executives. Most were exclusively focused on deal making. Topics such as valuation, strategic fit, pricing, and financing were their priorities. When asked about integration, most M&A leaders dismissed it as a secondary issue to be addressed after the closing. In their opinions, *integration* was not critical to the success of the deal.

Moreover, their advisers—investment bankers, lawyers, and consultants—were not very interested in integration either. For them, doing the deal was everything. Once the deal was done, they walked away and on to the next deal. Making the deal work and delivering value to investors after the closing were not their responsibility.

Sadly, however, many executives have learned over time that often the deals they have struck have not created the value they had promised their investors. In fact, the cumulative evidence from research by academics and consulting firms supports these intuitive conclusions. Simply put, *mergers and acquisitions, on average, are not profitable and do not create value for the buying company's shareholders.*

In spite of these results, M&A activity marches on. In fact, the last decade of the twentieth century can be characterized as the largest M&A boom in the history of the world. It is paradoxical that while M&A activity is so strong, the results are so poor.

A number of reasons have been advanced for the poor results. Increasingly, both experience and research are pointing to the importance of integration. Topics such as culture clash, selection and retention of key people, value leakage, integration teams, and "the soft side of due diligence" have entered the vocabulary of executives as they plan a merger or an acquisition. Why? Simply put, executives have come to realize that deal making is a theoretical exercise that attempts to forecast earnings and cashflow and thus the value of a target or merger partner. They have also come to realize that it is only after the closing when earnings and cashflow materialize.

Beyond this, they have found that:

1. Many deals require a premium to be paid to the target to get them to do the deal.
2. Premiums require synergies to justify the investment.
3. Synergies require changes to either the target or the acquirer.
4. An orderly, well-managed integration process can determine whether changes and synergies are captured, earnings and cashflow materialize, and investor value is created.

Research and experience indicate that integration is a critical management process that must be taken and managed seriously. Integration is not just a few random activities that can be handled after the closing, but a series of well-orchestrated activities that begin long before and continue long after the closing. There is a clearly defined process combined with a series of tested activities and approaches that can help executives ensure that a deal is theoretically sound, that it can be effectively integrated, and that the hypothesized results can be delivered.

As the M&A parade continues, the keys to success are to get the marching band to stop the drumming long enough to make sure all the players are in the right position, all the instruments are properly tuned, and each member is playing from the same sheet of music. It is to this end that I offer the thoughts in this book.

In the 10 chapters that follow, you will find an integrated framework with practical tools, checklists, models, and illustrations to help you effectively manage your integration process and create value for your investors. A more detailed description of the framework and the remaining chapters is presented in Chapter 1. My hope is that the ideas presented will stimulate your own, and that the resulting synergies will justify your investment in focusing on the value of integration.

As part of an ongoing commitment to improving our understanding of the integration process, I invite you to become involved in a continuous best-practices study and interactive learning community. The objective is to capture what companies are doing to more effectively manage integration in the pursuit of synergies and value and to share the aggregate findings with those participating in the study and with the scientific community at large.

If you are interested in participating in the study, please contact me at DMS@Schweiger-Associates.com.

ACKNOWLEDGMENTS

Integrating a merger or an acquisition is a complex process that requires the knowledge, insights, and energy of many people. So too is writing a book. Although I would like to take credit for all the ideas contained in this book, I cannot. There are many people and organizations that have contributed to my education, and without them I could not have written even one chapter. It is impossible to recognize every one of them, but you know who you are. There are, however, several that deserve special recognition.

I would like to begin by thanking several close friends and colleagues with whom I have worked closely over the years: Tugrul Atamer, Ernie Csiszar, Victoria Emerson, Rob Lippert, Peter Topping, and Philippe Very. Thank you for the stimulation, encouragement, and education.

Thanks also go to several key executives who have given me valuable feedback on this book: Dr. Roger Birkman (Birkman International), Glenn Tilton (Chevron/Texaco), Bill Rusak (BBA Nonwovens), Don Benson (Methodist Healthcare System), Harris Deloach (Sonoco Products), Gary Butler (Verizon), and Joel Smith (Moore School of Business). Thank you for the dose of reality.

I am grateful to the leadership of the Moore School of Business, University of South Carolina, who have given me the time, support, and freedom to acquire the practical skills and knowledge required to write this book. In particular, I would like to thank Joe Ullman, Susie VanHuss, and Hoyt Wheeler, who over the years have encouraged my efforts to integrate practice with academic research and theory. The Center for International Business Education and Research and the Riegel and Emory Human Resources Research Center at the University of South Carolina deserve recognition for their continued financial support of my research on mergers and acquisitions. Thank you all for creating a productive work environment.

And I would be remiss if I did not thank the many students I have taught in my graduate M&A classes and in my executive education seminars. You have provided me with stimulation and knowledge to undertake this project.

I would also like to thank the many clients and researchers who have over the years provided me with the knowledge and material for this book. Without you this would not be possible.

Last, but not least, I would like to thank my editor, Kelli Christiansen, my editing supervisor, Janice Race, and the editorial staff at McGraw-Hill for their support. I appreciate your confidence in me and your help in making this book better.

M&A INTEGRATION

1

THE PROMISING WORLD OF MERGERS AND ACQUISITIONS

We believe that the merger of Chrysler Corporation and Daimler-Benz AG to form DaimlerChrysler is a historical step that will offer Daimler-Benz shareholders exciting perspectives. In addition to participating in the growth of two very profitable automobile companies, the merger offers the opportunity to benefit from the additional earnings potential that we believe will be generated by the merged activities of the new company.

We have already identified opportunities to increase sales, to create new markets for Daimler-Chrysler, to reduce purchasing costs and to realize economies of scale. We are well-positioned to capitalize on these opportunities to increase the earnings power of DaimlerChrysler AG. In the short term, we see synergies of $1.4 billion that we expect to more than double in the medium term. Even beyond that, given the creativity and inventiveness of our teams, we expect to be able to identify substantial additional benefits as the integration process accelerates.

Jurgen E. Schrempp, Chairman and CEO, Daimler-Benz AG[1]
Robert J. Eaton, Chairman and CEO, Chrysler Corporation

Telecommunications is the most dynamic and exciting industry that we will see in our lifetimes, and the rapid and dramatic changes around us have created tremendous opportunities for companies that are willing to seize the moment. GTE's proposed merger with Bell Atlantic works in this environment because it will help us capture those emerging opportunities more effectively than we could on our own. The challenge that faces us, of course, as we move toward merger completion is to meld two strong, dynamic companies into one that can keep growing and evolving without missing a beat. To do that, we must blend not only our management and our operations, but we must blend our cultures and work styles.

Chuck Lee, Chairman and CEO, GTE (Now Verizon)[2]

This is a merger that truly constitutes far more than the sum of the parts. The new company will be able to take advantage of uniquely complementary geographical reach, product portfolio, pipeline and R&D strengths. As a result of the merger, Pharmacia & Upjohn will have extensive financial and operating resources, market scope, and earnings potential. Consequently, we fully expect the new company to achieve additional growth in expected 1996 EPS as well as accelerate future earnings growth. Above all Pharmacia & Upjohn is expected to generate significantly enhanced value for shareholders.

John L. Zabrisie, Chairman and CEO, Upjohn

These comments made prior to the merger of Daimler and Chrysler, GTE and Bell Atlantic, and Upjohn and Pharmacia are typical of those made by many companies in the throes of mergers and acquisitions (M&As).[3] They capture the optimism reflected in these deals as CEOs court their shareholders and employees and encourage them to support the deal. The CEOs promise that synergies will be realized, customers will benefit, employees will be excited, and investors will prosper.

Yet in spite of all the pronouncements, the evidence suggests that much of the exuberance and promised synergies and value never come to fruition, only to leave customers, investors, managers, and employees disappointed. Nevertheless, M&A activity marches on!

THE NEVER-ENDING QUEST TO MERGE AND ACQUIRE

Since the beginning of the twentieth century, M&As have become a common part of the business landscape. During this relatively short period of time, trillions of dollars in deals have been struck and tens of millions of people have been affected. As the twentieth century opened, there was a wave of M&As characterized by horizontal consolidation. Since then, M&A activity has remained a consistent and growing part of business, characterized by a number of major and differing waves.

As we end the twentieth and begin the twenty-first century, we are again in the midst of another major wave. From 1992 through 2000 there have been eight straight record years of worldwide M&A activity, although such activity slowed at the beginning of 2001.[4] This wave is the largest in history and is being driven by globalization, technological change, and market deregulation and liberalization. The escalation in the price of many companies' stocks during the stock market boom of the 1990s also provided a currency that fueled the M&A boom. So far, the new millennium has not been as helpful for equity-based purchases.

Unlike the conglomeration movement of the 1960s, the latest wave appears to be strategic. Companies are attempting to improve their current and future strategic positions domestically, regionally, and globally, and are doing so by acquiring new technologies, products, and services; gaining access to new customers; expanding geographic presence; and consolidating within the markets in which they compete or hope to compete. Whether through mega-mergers or industry roll-ups, M&A activity goes on. Just a small sample of the deals transacted on a worldwide basis during the last five years of the twentieth century include:

- AOL –Time Warner
- Chevron-Texaco
- BP-Amoco-Arco
- Daimler-Chrysler
- Sandoz–Ciba Geigy
- SBC-Ameritech
- Bell Atlantic–GTE
- AT&T–TCI
- Vodaphone-Mannesman
- Travelers-Citicorp
- Bank America–Nations Bank

In addition to these mega-mergers, numerous other fragmented industries have been consolidating. Most of these deals involve larger players acquiring small and medium-sized companies as they attempt to "roll up" their industry. Some examples include the funeral home, security monitoring, and banking industries. It is almost impossible to find an industry where merger or acquisition activity is not taking place.

Given the pervasiveness and growth of M&A activity and the volume of capital involved, it is critical that we understand as much as we can about the dynamics underlying M&As and whether they create value for investors.

DO MERGERS AND ACQUISITIONS CREATE VALUE?

Numerous studies have investigated the relationship between M&As and financial performance. Using a variety of financial measures (e.g., profit, stock price) and nonfinancial measures (e.g., firm reputation) and time frames (e.g., premeasurement and postmeasurement, initial market reaction and four years after a deal), these studies demonstrate that, on average, M&As consistently benefit the target's shareholders, but not the acquirer's shareholders. In fact, there are varying results with respect to the buying firms' performance.[5]

For example, financial economists have found that, on average, M&As lead to no gain or a slight loss (over a variety of time frames) in both stock price and profit to the buying firm following closing. However, stock price gains to target shareholders average between 20 and 30 percent depending upon the particular study. Various consulting firms have also estimated that from one-half to two-thirds of M&As do not live up to the financial expectations of those transacting them, and many resulted in divestitures. One study even estimated that the merger and acquisition failure rate is equivalent to the marriage divorce rate in the United States!

Clearly the evidence for the shareholders of acquiring firms is not encouraging, at least not encouraging enough to make executives jump up and do as many deals as they can. As importantly, numerous studies and practical experience have also demonstrated that the impact of M&As on managers and employees can be traumatic. Studies have shown that M&As often result in job loss for people, as acquirers pursue cost synergies through the elimination of redundant jobs. Often the numbers of jobs lost in a particular deal can range into the thousands and even tens of thousands. Studies have also shown that M&As can affect employees' health, stress, loyalty to their organization, productivity, absenteeism, and the like, all elements that are essential to a well-functioning organization.

Given the evidence to date, is it unrealistic to expect that M&As can create value for investors? Is it ridiculous to conceive that M&As can be beneficial to employees, or at least do no harm? If the answers to these questions are no, then it would be crazy for executives to continue doing deals. But as in most cases, there are no simple answers. Most of the studies reported and summarized represent averages, and where there are averages there are variances. The bottom line—some M&As create value, whereas others do not. Thus, the key is to understand what differentiates those that do from those that do not.

VALUE CREATION AND DESTRUCTION[6]

Before going any further, it is important to briefly define value creation. For the purposes of this book, value will be defined as the extent to which the return on investment over a period of time exceeds the cost of capital for that investment. The cost of capital is a function of the risk of an investment. Return is a function of cashflow and amount of investment. A more detailed discussion of value and its formulation is presented in Chapter 2.

From the perspective of a merging or acquiring firm's shareholders, the decision to acquire should depend on whether an investment produces realistic expectations of potential future returns on investments. If not, it simply ought to be avoided. (Easier said than done!) Accordingly, the executives of merging or acquiring firms face two formidable tasks.

First, they must determine what returns a merger or an acquisition can be expected to create. This is not an easy task since it requires executives to predict, with considerable accuracy, the sources of value and the future cashflows of three different entities: the target, the acquirer, and the combined firm. Also included in these predictions is an equally difficult assessment of the likelihood that these future cashflows will indeed be realized over an appropriate time horizon.

Second, executives must convince shareholders that a merger or an acquisition will add the value that management expects. The executives can achieve this in one of two ways: by convincing shareholders to share their positive expectations or, absent such shared expectations, by proceeding with the deal and succeeding in creating the value they promised. The statements made at the opening of this chapter reflect such expectations, as executives attempted to convince their shareholders, employees, and customers of the inherent value of a merger and ensure that such value would be realized after the deal was closed. Neither would be an easy challenge.

Not meeting these expectations destroys whatever increase in value might have been achieved as a result of the initial (and ultimately false) expectations; and not realizing the value that management expected, obviously, damages the acquirer or merging partners. Moreover, unmet expectations are likely to generate reservations about management's competence and, hence, are likely to fuel adverse expectations with respect to management's future performance. Neither bodes well for an executive's career.

How, then, can the executives of an acquiring firm determine what value to expect from an acquisition? What can they do to ensure their expectations are met? What is the nature of the process whereby value can be created? These questions have been debated by both practitioners and academics for years and have resulted in many proposed answers.

A FRAMEWORK FOR CREATING VALUE

Two sources of value are possible in a merger or an acquisition:

- Value from the purchase of a target for less than its intrinsic or standalone value (i.e., an undervalued target)
- Value from synergies that can be created by integrating two firms

Whether a "good deal" can be had or synergies can be realized is a function of inflows and outflows of value that occur during a merger or an acquisition. If the inflows exceed the outflows, then a merger or an acquisition will add value to an acquirer. If the reverse holds true, a negative impact on value is to be expected. Accordingly, it is necessary to specify the inflows and the outflows that an acquiring or merging firm can expect. These are summarized in Figure 1-1.

Inflows of Value

There are two categories of inflows: the intrinsic value of a target and synergy value.

Intrinsic Value of a Target

This is the true stand-alone value of a target firm. It is determined by the actual cashflows, adjusted for risk, that a firm generates. The true intrinsic value of a firm at any given time can only be established retrospectively, as time unfolds and expectations of future cashflows turn into historical events. The best an acquiring firm can do is to approximate intrinsic value by formulating realistic expectations about the future cashflows of a target.

Since neither a buyer nor a seller can know for certain what a target's true value is at the time of a transaction, both parties are subject to the potential for error. When a target errs by underestimating its own true value, an acquiring firm has an opportunity to create value for itself by taking advantage of the error. More specifically, this opportunity arises when a target underestimates its full prospective cashflow potential or overestimates the risks that attend these cashflows. If an acquiring firm can realistically expect to exceed a target's self-assessed expectations of its future cashflows, value can be created.

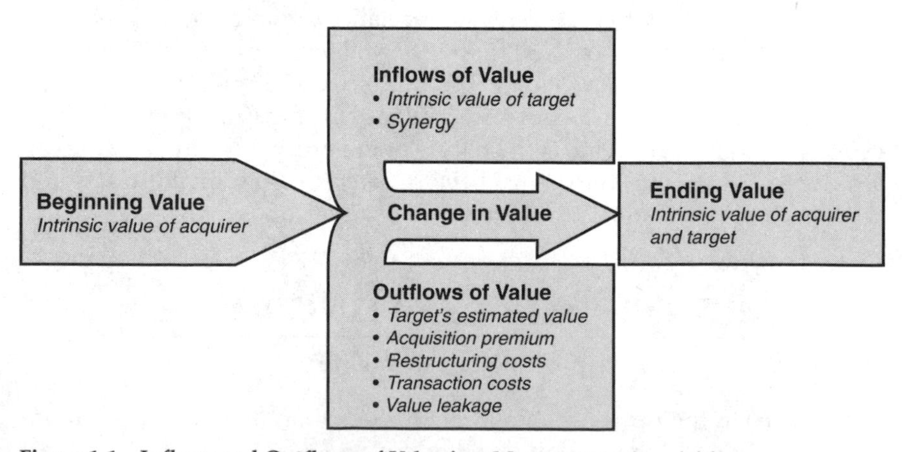

Figure 1-1 Inflows and Outflows of Value in a Merger or an Acquisition

While such a situation is theoretically possible, in actual practice it is exceedingly difficult to achieve. In the case of a publicly traded target, for example, an acquiring firm would have to outguess the market with respect to a target's prospects. One need not assume a fully efficient market to suggest that the presence of highly sophisticated market participants make such an outcome extremely unlikely. Perhaps the case of an undervalued private target is easier to imagine. However, the strong emotional attachments that private owners have to their firms, often the product of several generations' work, typically lead these owners to overestimate rather than underestimate the value of their firm.

Synergy Value

An acquisition can create opportunities to increase revenues, reduce costs, reduce net working capital, and improve investment intensity. In order to assess the opportunities created by synergy, an acquiring firm must not only identify the changes that are likely to enhance cashflows but also estimate the probability of implementing these changes. Yet many firms satisfy themselves with very broad or global assessments of this potential, as in the opening statements of this chapter. Such vague assessments, even if quantifiable, are much too general to permit the formulation of realistic expectations with respect to an acquisition, particularly expectations about how such "synergies" might eventually be implemented.

Acquiring firms could profit from more accurate and refined calibrations of this potential, whether that be by gaining a more realistic appreciation of the value that can be expected to be delivered or by determining that the transaction is not worth the price. More is said about this in Chapter 2.

Outflows of Value

There are five categories of outflows. They include the target's estimated value, acquisition control premium, restructuring costs, transaction costs, and value leakage.

Target's Estimated Value

For a publicly traded target, the market sets a benchmark for estimating its value. For a privately held firm, no such benchmark is available. Regardless of whether a target is a public or a private company, however, both a target and an acquirer need to estimate the intrinsic value of the target if for no other reason than to establish the parameters for a fair acquisition price. These estimates will be based on each firm's assessment of a target's prospective cashflows. Since these estimates are likely to derive from differing perceptions of a target's future performance and valuation methodologies, the possibility exists that a target will overestimate its intrinsic value. In this case the difference between this value and the intrinsic value will result in an outflow.

Acquisition Premium

Mergers and acquisitions typically require an incentive payment in order to induce the owners of a target to sell their interest in a firm. In a publicly traded firm, this premium is simply the portion of the purchase price that exceeds the firm's market value. With a private firm, the parties are more likely to conceive of the transaction in terms of a "bulk" purchase price. Nonetheless, it is important for executives of acquiring firms to develop a clear distinction between that portion of the price that represents its estimate of a target's intrinsic value and the portion that represents the premium. The importance of this distinction lies in the fact that if value is to be created, the premium most likely must be recovered from something other than the intrinsic value of a target (i.e., synergy).

Restructuring Costs

These are the costs incurred in implementing the changes that are necessary to realize the potential value added by combining two firms. These may include such costs as severance benefits and the costs incurred in bringing certain facilities up to OSHA standards.

Transaction Costs

Transaction costs arise from the transaction itself, including attorneys' fees, investment bankers' fees, financial commitment fees, consultants' fees, etc.

Value Leakage

Value leakage occurs when there is a loss of cashflow during the M&A process. Two possibilities give rise to the potential for value to leak during a merger or an acquisition. These include the dissipation of the potential value of combining due to:

1. The potentially negative impact the act of acquiring has on the intrinsic value of either firm (e.g., loss of productivity, employees, and customers)
2. External environmental changes before implementation (e.g., economic downturns)

To summarize, a merging or an acquiring firm must determine which of these potential inflows and outflows of value are applicable to a particular merger or an acquisition. The difference between the sum of the inflows and the sum of the outflows determines the change that an acquiring firm should expect from a merger or an acquisition. The objective in a value-creating merger or acquisition is to ensure inflows exceed outflows. Ensuring that this happens is the core responsibility of executives and depends upon a number of critical factors:

1. An appropriate merger or acquisition candidate must be targeted, and a basic understanding of how value can be created from a deal is developed.

2. Realistic expectations (i.e., pro forma) of a future target's revenues, costs, net working capital, investments, and the sources of them must be estimated.
3. Pro forma financial statements must be established based on detailed assessments of how specific functions of the target will be integrated — or, at least enough functions to recover any premium paid.
4. Based on pro forma statements and other methods (e.g., market multiples, asset values), values for a target must be developed.
5. Estimates of value from a target must be continually refined based on securing due diligence information (legal, strategic, financial, organizational).
6. Effective bargaining and negotiating with a target must be undertaken to ensure that the right price based on the valuation models is paid. Poor negotiations can lead to overpayment.
7. Actions must be undertaken to ensure that the acquisition process does not destroy existing value of either a target or an acquirer (e.g., uncertainty or confusion about the implications of the acquisition may lead to the defection of key employees or customers, productivity losses, poor customer service, etc.).
8. Actions must be taken to ensure that integration is achieved and that synergy value is realized.

Throughout this chapter, I have outlined a balanced view of the many elements that affect value creation in M&As and the challenges executives face in managing them. Although all the elements are important, one in particular, integration, has historically been among the most neglected, most underestimated, but the most difficult process to manage by executives.

THE IMPORTANCE OF INTEGRATION

Why is integration so important? As the discussion above suggests, most of the elements in the M&A process take place prior to the closing of a deal. They are theoretical activities to help arrive at and negotiate a "reasonable" purchase price. Once the deal is closed, the challenge first begins. Now the organizations and the people of the combining organizations have to be managed in such a fashion that all the assumptions about synergies, cashflows, and earnings are converted to reality. Enamored with the excitement of doing deals and preoccupied by financial and strategic issues, executives have not, historically, focused much attention on integration. Increasingly, however, that has been changing. Burned by a lack of results, many executives have come to appreciate the importance of the roles integration and people play in the success of M&As and their ability to create value for investors. Growing research in this area has also demonstrated that many disappointing mergers and acquisitions may be attributed to failure to plan for and execute integration. [7]

MANAGING THE INTEGRATION PROCESS

Figure 1-2 illustrates the key elements of the integration process and serves as the framework for the rest of this book. The process starts with the strategic and financial objectives underlying a merger or an acquisition. The first major premise of this book is that for value to be created, the integration process must be aligned with and be driven by these objectives. These objectives are discussed in depth in Chapter 2.

The second major premise of this book is that integration activities should not begin after closing. Integration begins at the point at which a target or merger partner is considered and continues until well after closing when a merger or an acquisition is actually integrated. To better understand the complex integration process, the discussion will be divided into three interrelated stages: transaction, transition, and integration. Each stage and the activities to be performed during them are briefly described below and are discussed in depth in Chapters 3 through 8.

The last element in the framework focuses on evaluation. It is the third major premise of the book that continuous evaluation and improvement are critical to success during integration and that what is learned is applied to future deals to improve subsequent integration efforts. Evaluation is discussed in Chapter 9.

THE STAGES OF THE M&A PROCESS

Let's begin by eliminating a myth: namely, that the integration process should begin after the deal is closed. Most experienced and successful acquirers recognize that the process should begin as early as possible in the life of a deal (e.g., when a target firm is being considered). The earlier that information pertinent to the integration is collected and the planning of the integration is begun, the better! These steps create the speed and momentum needed to integrate the firms after closing. However, this is not always possible. Two elements drive the timing of integration activities: availability of accurate and relevant information and access to and cooperation with a target.

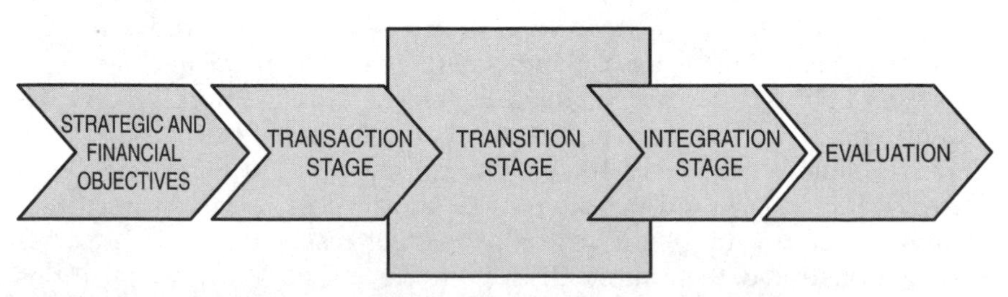

Figure 1-2 Key Elements of the Integration Process

Accurate and Relevant Information

As noted earlier, a buyer's ability to forecast earnings and cashflows is central to an accurate valuation. Being able to analyze and understand the issues (e.g., cultural fit, retention of key people, information systems compatibility) that might affect the success of the integration is more likely to lead to an accurate valuation. After all, cashflows and earnings can only be realized after closing! For example, a buyer forecasts a certain cashflow in the first year after the closing, which typically serves as the basis of future cashflows and the terminal value. Let us assume that such a forecast is based on revenue synergies that presume cross-selling of products between complementary sales organizations. To the extent that a buyer understands the likelihood that cross-selling can be implemented and effectively managed in the merging sales forces or distribution channel, the greater the likelihood that the valuation will be accurate. Failure to anticipate and understand the integration issues that affect cross-selling will probably lead to a poor forecast and the likelihood of overpayment—if, of course, the price assumed the presence of sales synergies. These assumptions point to the importance of obtaining early information and analysis. This gives the time needed to devise strategies for ensuring that plans are put in place to manage these issues once a deal has closed.

If integration information is not available during the selection of a target, then it is essential that a buyer attempt to gather it during due diligence. Knowing that sales synergies are critical to the valuation, the buyer needs to conduct a proper investigation to verify the presence and likelihood of that synergy. Chances are that this will include questions concerning the capabilities of the sales staff, the customers they serve, the likelihood that products or services are transferable, and the incentives that are provided to the sales staff. If such questions cannot be answered until after the deal is closed due to lack of availability or access to information, then two problems are created.

First, the presence of synergies becomes a guessing game, as does deciding on the price that should be paid. Second, the buyer then has to wait until after a deal has closed to determine whether synergies exist and how to capture them. When this happens, there is a tremendous slowing of momentum of the integration and a lower probability that the earnings and cashflows that were forecasted earlier in the process will be realized. Moreover, the buyer may have to find unanticipated ways (e.g., cost cutting), with unanticipated consequences, to improve earnings and cashflows after the deal is closed. After all, no one wants to fail to meet expectations.

Information Access

Access to information about a target and the timing of when that information can be secured is essential to effective integration. Obviously, with a publicly traded target, information is more readily available. This is also likely to be the case with a large and visible target. The greatest difficulty is with small, privately held companies. Access to information is often a function of:

- The trust an acquirer can generate with a target's management/owners and assurances as to the acquirer's "seriousness" about doing a deal
- A target management's concerns about employees learning that the target is up for sale

An acquirer must be prepared to conduct assessments during this phase with varying levels of access and to decide what risks to take if not permitted sufficient access. Note that some of the risks may be mitigated through warranties, representations, and indemnification clauses written into the acquisition agreement.[8]

Stages of Information Gathering and Analysis

It is important to keep in mind that there are two separate stages of information gathering and analysis: assessing the target before formal contact and after formal contact.

Stage 1: Assessing the Target Prior to Formal Contact

This would involve discreetly collecting information through primary sources (e.g., knowledgeable personal contacts) or secondary sources (e.g., public databases and periodicals). On the basis of such an analysis, a buyer can develop a preliminary understanding of the target.

Information gathered at this stage may be related to product lines and markets (including customers, distribution channels, etc.), functional area capabilities, work processes and strategies, support area capabilities (e.g., MIS, accounting, human resources), financial situation, legal situation, organizational culture, organizational structure and staffing, and key management and employees. Although preliminary, this information prepares an acquirer for integration issues that may require further analysis.

As soon as contact with a target is established, the integration process begins. It starts before the closing, beginning at the time of the initial entrée, and continuing through negotiations, due diligence, integration planning, and the integration process itself. Why is this the case? From the point at which contact begins, a buyer and target establish a relationship and create a history. They learn about each other's values, culture, behaviors, etc., all of which send signals about what life is going to be like after a deal is closed. Moreover, the parties will remember how the other treated them, which will establish a base for future cooperation, or conflict. For example, if the people sent by the buyer to conduct due diligence are insensitive to the target's people, or treat them like second-class citizens, the latter will likely remember it after the closing—if, of course, they decide to stay around. It will not take them very long to become defensive and will not create the cooperative atmosphere needed for the success of the subsequent integration.

The discussion above suggests three important elements. First, collecting integration information early in the M&A process helps ensure that the valuations and needed integration are aligned. Second, establishing a cooperative atmosphere early in the M&A process facilitates the ensuing integration. Third, beginning the integration planning as early as possible creates the momentum to integrate after the closing.

Stage 2: Assessing the Target after Formal Contact and Cooperation Have Been Established

This may not happen until the transition or integration stages. This would involve in-depth assessments of the current state of the target and/or similarities and differences between it and the acquirer.

PREPARING FOR SUCCESS DURING THE TRANSACTION STAGE

The transaction stage characterizes the period after which an acquirer identifies a target and culminates when there is commitment to "do a deal." This commitment is typically reflected in the signing of a merger or an acquisition agreement and the announcement of a deal.

During this stage the acquirer or merger partner attempts to gather enough information to decide whether to do the deal and what issues must be managed to successfully close the deal. Information pertains to valuation, pricing, due diligence, and negotiations. Typically, acquirers and merger partners focus on strategic, financial, and legal considerations during this stage. Rarely do they seriously consider significant organizational issues that affect integration, especially in the case of an inexperienced acquirer. Organizational issues, with the exception of payroll and benefits costs, are often considered too soft and difficult to quantify and as such are given less attention. Increasingly, however, experienced buyers have come to realize the importance of organizational issues (e.g., cultural fit, the caliber of key personnel, etc.) and the impact those issues can have on the success of the deal, and have begun incorporating them into the transaction stage. A study of 350 European mergers and acquisitions[9] supports the conclusion that the issues listed below were insufficiently considered prior to closing:

1. Communication plans
2. Organization of the new entity
3. Culture
4. Assessing target management

Transaction-Stage Objectives

During the transaction stage there are four objectives that an acquirer or merger partner should focus on. These are:

1. Gather and analyze information (i.e., due diligence) to learn as much as possible about a target. In particular, the acquirer must decide whether the target and the deal make sense from four perspectives:
   a. *Strategic*. Will the deal allow the company to achieve some or all of its strategic objectives? Can enough synergies be documented to support the strategic objectives and justify the price being paid?
   b. *Financial*. Will the deal likely deliver the financial results hoped for? Are the cashflow and earnings forecasts accurate? Is the valuation model correct? Do we have an accurate assessment of the assets and liabilities?
   c. *Legal*. Do we understand all of the target's off-balance sheet liabilities and their impact? Have we complied with all laws and regulations?
   d. *Organizational*. Do we have an accurate assessment of the people and organizational cultures? Do the two organizations fit together enough to ensure that the deal can be integrated and synergies can be captured?
2. Negotiate the right price. Based on all the information gathered, the acquirer must not pay a price beyond what a target is worth. This requires accurate valuation and objectivity during the negotiation process.
3. Ensure both that the behaviors of all acquirer personnel who come in contact with the target and that the activities conducted during this stage create a constructive environment for successful integration and preserve the value of the acquirer and the target.
4. Anticipate roadblocks that need to be managed for effective integration. These may include technical, political, or cultural issues.

Transaction-Stage Activities

Several key integration activities should be performed during the transaction stage. Although numerous activities are required to close a deal, our discussion will focus only on those that pertain directly to integration. These include:

1. *Organizing for information gathering and analysis*. Creating, developing, and managing teams of people to perform an effective and efficient due diligence is critical, especially if time available to do so is limited. The information gathered here provides an early view of the integration issues to be managed.
2. *Assessing the culture of the target*. It is increasingly becoming common knowledge that differences in culture between merging firms are a

major source of conflict in M&As. As such, it is necessary that an acquirer assess the cultures of both a target and itself to:
   a. Determine whether culture is important to a deal
   b. Determine whether differences are so severe that a deal should be killed
   c. Employ interventions that can ensure that differences become a source of value rather than destructive conflict
3. *Assessing key target people.* As will be demonstrated throughout the book, identifying and assessing people in both an acquirer and a target who might be important to either the success of the transition or the long-term viability of the combined organization is essential. Without qualified people an organization cannot function effectively.
4. *Guiding the behaviors and attitudes of negotiators, due diligence teams, and negotiators.* As noted above, the integration process begins the minute that people from an acquirer and a target come in contact with each other. Thus acquirer's people should be trained in how to properly interact with the target and create a context for cooperation.

PREPARING FOR SUCCESS DURING THE TRANSITION STAGE

The transition stage begins when the acquirer and the target or merger partners formally announce a deal and sign a merger or acquisition agreement. At this point there is likely to be significant speculation by both employees and customers about the implications of the deal and its impact on them and their organization. There will also be greater interaction among people from both organizations, and the acquirer will have access to the target. As noted above, this stage may involve completing the activities that were not finished during the transaction stage due to limited access to the target.

Transition-Stage Objectives

There are four objectives during the transition stage:

1. Ensure that the activities conducted during this stage continue to create a constructive environment for successful integration.
2. Ensure that the value of both the acquirer and the target or merger partners is preserved.
3. Ensure that any preliminary integration analyses and assessments begun during the transaction stage are either completed or conducted in more depth.
4. Conduct the integration planning process.

Transition-Stage Activities

Several integration activities need to be performed during this stage. These include:

1. *Create an integration transition structure.* A structure to manage the process of taking two independent companies and creating one can help create an orderly integration. The complexity of the structure will vary depending upon the nature and level of the integration process.
2. *Articulate integration guiding principles.* Numerous activities are performed during this stage, and many people are involved. Thus, it is impossible to control everything tightly. Guiding principles are broad enough to help ensure that the basic philosophy underlying the integration is understood and that the decisions and behaviors of those involved are in concert.
3. *Decide what to integrate and how to do it.* What areas to integrate and how best to integrate them needs to be defined. Considerations at this point include using best practices or innovating new practices.
4. *Develop an integration project plan to drive implementation.* It is almost impossible to manage the many activities involved in integration unless there is a coherent and organized plan for doing so. Project planning methodologies can be of great help.
5. *Manage communications with all stakeholders.* Although discussed in the transition stage, communications should be a key component in every stage of the integration process. From the point at which rumors begin to circulate about a possible merger or acquisition throughout the integration stage, communication with stakeholders will be critical, especially if the changes being created impact them.

PREPARING FOR SUCCESS DURING THE INTEGRATION STAGE

The integration stage begins after closing and continues until after the target or merger partners are integrated. Closing is a critical event since it is the point at which the acquirer formally owns the target or a new merged entity is created, control has shifted, and changes can "officially" be made. Prior to that point an acquirer or a merger partner can only recommend changes to the other management team.

Integration-Stage Objectives

There are three objectives during integration. These include:

1. Complete any analytical activities that were not completed prior to the closing.
2. Execute actions to physically integrate the target or merger partner.

3. Rebuild the organization into a stronger, more competitive entity capable of realizing financial and strategic objectives.

Integration-Stage Activities

Several integration activities need to be performed during this stage. These include:

1. *Demonstrating a committed and open-minded leadership*. Since integration involves change, it often requires a strong leader to drive the effort. In fact, strong and committed leadership is often cited as a key element in any change effort.[10]
2. *Building teams and work units*. Often in a merger or an acquisition, teams of people who have never worked together are created. Creating a cooperative context in which this can happen can help facilitate the ease and speed of the integration.
3. *Focusing on financial and strategic objectives*. It is very easy for people to take their eyes off the business during the integration process as they deal with their many personal issues. Moreover, as work units change, it is very easy for them to fall out of alignment with the broader organizational financial and strategic objectives. Alignment must therefore be managed to ensure this does not happen.
4. *Remaining flexible—things change*. No matter how well transition planning was conducted, many elements cannot be forecasted accurately. Executives and managers must therefore be prepared to make adjustments to plans as events change.
5. *Developing capable and motivated people*. It is a mistake to assume that people will be able to step into new positions and perform well after a merger or an acquisition has closed. It is essential that executives put into place elements that help people develop the proper capabilities and motivation.
6. *Assimilating new people*. Many people in a merger or an acquisition want to succeed in the new organization. Care must be taken that they are properly assimilated and are provided proper coaching and information on how they can succeed in their new positions.
7. *Achieving cultural integration*. As new units and teams are created with people from different organizations, the opportunities for culture clash are significant. Rather than wait for a clash, there are approaches that executives and managers can employ to ensure cultural learning and cooperation. These can greatly improve the speed of and the impact of the integration effort on the financial and strategic considerations.

EVALUATING THE INTEGRATION PROCESS

Central to the effectiveness of the integration is the need to continually improve the process. This must occur in two ways. First, a process must be developed where learning and improvement can take place during the integration effort. Thus, when deviations from the plan are found or problems arise, they can be corrected. After the merger or acquisition is "completed," it may be too late. Value may have leaked, and synergies may have not been realized.

Second, there are many opportunities for executives to learn from each integration effort and improve subsequent efforts. I have learned over the last 20 years from research and consulting that there is always something new to learn and new ways to improve the integration process. Unfortunately in most organizations there is no process for institutionalizing learning. What has been learned often resides in the minds of a few people. Sometimes they share what they have learned, and sometimes they do not. Sometimes they leave before they have had the opportunity to do so. The result is that companies repeat mistakes and miss opportunities.

THE LAST CHAPTER

Thus far I have presented the conceptual framework for the book and the 9 chapters that support it. However, there is one last chapter. While it does not directly fit within the framework, it nevertheless is of importance to the success of the integration effort and to those who participate in it.

Chapter 10 presents a personal perspective on M&As and strategies for how executives, managers, and employees can personally prosper during them. Many of the insights in this chapter are drawn from psychological disciplines, personal experience, and interactions with thousands of people who have both prospered and suffered during M&As.

This chapter is important for two reasons. First, I learned a long time ago that if people cannot successfully manage how they deal with challenging events, they have little chance in successfully managing others going through them. Second, many people needlessly suffer during M&As and other traumatic organizational changes. The hope is that this chapter will provide some insights to help manage oneself and others during these challenging times.

Now that the overview of the book is complete, we will turn our attention to creating value through the integration process. The next chapter will focus on the strategic and financial objectives driving integration.

2

STRATEGIC AND FINANCIAL OBJECTIVES: THE DRIVERS OF INTEGRATION

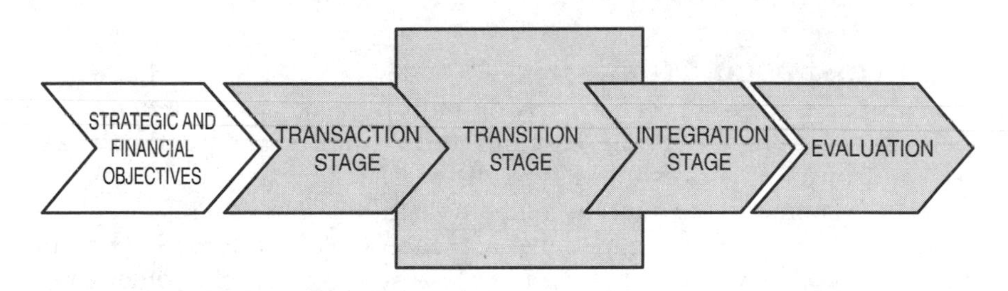

The financial and strategic objectives underlying a deal must first be understood before an approach to integration is chosen. This chapter specifically illustrates how both objectives shape the integration process.

For M&As to succeed, they must be driven by a sound business strategy. Contrary to what some executives might think, M&As are not strategies in and of themselves. They are only tools of implementation, much like joint ventures, alliances, licensing agreements, and internal investments. Although each has different attributes and pros and cons, they are essentially interchangeable. Of importance is what they accomplish for a firm. For example, do they allow a firm to extend its geographic scope of operations; sell to new customer groups; improve its cost position through economies of scale; acquire new products, services, and technologies; control supply and distribution; or all of the above? Essentially, do they allow the firm to grow revenues profitably and improve competitive advantage? If not, then it is unlikely they will create value for investors.

Strategy alone is not sufficient to create value for investors. M&As must satisfy financial objectives as well. If the strategy is sound but the deal is unable to provide the right return, value for investors will be lost. Throughout the remainder of this chapter I discuss how strategic and financial objectives shape the integration process. Additionally, I demonstrate that the true purpose of the integration process is to ensure that both strategic and financial objectives are indeed realized and provide a framework for guiding the integration process.

CREATING VALUE—THE VALUE OF A COMPANY AND THE PRICE PAID

It is essential to understand the relationship between valuation and pricing. Although a simple idea, it is quite complex in practice. When making an acquisition or undertaking a merger, most companies employ several methods to valuation. The two most influential are (1) cashflow models such as discounted cashflows (DCF) and real options and (2) market-based models such as comparable company and comparable acquisition transaction analyses. Publicly traded companies also examine earnings-per-share (EPS) dilution effects. These are critical drivers of the results that must be achieved during the integration and ultimately determine the success or failure of a merger or an acquisition. In this section I briefly review valuation methods and illustrate how they affect integration.

Market-Based Measures

Market-based measures usually rely on multiples such as price to trailing 12-month earnings, EBITDA (earnings before interest, tax, depreciation, and amortization), or cashflow. Typically a particular merger or an acquisition is compared with a recent comparable transaction or with a publicly traded company to determine what an "acceptable" multiple is (e.g., 10 times EBITDA). A market-based multiple only suggests what other comparable companies are valued at or have sold for in the marketplace and often establish the purchase price for a target. It does not indicate what a company might be worth to a particular buyer; it may be worth more to one buyer than to another due to differences in their organizational capabilities and the role that a target plays in enhancing the buyer's competitive position. In other words, there may be synergies available to one acquirer but not to another. Moreover, a market multiple may change without any fundamental change in a target's intrinsic or stand-alone value.

Earnings-per-Share Approach

An EPS approach is typically used by publicly traded acquirers. EPS is an important measure that shareholders and analysts use to assess a firm's performance. It is not a valuation measure but does demonstrate the impact of price paid as an important predictor of stock price. Essentially, the acquirer examines an acquisition to determine whether it will be dilutive or accretive. A dilutive acquisition is one in which the initial and subsequent combined earnings of the acquiring and acquired firms do not at least sustain the acquirer's EPS. An accretive acquisition is one in which EPS is improved. In publicly traded companies, where EPS seems to influence stock price, this is an important consideration. This is especially important in cases where an acquirer has issued stock as currency to make an acquisition. For example, this was a critical part of Worldcom's growth strategy. As the multiple paid increases, so do the earnings needed to sustain EPS. An example of dilution-accretion is as follows.

Telecom is interested in buying Terrestrial Communications. Both companies are publicly traded. Telecom will purchase 100 percent of Terrestrial Communication's stock by issuing new shares of its own stock. However, Telecom is concerned about possible dilution. Table 2-1 presents some basic statistics on both companies' financial situations.

To examine possible dilution, Telecom conducts the following analysis. First Telecom must determine how many shares of its stock it must issue to acquire all of Terrestrial's stock. After initial valuation and negotiations, Telecom offers $65 per share. To determine how many shares of its own stock Telecom must exchange, the following calculations are made:

Exchange ratio = offer price per share for target/share price of acquirer

Exchange ratio = $65/$150 = 0.43 share

Given Telecom's stock price and the offer price, Telecom will offer 0.43 share of Telecom for each share of Terrestrial Communications.

Total shares = (offer price)(total target shares outstanding)/price of acquirer

Total shares = ($65) (2,000,000)/ $150 = 866,667.67 shares

Given that there are 2,000,000 shares of Terrestrial outstanding, the total number of shares of Telecom required is 866,667.67. The following analysis allows us to calculate initial dilution-accretion.

Initial EPS of Combined Firm

Combined earnings = $50,000,000 + $10,000,000
Total shares outstanding = 5,000,000 + 866,666.67
Preacquisition EPS = $10
Postacquisition EPS = $60,000,000/5,866,666.67; Postacquisition EPS = $10.23

In this case the merger is accretive since the EPS increases after the deal is done. The sensitivity of the initial EPS to offer price is as follows:

At $65 EPS = $10.23

At $90 EPS = $9.68

In general, dilution occurs whenever the P/E paid for the target exceeds the P/E of the buyer.

Table 2-1 Financial Statistics for Telecom and Terrestrial Communications

	Telecom	Terrestrial Communications
Present earnings	$50,000,000	$10,000,000
Shares outstanding	5,000,000	2,000,000
EPS	$10	$5
Stock price	$150	$50
Price/earnings	15	10

P/E paid = \$65 / \$5 = \$13 < \$15

P/E paid = \$90 / \$5 = \$18 > \$15

The following calculation determines the maximum offer price where there is no dilution:

Maximum nondilution offer price = (buyer P/E) (target EPS)

= (\$15) (\$5) = \$75 per share

The above analysis can be applied to forecasted earnings for subsequent years following the initial combination as well. If forecasted earnings of the combined firm decline or do not increase (given initial dilution), then the deal will likely lead to future dilution and will be value-destroying. If it increases, the deal will likely be value-enhancing. Why is this important? It clearly indicates the level of earnings that will be required after the deal to avoid dilution. If the target's earnings are not sufficient to sustain EPS, then dilution will occur. To avoid this, earnings will need to improve. The result: The need for synergies. The implication: The need for successful integration.

Discounted Cashflow Approach

Often, companies rely on some form of discounted cashflow to value a target.[1] Under this approach the value of a target is essentially the stream of its future cashflows (usually five years) plus a terminal value discounted at the combined firms' weighted cost of capital. Cashflows for the projected time period and the terminal value are discounted and added to determine the total value of the target firm.[2]

From this perspective it is apparent that value creation is dependent upon the total capital invested (i.e., purchase price) in an acquisition and the cashflows generated from it. If the DCF value is less than the purchase price, then value is destroyed. If it is greater, then value is created. Based on this model, economic value is created when the return on capital employed in an acquisition exceeds the target's weighted-average cost of capital.[3] The final valuation will vary depending upon the weighted-average cost of capital, the forecasted cashflows, and the terminal value chosen.[4]

To illustrate this, an example of a privately owned company that is being acquired as part of an industry roll-up is presented. The industry is growing at a modest 2 percent rate and is highly fragmented, with small, privately held companies. There is some overcapacity in the market, prices have been declining, and cost of goods sold is growing annually at a 1 percent rate. Thus, margins have been shrinking. Most of the companies have been around for many years and increasingly have come up for sale. The buyer sees a number of synergies that can be accrued from consolidation and has embarked on an active program to do so.

A DCF model is built from the income statement and elements of the balance sheet (see Part A of Table 2-2). First, beginning with a partial income statement, a five-year pro forma is developed. Critical to the pro forma are forecasts of sales volume and pricing; cost of goods sold; sales, general, and administrative expenses; and profit margins. With the use of the partial balance sheet, a net working capital (i.e., inventory plus receivables minus accounts payable) and an investment pro forma are then developed.

A pro forma is first developed for the target as a stand-alone company, i.e., as an ongoing business without any synergies created through acquisition.[5] Then forecasts are developed for each synergy that is hypothesized. Essentially, a pro forma is developed to reflect the incremental value created by each synergy. The purpose of this exercise is to understand what incremental values are related to the achievement of specific synergies, and ultimately what integration issues are related to the achievement of specific synergies.

Based on the income statement and balance sheet, cashflow statements are then developed. As noted below, cashflow analyses are developed for the stand-alone value and for each potential synergy. The weighted-average cost capital for the target, which is used as the discount factor, is 10 percent based on its capital structure, the cost of its debt, and the cost of equity.

As can be seen from the DCF analysis in Part B of Table 2-2, the stand-alone value of the company is $35,526,770. Synergy values are derived from a number of sources. The first source is a 5 percent cut in sales, general, and administrative costs through the elimination of duplicate corporate offices and services and some limited pruning in the sales organization. The second is a 3 percent increase in sales due to opportunities to cross-sell products. In particular, the buyer has a number of products that it has developed that can be sold through the target's distribution channels. The third is a price increase of 1 percent through the elimination of some capacity from the marketplace. The last source is a 5 percent cost saving in raw materials through the superior purchasing power of the buyer. As illustrated in Part C of Table 2-2, the total value of the synergies is worth $13,388,540.

From the example presented above, it is clear that the analysis yields a range of values. The values depend upon the assumptions made concerning the drivers of cashflow. For example, in Table 2-2, Part A, it is assumed that sales volume would grow 2 percent; cost of goods would grow 1 percent; sales, general, and administrative expenses would remain at 5 percent of sales; and investment would equal the rate of depreciation. The numbers were derived from historical averages. Clearly, there are numerous ways in which to forecast these numbers. In the stand-alone case, the valuation is based on the target firm as an ongoing concern with no synergies created by the acquirer. In this case, the greatest managerial challenge is to do no harm to the target, sustain the projected cashflows, and thus realize the value that is inherent in the business.

If the buyer can acquire a target for the stand-alone value ($35,526,770) or less, the implementation challenges are fewer. Synergies are not required to create value. However, valuation is subject to the

Table 2-2 Financial Statements, Part A (All numbers reported in $,000)

Partial Pro Forma Income Statement							
	Year 0	Year 1	Year 2	Year 3	Year 4	Year 5	
Revenue	$40,000.00	$38,760.00	$39,044.58	$39,330.98	$39,619.19	$39,803.10	
Price	$ 20.00	$ 19.00	$ 18.95	$ 18.90	$ 18.85	$ 18.75	
Volume	$ 2,000.00	$ 2,040.00	$ 2,060.40	$ 2,081.00	$ 2,101.81	$ 2,122.83	2% growth
Cost of goods sold	$30,000.00	$30,300.00	$30,603.00	$30,909.03	$31,218.12	$31,530.30	1% growth
Gross margin	$10,000.00	$ 8,460.00	$ 8,441.58	$ 8,421.95	$ 8,401.07	$ 8,272.80	
Sales, general, administrative costs	$ 2,000.00	$ 1,938.00	$ 1,952.23	$ 1,966.55	$ 1,980.96	$ 1,990.16	5% of revenue
Depreciation	$ 1,000.00	$ 950.00	$ 800.00	$ 600.00	$ 800.00	$ 900.00	
Earnings before interest and taxes	$ 7,000.00	$ 5,572.00	$ 5,689.35	$ 5,855.40	$ 5,620.11	$ 5,382.65	
Interest	$ 1,000.00	$ 958.00	$ 1,011.00	$ 1,032.00	$ 980.00	$ 650.00	
Earnings before taxes	$ 6,000.00	$ 4,614.00	$ 4,678.35	$ 4,823.40	$ 4,640.11	$ 4,732.65	
Taxes @34%	$ 2,040.00	$ 1,568.76	$ 1,590.64	$ 1,639.95	$ 1,577.64	$ 1,609.10	
Net income	$ 3,960.00	$ 3,045.24	$ 3,087.71	$ 3,183.44	$ 3,062.48	$ 3,123.55	
Additional Information							
Capital expenditures		$ 950.00	$ 850.00	$ 600.00	$ 800.00	$ 900.00	Equal to depreciation
Changes in net working capital		$ 8.00	$ 3.56	$ 119.63	$ 126.26	$ 133.49	
Partial Pro Forma Balance Sheet							
Assets:							
Inventory	$ 5,000.00	$ 5,050.00	$ 5,100.50	$ 5,151.51	$ 5,203.02	$ 5,255.05	
Receivables	$ 1,000.00	$ 1,008.00	$ 1,016.06	$ 1,024.19	$ 1,032.39	$ 1,040.65	
Fixed assets	$10,000.00	$10,000.00	$10,050.00	$10,050.00	$10,050.00	$10,050.00	
Total assets	$16,000.00	$16,058.00	$16,166.56	$16,225.70	$16,285.41	$16,345.70	
Liabilities and equity:							
Accounts payable	$ 500.00	$ 550.00	$ 605.00	$ 665.50	$ 732.05	$ 805.26	

Table 2-2 Financial Statements, Part B (All numbers reported in $,000)

	Stand-Alone Value						
	Year 0	Year 1	Year 2	Year 3	Year 4	Year 5	
EBIT	$ 7,000.00	$5,572.00	$5,689.35	$5,855.40	$5,620.11	$5,382.65	
Taxes	$ 2,040.00	$1,568.76	$1,590.64	$1,639.95	$1,577.64	$1,609.10	
EBI after taxes	$ 3,960.00	$3,045.24	$3,087.71	$3,183.44	$3,062.48	$3,123.55	
Depreciation	$ 1,000.00	$ 950.00	$ 800.00	$ 600.00	$ 800.00	$ 900.00	
Cashflow from operations	$ 4,960.00	$3,995.24	$3,887.71	$3,783.44	$3,862.48	$4,023.55	
Change in net working capital		$ 8.00	$ 3.56	$ 119.63	$ 126.26	$ 133.49	
Capital expenditures		$ 950.00	$ 850.00	$ 600.00	$ 800.00	$ 900.00	
Free cashflow		$3,037.24	$3,034.15	$3,063.81	$2,936.22	$2,990.05	
Free cashflow		$3,037.24	$3,034.15	$3,063.81	$2,936.22	$2,990.05	
Terminal value						$42,715.036	$24,097.06
Discount factor =10%							
Present value per year		$2,761.13	$2,507.06	$2,301.19	$2,004.67	$1,855.66	
Stand-alone value	**$35,526.77**						

Table 2-2 Financial Statements, Part C (All numbers reported in $,000)

		Synergy Values					
		Year 1	Year 2	Year 3	Year 4	Year 5	
SGA Expenses Cut of 5%							
Incremental EBIT		$ 96.90	$ 97.61	$ 98.33	$ 99.05	$ 99.51	
Taxes		$ 32.95	$ 33.19	$ 33.43	$ 33.68	$ 33.83	
Incremental free cashflow		$ 63.95	$ 64.42	$ 64.90	$ 65.37	$ 65.68	
Terminal value increment							938.2160083
Present value per year		$ 58.14	$ 53.23	$ 48.74	$ 44.63	$ 40.76	$ 529.28
SGA increment total	**$ 774.79**						
Increase Sales Volume 3%							
Incremental EBIT		$ 60.00	$ 61.20	$ 61.81	$ 62.43	$ 63.05	
Taxes		$ 20.40	$ 20.81	$ 21.02	$ 21.23	$ 21.44	
Incremental free cashflow		$ 39.60	$ 40.39	$ 40.80	$ 41.20	$ 41.62	
Terminal value increment							594.5131142
Present value per year		$ 36.00	$ 33.38	$ 30.64	$ 28.13	$ 25.83	$ 335.39
SGA increment total	**$ 489.36**						
Increase Prices 1%							
Incremental EBIT		$ 0.20	$ 0.19	$ 0.19	$ 0.19	$ 0.19	
Taxes		$ 0.07	$ 0.06	$ 0.06	$ 0.06	$ 0.06	
Incremental free cashflow		$ 0.13	$ 0.13	$ 0.13	$ 0.12	$ 0.12	
Terminal value increment							1.777285714
Present value per year		$ 0.12	$ 0.10	$ 0.09	$ 0.09	$ 0.08	$ 1.00
SGA increment total	**$ 1.48**						
Reduce Cost of Goods Sold 5%							
Incremental EBIT		$1,500.00	$1,515.00	$1,530.15	$1,545.45	$1,560.91	
Taxes		$ 510.00	$ 515.10	$ 520.25	$ 525.45	$ 530.71	
Incremental free cashflow		$ 990.00	$ 999.90	$1,009.90	$1,020.00	$1,030.20	
Terminal value increment							14717.11386
Present value per year		$ 900.00	$ 826.20	$ 758.52	$ 696.39	$ 639.35	$ 8,302.44
SGA increment total	**$12,122.91**						
Total synergy value	**$13,388.54**						

vagaries of predicting revenues, costs, margins, net working capital, and investments. Once the buyer has to pay above the stand-alone value, the challenge becomes more interesting.

PAYING PREMIUMS AND ACHIEVING SYNERGIES (PRICING AND VALUE)

The real challenge in creating value is to ensure that the price paid for an acquisition does not exceed its value to the buyer. As Figure 2-1 illustrates, there are three key elements to consider. First is the stand-alone value of a target. Second are the synergies that can be accrued from the acquisition. Third is the price a buyer will have to pay to gain control of the target.

If the price (Price 1) is lower than or equal to the stand-alone value (e.g., $35,526,770 in the example), then the buyer is likely to have few difficulties in creating value (unless, of course, the buyer overestimated the stand-alone value, has value leakage, or did not uncover critical hidden liabilities during due diligence that lower future cashflow projections).

If the price (Price 2) paid is higher than the stand-alone value, then the buyer must capture synergies to justify the price. In the example, this

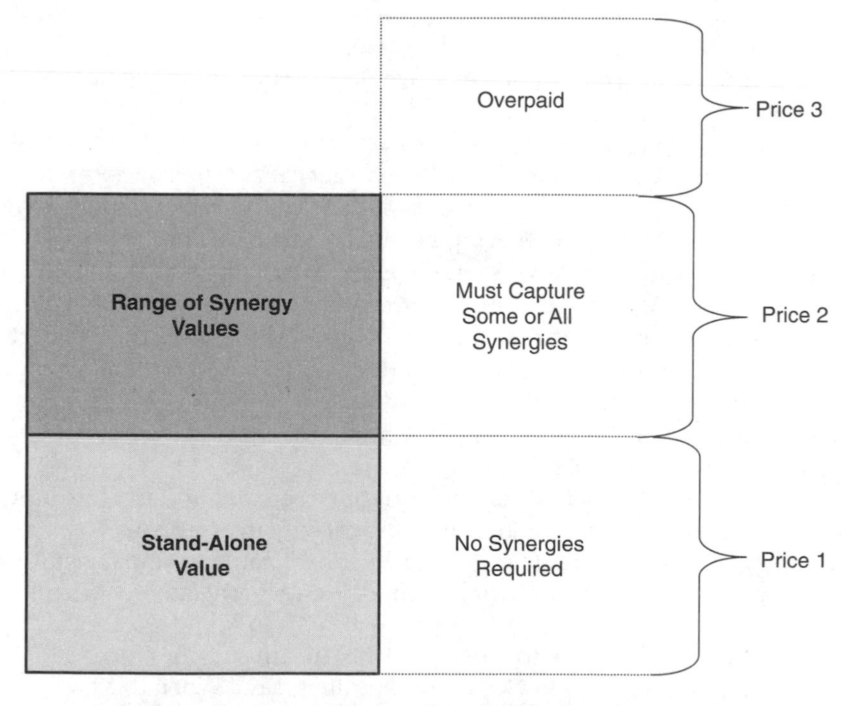

Figure 2-1 Pricing, Synergy, and Value Creation

incremental value of synergies ranges from $1,480,000 to $12,122,910 and totals to $13,388,540. Failure to do so clearly leads to overpaying. Theoretically, the target is worth anywhere from $35,526,770 to $48,915,320. At the high end, all synergies must be captured through effective integration.

As Mark Sirower,[6] a consultant and former professor at New York University found, however, that firms almost always pay a premium (above the stand-alone value) to gain control of a company, and thus have to find synergies. The capture of synergies is not an easy task. Those that can be easily documented and captured immediately are the ones a firm is most likely to realize. These often are immediate and obvious cost reductions. As a buyer has to realize more difficult synergies (e.g., cross-selling among sales organizations or distribution channels), the challenges become greater and the likelihood of success becomes lower. Sirower also noted that for M&As where a premium has been paid, the likelihood that value will be created is lower.

Finally, if the price paid (Price 3) exceeds the combined stand-alone and synergy value that can "reasonably be expected" (e.g., $48,915,320), then the buyer has overpaid. In such cases there is little hope that value can ever be created, unless of course the stand-alone cashflows or synergies that were forecasted were underestimated. Rarely is this the case, especially when a buyer is eager to do a deal.

As consultants Robert Eccles, Kersten Lanes, and Thomas Wilson note, "Ultimately, the key to success in buying another company is knowing the maximum price you can pay and then having the discipline not to pay a penny more."[7]

Now you might be thinking why anyone would do anything so foolish. There are several reasons. First, a buyer may get caught up in a competitive bidding process and just pay too much. This has come to be known as the "winner's curse." The bidder won, but value was lost. That happened in the security monitoring business in the late 1990s. Both SecurityLink from Ameritech and ADT were rolling up this highly fragmented industry. Over time it became clear to sellers that these two companies were eager to do deals. Within one year prices for the targets (based on market multiples of recurring monthly revenues) doubled, without any appreciable increases in the stand-alone values of the firms (i.e., earnings and cashflows). The pressure for synergies just escalated!

Second, many acquisition negotiations create an escalation of momentum. This is a psychological state whereby the buyer has invested time, energy, and resources (e.g., legal, investment banking, and consulting fees). Given these sunk costs, it becomes increasingly more difficult to walk away, even when it might be prudent to do so.[8]

Third, a buyer wants to do a deal because he is convinced of the strategic reasons regardless of what the "numbers say." When this happens, objectivity is dismissed and the numbers are crafted to justify the deal. It is not uncommon in such cases for buyers to adjust forecasts in a DCF model to generate a value that supports the price demanded by a target.

Finally a buyer underestimates the difficulties involved in integrating the firms, and so synergies are never realized. Although many synergies are identified, they cannot be achieved due to problems such as culture clashes, loss of key people, and loss of customers. (A more comprehensive discussion of these issues is presented in Chapters 3 to 8.)

To create value the buyer must be realistic about the synergies that can be realized. Buyers should not pay a premium above the intrinsic and synergy values, and they should develop and implement an integration process to ensure orderly capture of synergies.

Value Creation and the Timing of Cashflows

Of critical importance to valuation models is the timing of the forecasted earnings and cashflows. For example, if certain synergies are forecasted to take place during the first year after the closing but are not realized until the second year, the results can be dramatically different. For instance, in Table 2-2 if the cost of goods sold take an additional year to realize due to integration problems, the value of the synergy drops from $12,122,910 to $11,222,910. This clearly suggests that forecasted synergies are quite sensitive to the realization and timing of synergies, which in turn are dependent upon the management and success of the integration process.

STRATEGIC OBJECTIVES AND POTENTIAL SOURCES OF SYNERGY

Now that the financial objectives underlying M&As have been examined, it is important to focus on strategy. Various strategies represent different potential sources of synergies and the opportunity to realize value. Regardless of how good a strategy may appear, it is dangerous to argue that a deal should be done based on "conceptual definitions" of strategy and synergies alone. The business landscape is lined with many M&As that made conceptual sense, "were made in heaven," and delivered no value. The following comments reported in Eccles, Lanes, and Wilson summarize my key points perfectly:

> Assume that the numbers don't add up, but people in the company still claim there are compelling strategic reasons for doing the deal anyway. What's next? The most disciplined thing to do is walk away.
>
> Doubtless there are deals that should happen for strategic reasons even when the numbers don't sound promising, but they are few and far between.

> "We have a rule on the Executive Committee," says Harry Tempest of ABN AMBRO. "When someone says 'strategic,' the rest of us say, 'too expensive.'"

This is not to argue that the numbers should drive the decision. The very specific strategic benefits that a deal delivers and how that translates at some point into earnings and cashflow must also be taken into consideration.[9] Even if it may take 10 years to realize the benefits of a strategy, an attempt must be made to quantify and capture it. Although DCF models are as much art as they are science, they do force managers to articulate their assumptions about industry and organizational factors that drive cashflows and earnings. This exercise is often sobering and useful, especially if attempted with some level of objectivity.

As illustrated below, a number of strategic objectives drive a deal. Each has the potential to deliver certain synergies. These are key to creating value—of course, depending upon the price paid!

Sources of Synergy

There are basically four sources of synergy: cost, revenue, market power, and intangibles. Cost synergies are often the easiest to document and capture in a merger or an acquisition. Revenue, market power, and intangibles, on the other hand, are increasingly more difficult. Each is described below.

Cost Synergies

Reducing costs is one clear way to increase earnings and cashflows. It has historically been the most common form of synergy and is often the easiest type to capture. There are two types of cost synergies:

1. Fixed-cost reduction
2. Variable-cost reduction

Fixed-cost reduction is often associated with economies of scope and scale and productivity. It is also associated with reducing general, administrative, and sales expenses through headquarters and support function consolidation; gaining economies of scale in operations, sales force, and distribution optimization; and reducing transaction costs in the supply chain. Variable-cost reduction is associated with increased purchasing power and productivity. Both forms of cost reduction often come with the physical consolidation of activities between the combining companies. The synergies that can be accrued here depend very much on the nature of the cost structure of the business model being employed by an acquirer.

Cost synergies are present in almost every M&A. They have been central elements behind deals transacted in the banking, pharmaceutical, automobile, airline, and security monitoring industries, to name just a few.

Revenue Synergies

Revenue synergies are often hoped for but rarely realized in M&As. Typically, revenue synergies are associated with cross-selling products or services through complementary (i.e., nonoverlapping) sales organizations or distribution channels that serve different geographic regions, customer groups, or technologies. A key assumption underlying this source is that complementary markets desire the same products and services.

In addition, revenue synergies can be derived from broadening a company's products and services to provide needed bundling or a more complete offering. Critical to this synergy is to leverage complementarity without adding additional costs. This includes:

1. Increased sales productivity by selling more volume with the same number of or fewer salespeople (this may also create cost synergies)
2. Cross-selling products through complementary sales organizations and distribution channels
3. Reducing fixed new-product development costs by utilizing complementary products (i.e., reducing the per unit cost of each product or service through increased volume)

In the 1999 merger between SBC and Ameritech, revenue synergies were captured. In particular, new products were brought from SBC to Ameritech in the directory services (i.e., Yellow Pages) business. Revenues per employee were increased in the Ameritech organization without any additional new-product development or fixed sales expenses.

Revenue synergy was also a critical element behind the Pharmacia and Upjohn merger, where there was geographic complementarity. Pharmacia had a strong presence in Europe, whereas Upjohn had one in the United States. This provided a potential opportunity to cross-sell products. There were differences in customers served and local regulations, however, that limited the benefits that could be realized.

In the 1998 Travelers and Citicorp merger, complementarity existed in customer groups served and in distribution channels employed. Originally, Travelers' insurance products focused on mature adults, whereas Citigroup's banking products emphasized younger customers.

Hilton Hotels has taken advantage of its worldwide reservation systems to cross-sell room inventory for all the brands it acquires. Hilton has used five U.S. call centers to cross-sell through manual call transferring, accounting for more than $100 million in incremental revenue. The centers have become a leverage point for additional acquisitions.[10]

Of course, revenue synergies assume that sales and distribution channels are capable and motivated to sell complementary products. This, however, is not always the case.

Market Power Synergies

This type of synergy results from the elimination of competitors and capacity from a market. This synergy has been a critical element in many mature market consolidations where there is overcapacity. It allows an acquirer to maintain or increase prices in the market, thereby improving margins. An excellent example of this has been the paper core and core board market in Northern Europe. With the market fraught with overcapacity, prices declined in the late 1990s. Through consolidation, capacity could be taken out of the market and competitors eliminated. The net result was increased market power, prices, and margins for the remaining players.

Intangible Synergies

This type of synergy is the most difficult to achieve. It does not easily lend itself to quantification. Intangibles include brand name extensions and the sharing of knowledge and know-how. Rarely do they accrue through the physical consolidation of activities. They rely on the ability to transfer the intangible capabilities of one firm to the other.

This source of synergy was the basis of many acquisitions made by the French company LaFarge, one of the largest cement and concrete manufacturers in the world. In its acquisitions, little opportunity for physical consolidation and economies of scale in operations existed since cement manufacturing is highly localized and decentralized due to transportation costs. What their acquisitions did, however, was to provide excellent opportunities for the transfer of best practices to improve the operations of each manufacturing facility acquired.

Negative Synergy

All the types of synergies described above focus on the creation of value. However, it is important to note that M&As are interventions in organizations that can create disruptions that destroy the intrinsic value of a firm. We call this *value leakage* or *negative synergy*. Thus, while it is critical to manage for positive synergies, it is also important to manage against negative synergies by developing a value preservation plan.

This was an issue, for example, in the sale of a privately held company in California (i.e., the target) that manufactured and sold fans for cooling the chips in personal computers. The target was sought by a Japanese company that wanted access to the U.S. market. Upon examination of the target's balance sheet, it was clear that the price being asked for the target was far greater than its tangible assets. The value provided by the target was its ability to generate cashflows through its extensive distribution network and design and engineering capability. Inability to maintain these, especially during due diligence, would have led to a leakage of value. This was especially critical since key employees and distributors were concerned about the impact of dealing with a large Japanese owner. In fact, the loss of one key distributor may have represented a loss of 10 percent of sales volume, without any clear alternative for regaining it. To combat this, a value preservation plan that included communications and incentives was put into place.

Rarely in a merger or an acquisition is only one form of synergy present or sought. Depending on the particular deal, the number and importance of possible synergies will vary. Moreover, the realization of each form of synergy cannot be assumed. The integration process must be managed with the achievement of each synergy in mind.

ASPECTS OF INTEGRATION

At this point it is necessary to take a closer look at the concept of integration. All too often integration is viewed as a simple concept that implies two organizations are either integrated or left autonomous.[11] In practice the term *integration* is not that simple. It has different meanings, and therefore different implications for how two firms might be combined. There are four primary dimensions of integration. These are:

1. *Consolidation.* The extent to which the separate functions and activities of both the acquirer and the target firms are physically consolidated into one.
2. *Standardization.* The extent to which the separate functions and activities of both firms are standardized and formalized, but not physically consolidated (e.g., separate operations may be maintained, but the operations are made identical). This is typical when acquirers formally transfer best practices across firms.
3. *Coordination.* The extent to which the functions and activities of both firms are coordinated (e.g., one firm's products are sold through the other firm's distribution channels).
4. *Intervention.* The extent to which interventions are made in the acquired firm to turn around poor operating profits and cashflow, regardless of any inherent sources of synergy value (e.g., change management, drop unprofitable products).

STRATEGIC OBJECTIVES, SYNERGIES, AND INTEGRATION: PUTTING IT TOGETHER

Based on the discussion above, it is important to understand how the strategic objectives driving a merger or an acquisition are related to the achievement of synergies and thus the different dimensions of integration. Simply put, different strategies result in different sets of potential synergies and require different dimensions of integration. Presented below are a series of strategic objectives and the synergies underlying them. Also discussed are some of the integration implications associated with achieving these synergies. It is important to note that an acquirer may be seeking multiple strategies and synergies in a particular merger or acquisition. More will be said about this later.

Consolidate Market within a Geographic Area

When this objective is employed, the basic goal is to acquire competitors in the same geographic market. Depending upon the nature of the market, it may include a region within a country, a country itself, a continent, or the globe.

For example, this was the strategy employed by a major U.S. paper manufacturer in Northern Europe. The market was fragmented with many small, privately owned companies and suffered from overcapacity and high fixed costs. As a result, prices were crashing. In a high-fixed-cost business, volume is critical to success.

Consequently, the company began a process of consolidation through acquisition. The objectives were to take capacity out of the market by closing inefficient plants, eliminate redundant sales organizations, reduce general and administrative overhead, increase power vis-à-vis suppliers and customers, and utilize complementary products. The net results were better gross profit margins through higher prices and reduced raw material costs, lower fixed costs through elimination of redundancy, better capacity utilization through increased market share, and thus better return on net assets (i.e., return on capital employed).[12]

On a global level, consolidation has been a driving force in the auto industry. Due to overcapacity, many of the auto companies have made acquisitions, not only to broaden product lines, but also to eliminate capacity and increase economies of scale from manufacturing, product development, and distribution. They have also attempted to reduce general and administrative overhead and increase purchasing power through transactions with suppliers. This has been an objective behind many of the banking and security monitoring M&As that have taken place as well.

The potential sources of synergy in this strategic objective thus include:

- Lower variable costs of raw materials through increased purchasing power
- Lower fixed costs through the elimination of redundant functions, e.g., corporate staff, information technology, sales staff
- Lower fixed costs through better utilization of fixed assets, i.e., economies of scale
- Higher prices through elimination of capacity from the marketplace
- Economies of scope in the sales organization through sharing of products and services developed by each organization

Market consolidation requires high levels of organizational consolidation, standardization, and coordination. This means that:

- Most, if not all, organizational functions and activities will be consolidated and standardized.
- High levels of redundancy of management and employees exist, and reduction in force will likely take place at all organizational levels. Retention of key people in nonconsolidated areas, or highly competent people in general, may be important.
- Differences in organizational culture, identity, and management practices between the acquirer and the target will have to be resolved.
- Differences in strategy, policies, operations, brand names, etc., will have to be resolved.

Extend or Add Products, Services, and Technologies

Typically, opportunities exist to increase competitive capabilities in the marketplace by acquiring new products and services, skills and technology, and access to complementary distribution (if products or services utilize different distribution channels).

This strategy has been a primary driver of many companies in telecommunications equipment manufacturing. For example, Cisco, Alcatel, and Lucent have used acquisitions to expand their technological capabilities and products in Internet protocol and optronics (e.g., optical switching). In industries where numerous start-up firms are developing new technologies, acquisition is often a relied-upon vehicle utilized by larger players in the market. On the telecommunication-provider side, AT&T has relied upon acquisitions to enter both the wireless and cable businesses. Where companies are seeking bundling (i.e., providing a full range of products and services to customers), acquisition remains an important tool.

The elimination of the Glass-Steagall Act has led also to large consolidation in financial services. Today many commercial banks are merging with insurance companies and investment banks. Such mergers eliminate many backroom fixed costs and provide bundled products and services that allow both cross-selling opportunities and "one-stop shopping" for customers.

This strategy has also been employed by many consumer goods companies that have sought to round out their product offerings and by pharmaceutical companies that have attempted to improve their pipeline of new products.

The potential sources of synergy in this strategic objective thus include:

- Lower variable costs through increased purchasing power, where acquired products and services utilize the same basic raw materials

- Lower fixed costs through elimination of redundant functions, e.g., corporate staff, human resources, and information technology
- Lower fixed costs through better utilization of fixed assets (i.e., economies of scale) where products share basic platforms
- Lower fixed costs through better utilization of fixed investments such as advertising and brand development, i.e., economies of scope
- Increased revenue through sharing of products and services developed by each organization
- Increased market share (i.e., volume and revenue) by providing a more competitive lineup of products and services

Extension requires moderate levels of organizational consolidation and standardization and high levels of coordination. This means that:

- Some functions and activities, especially with respect to general and administrative overhead (e.g., MIS, accounting, human resources, and sales), may be consolidated and standardized. Operations may be consolidated and standardized depending upon the extent to which new products and services can be provided within the existing operating infrastructure.
- Redundancy of management and employees and reduction in force will likely take place in those areas being consolidated. Retention of key people in nonconsolidated areas, or highly competent people in general, is important. This may especially be the case where the value of the target is largely tied up in intangible assets such as people.
- High levels of coordination may be required across organizations and sales forces if cross-selling is required.
- Differences in organizational culture, identity, and management practices between the acquirer and the target will have to be resolved.
- Differences in strategy, policies, operations, brand names, etc., will have to be resolved.

Enter a New Geographic Market

In this case, the objective is to extend the business into geographic areas where the firm has had no presence. Typically, this objective is employed by firms that are rolling up a fragmented industry and by firms that are taking advantage of market deregulation and liberalization.

In roll-ups the market is highly fragmented and characterized by numerous small firms with very small market shares. Usually, one or several firms see an opportunity to grow revenues and profitability. Often roll-ups begin by consolidation within a geographic area and then by geographic extension. This has clearly been the case in the banking industry. Nations Bank, for example, first began rolling up retail banks within state (e.g., North Carolina) and then across states (e.g., Florida, Missouri). Today, it is found across regions of the United States (through its merger with Bank of America). In this example there was an excellent opportunity to consolidate the fixed costs associated with information technology and backroom activities and to expand geographic presence.

Geographic expansion has also been behind the acquisitions driving the security monitoring business within the United States. Historically, the security monitoring industry was made up of many small, privately held firms that provided basic services within a specific geographic area (e.g., a city). The typical firm provided sales, installation, customer service, and security monitoring. Two large players, ADT and SecurityLink from Ameritech, saw an opportunity to consolidate this market and grow on a national level. Not only could they expand their geographic reach, but they could also significantly improve profitability. First, there was an excellent opportunity to better manage fixed cost. Many of the small firms had their own security monitoring call centers. In general, they were not very efficient. By acquiring enough firms the large players could build a nationally scaled centralized monitoring center. They could much more effectively amortize the costs of the center by acquiring volume than the small firms could. The same opportunity existed for support functions such as payroll, accounting, and sales and billing systems. They could also transfer the knowledge they accrued to bring best practices to the geographically decentralized sales, installation, and customer service organizations. The net result was growth and improved profitability.

This strategy was also employed in the hospital management industry. Columbia/HCA, for example, acquired numerous hospitals throughout the United States. In doing so, it was also able to reduce fixed costs throughout many administrative functions. It was also able to reduce variable costs through increased power over hospital supply companies. It was a lot different negotiating for 300 hospitals than for just 1 or 2.

Market deregulation and liberalization have influenced numerous industries. Essentially the regulatory changes have opened previously closed markets. An excellent example is the telecommunications industry. In an attempt to grow beyond their regulated markets, many U.S. telecoms began making acquisitions (and taking equity interests) in international companies. All these opportunities were driven by host governments' privatizing previously owned government utilities. Some acquirers took portfolio positions (i.e., purely investment positions), whereas others brought technology and knowledge to the target to improve operations and profitability. Many of these acquisitions were purely opportunistic with few synergies present. The acquirers were responding to privatization opportunities. In the future, however, as the industry globalizes, the game may change. For example, serving the needs of international business customers will mean that many providers such as Verizon, MCI Worldcom, and AT&T will have to provide seamless data service throughout the major markets in the world. This will require strategic acquisitions in key countries and integrated operations to achieve that kind of service.

Geographic expansion has been a critical competitive issue in the mobile telephone business as well. Several years ago a mobile telephone provider could survive by serving a small regional area. Today, survival requires that it be able to serve the entire United States without roaming and long distance charges. In the future, as technological standards are harmonized, the market may likely be the globe! It is unlikely that geographic reach will be achieved through organic growth. It will require mergers, acquisitions, joint ventures, and alliances.

The potential sources of synergy in this strategic objective thus include:

- Lower variable costs through increased purchasing power, where acquired products and services utilize the same basic raw materials. This will now be accomplished on a larger geographic scope than before.
- Lower fixed costs through the elimination of redundant functions, e.g., corporate staff, human resources, and information technology.
- Lower fixed costs through better utilization of fixed investments such as advertising and brand development over a broader geographic scope.
- Increased revenue through sharing of products and services developed by each organization.
- Increased sales volume through geographic expansion.
- Increased competitiveness by being better able to serve customers with needs for broader geographic coverage.

Market entry requires low levels of organizational consolidation where there is little geographic overlap, but may require high levels of standardization and coordination. This, however, is dependent upon the extent to which the firms can take advantage of doing things the same way across geographic markets. If each market is relatively independent due to strong pressures for localization, there may be few if any opportunities for synergies. If markets are interconnected in some fashion, synergistic opportunities increase dramatically. Certainly standard products across markets would lead to significant efficiencies in new-product development and operations, as well as development of a standard for a best practice.

This means that:

- Very few functions and activities will be consolidated. Some aspects of general and administrative overhead (e.g., MIS, accounting, human resources, sales) may be consolidated and standardized.
- Operations will not be consolidated, depending upon the economics of the business. They may, however, be standardized to the extent that one basic approach (e.g., best practice) for providing the product or service across all markets makes sense.
- High levels of consolidation and standardization within new markets (e.g., as in market consolidation) may take place if geographic entry is the first step in a regional market concentration strategy.

- Redundancy of management and employees and reduction in force will likely take place in those areas being consolidated. Retention of key people in nonconsolidated areas, or highly competent people in general, may be important. In geographic expansion, retention of people is important in nonredundant areas since acquirers neither have the internal talents available to staff the new operation nor have "deep knowledge" of the local area.
- High levels of coordination may be required across organizations and sales forces if cross-selling is required.
- Differences in organizational culture, identity, and management practices between the acquirer and the target will have to be resolved unless each geographic area is different.
- Differences in strategy, policies, operations, brand names, etc., will have to be resolved, depending upon the degree of standardization.

Vertically Integrate

In this case, the objective is to enter into either sources of supply or distribution. Such moves are made to increase value added into the business or gain control over more aspects of the business. Vertical integration requires very low levels of organizational consolidation and standardization but high levels of coordination. Companies such as Home Depot have acquired lighting, heating, and plumbing companies to better control sources of supply.

The acquisition of Medco by Merck is another excellent illustration. Merck, a traditional pharmaceutical company, acquired Medco, a distribution intermediary (i.e., pharmacy benefit manager). Medco represented third-party payers and self-insured companies that were trying to lower the cost of ethical drugs. The acquisition gave Merck access to Medco's mail-order business and patient treatment database. The latter allowed Merck to better understand the effectiveness of treatments and to guide product development. The former gave Merck access to an emerging distribution channel for chronic-care drugs, thus increasing the market share.

The acquisition of Citgo by PDVSA, the Venezuelan oil company, was also driven by vertical integration. PDVSA was looking for a source of refining and distribution for its heavy crude oil. Not comfortable with long-term contracts, it decided to acquire the downstream activities of Citgo.

Vertical integration is also the key element in the America Online (AOL) and Time Warner merger. It melds the content of Time Warner (e.g., entertainment, news) with the Internet distribution power of AOL.

The potential sources of synergy in this strategic objective thus include:

- Lower variable costs of raw materials through control over raw materials and value added retained within the new company. Accounting for the costs will depend on the transfer pricing agreements established within the new company.

- Lower overall costs through improved product development and manufacturing interfaces.
- Lower fixed costs through the elimination of redundant functions, e.g., corporate staff, information technology, sales staff. Costs associated with managing the new vertical relationship internally will replace costs of managing the external relationship (e.g., purchasing function).

This means that:

- No functions and activities will be consolidated, with the exception of cash management, treasury functions, and financial statements. Moreover, the senior management of the target will likely report into the acquirer's structure.
- Operations will be neither consolidated nor standardized.
- Key interrelationships will be established, as the new acquisition will support existing parts of the business.
- Redundancy of management and employees and reduction in force are not likely although some key people in the target may leave or be replaced. Retention of key people is important.
- Differences in organizational culture, identity, and management practices between the acquirer and the target will not be an issue unless there are certain aspects of the target firm the acquirer cannot live with.
- Differences in strategy and brand names will have to be resolved.

Enter a New Line of Business

In this case, the objective is to enter businesses where the acquirer has little or no previous experience. Typically, opportunities exist to grow revenues, add distribution, add new products and services, acquire new technologies, and acquire new management talent with different perspectives.

This strategy was used by conglomerates during the 1960s and 1970s. The objective was to diversify away from a company's core business due to limits to growth in the core business, antitrust challenges, and the desire to find opportunities with uncorrelated cashflows. The latter strategy was designed to lower the business's risk and thus cost of capital. Many conglomerates, however, never delivered value to shareholders. Unfortunately, it proved easier for investors to diversify their own personal investment portfolios than for companies to do so. There are a few exceptions, such as Berkshire Hathaway and General Electric, which have made numerous successful acquisitions.

The potential sources of synergy in this strategic objective thus include:

- Lower fixed costs through the elimination of a few redundant functions, e.g., corporate staff, information technology, sales staff
- Lower cost of capital for a combined firm by reducing firm risk through diversification

- Intangibles such as a broader pool of available management talent and business know-how

This means that:

- No functions or activities will be consolidated, with the exception of cash management, treasury functions, and financial statements. Typically, the acquired company will:
  1. Either operate as a division of the acquirer, whereby the senior management of the target will report into the acquirer's structure
  2. Or be a wholly-owned subsidiary whereby the acquirer controls the target through board representation
- Operations will be neither consolidated nor standardized because there are no sources of operational synergy (e.g., operational cost reductions or cross-selling opportunities).
- High levels of consolidation and standardization may take place in subsequent acquisitions in the new line of business if the initial acquisition is a platform for further market concentration, e.g., as in the case of General Electric and Tyco International.
- Redundancy of management and employees are not likely, although some key people in the target may leave or be replaced. Retention of key people is important since the acquirer rarely has its own people to transfer to the target.
- Differences in organizational culture, identity, and management practices between the acquirer and the target will not be an issue unless there are certain aspects of the target firm the acquirer cannot live with. Differences between the senior management teams may be an issue.
- Differences in strategy and brand names will not likely be an issue.

Table 2-3 summarizes the five types of strategic objectives and the synergies possible within each type. Each box presents the level of synergistic benefits for each strategic objective. Table 2-4 shows the level and type of integration that each objective is likely to require. Each box in this table presents the level of integration required.

WHEN MULTIPLE STRATEGIC OBJECTIVES ARE BEING PURSUED

The discussion of strategic objectives above is somewhat simplified in that more than one objective may be present in a particular merger or acquisition. Much of this will depend upon the scale and nature of the merger or acquisition. In the case of a small acquisition, a single objective and limited synergies may be all that are sought. In a mega-merger such

Table 2-3 Linking Strategic Objectives and Synergies

	Strategic Objective				
Type of Synergy	Consolidate within a Geographic Area	Extend or Add New Product or Service	Enter a New Geographic Market	Vertically Integrate	Enter a New Line of Business
Cost	High	Low	Low	Moderate	Low
Revenue	Low	High	High	Low	None
Market Power	High	Moderate	Low	High	None
Intangible	Moderate	Moderate	Moderate	Low	Low

Table 2-4 Strategic Objectives and Impact on Integration

	Level and Type of Integration		
Strategic Objective	**Consolidation**	**Standardization**	**Coordination**
Consolidate within a Geographic Area	High	High	High
Extend or Add New Product or Service	Moderate	Moderate	High
Enter a New Geographic Market	Low	Low to High	Low to High
Vertically Integrate	Low	Low	High
Enter a New Line of Business	Low	Low	Low

as in the case of Daimler-Benz and Chrysler, or AOL and Time Warner, multiple objectives and synergies are critical to the success of the deal. Obviously, in the latter case the nature and depth of the integration will be far more complicated and difficult to manage.

For example, in the acquisition of Chrysler by Daimler-Benz, multiple objectives and sources of synergy were hoped for. Objectives included market consolidation, geographic expansion, and extension of new products and technologies. Synergies included fixed- and variable-cost reduction, cross-selling of products, increased market power, and intangibles. The synergies from the deal five years out were expected to be $3 billion, with $1.4 billion in cost savings in the first year. This would be derived from several sources. First, savings would include reductions in general and administrative overhead, lower raw material cost (both companies combined purchase roughly $60 billion in materials from outside suppliers), lower advertising overhead, and more efficient utilization of R&D.

Second, it was envisioned that economies of scale could be achieved in components such as engines, transmissions, and car platforms, all of which consumers do not directly associate with the brand of their cars. Third, some opportunities for cross-selling were also envisioned since over 90 percent of Chrysler's sales came from the United States and over 60 percent of Daimler's sales came from Europe. Moreover, neither company had product offerings in the same segments (i.e., price points and car types). Fourth, sharing of technological know-how could be achieved. Daimler would bring airbag technology, ABS braking systems, an electronic stabilization program, and fuel cell development, among other technologies. It would also bring quality and durability know-how. Chrysler would contribute computer design technology that reduced development time and costs, and lean manufacturing that reduced development and manufacturing times and costs. On paper, this was another "marriage made in heaven." From a financial perspective, the deal was viewed as a great deal for Daimler. It purchased an undervalued company in Chrysler (U.S. auto stocks were depressed) using its own stock, which was flying high prior to the merger.

Although nice in theory, the success of these strategies, synergies, and improvement in profits and cashflow would depend upon whether they could be implemented in practice. As a worst-case scenario, Daimler had to preserve the stand-alone value of Chrysler. At best, it needed to secure synergies to improve the overall capabilities of both firms. Initially the deal proved to be a good deal for Daimler shareholders, especially with respect to EPS. Over time, this has been questioned. The preservation of Chrysler and the achievement of many synergies have been more challenging. The many cultural conflicts and problems between the management of both companies have been well documented.

RECENT PERFORMANCE HISTORY OF THE TARGET

It is vital to get a fix on the recent financial performance history (e.g., the last three years) of a target and the causes of that performance (e.g., management decisions, operating measures, market trends) before you can understand the nature of the integration effort. Such an assessment will enable you to determine the depth (e.g., replace management, change operating procedures, introduce new technology) and speed of interventions required by the acquirer in the target firm to ensure that projected earnings and cashflows materialize as predicted. These interventions are essential regardless of the synergies being sought.

If the target has been performing well, and is projected to continue to do so, little intervention may be required. If, however, the target is in need of a dramatic turnaround, significant intervention will be required.

PUTTING IT ALL TOGETHER

In this chapter the importance of valuation, pricing, and synergy in driving the integration process and the relationship among these elements in creating value was examined. These relationships are depicted in Figure 2-2. Throughout the remainder of this book, I address the activities that need to be managed during the transaction, transition, and integration stages to ensure that integration is effectively managed, value is preserved, and synergies are realized. When applicable, I describe how the activities may need to be managed differently depending upon the strategic and financial objectives outlined above.

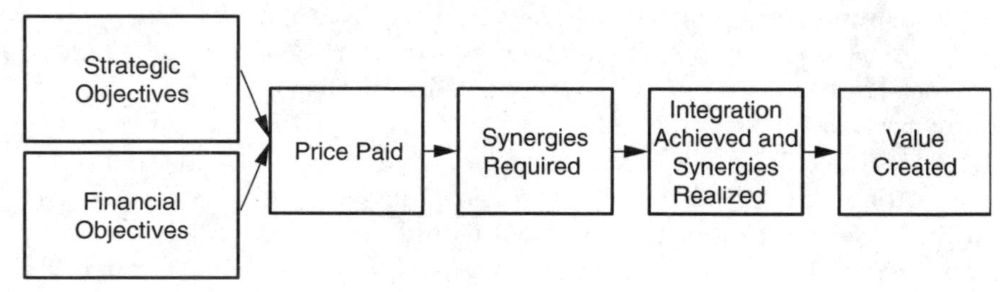

Figure 2-2 Key Relationships in Value Creation

3

LAYING THE GROUNDWORK: MANAGING THE TRANSACTION STAGE

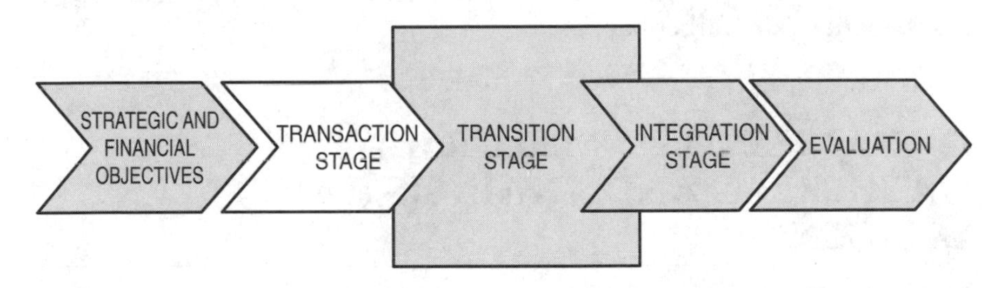

Integration should begin long before the closing. In fact, it should begin during the transaction stage when negotiations are taking place, due diligence is being conducted, and valuations are being performed. Since information is the lifeblood of sound decisions, gathering the right information at this stage can be invaluable. The objective of due diligence is to acquire factual information that helps the buyer understand:

1. The assets and liabilities of the target, both on and off the balance sheet
2. The sources of revenues, costs, and profits
3. Those factors that will either facilitate or hinder the successful integration of the target

From this information, decisions need to be made concerning whether to walk away from a deal, what price to pay for a target, and what issues need to be managed to ensure successful integration. Typically, due diligence focuses on items 1 and 2 above, with a heavy concentration on issues that can be quantified. They are often the domain of the legal and financial organizations and have been discussed in depth elsewhere.[1] Rarely are the "soft issues" that affect integration deeply examined. Rarely do they serve as "deal killers" when they should. Often, however, they do determine after the closing whether integration succeeded; if earnings, cashflows, and synergies were achieved; and whether value was created. The soft issues are often the top reasons why synergies are not achieved.

This chapter and Chapter 4 will focus on four integration objectives and activities that are paramount during the transaction stage. These are presented in Table 3-1.

In this chapter three primary activities are discussed. The first activity focuses on organizing for information gathering. The second addresses an often neglected but pivotal area of analysis, cultural assessment. The third concentrates on the behaviors of those individuals who come in contact with the target organization and negotiate deals. This early contact sets the stage for the ensuing relationship that forms between the acquirer and the target. The last activity, which is the focus of Chapter 4, deals with an area that has often determined the success of a merger or an acquisition, assessment of key target people.

ORGANIZING FOR INFORMATION GATHERING AND ANALYSIS (DUE DILIGENCE)

Efficiently and quickly gathering and analyzing useful information about a target as early as possible, but prior to the closing, is essential to the integration process. In particular, learning about similarities and differences between the acquirer and a target and their implications is pivotal. Therefore, an organized, systematic process for doing so must be created.

Table 3-1 Transaction Stage

Objectives
1. Gather and analyze information to learn as much as possible about a target
2. Negotiate the right price
3. Create a constructive environment for successful integration, and preserve the value of both the acquirer and the target
4. Anticipate roadblocks that need to be managed for effective integration
Activities
1. Organize for information gathering and analysis
2. Assess the culture of the target
3. Guide the behaviors and attitudes of negotiators, due diligence teams, and deal makers
4. Assess key target people

This includes (1) choosing someone to lead this effort and (2) creating and developing able and ready due diligence teams.

Companies vary on the sophistication of the due diligence effort, often depending upon their acquisition experience, the volume of deals they do, and their involvement with outside experts. An organized effort can be very important, especially when time or access to a target is limited.

The importance of an organized effort is exemplified in the due diligence efforts of a major U.S. telecommunications company that took a stake in a privatized European telephone company. The company was given one-week access to a data room to examine information that was made available. The company was not an experienced acquirer and had to quickly identify and assemble the resources it needed. Since there were multiple businesses interested in the European operation, the selling company had the power in the deal and controlled the due diligence process. To complete the activity effectively and efficiently, the U.S. company needed to:

- Identify the due diligence skill sets needed.
- Choose a team leader.
- Identify the people who possessed the skills sets.
- Brief the people on the target and country, on the local culture, and on the business environment.
- Provide people with the checklists and tools to conduct analyses.
- Ensure that the team members worked together.

Several elements ensure a successful due diligence effort. These include choosing a champion, creating a team of experts, and making the right assessments. Each of these is discussed in more detail below.

Choosing a Champion: Leading the Effort

One of the major challenges during due diligence, and throughout the integration effort, is fragmentation.[2] Many experts are involved in gathering and analyzing information. They may come from different functional areas, corporate staff, business units, and geographic areas. In their quest to quickly finish their jobs, there is a risk that there is little communication and coordination among them. Sometimes there may be competition among them as they seek to control the process. This can be problematic since among due diligence team members there is a need to share information. Sharing helps identify consistencies and inconsistencies in information and conclusions. This is the objective of due diligence. Moreover, it is essential that the information gathered and conclusions reached during due diligence are passed on to those who are responsible for integration planning and implementation. Often, this does not happen, and essential insights gained early in the M&A process are lost.

To avoid fragmentation it is best to assign a "champion" (e.g., an executive) with ongoing responsibility for overseeing and leading the M&A process through the transaction, transition, and integration stages.

Since not all M&As are alike, the role of the champion needs to vary. In the case of a mega-merger it is likely to be a CEO or a direct report that will have responsibility for the overall merger. It is not uncommon for the chief financial officer to assume this role. For a company that is acquiring multiple smaller companies, for example as part of a roll-up, the champion will have responsibility for the overall M&A process, involving multiple acquisitions. Depending upon the number of deals being transacted, different individuals, who report to the champion, may have responsibility for each deal.

The Champion ensures that:

1. A leader of the due diligence team is chosen for each acquisition, where multiple deals are being done.
2. A core due diligence team is available and able at any time to execute the activities necessary during the transaction stage.
3. Transition and integration teams are ready and available during the transition stage (see the discussion on integration transition structure in Chapter 6).
4. Continuity and communication among due diligence, transition, and integration teams takes place.

Creating and Building the Due Diligence Team

Based on the experience of a number of successful acquirers, I have identified 10 steps that characterize a well-functioning due diligence team.

1. Identify and recruit a limited number of the acquirer's people who are most knowledgeable in areas of the business to be analyzed and who have good project management skills to serve as project leaders.

On the basis of breadth of knowledge, skills required, and availability, a dedicated pool of people should be drawn from both inside and outside the organization. This does not mean that these people will be permanently assigned to due diligence activities, but that they are part of a network of people who are ready when needed. How often they are utilized will be a function of the level of M&A activity.

This pool includes people with financial, legal, sales, marketing, operational, R&D, and human resources skills, among others. The pool should involve more than one person for each area investigated in case one person is not enough or is not available. Temporary replacements for these individuals in their normal job should be identified if due diligence activities demand too much of their time. The decision to include people should be balanced with the need to maintain the secrecy of M&A negotiations and deals.

Where needed, outside experts and consultants should be utilized. In a recent study of international deals, a colleague and I found that outside experts were critical to success in acquisitions when a company was making an acquisition in a new country.[3]

2. Train the team members to:

a. Work together effectively and efficiently (through the use of team building).
b. Identify the specific issues to be investigated and the questions they need to ask (i.e., develop and use a due diligence checklist).
c. Identify the type of information they need and the source of that information.
d. Secure the information.
e. Operate in a sensitive and confidential situation.
f. Present their findings to decision makers in an interpretable format.

3. Assemble the team quickly when a potential target becomes serious. Team members will be responsible for particular areas of investigation and, depending upon the size of the acquisition and the magnitude of issues to be examined, may serve as project leaders who manage subteams of other people. For example, an assessment of a target's human resources practices may require a team of experts who understand compensation, benefits, leadership development, performance management, and legal compliance.

4. Use dedicated project leaders and team members throughout the duration of the due diligence effort, even though the tendency is not to do so. If necessary, team members may be used on an as-needed basis.

5. Co-locate the team in a secure facility when feasible and desirable, either in corporate headquarters or offsite if proximity to a target is critical.

6. Brief (to the extent confidentiality allows) the team and leader on as many of the strategic and financial considerations surrounding the acquisition as possible. This provides them with the needed background to intelligently identify and examine the issues critical to integration.

7. Organize the following after the briefing:

a. Develop and circulate a directory of all team members and how they can be reached at any time since communication among members is critical to validating information secured.
b. Choose a standard software package for reports (e.g., Microsoft Word), presentations (e.g., PowerPoint), and data analysis (e.g., Excel) to ensure a smooth integration of information gathered.
c. Organize and manage communications among team members.
d. Make a presentation of team findings to deal makers and negotiators.

e. Centrally locate and maintain an indexed library of critical documents, reports, and presentations at the team's work site to ensure quick and easy access.
f. Schedule meetings among team members.
g. Use a project management framework for the team to:
   i. Identify deliverables.
   ii. Clarify working parameters.
   iii. Define activities to be performed.
   iv. Set time frames and milestones.
   v. Assign accountability for major activities.
   vi. Define resources (e.g., people, financial) needed to support the activity.
   vii. Monitor progress and take corrective actions.

8. **Develop a strategy as a team for how to approach the target.** It is critical to remember that once an acquirer's personnel "enter" the target, a signal is sent as to the acquirer's culture and attitude. Invariably, the target's management and employees will react (either positively or negatively) to this. Due diligence team members should be as unobtrusive and respectful of target people as possible while ensuring that necessary information is collected.
9. **Meet as a team as needed—but no less than once a week—to report findings, share and validate insights, and deal with any interrelationships among team members.**
10. **Keep a select number of people from the team together through the transition stage to ensure continuity of knowledge and relationships with a target's people.** This is a crucial element in successful integration.

ASSESSING THE CULTURE OF THE TARGET

Abitibi Consolidated Sales Corporation, the U.S. subsidiary of Abitibi-Price of Canada, understands the important of cultural analysis during the transaction and transition stages. This largest producer of newsprint in the world attempts to gather cultural information from a target as soon as it can when making an acquisition. At the early stages of an acquisition, the company will simply attempt to observe a target from afar, noting cultural artifacts such as how the employees dress and answer the phone. As the company progresses into due diligence, it will attempt a full cultural assessment, including interviews with and surveys of target employees. In its merger with Stone-Consolidated, Abitibi Consolidated got the 20 people in both companies considered critical to the success of the merger together in an off-site meeting to analyze and discuss their cultures and aspirations for the new organization.

Before Compaq acquired both Digital Equipment and Tandem Corporations, its HR teams analyzed the cultures of both companies from afar. This gave Compaq key insights into the challenges it would face and the interventions to employ to successfully merge the combined companies. It also allowed Compaq to move quickly once the deals closed.

Southwest Airlines undertook a comprehensive cultural due diligence prior to its acquisition of Morris Air, a smaller entrepreneurial firm. Using cultural information, Southwest carefully managed the integration, which resulted in a profitable outcome. In contrast, USAir's lack of cultural assessment and awareness and its autocratic methods in its acquisition of Piedmont Aviation caused years of cultural warfare.

Despite some solid examples of success in cultural due diligence, the cultural fit between an acquirer and a target is one of the most neglected areas of analysis prior to the closing of a deal. Often culture is considered too soft and fuzzy. It does not have the precision of financial analyses or the excitement of potential synergies. Moreover, it is typically within the domain of the human resources organization, which is often not invited into the M&A process before the closing—perhaps with the exception of conducting analyses of benefits and compensation costs.

Although many definitions of culture exist, most experts agree that it characterizes the basic values, beliefs, and assumptions that members of an organization hold.[4] In many organizations, especially small and successful ones, culture can be very powerful in shaping how people think and behave and has been shown to have a direct impact on an organization's growth and profitability.[5]

In essence, cultural analysis is pivotal for two reasons. First, cultural differences may be so extreme that they can impede successful integration, thwart the achievement of synergies, and thereby lead to poor financial results.[6] When faced with an acquisition, a target's managers and employees become much more aware of their culture, especially if it is different from that of the acquirer. In such cases, the potential for "culture clashes" and dysfunctional conflict between the acquirer and the target increases greatly.

Second, understanding cultural differences early in the acquisition process serves to identify critical issues that will need to be managed to ensure a successful integration. Rather than wait for these issues to emerge after the closing, warranting a crisis management response, early understanding can ensure that such issues are managed from day one. In Chapter 8 interventions for facilitating cultural integration are examined.

The assessment of cultural differences is somewhat complex, with a variety of methodologies available for doing so. In this section I elaborate upon some of them and demonstrate how they can be used to facilitate the integration process.

The primary responsibility for assessing culture should lie with a human resources or organizational development expert or outside consultant knowledgeable of this area. This person should become a member of the due diligence team. With input from others, this person conducts the assessments, interprets the results, and determines the implications of the results.

There are several important steps in assessing the impact of culture on a merger or an acquisition. These include determining:

1. How important culture is to a particular acquisition
2. How similar and different the buyer's and target's cultures are
3. What impact such similarities and differences might have on the success of integration and synergy realization
4. What interventions should be employed during integration to capitalize on similarities and deal with differences

To that end, the remainder of this section is dedicated to making such assessments and increasing the probability of integration success. The relationship among the steps is presented in Figure 3-1 and discussed below.

Step 1 Determine the Importance of Culture

Although cultures may be different, some differences may not be important. To determine importance three questions need to be asked:

1. To what extent is the target going to be integrated? If little or no integration is planned based on the financial and strategic objectives presented in Chapter 2, then the impact of cultural differences is less likely to be an impediment. Impact will be felt the most in areas and activities that are being integrated and by executives after a deal is closed. Regardless of the strategic objectives underlying an acquisition, executives of a target will have to report somewhere into the acquirer's organization and conform to certain ways of doing things.
2. To what extent are interventions in the target planned? Similar to the question above, if no interventions such as productivity improvements are planned, then the impact of cultural differences is likely to

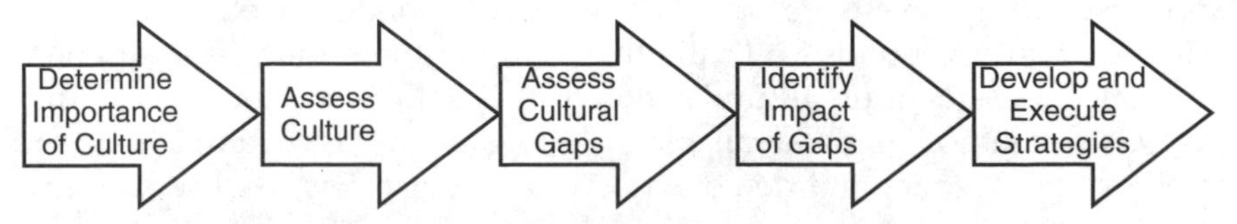

Figure 3-1 Steps in Assessing the Target's Culture

be minimal. To the extent that the performance of the target is inadequate, intervention will likely increase and cultural differences will have greater impact. For example, a buyer may decide to put a greater focus on accountability in the target than has existed in the past.

3. How tolerant is the acquirer of cultural differences? Regardless of strategic considerations, the acquirer simply needs to ask itself the extent to which it will allow a target to be different. Such differences may be critical to the success of an acquisition, especially if it is in new lines of businesses. Nowhere is this more important than when a large company acquires an entrepreneurial company or enters into a new country or region. Moreover, a target may bring valuable new ways of thinking to the acquirer.

Step 2 Assess Culture

There are two key components to cultural assessment. First, the acquirer should assess its own culture. In some companies this has already been done. Second, the acquirer should examine the culture of the target, preferably using the same approaches to measurement as it used in its own company.[7]

Cultural assessment of an acquisition can be a complex process and greatly depends upon access to a target. Also, more than one level of culture may be operating in a company, especially if the company is a large multidivisional one. Cultures may vary by divisions, functions, and geographic areas (especially in the case of international deals).[8] During due diligence, access and the depth of the assessment may be very limited, thus making it very difficult to make all these types of assessments, and the buyer may have to settle for a more generalized view of the target's culture.

If this initial assessment reveals no "deal killer," then deeper assessments to understand how to manage integration may be conducted during the transition, and if necessary the integration, stage. In the following sections (1) the dimensions of culture to be examined and (2) the methods available to assess culture are addressed.

Dimensions of Culture

The list below characterizes the dimensions of culture I have employed in my research and consulting work.[9] It is useful to assess how the target management behaves with respect to each dimension.

1. Centralized versus decentralized decision making
2. Speed in making decisions (slow versus quick)
3. Time horizon for decisions (short term versus long term)
4. Level of teamwork
5. Management of conflict (degree of openness and confrontation)
6. Risk orientation and entrepreneurial behavior

7. Process versus results orientation
8. Performance orientation (measurement orientation and goal achievement)
9. Focus on responsibility and accountability
10. Degree of horizontal cooperation and coordination (across functions, business units, and product lines)
11. Level of politics
12. Focus on rules and policies
13. Nature of communication (openness and honesty; speed; vehicles—written versus face-to-face, meetings)
14. Openness to change

Methods Available to Assess Culture

Assessment of culture is rather complex. There are direct and indirect methods requiring differing levels of contact and access to information with a target firm. These include secondary sources of information (i.e., little or no contact with a target) and primary sources (i.e., direct contact with a target). Each method is described below.

Secondary Sources of Information

By using these sources, a rough understanding of the target's culture can be pieced together without direct contact. Such sources of information include:

1. Internet
2. Newspaper, journal articles, and other periodicals
3. Speeches given by management
4. Interviews with your own employees who have worked for or closely with the target
5. Interviews with knowledgeable and trusted business brokers, consultants, and other industry participants (e.g., large customers, suppliers, other customers)

When secrecy of negotiations is important, the fourth and fifth sources may be problems since they could violate secrecy or disclosure agreements with a target. The first three, however, bear little risk of disclosure.

The dimensions of culture presented above should be used as a guide for assessment. When interviews are conducted, people should be asked to "describe how (the target) runs its business." They can also be asked to comment on each dimension as a probe (e.g., "Can you tell me about the level of cooperation among functional areas in getting work done?"). However, keep in mind that since most respondents will have observed the target as an outsider, or may have limited memory, such an assessment may be superficial.

As an example, a Catholic health-care system was interested in selling some of its hospitals to a publicly traded hospital management company (HMC). The hospitals in question no longer fit within the geographic scope of the seller's system. Before selling, the seller wanted to understand HMC's culture and what would likely happen to the hospitals after the deal was closed.

HMC had grown rapidly over 10 years by aggressively making acquisitions and engaging in joint ventures. The Catholic system's management had serious concerns, however, about whether the values and ethics of its hospitals would be compromised once they were sold to HMC. In anticipation of negotiations, it decided to quietly conduct an assessment of HMC. Since the seller did not want HMC to know about it, secondary sources were used. Appendix 3-1 contains the assessment that was conducted.

Through the use of an Internet search (based on information that included SEC documents, trade journals, newspapers, and the like) and select interviews with other hospitals that had dealt with HMC, the assessment was conducted. Since HMC was fairly high profile, such information was relatively easy to gather and a solid story could be pieced together. On the basis of this assessment, the Catholic system's management decided not to undertake the sale and looked for another alternative.

Primary Sources of Information

Primary sources permit a more detailed understanding of a target's culture to be pieced together. This approach, however, requires direct contact with the acquirer. Such sources of information include:

1. Observation of the target's behaviors during acquisition meetings and negotiations. This source is the easiest source to use. Primarily, it requires that managers from the acquirer who come in contact with a target keep notes on the cultural dimensions presented earlier. With some training, managers can keep notes on what they observe. Although their observations would not be based on a systematic assessment, it would provide additional data points for validation.

2. Examination of company documents and other artifacts (e.g., organizational charts, human resources policies, meeting minutes, company core values statements). This source requires more direct information from the company, but little interaction with employees. This, again, may be critical when a target's management does not want its employees to be contacted. Depending upon what information is gleaned, the depth of analysis can vary. Statements of values and culture articulate what a company's intentions are. They may reflect actual behaviors or not. More detailed documents on actual human resources policies such as measurement and reward systems, training and development programs, career management systems, and budgetary processes may be more revealing. The extent to which statements and practices coincide, the higher the probability that the assessment is valid. Observation of actual behaviors and company artifacts may be even more powerful. Some companies have even employed anthropologists and sociologists to assess cultures.

For example, Ciba Geigy's U.S. corporate staff, in anticipation of its merger with Sandoz, prepared a simple cultural assessment of its partner. When the organizational charts and management practices of the two companies were analyzed, it was apparent that there were two very different views on centralization and decentralization. Ciba had highly centralized staff activities located in New York. Sandoz, on the other hand, believed that staff activities should be decentralized and contained within divisions. Prior to the closing of the merger, the top-management positions of the soon-to-be new company, Novartis, were announced. As expected, most of the key positions went to Sandoz people. Based on the assessments, it was apparent that the new organization would likely be decentralized. And, indeed, it was.

Prior to the closing of its merger, Chevron and Texaco shared with each other numerous documents concerning each company's cultures and ways of operating. Chevron, in particular, shared a document "The Chevron Way" that "sums up who we are, what we do, what we believe in, and what our goals are for the future." The document clearly articulated the company's vision and values and thus how it was trying to behave. As in any case, the extent to which those visions and values were embraced and manifested in the behaviors of people is unknown and requires a deeper level of analysis.

3. Interviews and focus groups with target managers and employees, and surveys and questionnaires. The final two sources require the greatest contact with people, but may reveal the greatest amount of information about a target. In addition, they allow a broader and more systematic exposure to the organization. Therefore, the acquirer can assess the extent to which there is a "single" culture across the target organization. In small organizations, where the leaders are more likely to embody the culture, access to members of the senior management team may be sufficient to learn about the culture. In large companies characterized by multiple divisions spread across the globe, assessment may be more challenging. There are likely to be several cultures, with perhaps a higher set of national and corporate cultural attributes. In such cases, integration will probably vary as well as the cultural issues.

Focus Group and Interview Guidelines. When conducting interviews and focus groups the following protocol is recommended:

> "We want to learn more about how (the target) runs its business and would like to use your experience to help us understand that. There are no 'right' or 'wrong' answers. This is not a judgmental exercise. We would appreciate it if you would be as candid

as possible. We will not share your specific answers with anyone or identify who you are. The more realistic the information we receive, the more likely that the integration will go smoothly. I am going to ask a few questions and would like your insights on them.

"Describe how (your company) operates..."

You can let people talk for a couple of minutes and then ask them to comment on each dimension as a probe:

"Can you tell me about the level of cooperation among functional areas in getting work done?" etc.

"Perhaps you can identify and tell me something about some people who would be considered heroes in the company and why.

"Are there any aspects of the organization and the way it operates that people take particular pride in? Are there any aspects that are critical to the success of the company?"

You can give them some examples: events such as company picnics, awards received, awards given to employees, logos, songs. Depending upon the cooperation among the people, you may ask:

"Are there any aspects of the organization and the way it operates that people would like to change?"

In some cases, the acquirer may not have much access until an acquisition agreement is signed (i.e., the transition stage) or even until after closing. When this is the case, a detailed cultural assessment will have little impact on the decision to consummate the deal and pricing, but will play heavily in the integration. In general, when limited cultural information is available, the acquirer must assess how much risk it is willing to take in moving forward and consummating the deal.

To assess culture in this context, focus groups or interviews with representative people throughout the organization can be employed. People should be chosen from different divisions, geographic locations, and functions to ensure a representative picture and to capture differences across the corporation.

The final source of cultural information is a survey or questionnaire. Surveys and questionnaires can be distributed to managers and employees throughout the target. They can even be accessed online. They provide a numerical score and allow the acquirer to systematically examine the nature of the target's culture and the extent to which there is a "single" culture across the organization. Moreover, they can identify the importance of each dimension. There are numerous commercially available instruments on the market that basically address the dimensions above.

It is recommended, to the extent that time, access, and costs allow, that different approaches (e.g., questionnaires and interviews) to conduct the cultural assessment be used. Multiple approaches help minimize bias and provide validation. When there is convergence among more than one source, there is greater confidence in the conclusion. When there is a lack of convergence, discussions to understand why this is the case should be undertaken.

Step 3 Assess Cultural Fit Between an Acquirer and Target

Based on the cultural profile, document and discuss any gaps. This will provide insights into similarities that can be leveraged and built upon, and potential sources of clash that may need to be managed. Also, attempt to isolate those dimensions that the target feels strongly about or are important to its success. You can assess importance in two ways: (1) by rank-ordering each dimension or (2) by rating each dimension on a five-point scale (1—not very important to 5—very important).

As an example using the dimensions of culture presented above, I asked the senior managers of both an acquiring and acquired company to assess their own cultures. The buyer was a large corporation, whereas the seller was a smaller entrepreneurial firm that offered new products and possible cross-selling and joint new-product development opportunities. More importantly, the valuation and subsequent purchase price were based on the buyer's ability to capture the synergies. Interviews and a survey instrument were employed to assess both companies' cultures. The initial plan was for the acquired company to be integrated into a major division of the buyer. Both companies were internationalized, with multiple divisions and geographic locations around the world. Included in this process was the CEO of the selling firm and his staff, the division president of the buyer and his staff, country managers, and selective other personnel from both organizations, including those involved in sales and new-product development. This analysis was conducted during the transaction stage to get a sense of whether these companies could work together and what the integration challenges would be like after the closing. Both parties agreed to this analysis after a letter of intent had been signed and the parties were well on their way to drafting a definitive acquisition agreement. Neither party had contractually agreed to do the deal yet.

The results of the survey are presented in Table 3-2. The table is a map of the extent of differences for each dimension. Keep in mind that the results were a composite of the responses of a large number of people and that there were variations in perceptions even among people from the

Table 3-2 Cultural Profiles

	Always	Often	Elements of Both	Often	Always	
	1	2	3	4	5	
Centralized decisions		x			y	Decentralized decisions
Fast decision making		y		x		Slow decision making
Short-term focus		x	y			Long-term focus
Individual orientation		x,y				Team orientation
Confrontation of conflict			x,y			Avoidance of conflict
High-risk tolerance		x			y	Low-risk tolerance
Focus on results		x	y			Focus on process
People held accountable		x,y				People not held accountable
Horizontal cooperation		y			x	Silo oriented
High trust among people		y		x		Highly political
Bureaucratic		x			y	Entrepreneurial
Open and honest communications	y		x			Guarded communications
Fast communications		y		x		Slow communications
Direct face-to-face communications			y	x		Indirect communications
Resistant to change		x		y		Open to change

x = Target
y = Acquirer

Statistically significant differences [boxed]

same organization. These differences were in large part a function of the fact that across members of each organization there were variations in perceptions and in the culture itself. To determine whether differences between the acquirer and the target were greater than between members of the same organization, statistical tests were conducted.[10] The tests confirmed that in a number of cases the differences between the organizations were indeed significant. These are indicated in the boxed in areas in Table 3-2. By using these results, the impact of differences could be examined. Table 3-3 presents the average rankings of the importance of each dimension. To assess importance, respondents were asked to rank-order each dimension according to the impact it had on the success of the company.

Although interview and archival data were collected they are not presented here for sake of brevity. For the most part these data confirmed the survey results and provided many illustrations of how the culture manifested itself. The multiple approaches of cultural assessment strengthened the validity of the findings.

Steps 4 and 5 Identify the Impact of Cultural Gaps and Develop and Execute Strategies

The next steps in the process are to use the information in the cultural profile to assess the impact that the differences have and the strategies that need to be considered to manage such differences. Of importance here is to gauge the need to capture synergies (based on the valuation and pricing), the degree of cultural differences, and the nature and depth of inte-

Table 3-3 Average Rank Order of Cultural Dimensions

	Acquirer	Target	
Centralized decisions	1	1	Decentralized decisions
Fast decision making	9	3	Slow decision making
Short-term focus	3	13	Long-term focus
Individual orientation	4	5	Team orientation
Confrontation of conflict	7	15	Avoidance of conflict
High-risk tolerance	10	4	Low-risk tolerance
Focus on results	5	11	Focus on process
People held accountable	2	12	People not held accountable
Horizontal cooperation	11	6	Silo oriented
High trust among people	12	7	Highly political
Bureaucratic	6	2	Entrepreneurial
Open and honest communications	13	8	Guarded communications
Fast communications	14	9	Slow communications
Direct face-to-face communications	15	14	Indirect communications
Resistant to change	8	10	Open to change

gration required. It is also critical to determine the importance attached to the various dimensions and the level of resistance to change by either of the firms involved. Such strategies may include terminating the deal, adjusting synergy expectations and valuations, or working with the target to manage gaps. The latter will depend upon levels of access to and cooperation with the target. It may be the case that resolution of gaps has to wait until after an acquisition agreement is signed or until the deal is closed. At that point, however, it may be too late. Based on the steps conducted above, a table similar to Table 3-4 can be constructed. The table allows the acquirer to systematically examine the impact of differences on each dimension and choose a strategy for dealing with it.

In the example presented above, it was clear that there were a significant number of cultural issues that could prevent the deal from succeeding. After the profiling, this became quite apparent to the buyer. Although the acquirer's division president was prone to discount the results due to the strategic attractiveness of the deal, he chose to explore the implications of the deal further. Specifically, he put several options for consideration on the table. These included:

1. Walk away from the deal.
2. Lower the synergy expectations, valuation, and purchase price.
3. Decide whether he could live with the differences and whether they would preclude a successful integration and achievement of synergies. For example, an independent and autonomous division for the target was considered.
4. Integrate the target slowly.
5. Change the buyer to become more compatible with the target and vice versa.

After numerous discussions with his management team, option 2 was his first choice. Unfortunately, the seller would not drop the price low enough to justify the deal. After agonizing over options 3 to 5, the buyer chose to walk away. Although the target was a good potential strategic fit, he came to realize that the cultural problems would prevent a successful integration and achievement of the synergies that were the true source of value underlying the deal.

GUIDE THE BEHAVIORS AND ATTITUDES OF NEGOTIATORS, DUE DILIGENCE TEAMS, AND DEAL MAKERS

The negotiation process is another area in which the acquirer has the opportunity to interact with the target. It is critical for negotiators to realize that such interactions set the stage for the integration process. During

Table 3-4 Culture Assessment

Cultural Dimension	Culture of Target	Culture of Acquirer	Gap between Cultures	Importance of Dimension	Impact of Cultural Gaps on Deal or Integration	Strategies
Centralization of Decision Making	Highly decentralized	Highly centralized	Great	1	• Significant potential conflict • Trying to change culture of target will harm its performance	• Leave target culture alone • Change culture of acquirer • Change culture of target • Do not do the deal • Adjust synergy expectations and valuations

the negotiation process the target's management begins to learn about the acquirer's culture and what is in store for the target after the deal is closed. Therefore, it is essential that deal makers and negotiators attend to their negotiating style.

Further, negotiations with a target often entail more than just the purchase price, especially with respect to small firms. Early concerns with such issues as target managers' roles in the future, retention of employees, and compensation and benefits packages, among other issues, will be on the table. As such, deal makers and negotiators should:

- Quickly learn major integration concerns of the parties selling the business
- Examine what issues need to be resolved to do the deal
- Assess the subsequent effects any agreements might have on synergies, cashflow, earnings, and subsequent integration efforts

To this end, close communication between negotiators and the due diligence team is essential, as will be future communications with those responsible for integration.

APPENDIX 3-1 SECONDARY SOURCES OF CULTURE*

The preliminary study reported below was undertaken to help Catholic Healthcare System (CHS) develop a basic understanding of the culture (i.e., core values and management practices) and agenda of HMC. The study is based on a comprehensive search and analysis of public sources of information (e.g., journals, annual reports, news clippings) available on HMC, select interviews with hospital administrators currently or recently involved in joint-venture negotiations with HMC, and several reports by stock analysts. The interviews, however, were not comprehensive, but were with personal contacts who requested anonymity. As such, many of the conclusions drawn herein are speculative and limited and should be interpreted as such.

The report is divided into two parts. Part one discusses HMC's culture and agenda and part two addresses some thoughts I have on how to deal with them.

HMC'S CULTURE AND AGENDA

"Capitalist," pragmatic, and profit driven are the best ways to describe HMC's culture. The organization is led by James Smith, who in 1990 decided to aggressively change the paradigm for doing business in the health-care industry. In fact he has a paperweight on his desk that states "If you are not the lead dog, the view never changes." After an unsuccessful attempt to take over DEF in 1985, Smith, a health-care merger and acquisition attorney, and Oklahoma financier Robert Jones, formed HMC and bought two hospitals. With the support of a young management team and Smith's leadership, they have aggressively acquired close to 200 for-profit and not-for-profit hospitals over the past seven years to form HMC with approximately $10 billion in annual revenues. From an initial investment of $250,000, Smith, who is 40, is now worth $200 million. From all indications he continues to move aggressively and is well capitalized to do so. HMC has stated that it may operate as many as 500 hospitals within the next 10 years. It appears that Smith is committed to building a health-care empire. Based on his background, it seems that "empire" as opposed to "health care" is the key term here. Although it is speculation,

* The names of the companies involved, essential statistics, and geographic information have been changed to protect anonymity. The essence of the analysis and the conclusions reached have remained the same.

I suspect he would have been very happy to do what he is doing in any other industry if the same opportunity arose. As such, it does not appear that he has a driving philosophic commitment to providing "high-quality" health care. This is not to suggest that quality is unimportant, since it may be an important source of competitive advantage. It is just to suggest that low cost, profit, and growth may be more important.

It is very clear that HMC is being driven from an investor perspective, with financial results and stock price being of paramount importance. This suggests, consistent with my experience with other publicly traded companies and an examination of HMC's annual and other reports, that Smith and HMC likely have earnings per share growth and return on equity as their primary goals. Although it is speculation, I suspect that these goals would clearly take precedence over indigent care and "high-quality" health care if "push came to shove." To these ends, I further suspect that Smith, like most CEOs of similar-type companies, spends most of his time "on the outside," with the investment community, legislators and regulators, and major payers. As such, operational control is likely delegated to key senior managers, especially at the regional level. Smith appears to manage regions from a distance using financial indicators and does not seem to get involved in operations unless regional managers do not perform according to the indicators. Currently, investors believe in HMC's long-term strategy for the industry and its short-term performance. However, HMC may face numerous organizational challenges in the near future as it integrates the recently acquired B and D systems. Integration may be challenging given Smith's earlier unwelcome takeover attempt of DEF in 1985. Moreover, it is not clear how deep HMC's management talent is and how long it can organizationally sustain such rapid growth.

Smith's strategy for HMC is quite clear. Recently, he stated that "Our business is no different than a factory. We're building a nationwide network based on providing high-quality care at the most reasonable rate." Robert Jones recently described HMC as the Wal-Mart of health care. Again, comments such as these suggest that the primary focus will be on efficiency and profit. HMC's strategy (clearly demonstrated in Georgia where it dominates the market), not unlike others, is to create a highly efficient system with strong national supply purchasing power, regional economies of scale, and better facility utilization. It is are utilizing information technology wherever possible to facilitate efficiencies and effectiveness. Also key to HMC's strategy is to continue to grow its network of referring physicians.

In addition to hospital acquisitions and joint ventures, HMC is also acquiring and joint venturing with outpatient surgery centers and discussing joint ventures with nursing homes. In general, it prefers ownership to alliances and ventures and has aggressively targeted not-for-profits. Perhaps joint ventures may be useful to HMC in laying the groundwork for future acquisitions or for building relationships with physicians it can leverage in the future. It is important to note in the sample of joint ventures I examined that HMC had at least 50 percent ownership and equivalent board representation and management control. The implications of this position are quite important. It is unlikely that after the closing of a venture deal CHS would have much leverage over HMC beyond enforcing the venture agreement, or be able to muster a majority of board members to change the way the target hospitals are being run.

It does not appear that HMC has a particular agenda for meeting the needs of the poor and indigent. In a number of speeches, Smith has claimed, however, that HMC does a better job at that than do not-for-profits when one takes into consideration corporate income taxes and that not-for-profits have an unfair playing field. There has been some speculation that HMC will aim for better-insured customers, while Catholic not-for-profits will focus on the indigent. Noting that universal access is coming, HMC recently said, "I have no problem with their (Catholic canon of ethics). Their mission was to take care of charity patients. That mission is past."

However, in a recent acquisition of a DOC hospital, St John's, in Fort Lauderdale, Florida, HMC agreed to a certain amount of charity care and retained the hospice program. It does appear to be pragmatic enough to do what it takes to strike a deal. But, I think "pragmatic" versus "philosophic" is the key word in describing HMC's approach to charitable care. In Florida last year it did make $200,000 in charitable donations, with $80,000 going to local AIDS groups.

HMC has also been quite tough in its dealings. In fact, some have described Smith as a bounty hunter. According to a *Wall Street Journal* article, "HMC has employed big money, tough tactics and relentless pressure to become Georgia's largest provider of health care." In Atlanta, the state capital, it paid 26 lobbyists to push for tight restrictions on tax exemptions for not-for-profit hospitals, which are primary competitors and acquisition targets. To motivate management of one hospital to sell, HMC bought land near the hospital and allegedly threatened to build an outpatient surgery center to perform 70 percent of the operations performed by the hospital. To gain a contract with Jones County in Georgia, HMC slashed prices and released a study showing that the tax breaks given to competing Barnes Memorial Hospital and other not-for-profits were worth more than the charity care HMC provided. HMC won the contract. The Barnes Memorial situation led to a great deal of mud-slinging, but both sides claimed the other started it. In another case, HMC, soon after the owner of a local health-care company in Fort Myers, Florida, died, swooped in to purchase the business from her estate.

Three not-for-profit hospital administrators who are negotiating joint ventures and were interviewed said that HMC has behaved legally, professionally, and ethically thus far. They also noted, however, that HMC's managers are "staunch capitalists." In order to enhance its credibility and image of providing state-of-the-art health care, HMC is presently in various stages of negotiations with at least 17 academic health centers nationwide. Earlier this year a large medical school organization entered into negotiations with HMC to establish an extensive health-care network. In spite of the organization's history of entrepreneurial ventures, while providing indigent health care, it recently broke off negotiations with HMC. Hospital administrators cited a "clash of cultures" between the organizations as the main reason. The organization felt that HMC was too aggressive to consummate the deal, too capitalistic, and too rigid over who would be in charge. Another hospital administrator in Atlanta, who generally finds HMC more ethical than some hospital chains, notes that when presented with a difference in operating philosophy, "HMC may give lip service, but it is clear that they are in charge."

It appears to me, based on conversations I have had with a number of people in the industry, that HMC may be positioning long term for an HMO environment where covered lives may be the key to financial performance. As such, it may be positioning through acquisitions, alliances, and other means to maximize the number of persons enrolled in its managed-care plans. To support this, HMC has been very aggressive in building tight alliances with referring physicians by offering them equity interests in their local HMC subsidiary. Further, such interests are contingent upon the physicians signing noncompete clauses preventing them from investing in other health-care ventures. Moreover, a 1992 FAHCA (Florida) study of patient admissions by physician-owners at HMC's Jones Hospital, a 236-bed Miami institution, found Medicare patients that they referred there stayed an average of 8.48 days, while those sent to competing institutions averaged 13.5 days. While the Florida agency said the numbers were inconclusive, it points to possible profiteering, with more complicated, less profitable patients being steered to other hospitals.

DEALING WITH HMC

At this point I can only speculate, since I have no inside knowledge of HMC. It appears that HMC's core values, culture, and agenda are quite different from those of CHS, especially with respect to indigent and quality health care, i.e., basic core values. As such, I suspect that CHS will have great difficulty reaching a successful agreement with HMC.

There appear to be a number of risks from continuing negotiations and engaging in a venture with HMC. First, CHS must consider any reputational damage among its external stakeholders and employees and any co-optation of its mission. These are major core issues. I suggest that CHS ask itself whether "it could sleep at night" if it were involved with HMC. For example, if CHS partners with HMC, what impact would such a relationship have on potential affiliations with other Catholic hospitals? Would it appear that CHS "sold out"?

If CHS decides to continue joint-venture negotiations with HMC, it should do so *very carefully* and ask some tough questions. It is apparent that HMC is committed to growing rapidly and is aggressive in doing so, and wants to do a deal for the target. I suspect it would prefer to buy the target and not have to deal with CHS as a partner. However, HMC is so hungry to grow that it would settle for a venture, perhaps as an interim step. As such, a great deal of caution is warranted. HMC's agenda and goals are clear. Moreover, it is very pragmatic and may initially make concessions with respect to such issues as indigent care to do a deal. The real issue, however, is what life for the target will be like after the deal is closed.

From my experience with mergers, acquisitions, and joint ventures, not all issues can be specified in the written agreement, although as many as possible should be. In the end, however, many issues will have to be resolved outside the formal agreement. *Thus, CHS needs to feel confident that it can trust and work with the specific people and organization it will be involved with at HMC.* Since HMC is very large and regionally decentralized, it appears that the people and specific culture and agenda in Colorado (the location of the target) should be the focal point of further thought and analysis. Keep in mind, however, that the Colorado region will still likely reflect the basic core values, culture, and agenda of the overall corporation. Further analyses should focus on such day-to-day operating management issues as primary measures of organizational success; orientation toward indigent care and community service; tolerance of the canon of ethics; focus on employee empowerment and teams; performance management and reward systems; administration/medical staff relations; orientation toward quality-care approaches to conflict management and problem solving; philosophy of employee and management development; management control systems; and approaches toward promotion, staffing, and termination. Moreover, general perceptions of operating management's honesty, integrity, fairness, and credibility should be examined. To directly learn about these issues, interviews with local HMC managers and employees and other joint-venture partners, employee surveys and focus groups, facility inspections, and examinations of key records and documentation should be employed.

If CHS decides to continue negotiations, the governance structure of the venture and a definition of what "operating control" means should be thoroughly examined. These include management and board control; roles, responsibilities, and composition of the management team and board; bailout provisions for CHS; and mechanisms for making decisions and resolving disputes and conflicts.

Although it may be easy to halt discussions at this time because HMC appears to be "different," it may be worthwhile to continue negotiations and analyses. First, the venture may provide CHS with a good opportunity to learn more about HMC and how it operates. CHS may face HMC down the road as a competitor. Moreover, CHS may learn more efficient practices for operating a hospital. Second, if CHS divests itself of the target, its mission in Colorado will cease. This joint venture may be the only hope of preserving the mission.

Whatever course CHS pursues, it should do so objectively and with solid data and information. Failure to do so will likely result in a grave mistake.

4

Assessing Key Target People

With few exceptions, the selection and retention of key people during a merger or an acquisition is critical to the success of a deal.[1] Even in cases where there is significant redundancy, certain people will be essential. These may be people who are needed for the long term or long enough to ensure that the transition and integration process is successfully completed. Most companies are always in need of talented people, and a merger or an acquisition is an excellent opportunity to secure them. As such, an acquirer's ability to identify people key to the success of the merger or acquisition, and to assess whether they can effectively contribute and are willing to stay, is of utmost importance.

The sooner such assessments can be made, the better. Until people are named to key positions, the "me" question will preoccupy many people's minds. Good people are likely to update their resumes and start looking for new jobs. The net outcome is not likely to be positive, resulting in possible value leakage. Although it would be desirable to assess everyone in a target or merging organization, at this stage it is not possible. It would require too much time, access, and too many resources. Focusing on key people at this point is sufficient. During the transition and integration stages, these assessments will become essential.

This chapter presents several key steps required to determine the staffing of key positions. It also provides examples of tools for assessing people and making staffing decisions. Such decisions, however, are not easy to make. They require assessment of people in both the target and acquirer.

The person with the primary responsibility for assessing key managers and employees will be someone from human resources (HR), with the input of relevant line managers (i.e., to provide inputs on functional competencies) and outside consultants. This HR "point" person should be a member of the due diligence team and subsequently a member of the staffing integration team (see Chapter 6). The level of HR person involved will depend on the level of the positions being assessed.

A key to the success of an acquisition is having a sufficient number of people with needed talent, skills, competencies, style, and motivation. As such, the acquirer must:

1. Assess staffing needs to manage through the transition and afterward to run the business.
2. Assess the capability of the target and other sources to meet these needs.
3. Assess staffing time frames.
4. Develop strategies for closing any gaps in staffing needs.

Much the same as with assessing culture, the challenge in assessment is going to be the level of access to a target. It is recommended that both primary and secondary sources (see the previous chapter) again be considered.

STEPS IN THE ASSESSMENT OF KEY TARGET PEOPLE

The relationship among the steps are presented in Figure 4-1 and discussed below.

Step 1 Assess Staffing Needs

This requires that a rough pro forma of the consolidated postclosing organization be developed to determine the:

1. Basic organization structure
2. Key positions
   a. Number of positions
   b. Roles and responsibilities for each position (i.e., position description)
   c. Talent, skills, competencies, style, and motivation needed for each position (if profiles have already been developed, use them)[2]
   d. Target staffing costs (salaries and benefits) the acquirer is willing to sustain and what the actual costs are likely to be

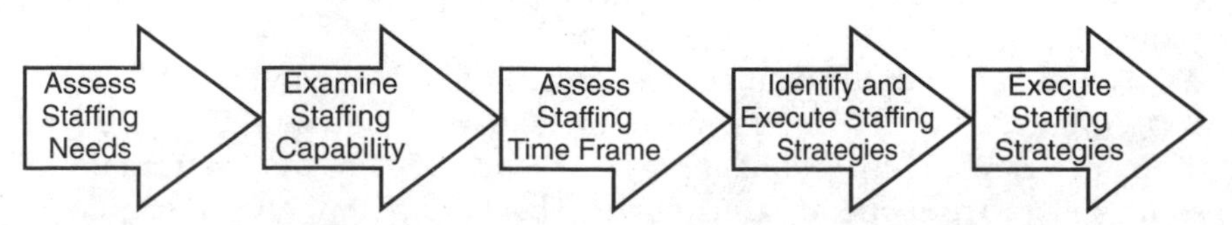

Figure 4-1 Assessing Key Target People

Financial and strategic objectives play a key role in this assessment. For example, where levels of consolidation and redundancy are high, there is not likely to be a shortage of people, although there may be a shortage of qualified people. Where there is geographic expansion and growth and where redundancies are few, acquired people may be critical to success, especially if there is a shortage of talent in the local market.

Step 2 Examine Staffing Capability

Next, examine staffing capability in both the target and the acquirer. It is recommended that such assessment be undertaken with the three highest levels of management and with other key people (including high potentials). Key questions to address include:

1. Who are the key people in the target? These may include people with:
   a. Technical knowledge (e.g., research and development and new-product development, marketing) that cannot be easily replaced
   b. Important relationships with key customers, employees, government officials, and other stakeholders
2. To what extent will target people "fit" within the acquirer's organization? If they do not fit, can the acquirer live with such mismatches, and how can they manage them?
3. How likely are key target people to remain with the acquirer and be motivated during the transition stage and after closing?
4. Does the target have capable successors to key managers and personnel? Are they likely to remain?
5. Does the acquirer have sufficient replacements if target people are not retained?
6. Can sufficient replacements be hired in the marketplace if target people do not stay?
7. How long will it take to find replacements, and how long will it take for them to be performing on the job?
8. How much will it cost to meet the staffing requirements?

Step 3 Assess Staffing Time Frame

Third, determine for how long key people are needed. Some people will be needed only for the duration of the transition but will have no future with the company, whereas others will be retained as long-term employees. This distinction is important because many companies fail to consider transitional needs.

Step 4 Identify and Execute Staffing Strategies

Finally, based on the staffing needs identified in the pro forma organization, and the staffing capabilities and time frame, identify any potential short-term and long-term gaps in key positions. Then develop a staffing strategy.

The strategy should focus on:

1. Retaining key target people (more will be said about strategies for retaining target people in Chapter 7)
2. Identifying possible successors in the target
3. Identifying the acquirer's replacements
4. Preparing to recruit replacements in the marketplace
5. Terminating the deal if critical people cannot be retained or replaced

Using the information you've gained from the steps conducted above, you can construct a staffing assessment table like the one shown in Table 4-1. After the table is constructed, the pros and cons of each strategy should be examined.

ASSESSING KEY PEOPLE

Four major questions are useful in assessing people:

1. Have the key people performed effectively in the past?
2. Do the key people have the talent, skills, competencies, style, and motivation to manage in the new organization?
3. What is the likelihood the key people will fit and succeed in this new environment?
4. What actions, if any, can be taken to ensure that key people will succeed?

Answering these questions is more an art than a science. No single source of information can provide answers to these questions. Moreover, each source has certain limits to validity. As such, to answer these questions companies must rely on a variety of approaches and tools.

As is the case in cultural assessment, there is no single or easy way to assess managerial capabilities or intentions. Also, since such assessments are more personal than are cultural assessments, they are likely to engender reactive responses. Great care must be taken during such assessment. It is suggested that primary and secondary sources be utilized with consideration of the following:

Target Company Documents

Various company documents can be examined. Such documents, however, may reflect past accomplishments and not accurately reflect future potential. In addition, depending upon the sophistication of the target, many companies may not ever have prepared such documents. Key documents to look for include:

Personnel records. These records identify staff, how they can be contacted, what their roles and responsibilities are, what development

Table 4-1 Staffing Assessment

Key Position	Number of People Needed	Target Candidates	External Candidates (Including the acquirer)	Readiness for the Position	Likelihood Person Will Take the Position If Offered	Retention or Recruitment Strategy	Cost of Strategy	Pros and Cons of Person

activities they have participated in, and what their salaries and benefits are.

Business plans and personal goals. These provide insights on results achieved by key managers.

Performance appraisals. These provide insights on how people have performed on key competencies and behaviors. Be careful, however, since many companies' appraisals are not very accurate or comparable across companies.

Succession plans. These identify successors to all key positions.

Development plans for high-potential managers. These identify any high-potential managers, their stages of development, development activities completed, and development needs remaining.

Interviews

Incumbents. Interviews should focus on what the key players have accomplished and how they have done so. Be careful not to reveal too much information about the acquirer's criteria for judging people, since these may elicit "socially desirable" responses. Any interview techniques that human resources has developed for interviewing prospective employees might be very useful.

Seller or senior management. Such interviews should focus on basic insights about who the key people are, how important their retention is, and what the downside risks are if they should depart. These insights should be tempered by the fact that the target management is interested in selling the company and might be interested in looking after its people.

360 degree interviews. To the extent possible, such interviews should focus on soliciting independent information on key managers from peers, subordinates, superiors, and other relevent parties (e.g., customers, suppliers).

Leadership Style and Psychological Assessments

There are numerous tools and testing companies available for assessing managers' psychological makeup and leadership style. These assessments may be useful in determining the extent to which people fit with the acquirer. Again, any tools human resources has developed for assessing prospective employees might be very useful here.

Resumes. Resumes may provide insights on people's work experience, including the:

- Number of jobs and positions they have held
- Frequency and changes in employment
- Types of companies and industries they have worked for and their tenure
- Major accomplishments
- Future goals and aspirations

Talent, Skills, Competencies, Style, and Motivation[3]

In putting a new organization together, the right mix of talent, skills, competencies, and styles is critical. Determining what kind of people will allow a merged organization to achieve its financial and strategic objectives is paramount in the process. Does the company want a by-the-book or a creative CFO? Does it want an entrepreneur who takes risks or a loyal and conventional manager? Does it want to put its key people in an environment where they will be strongest or where they will be continually frustrated? Does it want all to fit a cookie-cutter image, or does it want diversity in style, approach, and expertise?

Even when the right mix has been decided, the challenges are not over. Assurances are needed that the styles of the players on the new team will complement each other. Does the company know in advance how a new team member is likely to relate to the rest of the team and to the demands of the work environment? Would it help to know what really motivates key people or to be forewarned about what is most likely to cause them stress? Could executives benefit by knowing how to discuss individual differences so their teams could work more effectively? Most merger executives and managers say yes, and yet these are the issues that are often overlooked and in the end can make or break a merger or an acquisition.

Knowing what kind of talents, skills, competencies, and styles are available and how each "player" is likely to best succeed still isn't the end of the people side of due diligence. The next step is integrating the players in such a way that creates a well-coordinated team. More is said about this in Chapter 8. If the styles of the team fit together nicely, the sailing should be pretty smooth. If they don't, much more thought has to be given to whether that "newcomer" from the acquired or merged company who appears to have a totally different approach or style from that of the existing players is a challenge worth taking on. Given the way mergers have gone over the last several years, putting the wrong people in place for the sake of goodwill can be a costly mistake.

In this section, near mistakes and the successes that resulted from the people side of due diligence are explored. A "shortcut" process that can improve the accuracy of selection and accelerate the assimilation of new players into a team is laid out, and vignettes of how this process has worked in three merger situations is described.

The "Shortcut": An Up-front Assessment Tool

The shortcut proposed is no panacea, but aids significantly in determining whether people have the right combination of talent, skills, competencies, styles, and motivation to succeed in the newly created environment. In effect, the shortcut reduces the time needed to get both an individual and a team into place and in a productive mode once selection decisions are made and integration is under way. Instead of spending 6 to 18 months learning what motivates people's best performance and how they lead, make decisions, work with peers, adapt to change, or handle stress, the shortcut provides reliable indicators about talent and fit from the beginning. It enables executives and managers to identify, in advance, where managing the team will be nearly seamless and where trouble might begin.

A tool that facilitates us in this process is called the Birkman Method. It is a highly validated and reliable instrument used by over 5,000 organizations worldwide and has 50 years of research supporting it. Most organizations use it to assess the strengths and differences among individuals and to facilitate productive relationships. My colleagues and I use it not only for its team-building power, but for its strong predictive capability. From this predictive dimension, we are able to lay out a spreadsheet of the organization's talent and individual job strengths. Those who assess people during due diligence can thus zero in more quickly on missing talents, skills, and competencies, and confirm whether the desired candidate(s) appear to have the requisite styles and motivations. The assessors can also estimate whether the value of the talents, skills, and competencies brought by particular candidates is worth the costs of managing potentially significant differences.

Our process is a useful shortcut that supports the more complex and traditional way of determining the fit of new team members that rely on such measures as:

- Performance reports and past development plans
- Seniority
- Placement request forms
- Information gathered from board members, from peers, from subordinates
- Preestablished ratios set by the HR group for the desired mix of acquired and acquiring staff
- Information garnered from interviews

These are all useful methods for acquiring the data needed, but often, as noted above, they are not available. Moreover, the traditional methods only give part of the picture. They do not give us the insights needed to create the best mix of all the people available.

We go beyond these commonly used measures by adding our shortcut as a compensatory step. By that we mean that the assessment reports generated from our process support other data and do not stand alone in decision making about the selection of candidates. In every instance, this shortcut is used in conjunction with all the other sources of information available to the acquirer or merger partner. In fact, Birkman reports help us structure the way we look at and use the other traditional information. With insights from the assessment, we can dig deeper in interviews for areas of talents, skills, and competencies as well as look for comments in performance appraisals that support the indications of style or approach.

The tool's predictive assessment capability emanates from computer-generated reports completed by candidates for positions in the new organization. A computerized questionnaire to assess people takes only about 45 minutes to complete and can be easily accessed online. The resulting spreadsheets allow us to explain a team's profile, an individual's fit to specific job functions, and the motivations, behaviors, and reactions each person brings to the job. At a glance, integration leaders have available the kinds of data they need to make decisions about the selection of key target talent and about the fit of that talent to the existing team and the company's environment.

A walk through the five-step "talent fit" method, along with some due diligence lessons learned, demonstrate the power of this assessment process. I will draw from the following examples:

- An insurance company where the designated CEO-in-waiting really did not have what was needed to take the company to a new level of growth
- Two banks that moved to such different rhythms that all the senior management of one had to leave the dance floor to make room for those who could move to a faster beat
- A large energy company where the merger created simply more of the same

Five-Step Talent-Fit Decision Process

From the earliest stage of due diligence, we follow these assessment steps:

Step 1 Assess whether the targeted individual has the requisite talents, skills, competencies, and style to do the job. We look at:

- Whether this person really could do what needs to be done
- How well he or she compares with others who have significant tenure in the kind of position and environment this job represents
- What approach we could expect this individual to take in getting the job done
- How the person would see problems and attempt to solve them

Step 2 Assess the environments and relationships that motivate the targeted individual's "best" performance. At this point we want to know to the greatest extent possible whether the predominant relationships among the team and in the overall environment will bring out the best or cause stress in a newcomer. For example, we look at the fit of a candidate's profile to the overall "climate" of the work environment and to the typical interpersonal relationships in the new company. Where would this candidate thrive—would it be in an environment that is fast-paced or thoughtful, continuously changing or focused, competitive or collaborative, self-starting or highly directive, frank and straightforward or characterized by subtle and diplomatic communication, highly pragmatic or intuitive and feeling-oriented, risk taking or risk averse, conventional or individualistic? When it looks like the match of the team environment to the motivational needs of the candidate is not there, we dig deeper to determine what would have to happen for this candidate to perform well. In this step of the people side of due diligence, we have insights into how a person will do a job. We can use this information to conduct probing interviews and to glean past successes or failures from the candidate's professional experience.

Step 3 Assess the target individual's interest in the functional area proposed for him or her. If offered the position, would this individual really want to do it?

Step 4 Compare the fit of the targeted newcomer to the existing management team. Are there more similarities than differences in style? If there are strong differences, are there areas that might be considered irreconcilable?

Step 5 Determine whether to eliminate the targeted newcomer from consideration or to offer him or her a spot on the team. If the latter, determine whether special effort is needed to assimilate the newcomer into the existing team. Is the cost of taking this talent into the team minimal or excessive?

Talent Spreadsheet

The starting point is a talent spreadsheet, or what the Birkman Method calls "Organizational Strengths." It highlights the potential strengths and gaps of talent represented by members of a team or work unit. It also gives insights into the way members of the team manage and get things done. By knowing the mix of talents on the team, a leader can determine what strategies and tactics will create the greatest chance of success in managing that team.

What we look for first are the predominant management styles and the specific talents brought to the organization. At a glance, we can see the surfeits and deficits of a team. The talent spreadsheet in Table 4-2, from an insurance company we have renamed "Healthy Life," provides a detailed example of the kind of information we can have at our fingertips.

The spreadsheet consists of career functions and categories that, when interpreted, depict talent and style. Each category is ranked on a scale of 1 to 10 (with 10 being the highest fit to a talent or style category). In looking at the predominant strength of Healthy Life's top-management team, we see above the far left column of numbers that the tallest bar connotes strength in planning. The CEO, sales VP, EVP, and VP corporate planning and policy all bring a strong talent for innovation and vision to the team (scores of 7 to 10). In terms of other strengths at Healthy Life, the sales VP and the general counsel contribute talent in the realm of communicating and persuading. The VPs of operations and customer service, as well as the company's EVP, share a talent for expediting; while the CFO, the VP of corporate planning and policy, and the EVP show they have strong potential to

Table 4-2 Healthy Life's Talent Spreadsheet / Organizational Strengths

	Planning	Communicating	Expediting	Administrating	Knowledge Specialist	Directive Management	Delegative Management	Artistic Careers	Educational Careers	Social Service / Counseling	Employee Relations / Training	Medical Professions
Averages	**7**	**6**	**5**	**6**	**7**	**4**	**4**	**7**	**7**	**7**	**7**	**6**
CEO	7	5	4	4	8	2	2	8	8	8	8	6
VP sales	8	8	5	5	7	1	7	9	7	8	9	9
VP operations	3	4	8	4	2	10	4	5	2	2	2	3
General counsel	6	8	5	3	5	4	5	5	6	8	7	5
EVP	9	6	7	7	9	3	1	9	9	9	8	9
VP customer service	6	6	7	5	5	4	4	7	5	5	6	6
CFO	6	6	2	9	9	2	8	5	8	7	6	4
VP corp. plng. / policy	7	4	4	7	9	2	3	9	8	6	6	8
Dirk*	**1**	**1**	**8**	**5**	**4**	**10**	**3**	**2**	**1**	**1**	**1**	**2**

	Direct Tangible Sales	Direct Intangible Sales	Consultative Tangible Sales	Consultative Intangible Sales	Legal	Crafts / Technical	Police, Fire, and Security	Petrochemical	Engineering / Technology	Science	General Administrative	Numerical Administrative	Administrative Professionals	Banking and Finance	Accounting
Averages	**6**	**5**	**5**	**6**	**7**	**5**	**5**	**5**	**5**	**6**	**7**	**6**	**6**	**5**	**4**
CEO	6	4	2	5	10	4	4	3	3	4	8	4	4	3	1
VP sales	8	7	9	9	8	4	4	4	5	6	7	4	4	5	3
VP operations	5	4	4	2	5	9	9	10	7	5	5	7	2	2	1
General counsel	6	8	8	9	7	4	5	4	5	6	2	1	3	5	6
EVP	5	5	4	6	8	7	6	8	8	9	9	7	9	5	4
VP customer service	7	6	7	7	3	7	6	7	8	8	4	4	5	6	6
CFO	6	6	3	6	8	1	1	1	2	2	8	8	10	9	9
VP corp. plng. / policy	4	3	2	3	8	5	3	4	3	5	10	9	9	6	3
Dirk*	**1**	**1**	**2**	**1**	**1**	**8**	**6**	**9**	**9**	**8**	**1**	**3**	**8**	**5**	**9**

*Designated CEO-in-waiting

contribute in the administrative area. At a glance, we see that only planning is an overall corporate strength (meaning in the 7–10 "very strong" range). This is a company with innovative talent but no particularly strong implementation or sales "signature theme."

The situation faced by Healthy Life was as follows:

- Nontraditional competition was fierce.
- Signing up new customers was the only way to win.
- The company had just bought out a rival competitor.
- One of the conditions proposed in the acquisition discussions was that instead of naming co-CEOs, the current CEO of the acquired company would step into the role of EVP for 18 months and then take over as CEO when Healthy Life's current CEO was slated to retire. The current EVP would take a package and exit. Twelve months down the road, a new EVP would be identified.

We looked at the gaps between what was needed and what talents, skills, competencies, and style existed within the merging organizations. First, competition suggested that a strong "sales approach" was called for.

The board of directors was concerned that the demonstrated operational talent of the acquired CEO, Dirk Jones (name changed), duplicated strength the company already had, particularly in its current VP of operations. The board members felt new strength in relationship management both inside and outside the company was needed in their future CEO if the company was going to be competitive. It was the board that insisted on mapping talent to the new company's intended strategy.

Let's take a look at the talents Dirk brought to the newly created Healthy Life from the acquired company. He had a track record as an "expeditor," having come up the ladder from operations. His expeditor summary score was 8. He had 1's in planning and communicating and a 5 in administrating. His managerial style indicated he probably was very directive (10), and he scored in the 8's and 9's on technical, engineering, and administrative specializations. Extremely bright and well liked by the acquiring CEO, Dirk had moved up to the top in his former company very quickly because he was organized and precise and could deliver on time.

The concern was whether he had the strength to take Healthy Life to the next level by bringing in new business. If he did not, would the cost to the company be too great? Was there enough time to test out his approach before two other giants in the insurance industry combined? Were Dirk's strengths already present in the acquiring company's current VP of operations? In fact, it looked to a few board members as if the current VP had a stronger record in operations management than Dirk did. Did they need carbon copies of the same skill and talent set?

Career Predictors

Moving on from the talent spreadsheet, we focused on a report that dug into indicators that predict a match with those who have tenure in specific job categories and functions. This report, called interchangeably "Career Predictors" or the "Interview Guide," is not a measure of skills but a benchmark of how a person thinks compared with others who:

- Are typical of those with tenure in specific occupations
- Have been successful in specific ways of analyzing problems and creating solutions
- Share similar managerial style and responsibilities and the ability to adapt to stress, responsibilities, and organizational politics

The report tells us whether the candidate can match those who have significant track records in doing the job in question. In analyzing this report, we took into account the context of the merger, the organizational culture of the new company or team, and the positions to be filled. Higher scores on this report indicate more motivation and interest for traditional job responsibilities, functions, and managerial style. Lower scores indicate a nonconventional, often entrepreneurial, hands-on or risk-taking approach. Extensive research has shown that the degree of interest in something and motivation to work is linked to performance effectiveness.

As with all elements of our process, we use the "Career Predictors" report with other information about a candidate's education, past experience, and performance. It is an extremely useful tool for structuring an interview because it allows the interviewer to focus in on those talents, skills, competencies, and styles typically associated with particular roles and functions. What it does not tell us is whether the candidate will take on that job or role, or how the candidate would do it. That will be discussed later in the chapter.

First we looked at Dirk's scores in categories that related to occupations of a creative or social relationship nature (e.g., arts, education, social service, sales, and law; see Table 4-3). Every one of his scores on a scale of 1 to 10 were 1, indicating weak interest in being involved in those specific career areas or in using a particular style associated with careers requiring relationship skills. As we moved into production and administrative career categories, Dirk's scores moved up. His managerial style matched those of directive managers with significant tenure. While he may need extra incentive to work hard, his scores definitely matched those who adapt easily to the chain of command and who are loyal and committed to the goals of their organizations. In the area of adaptability to stressful situations and in social responsibility his scores were above average. We could now be fairly certain that Dirk had real strength of character and, if CEO, would take a conventional approach to managing the company.

What we discovered was that while Dirk's profile matched those of managers who are strong technical managers as well as good corporate citizens, he didn't match up with the requirement for Healthy Life's growth. Looking at the rest of the senior managers, we saw that only the VP sales and the general counsel had a match in business development

Table 4-3 Career Predictors (the "Interview Guide")

	Arts	Education	Social Services	Sales	Consultative Sales	Legal	Production	Enforcement	Engineering	Office Admin.	Admin. / Prof.	Fiscal	Knowledge Spec.	Directive Mgmt.	Delegative Mgmt.	Work Motivation	Self-Development	Corporate Adapt.	Social Adapt.	Social Respons.	Public Contact	Global	Conceptual
CEO	7	5	6	5	8	10	5	7	3	5	4	2	8	2	2	2	9	2	8	2	10	10	7
VP sales	9	1	4	9	9	8	2	4	4	7	4	3	7	1	7	5	8	7	8	6	10	7	4
VP operations	3	3	2	3	8	5	8	10	7	2	2	4	2	10	4	4	6	2	4	4	3	6	8
General counsel	2	4	6	10	9	7	2	5	5	4	3	3	5	4	5	4	8	7	5	6	6	8	3
EVP	8	4	8	3	5	8	7	2	3	5	9	2	9	3	1	4	9	10	9	6	8	4	9
VP customer service	4	1	4	7	6	3	4	7	6	4	5	5	5	4	4	5	7	6	5	4	6	3	4
CFO	6	9	8	4	1	8	5	2	2	9	10	10	9	2	8	7	10	6	8	7	2	8	10
VP corp. plng. / policy	10	9	4	1	1	8	6	3	2	9	9	3	9	2	3	2	10	2	7	6	6	8	9
Averages	**6**	**5**	**5**	**5**	**6**	**7**	**5**	**5**	**4**	**6**	**6**	**4**	**7**	**4**	**4**	**4**	**8**	**5**	**7**	**5**	**6**	**7**	**7**
Dirk	**1**	**1**	**1**	**1**	**1**	**1**	**9**	**3**	**9**	**6**	**8**	**8**	**4**	**10**	**3**	**3**	**6**	**10**	**7**	**7**	**1**	**1**	**6**

predictors, and the VP sales had a stronger blend of managerial and administrative strengths than did the general counsel. The VP sales, however, was not yet ready in terms of "seasoning" to take on the CEO role.

Perceptual Filters

At this point we examined the information from which we could glean clues about the ways in which Dirk might typically look at problems and invent solutions. Going back to the talent spreadsheet, a "perceptual filters" report was generated in order to get a quick picture of how he might be expected to approach work.

When we approach a work situation or when we are engaged in an interaction, our perception of what is going on is our individual reality. We get to that reality through the "perceptual filters" we use—those expectations and assumptions we bring to the table. When we begin to take the time to acknowledge that other people don't necessarily see things the way we do, a shift can occur. The degree to which we show tolerance and understanding of other approaches and views—of those "filters" through which other people see issues and approach problems—the greater the chance that each style can contribute something useful to the whole.

If we apply this concept to leading an organization, it is apparent that when leaders have an understanding of how people relate to vision, mission, and goals and to the structure of the organization and its culture, there is a much better chance they will be able to develop more integrated and accepted solutions to business issues. They can take valuable insights from those who are engaged in planning and operations and blend them with ideas coming from the marketing and administrative sides of the house. The key here is to develop and look for the ability to "understand" or "appreciate." Leaders do not have to accept every perspective, but by listening to the ideas that come through filters different from their own, an appreciation of the value offered by diverse perspectives is developed. When this occurs, they have a much better opportunity to build the integrated and supportive team needed to carry the merged organization forward!

Returning to our integration in the insurance company, Healthy Life, let us look at where Dirk came out in this filtering process. He very squarely placed in the operations and technical filter category. That meant he most often assumed that problems related to business growth could generally be related to technology, to a lack of insistence on results, or to just too much emotion interfering with "the facts." He would most probably expect solutions to come quickly through either his own or the immediate direct involvement and technical expertise of others. His dominant approach would undoubtedly be one of "Let's get on with it and get this project done." With such a focus on "results now," we could likely predict a tendency to ignore the subtle social and relationship issues that are important in both developing business and motivating others.

In Figure 4-2, we see that other filters are portrayed by the functions planning, marketing and sales, and finance and administration. Those who see things predominantly through a planning filter tend to view things in terms of the future. They focus more on long-range benefits and implications. They are most likely to assume that problems result from oversimplification, from a lack of analysis, from an inability to see the big picture, from the tunnel vision of others, or simply from a lack of appreciation for the originality of one's creative approach. A person who sees things through a planning filter would be expected to reach a solution by synthesizing all available information and by using holistic reasoning and long-range thinking. A planning filter approach tends to be strategic. When people lead through a marketing and sales filter, they get results through communication, persuasion, motivation, and enthusiasm. Those operating through a finance and administration filter focus on detail, control, consistency, and systems that have worked in the past.

We are now brought back to the observation we made in the beginning of our analysis of Dirk's style. He appears fundamentally a technical thinker who would exclusively use this filter's style in approaching issues in Healthy Life. For us this is a red flag, because the job called for at least equal strength in seeing and acting on issues from a "get-out-there-and-sell" communicating and persuading perspective. Healthy Life's current CEO, overwhelmingly planning-oriented but with a high

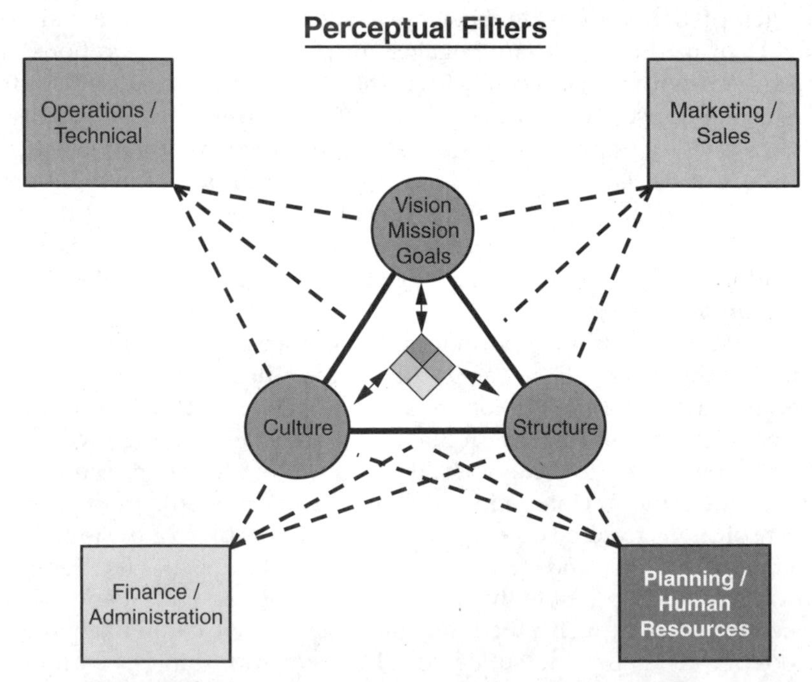

Figure 4-2 Perceptual Filters

need to have things done his way, was preoccupied with innovative new products and services. At this point, he just wanted to keep the place running, and he wanted the integration to move fast. He was sure the customers would be lining up to enroll in the creative new plans the company was poised to announce.

He saw that by bringing Dirk in as his EVP, he (the CEO) could make sure operations ran smoothly and products and services got off the drawing board and to the customers. He would let the future take care of itself. In this case, the future stemmed from a long past that the CEO had with Dirk's father. They had been college roommates and best golfing buddies over the last 35 years. He had known Dirk since he was a baby and had watched him grow into a responsible, action-oriented adult. When Dirk was recruited by a top insurance company out of his MBA program, Healthy Life's CEO was pleased for him. He knew Dirk would get onto a fast track through the company's management development program—but he hadn't estimated Dirk's rise to be so fast. He hadn't even had time to bring him into his own company! He had always said that one day he'd have Dirk on his team. He just never thought it would have come through an acquisition!

Even though he acknowledged that Dirk's social style was introverted, his solution would be to put a development plan together that would include sending Dirk to an Ivy League advanced executive management program. He estimated that would provide Dirk with a solid theoretical update of what it takes to lead a growing company. While interacting with other CEOs, Dirk would also have the opportunity to learn how important the social aspects of leadership really were. For Healthy Life's current CEO, it was a matter of putting information in and analyzing it, then taking actions around what had been learned. A second part of the CEO's plan was to take Dirk under his wing to "acclimatize" him to the required social routine that had proved successful for him during his tenure as Healthy Life's CEO. Despite his penchant for creativity, the current CEO had a real streak of impatience.

Assessing the Motivational "Drivers"

The talent spreadsheet, the career predictors, and the perceptual filters gave us insights into types of individual talents, matches with various occupations, the presence of certain traits, and the approaches and the styles Healthy Life's senior team (including Dirk) would bring to the job. These reports didn't tell us, however, the team's most productive ways of getting results. Like the board of directors, we wanted to go more deeply into how Dirk would exercise his talents. We knew the current CEO wanted to put Dirk in as his replacement. Already, we had seen enough signposts that warned us this could be a big mistake. While the CEO had brought us into the company, we had committed to the board to use every tool in our arsenal to identify the pros and cons of this choice. So we prepared for our next level of analysis.

We took Step 2 of our talent-fit method and turned to what distinguishes this tool from other assessment instruments. We wanted to understand what really motivated Dirk—what were the drivers in his personality that would describe to us how he'd achieve results for this company. We reviewed Dirk's specific motivational needs and most productive styles of achieving results in a vast range of personality areas—from communicating, to being sociable, to organizing, to competing, to directing, to using energy and emotion, to handling change, to making decisions. The report we used, dubbed the "Components," refers to the "strengths and needs" of one's personality. This report goes beyond a person's usual behaviors—those that others can observe and identify—to the hidden, underlying needs and values that are the reasons we tend to act productively or unproductively. The data also indicate what specific environment or interaction will likely trigger the type of performance desired in a particular role or job. Here we find the keys to *how* people use their talents, carry out career responsibilities, and personify desired styles of behavior and decision making.

We wanted to hone in on the areas that connoted leadership strength—strong communication style and an inclination to take risks, to be assertive, to delegate, to be involved with others, and to adapt easily to change or to stressful conditions.

Strengths and Needs

In this report (Table 4-4), personality elements are rated on a scale of 1 to 99. Low scores indicate one type of behavior; high scores, another. Scores of 50 are the median—a blend of high- and low-scoring tendencies.

In Dirk's case, we saw that he was motivated to work alone or with just a few individuals (low scores on "Acceptance"). This was the opposite of all other members of Healthy Life's senior management, whose scores were well above the 50 range and represented sociable, gregarious, team-oriented behavior. Dirk's penchant for working alone was reinforced by a style of communication ("Esteem") that was "to the point," if not terse. His communication scores indicated little motivation to engage in social conversation or chit-chat or just tune in to where other people were. In other words, it would not be common or comfortable for him to walk around and talk to people. Indicators of his approach to planning gave us clues that he would be very detailed and precise. He was probably a manager who liked to work to a plan and wouldn't necessarily be prone to either delegation or spontaneity.

Next we looked at how he gave and received direction. Against the backdrop of the talent spreadsheet and the "Career Predictors" reports we reviewed above, which had painted a picture of him as operationally and administratively oriented, we erroneously expected him to behave in a "chain-of-command" way. Instead, we were surprised by indicators that suggested he was probably the type of person who slid quietly into a leadership challenge when one presented itself. Where there was a vacuum in leadership, he was not afraid to take on that role; albeit, the role in which he was most comfortable was one of technical leadership.

Table 4-4 Strengths and Needs Report

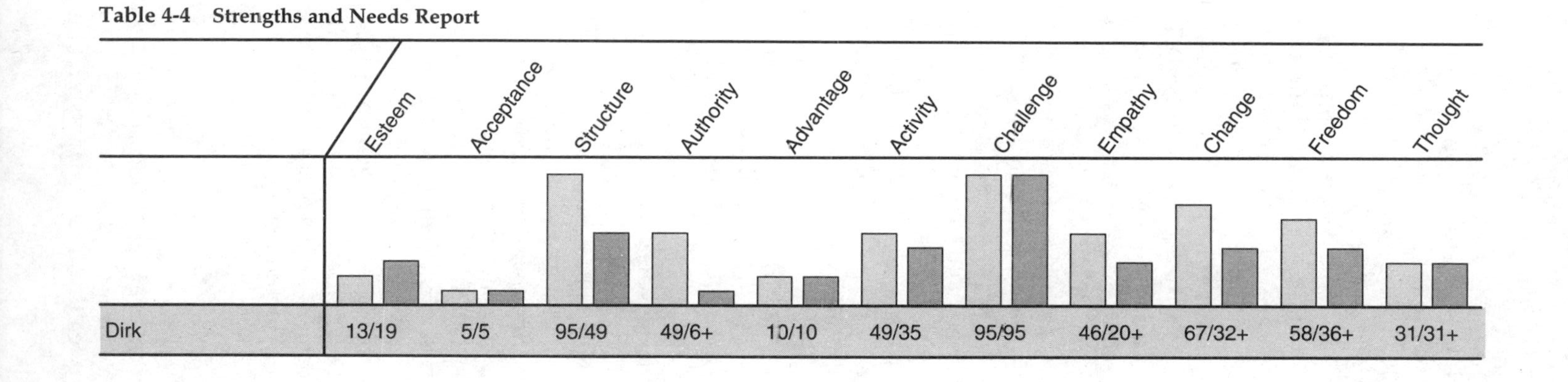

	Esteem	Acceptance	Structure	Authority	Advantage	Activity	Challenge	Empathy	Change	Freedom	Thought
Dirk	13/19	5/5	95/49	49/6+	10/10	49/35	95/95	46/20+	67/32+	58/36+	31/31+

His style of giving direction ("Authority"—average) indicated he was directive but in a slightly suggestive, nonauthoritarian way. This meant that most of the time he would leave people alone to be "self-directive" and that when he needed to, he would be there to direct the operation. For himself, he would flourish in an environment in which he was allowed to be self-directive but in which there were agreeable, pleasant relationships. He would have a tendency to avoid confrontation at all costs, except when he was not allowed to set his own course or when his judgment about a situation was questioned. When that occurred, we could expect to see a very different side of Dirk. Under stress (most likely when people were telling him what to do), he was likely to argue, become domineering, and exercise strong and direct authority.

Dirk's profile reflected an exceedingly strong achievement motivation. In fact, he was no doubt an "overachiever"—his performance records had proved that. His scores, however, indicated he did best when he had encouragement from others who could cheer him on. He needed lots of feedback to tell him how he was doing. We factored that in with the previous indication that he liked to work alone and was not easily prone to seek out others. On the one hand, this meant he probably wouldn't be stressed by "loneliness at the top," but we questioned how he might get his need for encouragement met if he tended to avoid being with people. We wondered if he could enjoy the role the board expected of the CEO, and if he did not, how long he would be able to sustain his drive to achieve.

Finally, we delved into Dirk's orientation to competition. It appeared Dirk mainly liked competing against himself (high "Challenge"). Other indicators ("Advantage," "Activity," "Empathy") showed he was more interested in opportunities to help other people than to compete against them. His motivation to negotiate or sell appeared negligible. All indications showed he would prefer a more thoughtful environment to one that was fast-paced, and he would not be prone to take an aggressive stance on issues. We further saw that his low "Advantage" scores, coupled with a low need for freedom (independence), meant he would probably shy away from taking risks. Additionally, his need for a steady income and for stability seemed stronger than any need he might have for influence.

As we checked off our leadership criteria, we saw that his strongest motivations were to achieve, but to get his "best achievement behavior" he needed the support of a low-key, noncompetitive, reflective, and stable environment where he could work alone and be his own boss. At this point, we didn't feel we had a match with either what the board wanted or what the competition demanded.

Interests

We were now ready to move the analysis of Dirk's profile to Step 3 (Table 4-5). Would he want the CEO job for which he was targeted? We know from research done on interests, that people are most likely to enjoy and succeed in areas in which they have a strong interest. Thus, we started with the number one need in Healthy Life—persuasive interest. We discovered

Table 4-5 Interests

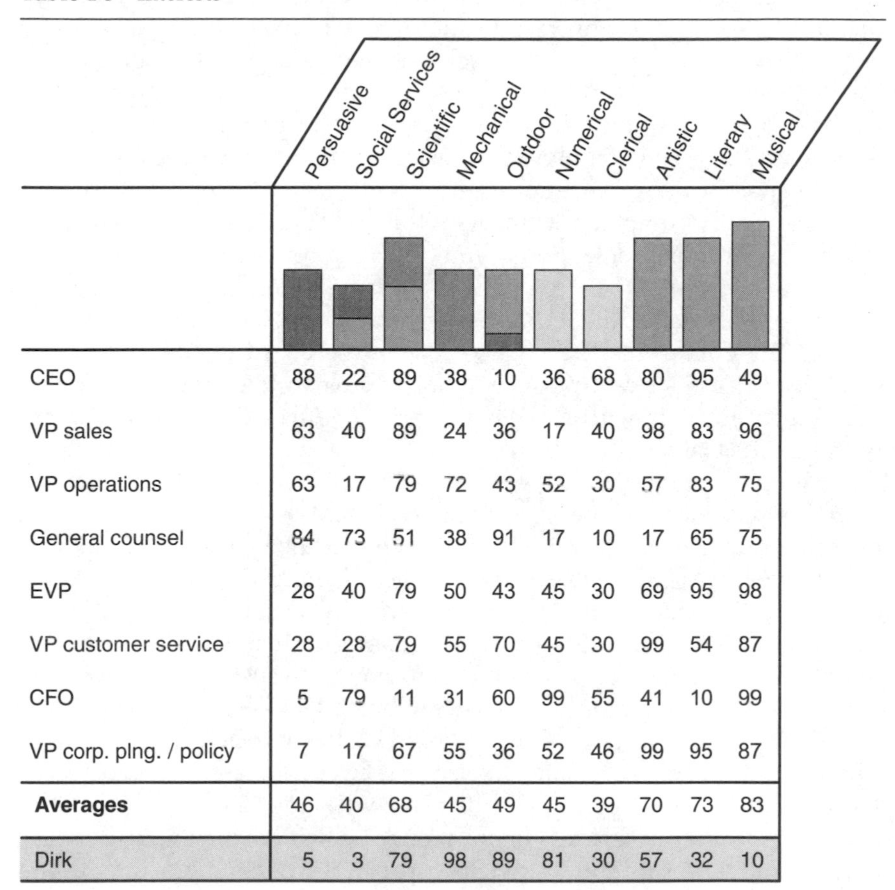

	Persuasive	Social Services	Scientific	Mechanical	Outdoor	Numerical	Clerical	Artistic	Literary	Musical
CEO	88	22	89	38	10	36	68	80	95	49
VP sales	63	40	89	24	36	17	40	98	83	96
VP operations	63	17	79	72	43	52	30	57	83	75
General counsel	84	73	51	38	91	17	10	17	65	75
EVP	28	40	79	50	43	45	30	69	95	98
VP customer service	28	28	79	55	70	45	30	99	54	87
CFO	5	79	11	31	60	99	55	41	10	99
VP corp. plng. / policy	7	17	67	55	36	52	46	99	95	87
Averages	46	40	68	45	49	45	39	70	73	83
Dirk	5	3	79	98	89	81	30	57	32	10

that only the current CEO and the general counsel had above-average persuasive interests. Dirk's score on a scale of 1–99 was a 5—way below the cutoff that could signal interest in the arena of selling ideas, concepts, or products. While only the general counsel and the CFO had above-average interests in relating to public issues or getting personally involved in being a champion for a cause, Dirk's score was 3. A low score like a 3 is not at all a strong indicator that he'd personally put himself into promoting.

Those interests that were above average in Dirk's profile clustered around scientific, mechanical, outdoor, and numerical activities. This told us he was probably drawn to technical, task-oriented, operational endeavors. All his scores in areas that signal strength in "relational" activities were below average, indicating it would be a stretch for Dirk to put himself in environments that required fortitude for socializing and influencing. Coincidentally, none of the other officers on Healthy Life's senior team appeared to have the complete mix of interest ingredients that would compel them to seek out opportunities to persuade or convince others.

We felt at this point we had enough information to make a recommendation on whether this target candidate, Dirk, was the right choice to become Healthy Life's next CEO. We packaged Steps 1 to 3 of our shortcut assessment together with Dirk's personnel history and interviews with peers, subordinates, and his board members, and presented our findings to Healthy Life's CEO and board. This information confirmed the board's hunch—what the organization would have in Dirk appeared to be a technically very competent manager, quite well suited for an operational leadership job. His profile did not indicate a strong underlying motivation or natural talent to lead the company in the increasingly competitive service arena. For that matter, other than the general counsel, no other member of the acquiring management team had what the board wanted in its next CEO. (*Note*: The general counsel was not a viable candidate because family issues prevented him from taking on the social obligations that went with the CEO job.)

We spent quite a lot of time with Dirk, reviewing his talents and motivations. In the end, he decided he really had never felt comfortable in his role as CEO of the acquired company when he was pushed into that job two years earlier. He was put there because he had done a great job in operations. It seemed to him that he was wearing a suit that did not fit him well. In addition, he really didn't like having to manage all the diverse issues that came up—from personnel, to finance, to customer relations. He wanted to have fun in his job, and so far, being CEO wasn't fun for him.

We explored what his dream job would be. It was to head the operations of a smaller and more technical, scientific, engineering-related company. We put him in touch with a headhunter who specialized in the petrochemical industry and in less than a month he had his dream job in a firm that was noted for its ability to deliver projects to customers. In addition to a good hiring package, the company was in a location that pleased both him and his family.

The board began a search for the current CEO's replacement, and after about six months the ideal candidate emerged. Her career experience was in banking, but she had all the relationship and leadership skills Healthy Life needed. She began working with the outgoing CEO and took over the reins of the company a year later. The integration of the two companies went smoothly in almost every respect, and the transition to new leadership was almost seamless. We had followed most of the five steps in our process and learned an important lesson or two. First, we learned to look beneath the top manager's desires for a certain individual to become his or her successor. There had to be some strong reason that Healthy Life's CEO wanted to put forth a candidate who from the earliest appeared to have neither the right mix of talent nor the necessary motivation for the challenge. Next, we learned that it pays to ask the candidate in question what he or she really wants out of his or her career—because it just might be something other than what top management had in mind!

The Case of Two Banks

This next example is one of a real clash of social and cultural styles. Here we focus on Step 4 of our talent-fit method by comparing the differences between an upstart entreprenuerial youngster and the refined stability of the granddaddy of regional banks.

In this merger of two banks (the names have been modified), we find an upstart acquiring an inveterate and respected institution. New Summit Bank was a young, 10-year-old bank with both progressive and aggressive vision and leadership. It was situated in a region of growing and dominant technology development. To better serve the younger affluent customer base coming into the area, the bank needed more branches. It chose as its acquisition partner, Golden Shores National Bank, a stable, historic, and conventional community bank with roots in the region for over 90 years. A prime consideration was that Golden Shores had more than 50 branches within the commuting radius of the technology corridor.

The corporate profiles of the two banks were very different (Tables 4-6 and 4-7). New Summit had real strength in strategizing for the future and creating a variety of products that appealed to younger, more technologically and consumption-oriented clients. It used the latest in technology and was noted for its internal focus on results. It was generally an efficient, friendly, fun place to work, where staff was on a first-name basis.

Golden Shores had an established and aging clientele. People banked there because their grandparents and parents had accounts with the bank. Its officers were leaders in traditional community organizations such as the Rotary Club and Chamber of Commerce. Its hallmark was the "upper-crust" polish it exuded along with the formal courtesy it extended to its customers. The offices were opulent and colonial in style. Products were geared to individuals who physically visited the bank. The bank's reputation was for meticulous accounting and personalized customer service.

When we looked at the talent spreadsheet of each bank in the context of the four major talent requirements (planning, communicating, expediting, and administrating), we saw that New Summit had almost equal strength in the first three requirements of planning, communicating, and expediting; the fourth, administrating, was below average. Conversely, Golden Shores came up very strong in administrating, made an average showing in communicating and expediting, and fell below average in planning talent. The intention of the merger was to expand the reach of New Summit through the network of Golden Shores' branches while emphasizing new products and new, more efficient, technology-linked banking services.

In essence, the deal was for "real estate." While due diligence had confirmed there would be a clash between the "visionary, sales, and delivery" leadership talent of New Summit and the "control mindset" of Golden Shores, New Summit's CEO did not want a backlash from Golden

Table 4-6 New Summit Bank—Talent Spreadsheet / Organizational Strengths

	Planning	Communicating	Expediting	Administrating	Knowledge Specialist	Directive Management	Delegative Management	Artistic Careers	Educational Careers	Social Service / Counseling	Employee Relations / Training	Medical Professions
Averages	**7**	**7**	**6**	**4**	**7**	**4**	**4**	**7**	**6**	**7**	**7**	**8**
CEO	8	8	7	5	7	5	4	8	8	9	9	9
EVP bus. development	8	9	3	2	8	2	7	9	2	4	9	9
VP commercial sales	9	8	4	6	9	3	5	9	9	9	9	9
VP lending	9	6	8	5	10	2	1	10	9	10	9	10
VP operations and CIO	5	4	9	3	6	7	2	6	3	5	4	7
VP customer service	8	8	6	2	10	2	2	8	8	8	8	9
CFO	1	3	6	7	1	10	8	1	1	1	1	1
General counsel	6	6	5	5	7	2	6	5	5	6	6	6

	Direct Tangible Sales	Direct Intangible Sales	Consultative Tangible Sales	Consultative Intangible Sales	Legal	Crafts / Technical	Police, Fire, and Security	Petrochemical	Engineering / Technology	Science	General Administrative	Numerical Administrative	Administrative Professionals	Banking and Finance	Accounting
Averages	**6**	**6**	**7**	**7**	**5**	**5**	**5**	**5**	**6**	**7**	**6**	**5**	**7**	**5**	**4**
CEO	8	8	9	9	7	7	8	7	7	8	6	5	6	5	4
EVP bus. development	8	7	9	9	6	4	2	4	5	7	5	2	5	5	2
VP commercial sales	8	8	8	9	7	4	4	4	4	5	8	7	5	6	3
VP lending	6	6	5	7	5	5	6	5	7	8	7	5	9	3	2
VP operations and CIO	4	3	5	3	5	9	9	9	8	9	4	4	3	1	1
VP customer service	6	6	5	7	3	4	3	4	5	6	9	9	10	8	6
CFO	3	2	5	2	3	6	6	7	7	6	2	4	10	7	10
General counsel	6	5	6	7	7	2	3	2	3	4	5	2	6	6	7

Table 4-7 Golden Shores National Bank—Talent Spreadsheet / Organizational Strengths

	Planning	Communicating	Expediting	Administrating	Knowledge Specialist	Directive Management	Delegative Management	Artistic Careers	Educational Careers	Social Service / Counseling	Employee Relations / Training	Medical Professions	Direct Tangible Sales	Direct Intangible Sales	Consultative Tangible Sales	Consultative Intangible Sales	Legal	Crafts / Technical	Police, Fire, and Security	Petrochemical	Engineering / Technology	Science	General Administrative	Numerical Administrative	Administrative Professionals	Banking and Finance	Accounting
Averages	**4**	**5**	**5**	**7**	**5**	**6**	**6**	**4**	**5**	**5**	**5**	**4**	**6**	**5**	**5**	**5**	**6**	**4**	**5**	**5**	**4**	**4**	**5**	**6**	**6**	**7**	**6**
CHM &CEO	4	8	3	5	2	7	10	4	3	5	7	2	9	9	8	7	7	3	4	3	5	2	1	4	4	8	7
President	3	6	6	6	3	9	5	1	2	4	5	1	9	6	7	5	4	5	7	5	6	5	1	1	3	4	5
VP operations	1	3	6	8	2	9	7	1	1	1	2	1	5	3	3	1	2	5	6	6	7	6	2	4	2	8	9
VP lending	7	8	4	7	5	5	10	5	8	8	9	7	9	9	9	8	7	4	6	3	3	2	5	6	8	8	7
VP customer service	7	3	4	7	10	4	1	7	8	7	6	7	2	1	1	3	9	5	2	4	3	4	10	9	10	5	2
VP fin./admin.	3	4	6	8	8	6	3	3	3	2	3	5	4	5	5	3	1	6	6	7	5	6	8	9	8	6	7
General counsel	6	6	3	9	7	1	5	7	7	6	6	6	6	5	3	6	10	3	2	4	2	2	10	10	9	9	8

Shores' established community customer base. His fear was that he would be known as the punk upstart who conquered the revered uncle, and publicity could hurt for awhile. He had to find a way to work through the differences in style. Our process provided him with a neutral tool to demonstrate to both the chairman and the president of Golden Shores that their senior-most leadership would not be comfortable with the aggressive approach embraced by New Summit's leadership. His goal was for them to see that the combined organization could benefit from the talent strength of both. At a glance they could see the talent "gap" in administration and New Summit and this "missing element" very much in evidence in Golden Shores' talent spreadsheet. Literally, all it took was a look at the comparative talent spreadsheets of these two organizations.

Although Golden Shores had the talent that New Summit lacked, the tenure of the officers overseeing administration, legal, and customer service was nearing its end, with each of these three officers 6 to 36 months away from retirement. The talent was there, but soon these three officers would be gone. This was enough for the leaders of Golden Shores to follow New Summit's logic. The numbers spoke the reality. New Summit's CEO felt that if each of these officers had hired in their own image, he would find similar "control strengths" in their direct reports. He also hoped these strengths would be combined with youth, with vision, and with a sense of urgency.

Together the two CEOs searched down the ranks of *Golden Shores* for individuals in administration and in customer service who were motivated by both competition and personal accountability and who could be expected to adapt most easily to the dominant leadership style of the new company. Though not so obvious at first glance, they found their new leaders—one and two layers, respectively, beneath the existing rank of top officers. It would take some straight talk to convince the staff being leapfrogged that their subordinates had what the new company needed and that these appointments were in the best interests of the entire company.

Next, given the ages and the motivational interests of the other three top Golden Shores officers, it was clear that they lacked, for the most part, the traits that favored adaptation to the aggressive atmosphere of the new company's senior management team. The decision among the leaders of both banks was (1) to create severance packages for the existing Golden Shores leadership team and (2) to immediately put the two newly identified Golden Shores leaders (administration and customer service) to work on the new company's integration teams. The chairman and CEO of Golden Shores decided to depart completely from the banking industry, while his president retired and accepted a seat on the new company's board.

With the addition of Golden Shores' talent to the new company's customer service organization, an immediate campaign was launched to reach out to Golden Shores' existing base of customers to:

- Explain the exciting new products available to them
- Assure them they would not become a number in a faceless computer

- Assure them that the same personalized service they had enjoyed at Golden Shores would become a trademark of the new company

The administrative talent tapped from Golden Shores took over, as the new VP of finance and administration replaced New Summit's VP, who was somewhat short on both vision and communication skills. Though not easy from an ego standpoint, this integration was completed more efficiently and smoothly than most of its kind. While information from our process was certainly not the only data used in the assessment decisions, it made the job much less contentious than other situations where mostly subjective or outdated performance information was used.

The key lesson learned in this case is that the integration effort can be facilitated by quickly assessing and choosing key people. The trick is to move and communicate quickly. That means explaining why certain people have been tapped for leadership roles and why certain systems and processes are being jettisoned or adopted. So long as both the "incoming" and "acquiring" staff understand the reasons behind the moves, there is a much better chance they'll accept changes in leadership, get on board, and work to integrate and be integrated into the newly created environment.

Speed cannot be overemphasized. The faster people are put in place and systems are changed, the better. The merger that decides not to put pressure on the "acquired team," and basically lets things sit to work themselves out, is the one that ultimately fails. This one went very fast—due to the entrepreneurial, action-oriented style of New Summit's CEO and the diplomatic style of Golden Shores' chairman and CEO.

Impact of the Organizational Life Cycle on Talent Needed

This last merger vignette is one in which two extremely large companies merged in order to stay alive in the face of recently merged competition. From a short-term financial perspective, the merger made sense. What was difficult to see, from our perspective, was that by coming together, they really didn't create anything new.

There didn't seem to be that important "value added" that would steal the competitive advantage from this new company's closest challengers. In the long term, we thought the financial gains would be eroded by competitors with newer and more efficient products and services. In this case, we entered with an analysis of where each organization was in its own life cycle so the organizations could see what they might be facing down the road.

Where a company is in its organizational life cycle (Figure 4-3) gives one a sense of what kinds of talents are needed at a particular time in history. When an organization is new and young, it needs structure and stability. When it is old and somewhat immovable, it needs to reinvent itself with new ideas, new flexibility, and new approaches to the marketplace.

The life cycle can be linked to the talent spreadsheets, like the ones we looked at in the cases of the insurance company, Healthy Life, and the two

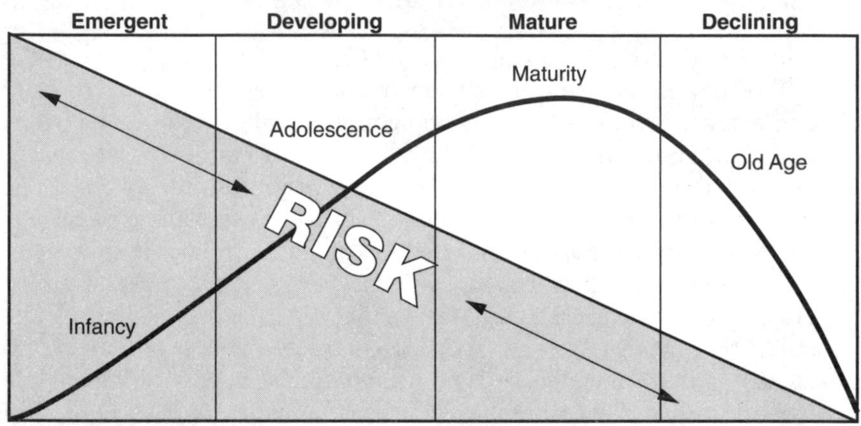

Figure 4-3 Life-Cycle Stages

banks, New Summit and Golden Shores. The typical life cycle for any organization looks like a bell curve. It begins as a start-up (or an emergent organization), and then moves into growth (or a developing organization), followed by maturity, and finally into decline.

At each of these stages, certain driving talents are required. During the emergence or infancy of an organization, the key talent required is innovation and strategic vision. Recalling from our talent spreadsheet that innovation and strategic vision are characterized by "planning," we call this start-up or infancy the "planning" phase of an organization's life cycle. It is here where ideas abound about products and markets.

As the company develops, it needs the talent to persuade its markets and promote its product. This can be referred to as its "marketing and sales" phase. It is where marketing and sales grow both in depth and in breadth. In maturity, the talent need is for implementation, delivery, and focused direction. Here, an organization establishes stronger production methods and processes, and it focuses on delivery targets. At this point, an organization is centered in its "operating phase."

As it heads into the declining or aging years, a company's talent is focused primarily on details and systems—keeping business going as usual. This is the "controlling" period of organizational life. Most organizations like to think they possess the requisite talent at each phase in their development. The fact of the matter is that if you look closely and scrutinize where the money is being allocated and where senior management targets most of its attention, there really is a predominant focus in each stage.

Take the case of a 100-year-old power company. Known for a century as a leader in power generation, renamed here as International Power and Energy Company (IPEC), it honed its skills to perfection in production and delivery. As the world changed, the company maintained its R&D by doing cutting-edge research on alternative sources of energy. But this futuristic preoccupation was just one pocket in a huge, lumbering organization where the top leadership continued to focus its talent on what it had always done best—build power-generating plants, produce, and deliver. It was squarely in the maturity stage of the organizational life cycle. Along came the Internet and deregulation, and companies that had been considered upstarts began to offer products and services that cut into the margins of the traditional power suppliers.

Although successful in acquiring other regional companies that enabled it to expand its reach (doing what it had done so well), IPEC was stymied by the mergers of other similar organizations. Eventually it was acquired by a well-established, but younger, power company that needed IPEC's international presence. A talent spreadsheet of the acquiring company (Midlands Power Company) shows that its predominant talents lie in vision and in sales. In essence it appears to be nearing the end of its "adolescence" as the "expediting" bar inches up in scale to the "planning" and "communicating" bars. Figures 4-4 and 4-5 present the talent spreadsheets of Midlands and IPEC and of the merged companies, respectively. The merged company spreadsheet shows the resultant mix of talents reminiscent of IPEC's original configuration.

Combined, the company brings nearly twice as much strength in expediting as it does in planning and communicating. Administration is the weakest of all the talent areas. Could this mean more of the same? By combining a mature organization with an aging adolescent, have we created a near carbon copy of what IPEC was at the time of its acquisition? Our concern is whether it has enough of a futuristic focus to enable the combined company to beat the creative competition in the long haul.

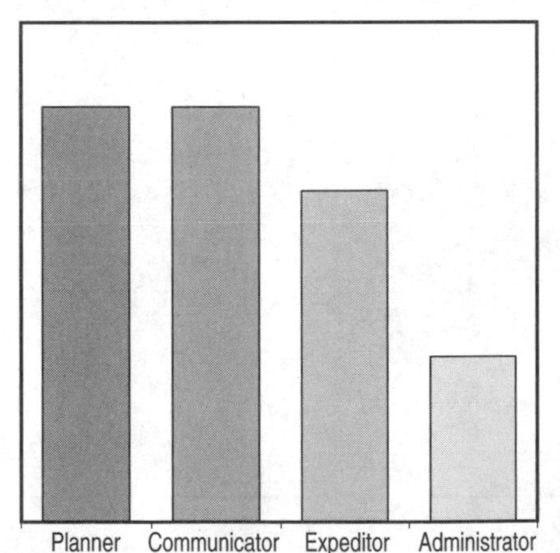

Talent Spreadsheet - Acquired Company
(International Power and Energy Co.)

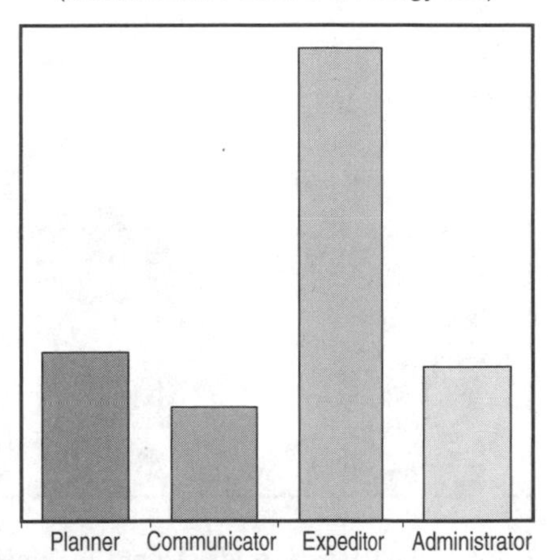

Figure 4-4 Talent Spreadsheet of Acquiring and Acquired Companies

To compete with the upstarts, who have brought changes to the way energy is marketed, this newly combined energy conglomerate will have to dare to bring in people who don't fit the mold of their predominantly operational leadership. We have shown them through the talent spreadsheets and historical precedents that they must step up to the challenge and bring in those who are far more visionary in outlook and ability. For the new company it means having the courage to take risks and not stick to what was done well in the past. If the planning and communicating strengths of the combined organization were on a par with its expeditor strengths, we would feel much more confident about the new company's ability to bring added value to the marketplace. Without this value added to galvanize the spirit and drive of the new organization, other possibilities could occur.

One scenario has to do with whether the more freewheeling adolescent acquiring company has what it takes to withstand the conventions and precedents adhered to by the IPEC contingent. Using the life-cycle diagram, the talent spreadsheets, the "Career Predictors," and the components, we were able to explore the opportunities and the pitfalls in selection and help the acquiring company make more appropriate choices in its key people. Our role in due diligence was to provide the merging organizations all the insights we could bring about what they have, what they lack, what the talents, skills, competencies, and style of the key players are, and how they may expect them to interact in productive times and in stress.

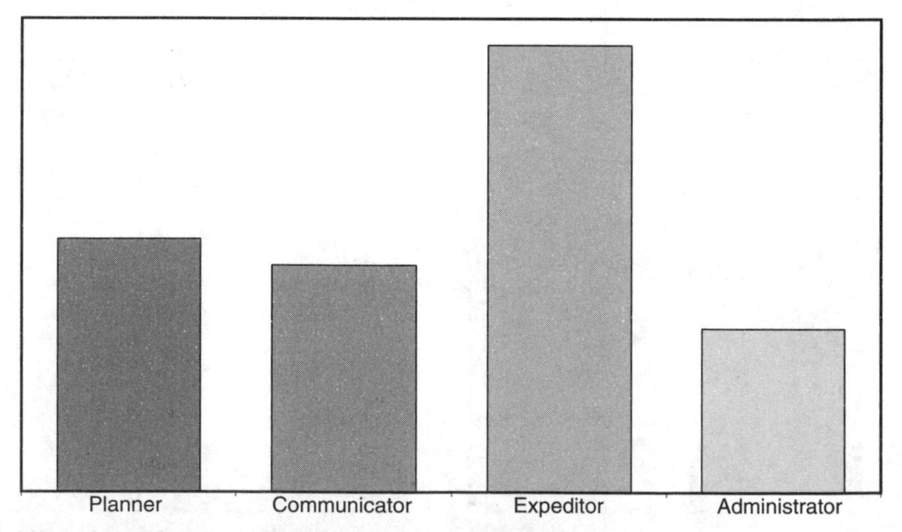

Figure 4-5 Talent Spreadsheet of Combined Companies

A FINAL NOTE

I have attempted to illustrate in this chapter and Chapter 3 several important elements of the integration process that need to be considered during the transaction stage and their potential impact on the success of the integration process and the accomplishment of strategic and financial objectives. Inability to manage these elements during this stage should not deter the acquiring and merging companies from doing it at later stages of the integration process. The earlier the better, but better late than never!

5

Preparing Stakeholder Communications and Value Preservation

Communicate, communicate, communicate! Almost every experienced executive who has managed integration and every expert who writes on the topic agree that you cannot communicate enough during this process. Most people, whether it is employees, customers, distributors, or investors, do not like uncertainty, especially if it is prolonged and involves issues that are likely to have a direct bearing on them.

It is a basic premise that most people have a need to make sense out of the world they live in so that they can adjust, plan, and take action. However, the process of making sense requires information and people who are resourceful and creative and will do what it takes to "figure things out." This will happen whether executives keep people informed of what is going on or not. In the absence of formal communications, people will turn to the rumor mill and other sources of less accurate information. They will also fill in additional details based on inferences and assumptions drawn from their previous experiences, from information publicized in the media, and from the experiences of others. People will also use their imaginations. The problem here is that all these sources are outside the control of executives and contain both accurate and inaccurate information.

The implications are clear. Failure to manage the communication process creates an uncontrolled and random process of making sense inside and outside the organization, which can lead to ideas and actions that are detrimental to both people and the merger integration itself. These include inaccurate perceptions, lost trust in management, morale and productivity problems, safety problems, poor customer service, and defection of key people and customers. It may also lead to the loss of the support of key stakeholders at a time when that support is needed the most.

However, regardless of how well executives communicate during a merger or an acquisition, uncertainty will never be completely eliminated. The objective is to minimize as much uncertainty as possible, especially with regard to issues that directly impact people and organizations.

The decision about when to begin the communication process is not an easy one to make. It requires a balance between the need for secrecy (e.g., to respect the target management's desires to keep the deal quiet, to prevent other buyers from entering the bidding process, or to fulfill legal or regulatory requirements) and the activity of the rumor mill. As such, it makes the most sense to consider communicating early (e.g., when discussions with a target have commenced) rather than later (e.g., with a formal announcement of the deal). The key, however, is to try and beat the timing of the rumor mill whenever possible. The impact of late communications and uncertainty was clearly felt in the acquisition of Digital Equipment by Compaq Computer. Compaq's senior management waited until after the acquisition closed before communicating with people. Tired of the uncertainty, a number of Digital vice presidents resigned from Compaq within a year after the merger and days before their severance agreement expired. On the other hand, companies such as Computer Associates and Cisco make communications with targets a high priority. They utilize rapid action teams that visit acquired employees within days to brief them on merger and acquisition plans.[1]

Acquiring executives should make communication a key discussion point with the target or a merger partner during the drafting of a letter of intent or memorandum of agreement. Although an acquirer does not have control over a target, the acquirer should strongly encourage the target management to initiate a communication process within its own firm. Again, this may affect the state of the target when the acquirer gains control. It also sends a signal about the acquirer's values and culture.

When dealing with a unionized work force, a partnership with the union should be attempted. If the union is cooperative, it may be worthwhile to use the union to help communicate with employees. Failure to include the union may lead to the creation of an enemy when one did not exist before. If the union is hostile, then the acquirer management may have to bypass it and wage a public relations battle.

In general, there is one major recommendation most successful acquirers give: Overcommunicate and overinform! The next section describes some basic, sensible steps to take to achieve effective communication.

KEYS TO EFFECTIVE COMMUNICATION

Consider these eight key elements when establishing a communication process:

1. Establish a communication philosophy.
2. Be timely and relevant.
3. "Walk the talk."
4. Be careful of secret meetings.
5. Understand what people want to hear.
6. Choose effective communication media.
7. Identify and communicate with all key stakeholders.
8. Develop and execute a communication plan.

Establish a Communication Philosophy

Before developing a communication plan, it is useful to determine the basic philosophy underlying it. The philosophy represents the core values driving the plan and guides managers in executing it. The acquiring and acquired companies need to begin this process by examining any core values they have articulated to run their own organization and any guiding principles they established to drive the integration (see Chapter 6) so that they can ensure that the communication process is consistent with them. However, regardless of the company's core values, several elements are essential to the success of any communication process.

Honesty Is the Best Policy

Honesty may sound a bit naïve when we consider the political gyrations that take place within and among organizations. However, not only is it morally the right thing to do, but it actually works! Why is this the case? There is a simple truism that applies to the communication process: "The truth happens whether it came from your mouth or not."

If the objective of an executive is to manipulate employees and other stakeholders in the short run, dishonesty is likely to work. Reassuring people that everything is fine and that "no one is likely to lose their job due to the merger" or "nothing will change as a result of the integration" may seem calming and perhaps comfort people in the short run. This assumes that they will believe these statements. However, the minute there is a loss of jobs or things do change, which is inevitable, people will clearly remember the reassuring statement that was made and assume that management deceived them. If all people are let go, such as in a plant shutdown, then we might not have to worry about the implications. No one will be left. Perhaps there will be some lawsuits and complaints. However, if there are people who remain, the situation becomes far more complicated. This is even more critical if the primary assets of the company are intangible and invested in people. Certainly customers, investors, and shareholders will also remember if they were misled.

For example, I was involved in the sale of a company in California. The purchase price being asked was far in excess of the value of the tangible assets reported on the balance sheet. The company, which made fans to cool chips in personal computers, owned very little property and equipment. The only real tangible assets were tied up in inventory and receivables, and they were not a significant part of the asking price. So what explained the value of this company? Most of the value was inherent in top-notch design engineers and relationships with customers and distributors. If these intangibles "walked out the door" or were significantly demotivated, the company would be worth very little. Knowing this led us to conclude that communications would be a key part of employee, customer, and distributor retention and of value preservation. It worked. The company had no defections. The stakeholders appreciated the company's diligence in keeping them informed during the deal.

A colleague and I tried to empirically determine whether honest communication really makes a difference to employees.[2] We conducted a study in two similar light manufacturing plants of a division of a *Fortune* 500 company preparing to be merged. The study was conducted prior to the merger. In one plant 126 employees were provided with an enriched "merger preview." The preview focused on giving employees frequent, relevant, and honest information about the merger through detailed newsletters, telephone hotlines, weekly meetings between employees and supervisors who were continually briefed by senior management, and meetings between individual employees and the plant manager whenever personal decisions had been made. Information communicated included background on the merger and information on layoffs and severance benefits, transfers, compensation and benefits, and integration plans for the combined firm. In the other plant there were no formal communications provided to the 146 employees other than an initial letter from the CEO explaining the rationale for the merger. This type of communication had been typical in the company.

We were interested in determining whether the communications had an impact on a variety of outcome measures related to the retention and well-being of the firm's intellectual capital. These outcomes included stress; perceived uncertainty; job satisfaction; organizational commitment; company's trustworthiness, honesty, and caring; intention to remain within the organization; and employee performance, absenteeism, and turnover. As shown in Figure 5-1, we collected data both before and after the merger announcement and before and after the merger preview was implemented. After the announcement of the merger there was a significant increase in stress, perceived uncertainty, and absenteeism. There were significant declines in job satisfaction; organizational commitment; company's trustworthiness, honesty, and caring; and intention to remain

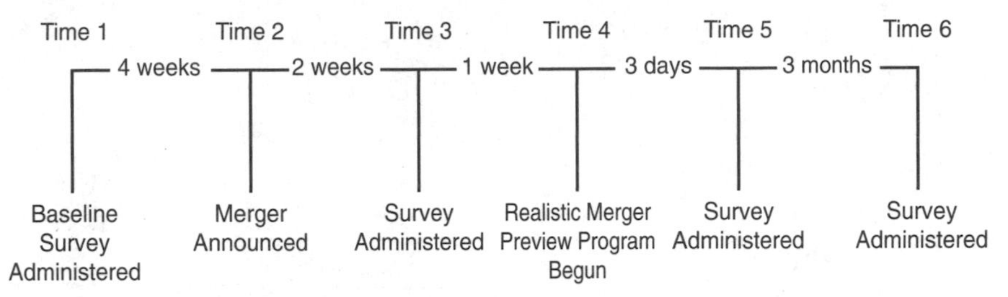

Figure 5-1 Time Line of Major Events

within the organization. Indeed the announcement of the merger did have a significant and negative impact.

The key question now was whether the merger preview would help ameliorate these negative outcomes. There was a significant difference between the plant receiving the merger preview and the one that did not. Specifically, the preview plant reported significantly lower perceived uncertainty, higher job satisfaction and performance, and greater commitment to and trust in the company and management. The merger preview appeared to stabilize the level of dysfunctional outcomes, and this effect continued over time. Figures 5-2 through 5-4 illustrate these effects for several outcomes. Of importance is that none of the merger preview outcomes were as strong in comparison to those prior to the merger, demonstrating the impact that such an event can have. It also suggests that communication cannot eliminate these outcomes—it can only hope to improve them. Indeed, honest and frequent communication does work!

Critical to the success of a merger or an acquisition is the ability to build a new organization. This requires that the best people be retained and motivated. Clearly manipulation does not work in this situation. Whether people remain motivated and stay will depend upon the credibility of those leading them. Often during integration, executives will need to ask people to trust them as the many complicated decisions are being worked out and are not quite ready to be communicated. The credibility quotient of these executives will be measured by the gap between what they say and do and what ultimately happens. The greater the gap, the lower the credibility. The lower the credibility, the less the likelihood they will successfully be able to lead.

As the preceding discussion suggests, executives are often going to have to ask people to trust them and to wait for answers. Thus, going into the integration they must draw upon their relationships with people. The critical issue is whether they are credible prior to the integration.

What does all this mean in practice? While people can always be honest, they cannot always be open; i.e., they cannot always tell others all the details of what is going on. As such, it is best to use the following three approaches in communicating:

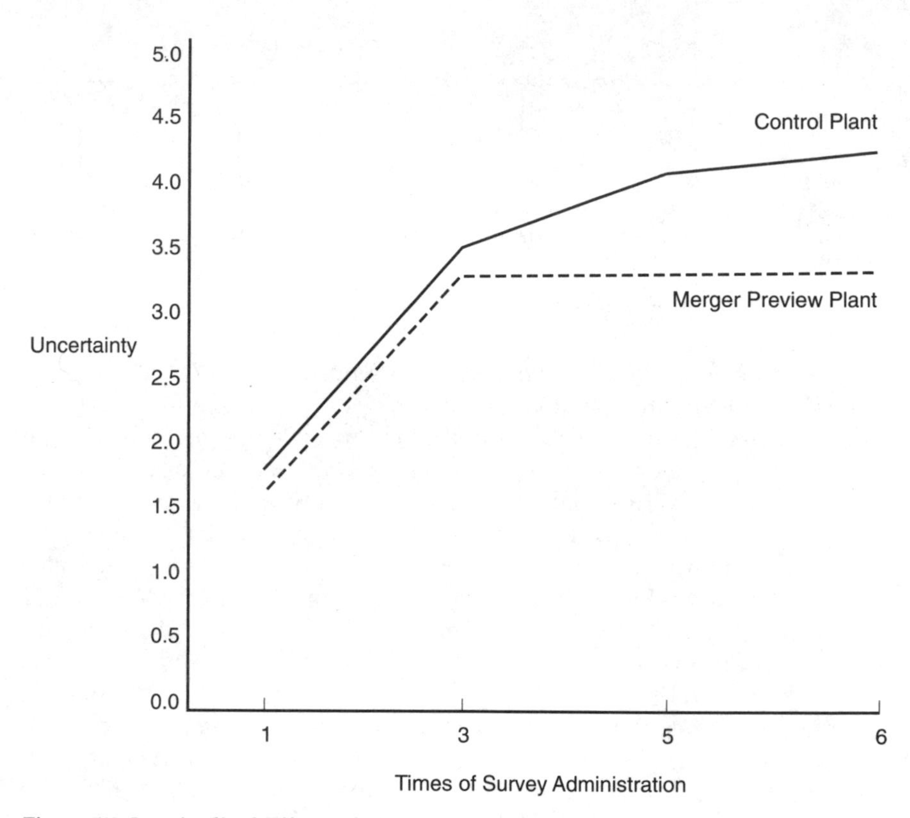

Figure 5-2 Longitudinal Effects of Merger and Realistic Merger Preview on Uncertainty

1. "If I can tell you, I will."
2. "If I do not know the answers, I will try and find them."
3. "If I cannot tell you, I will explain why."

I have found these responses to be quite effective. For example, I was assisting in the sale of one publicly traded company to another. The rumors concerning the buyer were rampant and in fact quite accurate. Moreover, the buyer was a direct competitor whom the employees were not thrilled to work for. Employees of the target kept asking management to confirm the rumors. Since the sale had not been made public, the company's executives could not confirm it. They were bound by SEC insider trading rules and obligated to announce the sale publicly before releasing a widespread communication within the company. To stem the rumor mill, they openly communicated that they could not comment due to SEC rules and explained the rules in simple terms to the employees. Although the employees thought such rules made little sense, they appreciated management's efforts. Soon after, the sale was then made public. As this

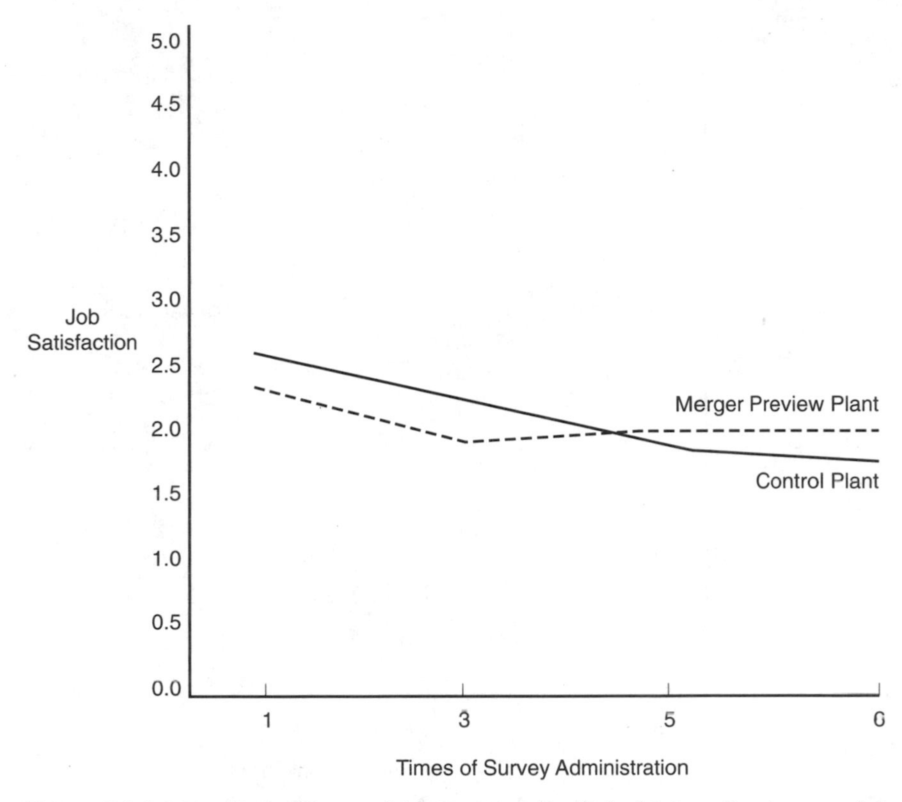

Figure 5-3 Longitudinal Effects of Merger and Realistic Merger Preview on Job Satisfaction

example illustrates, at some point you must be able to give tangible answers. Too many "I don't knows" will lead people to conclude that executives are withholding information or are ineffective. Neither bodes well for their credibility.

Further, executives must avoid giving unrealistic information. If they have either good or bad news, they need to deliver it. The best approach is to be realistic. People are capable of dealing with and responding to all types of news. Sometimes executives like to put a positive spin on communications. Either they are trying to manipulate interpretations of the facts, or they are trying to insulate people from the realities of a negative situation. Both are mistakes. My experience suggests that it is best to give people the facts so that they can have time to deal with them and plan how they will move forward. It is also best to avoid offering speculation instead of solid information. People often interpret speculation as information and will react in what may not, in the long run, be in their best interests or those of the company.

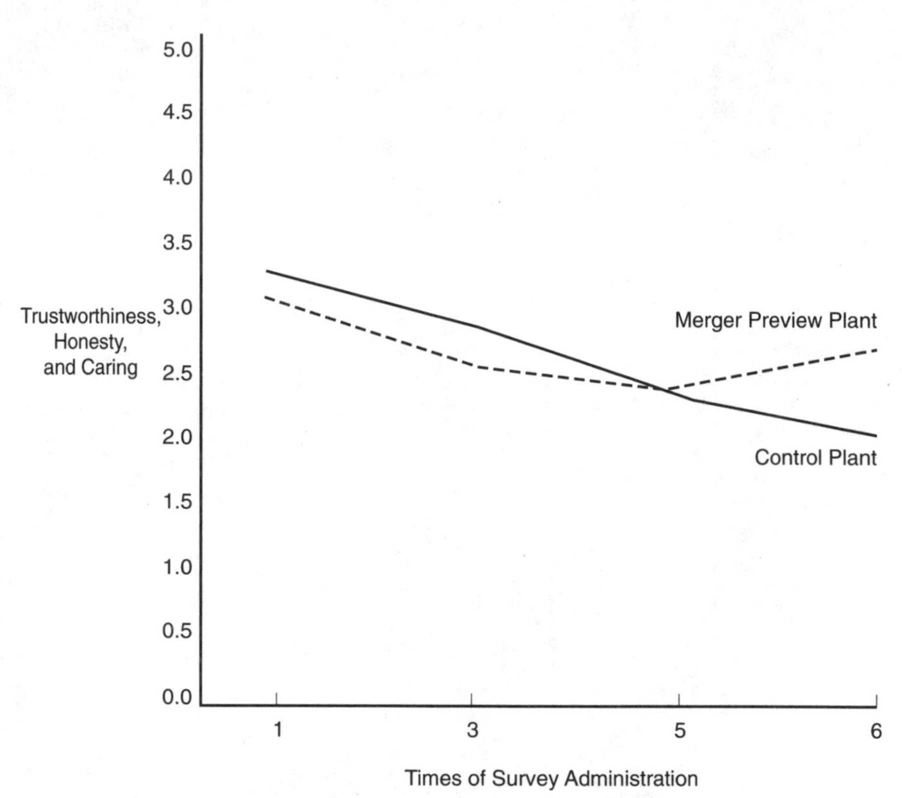

Figure 5-4 Longitudinal Effects of Merger and Realistic Merger Preview on Perceived Trustworthiness, Honesty, and Caring of the Company

Be Timely and Relevant

It is essential to provide information to people about issues that they are concerned with as early as possible, but no later than immediately following the formal announcement of the acquisition. Naturally, most employees want to know about what is happening to their departments and to them. Customers want to know how the deal will affect the service they receive, whether the company will be around, and the like. Until they do know, they will remain restless and maybe even defect.

"Walk the Talk"

Executives must be prepared to back up what they say (the credibility gap). If they make a commitment they cannot keep, they will be measured against it. If they speculate about something that will happen and it does not, they will also be measured against that. Trust and loyalty develop over time when there is consistency in word and action. Behaviors must conform to stated company philosophy, values, and policies.

Be Careful of Secret Meetings

Rarely is a meeting to discuss a delicate issue a secret, and it is prudent to begin such a meeting with that assumption. Secretaries often arrange such meetings, and it is human nature to share information. Employees notice that their manager or multiple managers are gone on a particular day and assume they must be up to something. Even meetings that take place at remote locations and times are difficult to hide. I have talked with numerous salespeople who have encountered executives meeting in secrecy in airport airline clubs. I even encountered an employee who learned about a clandestine meeting held by the executives of his company late one Saturday night. The company was rumored to be up for sale. On his way home from a party, he drove by corporate headquarters. He noticed a number of executives' cars parked in front of the executive office building. By Monday morning the rumors were running rampant and were quite creative.

In general it is safe to assume that someone knows the meeting is taking place. Therefore, it is wise to ensure that at such meetings the last item on the agenda should be communication. Specifically it is important to:

1. Develop a clear message. Avoid ambiguous messages.
2. Ensure that there is consensus among those participating in the meeting. Everyone needs to be "singing from the same sheet of music." I have found that employees from different work units communicate with each other and compare notes, especially through e-mail. If managers and executives deliver different messages or different interpretations of the same message, inconsistency of interpretation within the organization is likely. Not only will this fuel the rumor mill, but it will undermine the credibility of management.
3. Decide whether to communicate proactively or reactively. At a minimum, those attending the meeting should be prepared for "elevator talk"; i.e., what should I say if I am approached by someone? This is a moment of truth when employees will be waiting for an unambiguous, unflinching response. Anything short of that will send a mixed message.

Understand What People Want to Hear

I learned about what is important to people while traveling with a CEO of a merged company. It was just after the closing and we were visiting all the operations of the acquired company. He was in the process of visiting 15 locations in 20 days. He was conducting cafeteria-style meetings to explain the vision behind the new company and to announce organizational changes that had been made. In particular, the top two levels of the combined organization had been named, but many positions below these levels were still in the process of being decided. It was early in the trip, and the

CEO asked me if I would sit among the employees and give him my reaction to his presentation after he was finished. After being introduced to the audience as the consultant assisting with the integration, I took a seat. During the "vision" presentation, an employee on my left nudged me and asked me if I knew whether he had a job or not. I told him I did not know. Then he asked me if I would deliver a message to the CEO. I agreed. He asked me to tell the CEO: "If I have a job, this is the best vision I have ever heard and will support it. If I do not have a job, I could care less." On that day it became clear to me what people are really interested in hearing about. This is not to argue that people are not dedicated to their jobs or care about their companies. It is to illustrate that until the "me" issues are taken care of, it is very difficult for people to embrace a merger.

If the issues that management presents during merger presentations and the issues people want to hear about are examined, you get two very different stories. Table 5-1 provides examples of these two perspectives. Although executives do not always know the answers to "me" questions, it is important to realize that the sooner they answer these questions, the sooner people will be able to move on and start the process of building the new organization.

Choose Effective Communication Media

Once the communication philosophy and the message are established, the media need to be determined. The most effective way to communicate daily with employees is through face-to-face communications with supervisors and managers.[3] The best way to communicate major changes is through *dialogue* with senior managers in town hall–type meetings. This

Table 5-1 What People Want to Hear About

What executives think are important	What employees think are important
• Vision for the merged organization • Strategic benefits of the merger • Reasons for changes and transitions • Changes in the company name • Changes in organizational structure and management • Changes in product lines, etc .	• Will I have a job? • What will the company *and I* gain/lose from it? • How can I be successful in the new envi ronment? • Changes in benefits and compensation • Changes in job and role • Changes in perks • Greater or fewer career opportunities • Provisions for layoffs • Severance benefits • Internal transfers ("voluntary") • Outplacement services • Changes in company systems, policies, etc.

means two-way communications! The same approach often works with key stakeholders. They would like to have a dialogue with key executives and managers concerning changes that will significantly impact them. Other media that can be used to communicate include:

1. Rumor mill. Create employee communications committees within your organization to improve information channels. Such committees should be made up of a cross section of informal leaders.
2. Videotapes, memos, Intranet sites, or e-mail for hard-to-reach groups.
3. Normal company newsletter.
4. Transition/integration newsletter.
5. Bulletin boards.
6. Intranet and Internet sites.
7. Telephone hotlines.
8. Internal publications of press releases.
9. Brochures.
10. Training sessions.
11. Employee assistance program representatives.

It is best to examine the media that employees are most likely to respond to and consider valid sources of information within the acquirer and the target. Rather than guessing what works, it is more useful to assess options directly and use the media that are most likely to have the desired effect. I have conducted several studies with companies to determine the usefulness of their media in the eyes of employees. Particular focus has been given to the availability of information, the believability of information, and the usefulness of information. In addition to the 11 items noted above, I have also examined outside sources such as customers, suppliers, local media, and friends. The results are usually eye-opening and often challenge assumptions that executives have about various media. In one study it was clear that the president of the company was the most useful and believable source of information. In another, the president lacked credibility. However, his executive vice president was highly respected. Whom would you send out to visit with the troops?

It is also important to provide all employees who interact with key stakeholders (e.g., joint-venture partners) with information so that they can effectively respond to questions about the status of the integration. Otherwise employees will be perceived as ineffective and out of the communication loop.

Identify and Communicate with All Key Stakeholders

Although the discussion above has primarily focused on employees, it is important that an acquirer communicate with other key stakeholders as well. Key stakeholders are those that might be affected by integration, or perceive that they will be, and can have a direct bearing on the success of an acquirer, a target, or the integration. Typical stakeholders include:

1. Customers
2. Distributors
3. Financial analysts and consultants
4. Trade and business press
5. Government agencies
6. Communities in company locations
7. Shareholders
8. Unions
9. Joint-venture and alliance partners

This list of stakeholders may grow or shrink, depending upon the companies and situation involved. In general, much like employees, these stakeholders will be concerned with how a merger or an acquisition will affect them or the groups and individuals they represent. For example, a union has the capability of striking or restricting organizational changes that can be undertaken. For a military contractor, the Department of Defense can have a significant impact on new contracts and the preservation of existing ones. In an international context a government may have a significant impact on changes created by the merger of two oil companies. Financial analysts' assessments of the status of integration can also have an impact on an acquirer's stock price. And the list goes on!

Develop and Execute a Communication Plan

Regardless of the stakeholders, an organized communication plan is essential. It ensures that the right communications are provided to the right stakeholders at the right time.

Table 5-2 illustrates the basic elements required in any sound communication plan. The plan must identify:

1. The objective behind the communication
2. The message to be communicated
3. The target audience (stakeholder) of the message
4. The most effective media (including people) to employ in influencing the stakeholder
5. The timing of the communication

Table 5-3 illustrates a more detailed employee communication plan that was used by an acquirer in the process of making multiple acquisitions. The plan was designed for employees and managers of acquired companies, during the transaction, transition, and integration stages:

Table 5-2 Basic Communication Plan

Who says	What To	Whom Using Which	Media Pursuing Which	Objective	When

- To help them understand:
  - Why their company was bought
  - How it would be integrated with the acquirer
  - Changes that were being made and implemented
  - How changes would affect them
- So that they would:
  - Remain with the company
  - Support the changes
  - Maintain levels of performance
- Using "believable" media that allowed people to:
  - Get information when they needed it
  - Engage in two-way communications
  - Resolve issues in a timely manner

Although the format of the plan presented in Table 5-2 is somewhat different, it still addresses the elements presented in Table 5-3. A more detailed stakeholder communication plan that was developed for a large acquisition is presented in Appendix 5-1.

Ensure Coordination and Consistency

The management and coordination of communications is as important as the plan itself. All communications must be coordinated to ensure consistency among media and over time. When inconsistent information is delivered across multiple media or over time, it sends a message to employees and stakeholders that the executives of the companies involved in the merger or acquisition either are totally disorganized or are manipulating them. Neither is useful.

Single-point coordination and communication guidelines can help avert inconsistency. I have found that a communication integration team

Table 5-3 Employee Communication Plan

Stage	Communication Messages	Media
Transition Stage (Following the Formal Announcement of the Acquisition	• History of the acquirer • Vision for business unit • Why target was chosen and strategy of combined organization • Need to focus on customers and day-to-day operations • Process that will be used to integrate the acquisition • Need for intercultural cooperation • Key decisions that have been or will be made	• Initial visit to target by the acquirer's business unit executives with possible support of target firm's president • Immediate follow-up through written or electronic media
Transition and Integration Stages	• Status of integration process • Changes being made and impact on strategic objectives • Impact of changes on people and how they will be managed • Integration successes achieved during the communicaton period • Orientation to the acquirer for newly acquired people	• Major changes announced by the acquirer's business unit executives during site visits or videos • Follow-up through written or electronic media • More routine changes through written or electronic media • Personal impacts and changes through face-to-face communications with direct managers

can be of great help. This team, working with other teams as part of the integration process, becomes the central clearinghouse for messages to release to employees and other stakeholders. The ultimate responsibility, however, for what messages are communicated lies with the leaders of the integration process. The team advises on messages, media, and timing and serves as the watchdog for consistency. This team should include those involved in employee communications, media relations, and public relations. The team needs to continually interact with other integration teams to understand the many issues requiring communications and their status. (More will be said about the integration transition structure in Chapter 6.)

Develop a Workable Communication Process

In addition to coordination, it's vital to have a process in place for ensuring that communications reach people and that issues are resolved on a day-to-day basis, especially during the transition stage. Too often, those sending communications have a sense of relief once a message has been sent. They can now check that item off their long list of activities that need to be performed as part of their plan. Unfortunately, once the message is sent, the work only begins. Was the message received and understood? Was the issue resolved? If not, then the entire communication process has been a waste of time.

A workable process requires an understanding of the organization and people involved and some creativity in developing an approach that ensures that messages went through and issues were resolved.

For example, I consulted with a company that was making several small to medium-sized acquisitions a month. Backroom activities were to be centralized by the acquirer. Many of the target's field activities were to remain geographically decentralized but standardized to best practices within three months after the closing. There were many activities to manage and many issues and questions that would arise. The level of activity within the acquirer was frenetic, and the opportunity for issues to fall between the cracks was great. The acquirer also had a shortage of integration staff. One area of concern was communication. Target employees did not always know whom to contact when they had questions or needed to get issues resolved. To manage the problem, a simple but consistent and workable communication process was developed. Several key roles were created: a transition team communication leader who attended all meetings of the transition teams and a key communication contact located in each field or branch location of each acquired company.[4] The role of the new positions are described as follows:

Transition Communication Leader (TCL)

This person would:

- Attend all weekly transition team meetings.
- Frequently interact and communicate with other members of the transition team.
- Prepare weekly (or more frequently as needed) communication updates for the acquisitions, presented in either the company newsletter, a special integration newsletter, or faxes and e-mails.
- Manage the execution of the transition communication plan.
- Be a central point for tracking, escalating, and resolving problems and issues coming from the acquisitions. This would include:
  - Compiling weekly tracking reports.

- Notifying transition team members of issues impacting their area.
- Reporting on issue resolution and channeling issues to functional area executives (i.e., sales, operations) or transition team members for resolution.
- Coordinate all communications with transition team leaders.

This process would ensure that:

- All integration communications are coordinated.
- There is a close connection between integration decisions and activities and communications.
- Someone is dedicated to, and responsible and accountable for, managing and implementing integration communications.
- All important issues and problems coming from the acquisitions are tracked and documented, and reports are submitted to senior management to keep them informed.
- Solutions needed by the acquisitions are provided in a timely manner.

The TCL would:

- Report directly to, and clear all messages and media with, the senior leadership team.
- Review all messages with the integration champion and other transition team members to ensure accuracy and consistency.
- Respond to all problems and issues that come from the key contact person by:
  - Either directly answering them.
  - Or routing them to relevant transition team members or other relevant parties.

Key Communication Contact (KCC)

For each acquisition, an acquired manager, based at the acquired company, would be appointed as a key communication contact person. This person would ensure that clear lines of communication exist between the acquired firm and the TCL.

The KCC would:

- Work with branch managers and regional managers to try and resolve their problems directly.
- Work with the TCL to ensure that critical problems and issues that cannot be resolved locally are brought to senior management's attention and are addressed.
- Ensure that all issues and problems that are encountered, as well as solutions that have been implemented, are documented and sent to the TCL, and be responsible and accountable for ensuring communications are disseminated to the relevant acquired organization's personnel.

Once the roles were created the next issue would be how the communication process would work. Within each acquisition there were several branch operations and thus branch managers. Below is a process that we employed to effectively facilitate the communications between the branches and the ICL. (See Figure 5-5 for a diagram of the process.)

Branch managers would contact the KCC directly with questions, problems, and issues. The KCC would first try to resolve the issue at the local level. If the problem was resolved, the KCC would submit a completed Issue Tracking Form (see Table 5-4) with the solution to the TCL. Then the KCC would communicate the resolution directly to the branch personnel who submitted the request. The tracking of locally resolved issues was essential for the TCL to maintain a complete understanding of the progress and obstacles in the integration project.

If the issue could not be resolved locally, the Issue Tracking Form was completed and sent to the TCL. The TCL would then review the issue and assign it to the appropriate transition team member or whoever was deemed best able to resolve the issue. The issue would then be added to the Issue Tracking Report and assigned a priority code of red, green, or yellow.

- Green was assigned to routine issues that the TCL believed would be resolved by the next reporting period.
- Yellow was assigned to those issues where the time frame was long, the cost was high, or the impact would be widely felt.

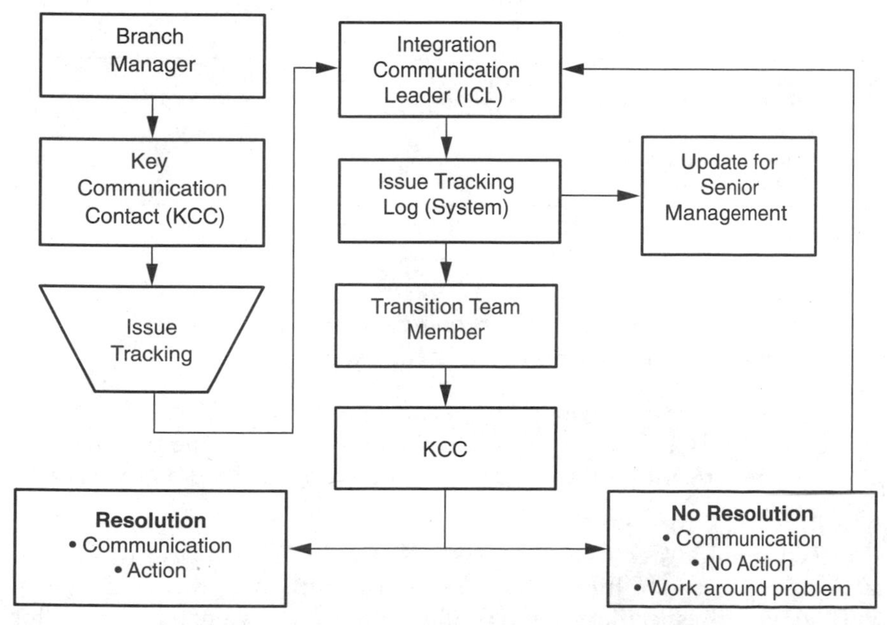

Figure 5-5 Communication Process

Table 5-4 Issue Tracking Form

Submitted by ________	Phone Number ________
Location ________	Date Issue Submitted ________
Branch Submitting ________	Key Contact at Branch ________

What is the issue we need to resolve?

Was the issue resolved at the local level? And if so, how and when?

Who in the branch/functional area experienced the problem?

Was the issue raised by a customer or in the presence of a customer? If yes, please explain.

Does the issue impact other employees in the branch? If yes, please explain.

What other areas are impacted by this issue?

In what format should the resolution be communicated?
Newsletter
E-Mail
Memo
Fax
Phone
Other

Could customer communication be required?	Y or N
Could customer communication be desired?	Y or N
Is there a customer impact?	Y or N
Could training be required?	Y or N
Is follow-up needed?	Y or N

- Red was used for issues or problems that were considered general roadblocks to the progress of the assimilation project.

All issues coded red would appear on a daily progress report submitted by the TCL and the transition champion. A red issue remained on the daily report until it was resolved or the status justified a green code.

The Tracking Process

The TCL would track all assigned issues along with their priority code in a weekly report submitted to the transition champion. The transition team and others with specific issues or problems to resolve were responsible for submitting a progress report to the TCL by Thursday of each week. This update was critical for the issue tracking and resolution process. The resolution would be submitted to the TCL, who would then communicate with the KCC. Staying "in the loop" allowed the TCL to accurately report progress to the integration champion.

If no resolution could be reached by the transition team or others assigned to the issue or problem, the TCL escalated the issue by first contacting the appropriate vice president.

Due to the overwhelming number of inquiries being fielded by the integration team, an effort was made to filter all questions from the branch personnel through the managers in the branches. Therefore, the only branch personnel who should be contacting the KCCs were general managers, operations managers, service managers, and installation managers.

Although this filtering process may have been perceived as cumbersome by branch personnel, the process was necessary for a number of reasons.

- Limiting the number of calls to a manageable level allowed the KCCs to field questions and communicate solutions in a timely manner.
- The filtering process required the managers in the branches to review all operational problems or issues occurring in their branches and to understand the solutions.
- The managers had the opportunity to review the issues for impact on other employees in the branch and decide if other branch personnel needed to be briefed on or involved in the issue.

The KCCs and the TCL needed to review each issue and eventual resolution for applicability throughout the company. The KCCs would review issues escalated to them from the branches for impact on other branches. In other words, should the problem and resolution be communicated to all other branches in the KCC's market? Such decisions should also be approved by the regional manager. In a like manner, the TCL needed to review problems and resolutions for applicability and impact to all branches in both the acquired companies and the acquirer's system.

The KCCs would complete an Issues Tracking Form for all problems that were raised by branch personnel. The TCL would input the information from these forms into a log that could be used to produce the weekly tracking reports. When contacting the branch personnel with the resolution to the question raised, the KCC could fax, e-mail, or phone the employee with the information. The TCL would follow up with a phone call for those resolutions that were judged to be complex, or that deviated greatly from the branches' current procedures. All branch personnel would be provided within 24 hours of their request with a report on the status of the issue. The branch personnel submitting the request would be updated weekly until the issue was resolved. These updates were delivered by fax, e-mail, or telephone. The final resolution would be added to the weekly tracking report. The example presented above illustrates the importance of proactively communicating and resolving target company issues in a timely manner.

HANDLING EMPLOYEE TRAUMA

Regardless of how well executives communicate with employees during integration, many employees may still have difficulty dealing with uncertainty and the actual events unfolding around them. As Figures 5-2 through 5-4 illustrate, many measures of employee well-being do not come back to "normal," even with a sound communication process. Therefore, executives must be prepared to deal with the trauma that employees might have. Keep in mind that trauma may vary depending upon the situation and the people involved. Where significant changes such as job loss, relocations, and new work processes are likely, trauma will be greater. Where the integration process drags out and the period of uncertainty is lengthened, trauma will also be greater.

Finally, not all people handle difficult situations similarly. Their psychological makeup and broader personal situation can have a dramatic impact. Clearly, it is not possible to control how people will react, but it is possible to understand, anticipate, and take some actions to help deal with people's reactions. In this section some insights on how to do so will be presented.

Set an Example

The behavior of executives and managers during a merger has a significant impact on the behavior of employees throughout an organization. It sets the tone for people and communicates what is acceptable and what is not. This is so, regardless of what managers say. During a merger or acquisition, people's emotions are likely to be higher than normal, as people are concerned, and even worried, about what is going to happen to them. As noted above, they are looking for every bit of information they can find to figure out what is going on. This includes watching managers' behavior and reactions, sometimes with the precision of a microscope. They attend to the words, voice tone, and body language. Often employees attach meanings to these, even when they are virtually meaningless or irrelevant to their own situation. The following is a case in point.

The vice president of an information technology group in a large company was responsible for consolidating his operation with that of an acquirer. His operation was to be shut down. Several people were to be retained and transferred to the acquirer's operations, and a number of people were to be let go. Decisions concerning individuals to be retained were pending.

During one weekend the VP was facing serious personal family problems and was quite upset. (The problems had nothing to do with the merger.) He came to work on Monday preoccupied and stressed. He had not slept much of the weekend. As he walked to his office to begin the day, a programmer passed by him and greeted him. Wrapped up in his own problems, the VP did not acknowledge her. In fact, later, he did not really remember having met her. An hour later the programmer was in the personnel office distraught that she was losing her job. She was convinced that the VP avoided her because he was afraid to tell her the bad news. She was upset that he did not look at her or even wish her good morning.

This example is typical of how many people behave during such times. Now, was the VP entitled to be in a bad mood? Absolutely, he is human. Was it prudent for him to demonstrate it? That is an interesting question. People are entitled to behave any way they want, but when they are in a perceived position of power, their behavior, intended or not, can have a dramatic effect on people. Be sensitive and be careful. People are quite creative in attaching meaning to and correlating things that are not related.

Kubler-Ross's Five-Stage Model[5]

A number of years ago a well-known psychologist, Elisabeth Kubler-Ross, developed a model for how people cope with traumatic events. The model depicts five stages. Each stage is part of a transition process that people typically go through. It is important to note that not everyone goes through all the stages, and the duration of each stage may vary. Simply put, some people are able to deal with the event and move on quickly, whereas others are not. Regardless, the framework gives you some understanding of where people are in the process and why. It helps you better deal with them. The stages are discussed below.

Disbelief and Denial

Stage 1 is characterized by a failure of people to recognize and accept what is happening. In a sense it is a defensive reaction that helps people insulate themselves from an uncertain and unpleasant situation. Essentially, people do not believe the events are happening. This is typified by reactions such as "There is no way that this merger will take place," or "They would be crazy to make changes to our organization—we have been very successful." These comments are often made when there is evidence to suggest otherwise.

The best thing a manager can do in this situation is to continue to present people with factual information about what is happening. Often, pleas to people to face reality do not work. It is more than just an intellectual exercise. For some, it just takes time to face up to the truth. Others are able to adjust quickly.

Anger
This is an extremely dysfunctional stage where people come to understand the reality. Rather than constructively accept the events and move on, they react emotionally. They may keep their anger inside or may lash out. This can range from grumbling, to open confrontation, to violence. Often, people will blame others for what is happening. Typical comments include "How can the idiots in management agree to this deal," or "This deal is likely to ruin our company." This stage can be dangerous, depending upon the individuals involved. It is best for you to get professional advice. Employee assistance program representatives or the human resources organization may be of help.

Bargaining
In stage 3, reality is beginning to set in, but people have not quite come to fully accept it. They still believe there is an opportunity to reverse decisions and outcomes, even if it is not possible. They may try to negotiate. If they are part of a layoff, they may try to bargain to get their name off the "list." They may even plead and explain why theirs is a special case. They still are holding onto a probability when, in fact, the reality is a certainty. The key for managers is to maintain their position and continue to provide accurate information. You may feel pressure to give people encouraging signs, but do so only if your encouragement is based in truth.

Depression
In this stage, reality has set in, and people may feel helpless because events are out of their control. They may feel they have no option. This may lead to a sense of hopelessness and thus depression. Depressed people show all sorts of dysfunctional behaviors, including lethargy and lack of caring.[6] They may retreat from the situation and either fail to come to work or not produce when at work. In this stage it is best to help someone seek professional assistance. It is clearly beyond the scope of managerial competencies unless the manager is certified in counseling, psychology, or psychiatry.

Acceptance
Clearly this stage is the most healthy and productive. This is the point where people accept what is happening and are ready to move on and deal with the situation. Recognizing, creating, and acting upon alternatives is the key here. This is an excellent time in which you, as an executive or manager, can help people do this. This may include transfering people to other operations or helping them avail themselves of company-sponsored outplacement and job search activities.

Regardless of the stage in which people find themselves, it is crucial to remind yourself that there are limits to your own capabilities in assisting employees traumatized by a transition. The most dangerous thing managers can do is to "play psychologist." The most productive thing they can do is to help people identify resources available to help them.

How People Cope with Change and Transition[7]

It is obvious just by watching people that they do not all have the same psychological makeup and that they do not all react to change the same way. It is important that managers recognize why people react differently to the same situation. It may provide managers with insights on how best to deal with people. The key point to understand is that not everyone will react the same way. Someone's opportunity is someone else's threat. Four key elements affect how people react: situation, self, supports, and strategies. Each is described below.

Situation

There are aspects of each person's situation that affect the way he or she reacts. Often, managers are unaware of these, and the work environment is just one aspect. For example, a 25-year-old with no family and no mortgage may view a merger-related relocation across the country as a great opportunity. It is a chance to live somewhere new and develop career opportunities. For someone who is 50, with elderly parents and with children in high school and college, relocation may be a dreaded threat. Although the opportunity to relocate may objectively be the same, the reaction will be entirely different. Some aspects of the situation to consider include:

1. Does the person see the transition as positive, negative, expected, unexpected, desired, or dreaded?
2. Did the transition come at the worst or best possible time?
3. Is it surrounded by other stresses?
4. Is it voluntary or imposed?
5. Is this the transition's beginning, middle, or nearly the end?

Self

Clearly, aspects of each person's psychological makeup contribute greatly to the person's reaction to an event. Experience in having made a significant transition is extremely important. People who have gone through such an experience are more likely to understand how the transition unfolds and what it feels like. More importantly, experience helps people realize they can successfully get through a new transition. I have observed that people who have been through a merger or major acquisition are far more equipped to deal with one the second time around. Also key to understanding people's reaction is whether they see that they have options. If they believe that there are no options other than the status quo, they will feel trapped and dependent. These are most likely to elicit strong reactions. Some aspects of the person to consider include:

1. What is the person's previous experience in making similar transitions?
2. Does the person believe there are options?
3. Is the person basically optimistic and able to deal with uncertainty and ambiguity?
4. Does the person have high self-esteem?

Supports

Support systems help people cope with transitions. Two in particular, social and financial support, help explain people's reactions. As many of us have found, we often lose perspective of a situation, especially when under stress. Having others to talk with allows us to vent and to have the assumptions we make about events challenged and brought back to reality. When people have no social supports, they can easily exaggerate the negative aspects of a situation and develop stronger reactions. Financial support provides people with a cushion to help them withstand a loss of employment. It also takes away the potential threat of job loss, since people's perceived dependency on the job is reduced.

Strategies

How individuals perceive a situation and the capabilities they have for dealing with it also explains their reactions. When people feel they have no control of events and don't have an accurate understanding of how the events are unfolding and the impact the events are likely to have, they are more prone to react strongly. That is why advanced and honest communication is essential. It gives people sufficient time to plan realistic strategies for how they will manage their personal situation. Some aspects of the strategies to consider include:

1. Does the person have the ability to change the situation?
2. Is the person's interpretation of the situation in need of change?
3. Does the person know how to manage stress?

How Managers Can Help

Given that people are likely to react differently during integration, what can managers do to help? First and foremost is to realize they are not psychologists. It is not the intent of this section to train psychologists, but to develop a sensitivity to and an understanding of how people deal with transitions. As such, it is suggested that managers do not attempt to provide personal psychological counseling. If they do so, they may be stepping beyond their knowledge base and hurt people rather than help them. Moreover, they may be putting themselves in jeopardy, since one often does not know how a person will react to advice.

Managers should counsel work performance issues. They should assist people in getting the proper help they need. When such situations arise, contact an employee assistance program representative or someone in human resources. Often they understand the best approach for getting someone help. Moreover, it is helpful to them in discerning whether a pattern is developing in the organization that requires a more systemic approach.

There are a number of general initiatives that can be taken to help employees. First, human resource departments are likely to have stress reduction and change sensitization workshops available. These can range from brown-bag lunch sessions to all-day sessions. These meetings provide people with basic skills for managing through a transition.

Second, meetings with employees to share and solve common concerns are quite helpful. Avoid general "bitch" sessions, because they only lead to venting. Sessions that are solution-oriented help people move forward and focus on things within their "sphere of influence," i.e., things they can control. Third, help people understand what their real work options are and how they can best take advantage of them. Choices here may include job transfers, resume writing, interviewing skills, job search, and the like. Managers should also provide whatever insights they can, but should direct people to get professional help when they do not have the knowledge or skills themselves. The human resources department may have programs or books on the topic.

MANAGE CUSTOMER RETENTION

Customer retention is central to ensuring the financial success of a merger or an acquisition. It is critical to set clear and achievable retention goals emphasizing quality (value) of customers retained as well as the overall retention figure. In other words, retention of all customers may not be important, such as the desired loss of unprofitable customers. To establish a reasonable retention goal, the target's customer base will need to be segmented into categories with known profitability levels. The categories can be the target's established segments if the profitability of their segments has been tracked. If not, the customer base will need to be segmented using the acquirer's standards. Once a retention goal is set, a retention plan should be developed.

A retention plan should be implemented immediately after approval by the transition team leader and the champion. The retention plan should include the following components:

- Communicate with customers, as discussed above.
- Use employee incentive plans.

- Use employee and point-of-contact tools.
- Create a customer retention SWAT team.

Use Employee Incentive Plans

Encourage customer retention among target employees by introducing upbeat incentive programs focused on retention of target customers. Provide awards and recognition for those employees who have direct contact with customers. Provide retention tools to support point-of-contact retention efforts. These could include:

- Calling lists with points on how to make effective retention courtesy calls
- Monthly retention tracking reports to show ranking of employees or locations
- Customer account recovery process (questions to ask before customer closes out relationship)
- Thank-you notes to sign and send to customers

Create a Customer Retention SWAT Team

This team (probably placed with the customer service unit) would be staffed with experienced telephone personnel who will handle outbound retention calls to high-value customers and inbound calls from employees and high-value customers. It is recommended that this group be empowered to extend special offers to target customers.

A FINAL COMMENT

Communication and value preservation are clearly major challenges throughout all stages of the integration process. For many executives it seems like a perpetual uphill battle. Issues are always changing, uncertainty continues to mount, and people want to know what is going on and how it will affect them. Effective leaders must rise to the challenge and continue to communicate with all stakeholders even when they feel overwhelmed. Failure to do so is likely to lead to value leakage and unrealized synergies.

APPENDIX 5-1 MERGER STAKEHOLDER COMMUNICATION PLAN

Below is a stakeholder communication plan (see Table A5-1) that was employed in an acquisition. The acquirer manufactured products for the defense industry and acquired a company that would help diversify it toward a balance between defense and commercial customers and products. The plan identifies communication objectives, stakeholders, messages, media, and stages in the integration process when certain messages should be delivered.

Communication Objectives

1. Promote positive attitudes toward new company through timely education of stakeholders about all aspects of merger.
2. Introduce the new management team and organization:
   a. Background and personality
   b. Organizational structure
   c. Commitment of management team
3. Communicate management's:
   a. Philosophy on industry
   b. Vision for success
   c. Business strategy
   d. Viability of new company
4. Minimize speculation and anxiety due to changes taking place.

Stakeholders (Target Audiences)

1. Employees
2. Customers
3. Distributors
4. Financial analysts/consultants
5. Trade and business press
6. Government agencies
7. Communities in company locations
8. Shareholders

General Messages

1. This is a "new" company rather than an extension of either ABC or XYZ.

Table A5-1 Communication Plan

	Transaction (Pre-Announcement)	Formal Announcement	Transition/Integration (Post-Announcement)
Customers	Managed letters Telephone hotline Key customer visits Internet messages Trade show guidelines	New customer newsletter Advertising and promotions	Direct mail on changes
Distributors	Trade show guidelines Management letters key distributor visits	New distributor newsletter Advertising	Direct mail
Press and Communities	Press materials Expand news bureau Announce milestones through briefings	Press/analyst tour Wire photos News releases Meetings with community leaders	New company profiles
Shareholders	1st-quarter report October annual meeting	Personal letter	February analysts' meeting
Government Agencies	DOD briefings Personal letters Visits with key agencies and people Crisis plan Attend critical meetings	Advertising Press coverage	
Employees	Newsletter inserts Site visits Executive memoes, e-mails Video interviews Telephone hotline Intranet messages	Newsletter/transition newsletter Celebration Management and supervisor briefings	Social gatherings Company meetings Leadership training

2. We are not conquering XYZ but building a stronger transformed company:
   a. The integration of employees from both organizations offers a truly unique opportunity to strengthen and restructure.
   b. The new company is committed to drawing on the best talents from both ABC and XYZ.
   c. The new company is committed to the ongoing welfare of ABC and XYZ employees.
3. This acquisition was part of a planned, ongoing company strategy.
4. XYZ is an ideal fit for ABC in terms of products and markets:
   a. Minimal duplication—areas of overlap between the firms are few
   b. Complementary product offerings in similar markets
   c. Broader international presence
   d. Greater commercial market emphasis resulting in faster growth—if we can successfully manage the integration
   e. Enhanced military offerings for ABC through complementary products from XYZ
5. The new company will be:
   a. The only major manufacturer driven by niche marketing growing faster than either previous entity
   b. Innovative in developing niche products and technology for market segments:
      i. Custom applications complemented by standard product lines
      ii. Able to serve broader markets with these products
      iii. Better able to serve military, industrial, and commercial markets
6. The new company will be committed to niche marketing because:
   a. There are greater opportunities for profits.
   b. The new "balance" of served markets fosters greater stability.
   c. It has historic expertise and specialized capability in niche marketing.
   d. These markets have a greater barrier to entry.
   e. The new company has critical mass required to do so in the 1990s and beyond.
7. The new company is committed to economies of scale driven by market opportunities.
8. The combined companies will guarantee a long-term domestic source of U.S. military technology.
9. The new company will merge the ABC and XYZ entities with maximum speed.

General Approach

1. Take advantage of brand name/corporate names and logos while working toward integration.

2. Combine ABC and XYZ logos in advertising treatments.
3. Centralize all product introductions.
4. Focus on a tag line that speaks to consolidation:
   a. "The vision of one"
   b. "The power of one"
5. Utilize one corporate typeface and colors.
6. Focus media spending on short blitz versus slow build.
7. Develop communications plans for all external and internal announcements.
8. Employees will be notified first on important news prior to releasing it to the press.

Initial Activities

1. Form central communication committee:
   a. Membership from both ABC and XYZ
2. Weekly input to and from Merger Integration Office (MIO):
   a. Long lead time notice of impending action
3. Establish approval process for communications actions: Recommendation of steps:
   a. Legal review
   b. XYZ concurrence
   c. Final approval (MIO leader, CEO)

STAKEHOLDERS AND COMMUNICATION MEDIA CUSTOMERS

1. "Executive briefs" outlining key issues:
   a. Personal briefings for key customers
   b. Personalized letters for other customers
2. Toll-free hotline number:
   a. Answered by customer service
   b. Provide specific questions and answers
3. Newsletter:
   a. Quarterly in first year
   b. Launched at announcement
   c. Series of stories on acquisition and integration
4. Site visits for key customers
5. Direct mailings:
   a. Theme-oriented publications
   b. Office or home keepsake
   c. Tied to advertising message

6. Advertising:
   a. Image-oriented
   b. Product-oriented
   c. Corporate guidebook for logo, typeface, colors
7. Media coverage:
   a. Reprint mailings
8. Customer briefing center update
9. Trade shows:
   a. Audit current shows
   b. Utilize new-sector theme
   c. Look like billion dollar company through:
      i. New presence/new booth
      ii. New corporate guidelines for:
         (1) Graphics
         (2) Message
         (3) Shows attended
   d. Question and answer sheet for booth staff on tough questions
   e. Eliminate controversy and conflict in messages between ABC and XYZ booths
   f. Gifts denoting new company

Press and Communities

1. Formal briefings
2. Meetings with influential industry consultant (i.e., Dataquest)
3. Personal meetings with company spokesperson
4. Preparation and mailing of press materials:
   a. Photos
   b. Bios
   c. Organizational chart
   d. New company press contact and number
   e. Feature on the future of the company
   f. New company capabilities brochure
5. Press tour (domestic and international):
   a. Trade
   b. Business and financial
   c. Industry analysts
6. General business publicity:
   a. Radio tapes
   b. Teleconferences
   c. Wire service photos
7. Expand existing news bureau:
   a. Identify and train spokespeople
   b. Clarify who talks to whom
   c. Decide how to handle incoming press calls

8. News releases:
   a. News of transition team
   b. Announcements:
      i. Business and trade
      ii. Photo opportunity
   c. New appointments
   d. Reorganizations
   e. Products:
      i. New introductions
      ii. Distributor assignments
   f. New company thrust and focus
9. Meeting with community leaders:
   a. Reassure community leaders of continued support (grants, charity, participation)
   b. Develop crisis plan in event of layoffs or facilities close

Distributors

1. Message development on new distributor strategy
2. Communicate through:
   a. Personal briefings
   b. Personal letters
   c. News stories in their publications

Shareholders

1. Special section in *FYI Magazine* (for shareholders)
2. First- and second-quarter report
3. Personalized letter from management at announcement
4. February financial analyst meeting:
   a. Invite industry analysts
5. Special financial analyst briefings:
   a. At announcement
6. Announcement at October annual meeting
7. Coverage in annual report
8. Corporate/image advertising

Government Agencies

1. Contingency plan:
   a. Department of Defense (DOD) briefing:
      i. Between ABC and XYZ
   b. Editorial boards with government books
   c. Crisis plan:
      i. Question and answer preparation
      ii. Releases

iii. Press calls
iv. DOD calls
v. Position paper (ABC commitment)
vi. White paper (issue-oriented to fewer government suppliers is better)
vii. Legislative mailing
viii. Speakers bureau
  (1) Need for on-share suppliers in industry
  (2) Personal letters from ABC management
  (3) Special conferences:
    a. Attend quarterly meetings

Employees

1. ABC/XYZ newsletter and e-mail and Intranet insert—"The power of one update":
   a. Transition to single employee newsletter
   b. E-mail
   c. Intranet site
2. Visits to operations of ABC and XYZ by both CEOs:
   a. Internal version of company presentation
   b. Question and answer session
   c. Follow-up video distribution
3. Executive e-mail and Intranet briefings:
   a. Key breaking events
   b. Announcements
4. Video conferences by CEOs via satellite and Intranet when needed and where possible
5. Merger hotline
6. Company meetings:
   a. Use regular meetings for question and answers
   b. Arrange special meetings when needed
7. Theme promotion:
   a. Buttons, posters, banners
8. Leadership training programs
9. Social gatherings:
   a. Picnics
   b. Open house

6

PREPARING FOR INTEGRATION: MANAGING THE TRANSITION STAGE

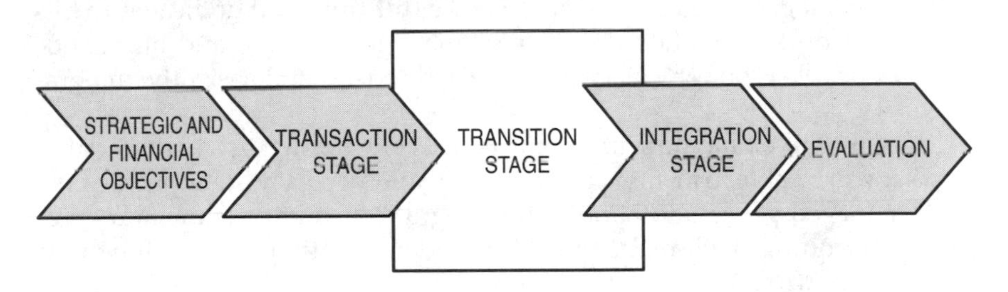

Now that the decision to do the deal has been made, the next interesting challenge emerges—figuring out whether and how to integrate the companies. How should these decisions be made, and who should be involved? Although these are seemingly simple questions, they are quite complex to answer in practice. There are numerous decisions to be made and people involved. Without a structured decision-making process, integration is likely to be chaotic and political, with many issues and decisions falling between the cracks.

The integration transition process typically begins after a formal merger or acquisition agreement has been signed, and should be completed prior to the closing. The extent to which integration plans can be developed earlier provides organizations the needed momentum to capture important changes identified during the transition process.

Unfortunately, thorough preplanning is not always possible. Sometimes, as in the case of a hostile takeover, there is a lack of cooperation prior to the closing, and planning can only take place after there is a change of control of the companies. Sometimes, as in the case of a merger between direct competitors, the parties are restricted in what they can talk about and jointly plan due to potential antitrust issues. Often the lawyers involved will guide this effort. Regardless of the timing, the need for a well-managed transition process remains a critical element in the success of any integration effort.

The basic objective of the integration process is to take two previously independent organizations and merge them together in some fashion. This requires that a process for managing the transition from "two to one" be created. The nature of this process will vary depending upon the:

1. Amount of concurrent acquisition activity being undertaken by the acquirer
2. Relative size and complexity of the organizations involved
3. Nature of the integration that is planned

The more the concurrent acquisition activity, plus the greater the relative size and complexity, plus the greater the depth of the integration, the more the process needs to be formalized, replicable, and staffed with dedicated resources. Simply put, a firm making an occasional small acquisition with little integration is less likely to need a full-time staff dedicated to this activity. It does need, however, a well-managed process and an ad hoc team of people who can easily be mobilized to lead and assist the integration.

On the other hand, a firm that is actively rolling up a fragmented market will be able to justify a full-time staff and need a more sophisticated, well-managed process to handle the integration activity. A mega-merger will also require a well-managed, dedicated integration process due to the sheer enormity of the work to be done.

STRATEGIC AND FINANCIAL OBJECTIVES AS THE DRIVER

As noted in Chapter 2, strategic and financial objectives and subsequent synergies should be the major drivers of the M&A integration process. It is most desirable if these have been thought out prior to doing the deal or at least during due diligence, but often they are not. In such cases, they must be addressed during the integration stage. Unless these elements are understood, it is extremely difficult to effectively set priorities, drive the integration process, and create value for investors. Sound decisions both with respect to organizational structures, systems, and process and with respect to people to retain will be impossible to make.

With smaller acquisitions the financial and strategic objectives may have been well thought out prior to the deal, especially if a buyer is clearly seeking targets that fit a particular strategic need (e.g., products, geographic entry). In such cases the transition process focuses specifically on how to integrate the target into the new organization.

In a large merger it may take more time before a clear strategy is developed. The merger may have been agreed to based on a vague vision, with many details of the strategy to be determined during the transition and possibly not until after the closing. It has been argued, for example, that some of the oil industry and automotive mergers were done for defensive reasons and that the strategies behind them were not thought out in much detail. General synergies, usually in terms of cost reductions, were identified early in the deal, only to be captured in detail during the transition and integration stages.

With the strategic and financial objectives as drivers, there are several key integration objectives to be accomplished and activities to be managed during transition. These are presented in Table 6-1 and discussed in the remainder of this chapter.

CREATE AN INTEGRATION TRANSITION STRUCTURE

GTE and Bell Atlantic created a transition integration structure to form Verizon.[1] To manage the many complex details involved in combining these two complex companies, they created the Merger Planning Office. It was jointly led by GTE's executive vice president of strategic development and planning and Bell Atlantic's executive vice president of strategy and corporate development. The office, which was staffed by a number of full-time staff members, was responsible for managing the overall integration planning process. This included key activities, timetables, financial results, synergy capture, and issue tracking and resolution.

The merger integration process involved three phases: (1) gathering and analyzing data on how the companies might fit together, (2) developing staffing and business plans, and (3) implementating the plans. For the data gathering and analysis phase, eight integration teams that focused on specific areas in both companies were created. These teams examined each company's practices, looking for synergies and best practices. Integration teams focused on areas such as:

1. Consumer and small business
2. Large business, federal, wholesale business, data/Internet working, technology and infrastructure management

Table 6-1 Transition Stage

Objectives
1. Complete unfinished analyses.
2. Create a cooperative integration environment.
3. Plan the integration.
Activities
1. Create an integration transition structure.
2. Articulate integration guiding principles.
3. Decide what to integrate and how to do it.
4. Develop an integration project plan to drive implementation.

3. Domestic wireless
4. Telecom network and operations
5. International and directories
6. Legal, regulatory, and government affairs
7. Human resources
8. Finance and headquarters support

Based on the recommendations obtained from phase 1, phase 2 began. This phase started six months prior to the closing and focused on the finalization of business strategy, organizational design, and the naming of the top leadership of Verizon.

Smithkline and Beecham began its transition integration structure by creating the Merger Management Committee (MMC), which consisted of an equal number of executives from each company. The MMC then created seven planning groups (i.e., integration teams) to identify the synergies and business opportunities that the combined organization could attain. Seven teams were formed for:

- Information, financial, and accounting systems
- Corporate headquarters
- Pharmaceuticals organization
- Pharmaceuticals manufacturing
- Pharmaceuticals R&D; marketing and sales
- Animal health
- Over-the-counter/consumer products

The seven teams were charged with developing strategies for their areas and creating five-year plans. Another group was formed to coordinate the work of all the other groups and to interface with the MMC. This group ensured that all tasks necessary for integration were identified and carried out and priorities were set; work was reviewed by the MMC in order of importance. A computerized master plan was employed to ensure that the work was properly monitored.

Based on due diligence and preliminary projections of the new company's performance, Fleet and BankBoston identified $600 million in cost savings through consolidation and $350 million through divestiture. They wanted to achieve these results in 18 months.

To accomplish these results, a Merger Integration Office staffed by both Fleet and BankBoston managers with expertise in mergers, organizational structure and dynamics, strategic planning, and risk management, among others, was created. The managers developed objectives, a process, and a timetable for accomplishing merger goals. They formed 66 integration teams of employees from both banks working within the business or staff areas to be merged. The integration teams were given support from 10 full-time cross-functional teams of employees from both banks. The 10 teams focused on communications, divestiture, facilities, finance, human resources, legal, marketing, revenue, risk management, and systems and operations.

The examples above characterize what other companies have done to manage the integration process. The key lessons drawn from their experiences are that to facilitate the integration process a transition structure should be created to ensure that:

1. The strategic and financial objectives underlying the acquisition drive the integration.
2. A comprehensive and effective integration plan is developed and executed.
3. Collaboration among and commitment of those needed to make the integration a success is garnered.

How elaborate the transition structure should be depends again upon the nature of the M&A activity. Regardless of the approach, some basic elements are common to all structures:

1. An individulal or a team needs to be accountable for ensuring that the integration and the necessary level of coordination among various people and groups are successfully accomplished.
2. Financial and strategic objectives must drive the effort.
3. All functional and support areas, lines of business, and geographic operations from both organizations need to be examined to determine whether and how they should be integrated.
4. An acceptable approach to making integration decisions must be agreed to.
5. A project-based implementation plan to ensure that all activities essential to a successful integration should be defined and executed.
6. Sufficient commitment among key individuals, groups, and other stakeholders to the implementation of the plan must be realized.

A general transition structure that has been effectively used by successful acquirers is discussed below and illustrated in Figure 6-1. The structure is built on a series of cascading teams with increasing levels of detailed responsibility for integration analyses and recommendations. The figure shows what the structure looks like for a single merger versus a company making multiple acquisitions as part of an industry roll-up.

Merger Integration Office or Integration Champion

A merger integration office (MIO) or integration champion (IC) has primary responsibility for leading the integration effort. In a merger this is likely to be jointly led by senior managers from both organizations (e.g.,

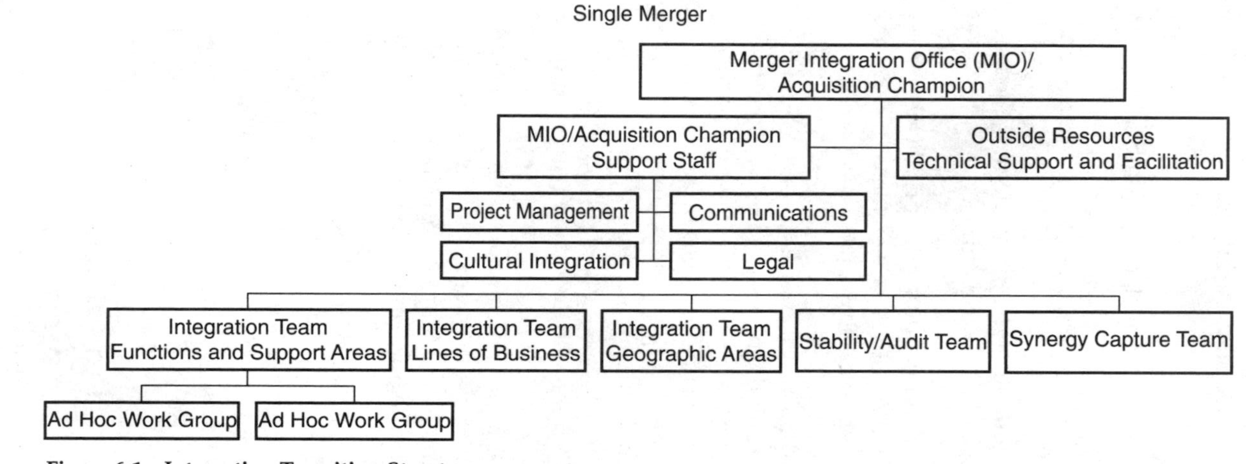

Figure 6-1 Integration Transition Structures

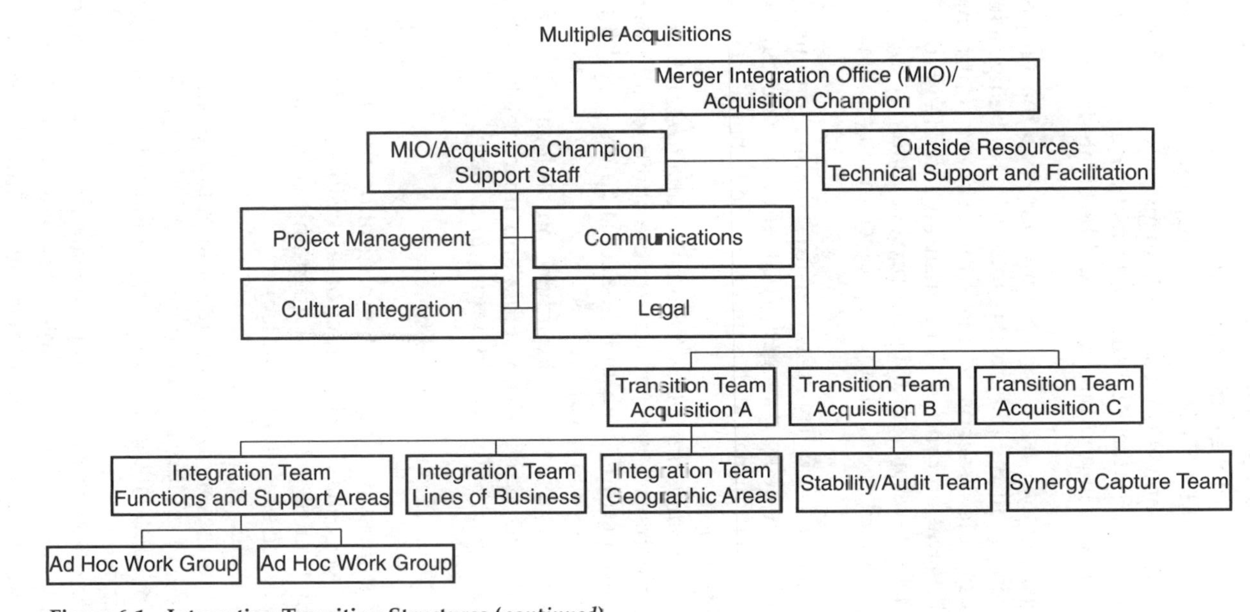

Figure 6-1 Integration Transition Structures (*continued*)

chief financial officers). These positions are typically named by the CEOs of the merging companies and report directly to them.

For a company that is making a series of smaller acquisitions it is likely to be an executive of the acquirer (e.g., M&A group, business development, CFO, member of the senior team) who oversees all the acquisitions. The MIO/IC should be provided with support staff to manage the numerous activities, and with outside help to give needed technical support and facilitation (e.g., for the MIO and the transition and integration teams). In particular, several support teams should be created:

1. *Project management team.* This team oversees a master project plan to ensure that all the integration activities are being managed and are on schedule. Essentially, this is the primary control mechanism for the integration process. All transition and integration teams are required to develop and execute project plans in their respective areas. More will be said about project management later in this chapter.
2. *Communications team.* This team ensures that communications to all stakeholders are being managed. The team ensures accuracy and consistency of all information disseminated. See Chapter 5 for a more in-depth discussion.
3. *Cultural integration team.* This team helps analyze and work through cultural differences that may impact the ability of all other teams to successfully perform their duties. See Chapters 3 and 8 for a more complete discussion of cultural issues.
4. *Legal team.* This team provides advice on all legal issues and guides all teams in recognizing acceptable and unacceptable activities and discussions (e.g., antitrust, SEC) prior to closing.

It is the MIO's/IC's responsibility to:

1. Clarify for those involved in the integration the strategic and financial objectives behind each merger or acquisition and the minimal synergies that must be captured (certainly unanticipated synergies should also be sought if they arise).
2. Create and charge:
   a. Transition teams to manage the integration of each acquisition in the case of multiple acquisitions.
   b. Integration teams to manage integration in the case of a merger or an acquisition.
3. Select transition team or integration team leaders for each acquisition.
4. Ensure that the guiding principles (discussed below) are adhered to.
5. Review and approve all major recommendations made by transition teams and integration teams.
6. Ensure cooperation among transition teams when more than one acquisition is being integrated.

7. Provide support to the transition teams and integration teams (i.e., provide resources, clear roadblocks).

Although the terminology differs, the concept of the MIO is basically the same as what has been used in many mergers including Chevron-Texaco, Baxter–American Hospital Supply, and Chase Manhattan–Chemical Bank. The MIO/IC should oversee the acquisition process from the transaction stage through the integration stage to ensure continuity of information and direction and should be led by executives or others with influence in the acquiring and acquired organizations.

Transition Teams

Depending upon the size, complexity, number, and importance of acquisitions being integrated at the same time, one or more transition teams should be created. For small and simple deals, one team may be able to handle several acquisitions. For multiple large deals, several transition teams will be needed. All will report to the MIO/IC, who will ensure that coordination among teams takes place. The teams ensure that each company being integrated receives the proper level of attention and support and that someone is held accountable for managing the transaction. If a company is making a single large acquisition or is involved in a merger, a transition team is not needed. In such instances, integration teams will report directly to the MIO.

It is the transition team's responsibility to:

1. Manage the transition phase of an acquisition.
2. Create and staff integration teams to examine all functions, lines of business, geographic locations, product lines, and activities considered for integration.
3. Ensure integration teams understand the strategic and financial objectives behind their acquisition and the minimal synergies that must be captured (certainly unanticipated synergies should also be sought if they arise).
4. Ensure integration teams are on schedule, and where necessary, are meeting and communicating with each other.
5. Create a standard methodology or process (e.g., best practices) for integration teams to use in making decisions.
6. Provide support to integration teams (e.g., provide resources, clear roadblocks).
7. Ensure cooperation among integration teams.
8. Make prioritized recommendations, including the business case, to the MIO/IC concerning the proposed integration of the acquired organization (e.g., products and services, organizational structure, management processes and systems, staffing, organizational culture, compensation, and benefits).

9. Set priorities for how the integration recommendations should be implemented.
10. Ensure execution of recommendations.
11. Ensure that both the acquirer and the target continue to function effectively (i.e., there is no value leakage) during the transition stage.

The following guidelines should be considered when staffing transition teams:

1. The team should consist of a transition team leader and integration team leaders (discussed below).
2. The transition team leader should:
   - Be an executive or a manager within an acquirer (depending upon the size, complexity, and importance of the acquisition).
   - Have a solid understanding of the businesses being integrated.
   - Understand the models and assumptions driving the valuation and pricing.
   - Be flexible and able to negotiate with a variety of people and departments.
   - Have excellent project management skills.
   - Have played a significant role during due diligence.
3. Involvement of target people on the transition team (e.g., as integration team leaders) should depend upon the size of the deal, the degree of integration required, and the level of involvement desired.
4. The team should meet weekly, or more often if needed, to discuss all aspects of the integration project, to talk about progress, and to ensure that issues do not slip through the cracks. More is said about tracking integration and project plans in Chapter 9.
5. The team should provide the continuity needed for the integration to proceed smoothly and without duplication or omissions of key tasks.
6. The transition team leader should be provided administrative support for managing the logistics of team activities, coordinating integration team materials, preparing presentations, communicating, dealing with cultural issues, and managing the project.

Integration Teams

Separate teams for each area (e.g., functions and support areas, lines of business, geographic area) of the business should be created. Typical functional and support areas examined include:

1. Strategy
2. Production
3. Distribution
4. Marketing

5. Sales
6. Engineering
7. Research and development
8. Human resources
9. Information technology
10. Legal
11. Procurement
12. Finance and accounting

Lines of business typically focus on major product lines. Geographic areas typically range from regions within a country (e.g., Southeast, Midwest), to countries themselves (e.g., United States, France, Venezuela), to continental regions (e.g., North America, Southeast Asia, Northern Europe), to the entire globe. To a large extent, these are dependent upon how the acquirer and target or merger partners have been organized in the past and how they intend to organize in the future. Again, a merger may be the catalyst that changes the way a company will compete in the future. For example, a merger between a U.S. and European telecommunications company could change the focus of two primarily domestic players to that of a global player. As a result, the types of teams that would be created and their focus may be very different than for the merger of two domestic companies.

It is the integration team's responsibility to:

1. Evaluate a specific function, line of business, or other area of each organization in a merger or an acquisition.
2. Identify how specific synergies can best fulfill the financial and strategic objectives of the deal.
3. Examine the viability of the best approach for managing each area and activity after the deal is closed.
4. Make specific recommendations, including the business case, on changes needed in either the acquirer, the target organization, or both to realize objectives, strategies, and synergies.
5. Make specific recommendations on what needs to be done to successfully implement changes.
6. Develop a detailed project plan for executing changes and implement it after it is approved.

All integration teams should be led by knowledgeable executives and managers from both the acquirer business unit and the target, and be made up of key people from both the acquirer and the target who represent diverse operations, lines of business, and geographic areas. Each transition team is typically staffed with between 6 and 10 people. The need for knowledge and representation should be balanced with the need to effectively and efficiently manage team dynamics. It is critical that the integration teams establish solid contact with people in their respective organizations so that the strengths of each company are understood and not overlooked during integration team deliberations.

Stability/Audit Team

This is an independent team charged with maintaining a satisfactory level of service to customers of both organizations during the transition period. The team's responsibility is to monitor employee and customer retention, service, profits, productivity, and other indicators that determine stability of both organizations. This team assures that sufficient attention is being given to the "business" during the integration. There is always a risk that integration activities consume so much time and energy that value leakage can occur.

The team leader of this group reports results to the transition team and to the MIO/IC. The team should include not only employees from audit and operations but also "generalists," who understand multiple functions.

Synergy Capture Team

Another independent team is responsible for identifying and tracking synergies. These include costs, revenues, net working capital, and investments (i.e., the components of earnings and cashflows). This team works directly with the MIO/IC and with the transition and integration teams that are working to identify and document synergies in each area. The focus is to track synergies over time, including the time after closing, to ensure they are realized. More will be said about tracking synergies in Chapter 9.

Ad Hoc Work Groups

Ad hoc groups are made up of key operational personnel from across the acquirer and the target. It is their responsibility to provide integration teams with specific technical advice and solutions to problems as they evolve.

These groups are formed throughout the transition stage as technical expertise is needed and are dismantled when each group's tasks are completed. The members of these groups would be part-time participants from across the acquirer or the target and would be considered "subject-matter experts." Provisions have to be made to ensure that ad hoc team members can be accessed since the integration is not their primary responsibility.

It is the ad hoc work group's responsibility to:

1. Review aspects of integration plans.
2. Recommend changes to plans.
3. Coordinate any conversions or changes.
4. Provide subject-matter expertise.

Developing Teams

To ensure that all teams work in an effective and efficient manner, it is important that time and attention be given early to the formation and development of the teams. Otherwise, the teams will likely waste time, if not flounder. Prior to beginning any work, transition and integration teams should be:

1. Briefed on the merger or acquisition and provided information on the merger partner or acquisition
2. Briefed on what is expected of them and how their day-to-day job will be handled
3. Provided necessary skills training (e.g., project management, best–practices assessment)
4. Provided intercultural sensitivity training and introduced to counterparts from the other company

Building partnership and cooperation among integration teams can go a long way in facilitating the integration process. In particular, it is useful to take members of the teams for an offsite retreat to set the context and ground rules for the management of the integration process. Below is an example of a three-day offsite session I conducted to help get integration teams off the ground prior to beginning transition planning.

Activities

The CEO, president, or another executive presents, in detail, to all attendees the strategic and financial objectives underlying the merger or acquisition and synergies that have been committed to. If these have not been fully developed, it is worthwhile that they be developed or completed prior to major integration activities. A preliminary version should be shared with attendees at the offsite retreat, with their input and revisions sought. The purpose of this exercise is to build an understanding of, and gain commitment to, a shared strategic direction. It is this shared direction that ultimately provides the glue for building the new organization and must drive the integration decision process, rather than expediency or local interests.

An educational session on merger and acquisition integration, the challenges it creates, and approaches for dealing with these challenges is useful. It gives attendees a realistic view of what awaits them and how to effectively manage through it.

An executive of each organization shares with attendees a history of his or her own organization, including its products and services, geographic presence, strategic direction, and organizational culture. To reduce tension, it may be useful to have members of each organization do a humorous skit during an evening to reflect their own culture. The objective here is to allow members of each organization an opportunity to discuss who they are. This helps eliminate stereotypes, "superiority syndromes," and arrogance that people of any one organization might have. In other words, it levels the playing field.

Following this discussion, small groups from each organization are formed and asked to address the following questions: (1) How would you describe your own culture? (2) How would you describe the culture of the other integrating organization? (3) How are they similar and dissimilar? (4) What elements of each organization's culture are most likely to support the strategic direction of the integrated organization? (5) Do we need to have a single culture throughout the integrated organization, and if not, how do we honor each organization's culture? (More will be said about this in Chapter 8.)

After the small groups present, the larger group of attendees can then focus on real versus perceived differences in culture and aspects of culture that are useful to the new organization. Often, many of the differences are perceived ones rather than real ones. This allows the group to eliminate incorrect stereotypes and focus on how to deal with real differences. Once real differences are isolated, then the group can discuss which aspects of existing cultures, if any, are useful to the new organization. Actions for resolving differences, or creating new aspects, can then be discussed.

A workshop using small mixed groups of attendees from the combining organizations can help anticipate, and begin to deal with, factors that might have a bearing on the overall success of the integration process. The groups meet to address the following questions: (1) What factors will support the integration of the organizations? (2) What factors will create roadblocks to effective integration? (3) What actions can be taken now to overcome the roadblocks and to leverage the support?

After these questions are answered, they are shared and discussed with the larger group. Common themes are identified, and actions to manage them are agreed to. Toward the end of the offsite retreat, teams should be given specific charges and ground rules, as noted above.

To facilitate interaction among members of all organizations, time for socializing in the late afternoon and evening should be planned. This may involve informal or formal activities. If formal activities are used, ensure there is a deliberate mix of people from both organizations. This socialization process facilitates working relationships.

Once integration teams have been formed, it is helpful to clearly outline expectations for each team. These should include:

1. The team's charge and scope
2. The team's authority, limits, and duration
3. Those to whom the team is accountable
4. Deliverables and time frames for completing specific work
5. Specific goals and success measures that the team should focus on, including cashflows, earnings, budgets, synergies, and any indicators that drive them (e.g., quality, safety, productivity)
6. Any specific methods the team should employ in conducting its analyses and making its recommendations
7. Budget and other resources needed

8. Composition of the team
9. Team members' roles and responsibilities
10. Team decision process (e.g., consensus)
11. Barriers to team performance (e.g., external political issues) and how they can be cleared
12. Project management approach to be employed in executing the team's work

It may also be useful for each team to have an independent facilitator. The facilitator should:

1. Encourage teamwork among the participants, regardless of company of origin.
2. Facilitate productive meetings ensuring that:
   - Agendas are distributed well in advance of a meeting.
   - Participants understand the issues to be discussed.
   - There is open discussion, and all issues discussed are clear.
   - Conflicts are constructively managed and resolved.
3. Advise team leaders and members of issues that need to be dealt with and items requiring resolution.
4. Be aware of issues, activities, and conflicts with other teams.
5. Ensure schedules are developed and communicated.
6. Continue to ask questions that provide clarity of issues.
7. Provide relevant information and feedback to those facilitating other teams.

The facilitator should be one who:

1. Has good organizational and political skills
2. Is willing to help others obtain results
3. Feels comfortable with limited or no authority
4. Can accomplish results by quickly building relationships and trust
5. Is insightful and analytical
6. Will maintain confidentiality

ARTICULATE INTEGRATION GUIDING PRINCIPLES

The integration of two firms can be complex, with numerous decisions having to be made. These decisions can have a great bearing on the people affected by the decisions. More importantly, they can have a great bearing on whether the strategic and financial objectives underlying the merger or acquisition are realized. Given the complexity of the integration process, and our inability to have a decision rule or tool available for every decision, it is important that a basic road map to guide those making the decisions be established. As such, many successful companies develop a set of integration guiding principles to serve as a road map and ensure that it is employed during the transition process.

In a merger, the guiding principles should be developed by the MIO. These principles foster consistency of actions throughout the entire transition and integration stages. It is incumbent upon the MIO to ensure that these principles are not hollow words but are adhered to throughout a merger or an acquisition.

In an acquisition the principles should be articulated and accepted by the acquiring executives and managers prior to the formal announcement of the acquisition and should be shared with the target through the IC. Below are some examples of guiding principles.

When Baxter acquired American Hospital Supply, it utilized the following principles:

- The organization will be based on doing what is best for the business.
- The best people will be retained regardless of company affiliation.
- The merger will proceed in an orderly fashion, but it must achieve early and visible benefits.
- We will seek decentralization to the extent that it serves our customers.
- The need to do it right will be balanced with the need to do it expeditiously.
- The integration will include participation from executives of both companies at every step.
- Management intends to conduct the merger integration in an unprecedented, model way.
- Employees of both companies will be treated in an open and honest fashion, and will be kept informed about the progress of the integration through constant communication.[2]

When Smithkline and Beecham merged, they committed to creating a new and transformed company. To guide this effort, they articulated the following principles:

- The merger will be one of equals, including shareholders, board members, management, and businesses. This will allow the company to become global without taking on a huge debt.
- Before the merger is finalized, management will plan how the companies will come together and identify the business expectations for the new firm.
- The merger integration will be accomplished as quickly as possible to capitalize on the energy and expectations of employees and before new ways of operating set in.
- The integration will involve as many individuals as possible. Managers understand the challenge and opportunities of their operations much better than a small group of headquarters executives.

Hence they will participate in the hundreds of project teams that will design the new company. Guidelines and standardized procedures will give them a sense of what the new company is trying to become.
- No appointment beyond the members of the Executive Management Committee will be made until the new company's organization structure has been defined. Then the best individuals from either firm will be selected to fill key slots. In the meantime, present members of senior management will observe leading candidates as they perform their current responsibilities and either lead or work in merger task forces.
- It is important to keep employees informed about what is happening, what will happen next, and what the company expects of them.
- Businesses that do not fit the strategic concept of the new company will be sold.[3]

I could go on with numerous examples of statements of guiding principles, but many of the principles used by companies are similar to those above. In general, the statements address the following areas:

- The involvement of people from both organizations in the integration process
- How people will be treated in:
  - Selection and retention decisions
  - Communications
- How the merger or acquisition integration processes will be managed
- The focus of the integration effort
- The focus on customers and strategic priorities during the integration

Although a number of principles can be articulated, I would like to highlight three that I have found to be of particular importance to successful integration. They are the degree of involvement of people in the integration process, the value of using a business and strategic perspective in making integration decisions, and the importance of treating people with dignity, respect, and fairness in decisions. These help ensure a well-managed value-enhancing outcome. It is also important to note that these principles should already be part of the principles that the merging or acquiring companies employ in their normal business activities!

Degree of Involvement

The extent to which people from *both* organizations participate in the integration of the combined organizations must be considered early. Involving the target's people is critical since:

- They have relevant knowledge about the target's situation and its history.
- They may have new ideas to contribute (e.g., best practices).

- Their involvement may be critical to gaining acceptance and commitment to decisions and retention.
- They may serve as important internal agents of change within the target.

In an acquisition in particular, the level of involvement should be determined by whether the target has performed well in the past and by whether the target's management and employees are competent and need to be retained. The level of involvement of target employees is characterized in Table 6-2.

When moderate and high levels of involvement are warranted in a merger, the MIO and integration teams should be jointly led and staffed. When moderate and high levels of involvement are warranted in small to medium-sized acquisitions, IC and transition teams should be led by executives and managers of the acquirer. Integration teams should be staffed with key people from both the acquirer and the target. When little involvement is warranted, a few select people who have necessary insights to manage through the transition or are to be retained should participate on integration teams.

Financial and Strategic Perspective

Those involved in the integration process must understand from the outset that decisions and activities must be aligned with the financial and strategic objectives underlying the acquisition, and should not be undertaken for the sake of expediency and local political interests. Failure to align will result in people and organizational units taking actions that do not support the acquisition objectives and detract from value creation.

Fairness, Dignity, and Respect

As decisions that affect individuals are made, caution should be taken that all managers and employees, regardless of organization of origin and whether they are retained or not, are treated fairly and honestly and with a sense of dignity and respect. Not only does this minimize the trauma experienced by those who are not retained by the acquirer, but it sends a very strong signal to those who are retained what the acquirer truly stands for (see the discussion in Chapter 7). Further, the integrated organization should be staffed with the best people, regardless of organization of origin.

Table 6-2 Level of Involvement of Target People

	Desired Retention of Target People	
Performance of Target	**Most**	**Few or None**
Solid	High Involvement	Little Involvement
Turnaround	Moderate Involvement	No Involvement

Similar to the last point, this sends a critical message to all the acquirer and target employees.

The remainder of this chapter outlines the key activities that must be managed for the principles discussed above to be successfully implemented.

DECIDE WHAT TO INTEGRATE AND HOW TO DO IT

After the integration transition structure is defined and communications begun, the MIO/IC must decide how it will manage the integration. There are two critical decisions to make here:

1. What areas of the companies should be integrated?
2. What approaches to integration should be employed?

What to Integrate?

Since integration can cause costly and time-consuming changes, it is suggested that the transition and integration stages engage the "principle of minimum intervention." Only those functions and support areas, lines of business, and geographic areas that are necessary to support the strategic and financial objectives and sources of synergy underlying the acquisition should be integrated.

However, in a transformational merger it is likely that almost every area of the business will be affected. This will necessitate a reassessment of both firms' business strategy and all aspects of the combined organization. As noted in Chapter 2, some mergers are transacted with only a rough understanding of how the organizations will compete in the marketplace and will be integrated. This is more likely to be the case in a merger between large multibusiness companies where there is significant overlap in some divisions and an opportunity to reposition the new combined company. In such cases, all aspects of both companies will be reevaluated during the transition stage, and many of the details will have to be honed.

This means that integration teams must examine each area of the business of both the acquirer and the target and then decide what to integrate. It is hoped that much of this was done during the transaction stage as those involved in due diligence and valuation thought about sources of synergy.

Preparing for the integration decision requires that two activities be performed:

1. The current state (i.e., baseline) of each area should be examined and compared. This includes the area's:
   - Vision, objectives, and strategies
   - Culture
   - Activities performed
   - Systems

- Business processes
- Operating and business models
- Organizational structure
- Positions, descriptions, and head count
- Operating and capital budgets

For the sake of simplicity, a side-by-side comparison of each of these elements should be made. Table 6-3 shows one way to do this. This comparison helps articulate each company's approach and the similarities and differences between the companies. Once these are understood, the teams can then begin to analyze what makes sense for the new company moving forward.

2. One or several scenarios for the end-state organizational design, based on financial and strategic objectives, should be developed. This provides a basis for understanding any gaps between what each organization is currently doing and what the new organization needs to be doing in each area.

For example, a German company involved in sorting and recognition systems used by postal authorities, priority shippers, and retail and distribution acquired a U.S. company after a careful strategic assessment. The acquisition expanded the German company's geographic presence in the NAFTA region, furthered its technological leadership, and strengthened its position as a total system supplier. After examining each company independently, the German company developed a pro forma of what the integrated organization would look like and then began to develop the details behind it. The concept set the stage for the integration teams. As illustrated in Figure 6-2, the primary scenario for the end-state organization was a transnational organization[4] where there would be localization of certain activities and global integration of others. Localization allowed needed responsiveness to the idiosyncrasies of country environments. Global integration allowed certain activities, such as product development, to be

Table 6-3 Assessing the Current Organizational State

Area	Topic	Acquirer	Target	Similarities	Differences
Strategy	Market focus				
Human resources	Medical plan				
Information technology	Software				
Manufacturing	Production process				
Purchasing	Supplier policy				

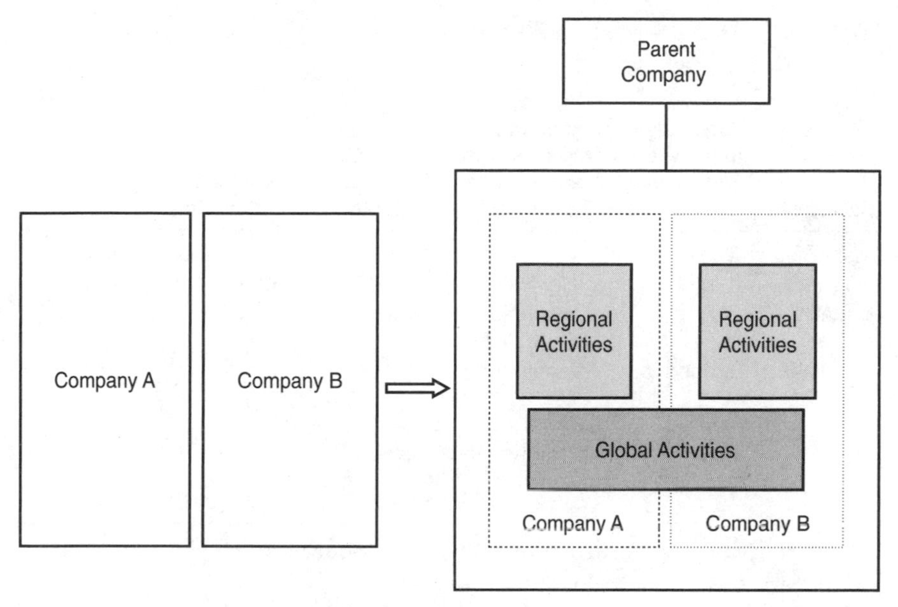

Figure 6-2 Pro Forma Organizational Concept

scaled such that the costs of development could be amortized over a worldwide volume. These activities would require some level of standardization. Thus it became the work of the integration teams to decide which activities would be global and which would remain local and how to realize that. First, the team had to detail the current state of each organization and then examine the pro forma. From there it had to identify the gaps between the two. Once this activity is completed, a methodology for deciding what and how to integrate must be chosen.

What Integration Approaches to Use?

As discussed in Chapter 2, and illustrated in Tables 6-4 and 6-5, integration decisions should be influenced by the financial and strategic objectives underlying a particular acquisition and the sources of synergy that are potentially available.

It is suggested that the areas of the companies to be integrated should be benchmarked to determine best practices and tested against the metrics that are deemed important to achieving the forecasted earnings and cashflows (e.g., variable and fixed cost, customer retention, quality, productivity). This will involve:

1. Using an integration template or best practice that the acquirer has already developed and can apply to new acquisitions
2. Using a best practice that has been developed by a target and applying it to the acquirer and subsequent acquisitions

Table 6-4 Linking Strategic Objectives and Synergies

	Strategic Objective				
Type of Synergy	**Consolidate Market within Geographic Area**	**Extend or Add New Products, Services, and Technologies**	**Enter a New Geographic Market**	**Vertically Integrate**	**Enter a New Line of Business**
Cost	High	Low	Low	Moderate	Low
Revenue	Low	High	High	Low	None
Market power	High	Moderate	Low	High	None
Intangible	Moderate	Moderate	Moderate	Low	Low

Table 6-5 Strategic Objectives and Impact on Integration

	Level and Type of Integration		
Strategic Objective	**Consolidation**	**Standardization**	**Coordination**
Consolidate Market within Geographic Area	High	High	High
Extend or Add New Products, Services, and Technologies	Moderate	Moderate	High
Enter a New Geographic Market	Low	Low to high	Low to High
Vertically Integrate	Low	Low	High
Enter a New Line of Business	Low	Low	Low

3. Using a best practice that has been developed by one of the merger partners and that can be used in the combined organization
4. Working in collaboration with the target or merger partner to develop a new best practice

Figure 6-3 provides a decision tree used to make integration decisions for a company that was engaged in an industry roll-up. The decision tree identifies three integration options: forced assimilation, voluntary assimilation, and innovation that the acquirer would need to employ to ensure that synergies were captured.

Gaining Acceptance and Commitment

In any one of these three methods, acceptance and commitment to new approaches will have to be secured. If not, resistance to change may

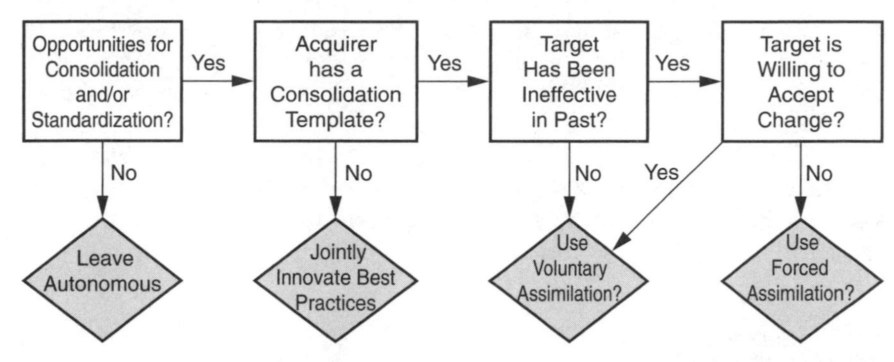

Figure 6-3 Integration Approach Decision Process

become a problem. This may not be a problem, however, if an acquirer intends to replace the acquired people! Thus, the following approaches and their implications should be considered:

Forced assimilation—where a target is *required* to adopt the practices of an acquirer. This is likely to be met with the greatest resistance to change by target people, as they feel like their cultures and practices are threatened. Many target people describe this as "superiority syndrome" by the acquirer and feel as if they are being treated as second class citizens. However, this may be necessary if the target has been ineffective in the past, requires change, and has not done so willingly. It may also be required if a large acquirer is folding a small target's backroom activities into its, regardless of who has the best practice. In such cases, it may be best to replace target people since their support and commitment may not be likely.

Voluntary assimilation—where a target *voluntarily* adopts the practices of an acquirer or a merger partner (or vice versa). A target may not have been as successful as the acquirer in the past and may be pleased to have a new approach. This is likely to be met with higher levels of support. However, some conflict and problems may still result for those who have to adapt to the changes. Moreover, it will greatly depend upon how the acquirer manages this process. See Chapter 7 for additional insights.

Innovation—where integrating groups decide to abandon existing practices in favor of newer and better ones. Typically, there is no sense of superiority by either the acquirer or the target, and the focus is on defining a new best practice.

To innovate, organizations often employ reengineering or process improvement approaches to develop changes that logically fit with the strategic and financial considerations driving the merger or acquisition. In the merger between Boeing, McDonnell Douglas, and Rockwell, the company utilized McDonnell Douglas's R&D center, Phantom Works, to drive the integration.[5] The center was used as a general technology generator to improve manufacturing processes throughout the entire corporation.

Challenges of adaption here will be similar to those of any work group going through a change process. The process may also require outside assistance or new people with fresh insights and ideas. Again, a merger or an acquisition may create an excellent opportunity to shake things up.

People will only voluntarily assimilate and support innovation when they:

1. Understand the strategic and financial objectives behind the deal
2. Participate in both designing and implementing new approaches
3. See the value each organization brings to the table
4. Understand how the solutions will benefit the combined organization
5. Realize they will personally benefit or not lose from changes

Mapping the Integration

The areas to be integrated can be mapped based on benchmarking, and then the changes in each area that need to be made and the impact of the changes on synergies can be detailed. For example, Figure 6-4 provides a simple representation of the integration of several acquired security monitoring companies by a large acquirer as part of an industry roll-up. The industry was fragmented, with opportunities to grow through both geographic expansion and consolidation within geographic markets. Almost all the players were small, privately owned firms concentrated in narrow geographic markets. There were opportunities to achieve economies of scale through cost reduction and transfer of best practices and innovation. To achieve these, the acquirer examined four core areas of the business: call centers, installation, sales, and customer service. After careful analysis, several conclusions were reached.

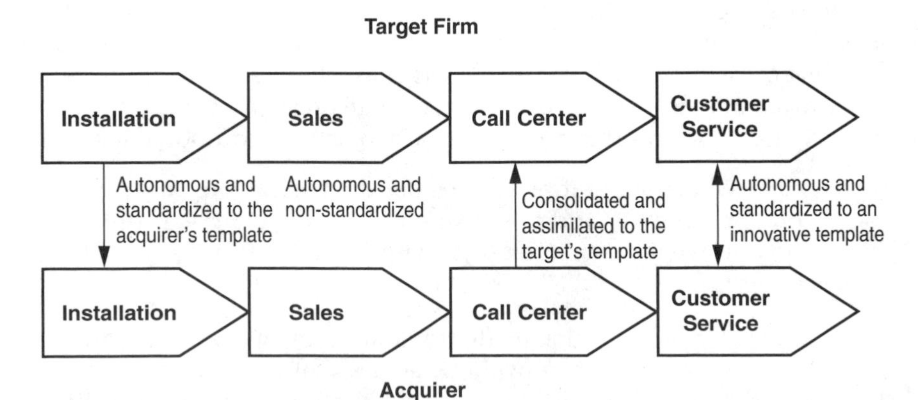

Figure 6-4 Representation of Integrating Acquisitions Selectively

First, many of the acquired companies had their own local call centers. None of them were very efficient, with high fixed costs. Based on a comprehensive study, it was decided that the individual call centers could be shut down and consolidated into two nationally scaled centers. Moreover, these centers could be located in geographic areas where employees could easily be hired and the lowest costs could be achieved. All that was needed was access to a telephone line, a key part of monitoring. The center design was developed as part of the roll-up strategy by the acquirer. As a result, significant efficiencies and cost reductions, and thus synergies, could be achieved. It is important to note that this strategy is quite similar to that used by major acquisitive banks (e.g., Sun Trust, Bank of America), whereby "backroom activities" such as information processing can be eliminated for each bank and centrally consolidated and redundant branches can be consolidated.

It was also found that each firm had a different approach to sales, installation, and customer service. Based on a best-practice study, it was decided that the acquired firms would be standardized to a best-practice model established by the acquirer. The model, which significantly reduced costs and improved response time, eventually became a template for future acquisitions. However, whereas the call center could be consolidated, these functions needed to be locally decentralized. The only consolidation that took place was when multiple acquisitions were made within the same geographic area and there was redundancy in people and physical assets.

Unfortunately, neither the acquirer nor the acquired firms had a very successful customer service capability. Thus, the acquirer used the acquisitions as a window of opportunity to innovate and develop a new approach that became the standard for the new company. This activity was carried out by an integration team, with the involvement of people from all the firms being consolidated.

The decision was made to leave the sales organizations relatively autonomous. A few procedures were standardized, but it was determined that there was enough variance in local markets not to force a standard model. Finally, a standard approach to installation, based on a best-practice template established by the buyer, was transferred to the acquired companies. Fortunately, through training programs, employee visits, and incentives, acquired employees embraced the changes.

It is important to note that the best-practices model identified the most effective organizational structure, activities to be performed, budgets, positions, physical assets, and head count that were needed to run each area. Moreover, the model carefully tracked cost savings in real estate rent and other overhead, salary reduction and elimination for branch operations and corporate staff, other corporate overhead, marketing, and other costs. Some capital expenditure would be needed. All the elements above were factored into both the valuation model and the impact on earnings and cashflow.

The illustration clearly indicates that there are multiple ways in which to integrate organizations and that multiple approaches need to be employed within each merger or acquisition. The approach chosen needs to be driven by both the strategic and financial objectives underlying the deal, but also by the judgment of integration teams as they attempt to learn the best way in which to manage the various parts of the business.

This was the case in the consolidation of the call center operations. The choice of physical location remained open to analysis by integration teams and was based on a sound methodology and goals (e.g., cost, quality, cycle time). For example, a call center could be centralized and performed either at an acquirer business unit; at the target, which may already have a best practice (i.e., center of excellence); or at a new and better location, yet to be determined.

Whether a target can serve as a center of excellence for a function or an activity will depend upon its history and prior success. Keeping an open mind about the capabilities and value that a target may bring will be helpful in finding better solutions to meet financial and strategic objectives and in building the support and commitment of target people.

In addition to practices, consolidation and assimilation of cultures, names, and identities of the organizations also need to be addressed. These are usually far more difficult to achieve than physical asset consolidation.

Managing How Fast You Go

There is considerable debate on how long the integration process should take. Speed can best be defined as the time it takes to make changes in the buyer, seller, or both and thus integrate the firms. Some argue that you should move quickly and integrate as fast as possible. People are expecting change, and delays prolong the uncertainty. As Sandy Weill, Citigroup's chairman and CEO, notes:

> Make decisions faster than you normally might, rather than slower . . . it will help you hold onto the good people and send the right message to everyone.[6]

Speed avoids periods of uncertainty in direction, both in the organization and in the marketplace. It also sets an early expectation that changes will be made and mitigates some of the buildup of political resistance to change.

Others argue, however, that integration should move more slowly, whereby careful assessments of how the organizations can be put together can be made. Moving slowly allows for a well-thought-out and planned integration. This argument is probably due to the incompleteness of the due diligence or preclosing acquisition integration planning process—all the more the reason to get as much analysis and planning completed as possible prior to closing.

Fortunately, there are a few studies that provide insights on this issue. A study by PriceWaterhouseCoopers[7] of 124 medium to large companies that executed a merger or acquisition within the last three years found that companies that managed the transition faster had more favorable gross margins, cashflows, productivity, profitability, and speed to market. Of those surveyed, 89 percent felt they should have managed the transition even more quickly. Unfortunately, there is not much precision in the definition of speed. Respondents simply indicated whether the transition was managed more or less quickly than their normal pace of work. Speed of integration of operating policies was also reported to have an effect on employee reactions. More rapid integration led to greater confidence in company direction, clarity of company direction, product focus, and speed of decision making. Also, more rapid integration was associated positively with acceptance of new vision, employee commitment and motivation, customer relations and communications to employees and customers.

Secondary findings of several other studies do provide some indication of the virtues of a fast versus slow integration process and the context in which one or the other may be expected to lead to greater postacquisition performance. In a case study of three international mergers,[8] a slow integration process was used to minimize conflict between the merging partners. Parity (i.e., balancing of management positions between the two companies), for example, was instituted between the power, responsibility, and authority positions of the combining firms' management teams. However, this process was later blamed for the combined firm's inability to develop cooperation within the board and management levels, along with a common identity necessary for postacquisition performance. The slow integration process used by these firms was actually found to inhibit, rather than enhance, integration.

Another study[9] found that the successful acquisition of Nokia-Data by ICL was the result of selectively and simultaneously utilizing both slow and fast approaches to integration. The study indicates that a key to the success of the merger was allowing time for each partner to learn about each other and for ICL to identify merger priorities. Change was phased in over time, without stripping either company of the areas it valued most. On the other hand, the two companies decided to begin to work on a new range of products, which appealed to the acquired employees who were weary of the acquirer's bureaucracy and potential inability to maintain the acquired firm's responsive decision-making practices. Furthermore, the decision was made to change every Nokia-Data sign in its home country of Finland to an ICL sign on the date of acquisition approval and to engage in press and other media campaigns to leave no doubt about the acquisition. This study clearly indicates that the speed of integration is complex, in that some facets of integration may be best suited for slow speed and others best suited for fast.

Based on research findings regarding the integration of R&D functions among combining manufacturing firms, another study[10] also suggests that speed is a complex issue. In this study it was found that human resources–focused integration plans and actions that help to promote a gradual process in which individuals from two organizations learn to work together and cooperate in the transfer of strategic capabilities improve postacquisition performance. It was also found that the centralization of R&D within the acquirer appeared to quickly provide clear strategic R&D objectives for the combined organization, resolute implementation of burdensome organizational changes, and avoidance of endless discussions on a joint R&D strategy. Speed, thereby, substantially reduced the uncertainty among the acquired firms' R&D professionals.

From a process perspective, a study[11] found that the speed at which integration occurred depends upon whether people were involved in a merger workshop. Those employees engaged in a workshop were able to develop a shared diagnosis or vision of an improved combined entity. This created increased organizational commitment and openness to postacquisition integration and, consequently, quicker integration. In addition, the study suggests that encouraging learning between the merging firms which combines both cognitive learning, based on rational processes, and behavioral learning, based on experimental learning, also improves the speed of integration.

Although the research is not conclusive, it suggests that integration should move purposefully and as quickly as possible. More importantly, speed considerations should be weighed against commitments to delivering earnings and cashflows. Premiums paid for an acquisition and commitments made to achieving synergies within a specified time frame should have a great bearing on speed There is certainly more than one executive who aggressively committed to achieving synergies within one year of the closing of the deal. Doing so becomes a critical acid test of the success of the deal and ultimately that of the executive.

However, one should be realistic about how long it might take to implement change. Some areas (e.g., information systems) may require significant time to integrate, even after integration changes have been agreed to. Experience suggests that fully integrating organizations (e.g., many areas, cultures) can take anywhere from one to five years, depending upon the relative size of the target and the extent of the integration. In the next section I will discuss how to put together an integration plan.

DEVELOP AN INTEGRATION PLAN TO DRIVE IMPLEMENTATION

The integration planning process requires that two key activities take place. First is the handoff between the due diligence and integration teams.

Otherwise valuable information, analyses, and insights gained during due diligence will be lost. Second, a project plan to ensure that the transition and integration activities are successfully completed should be developed and implemented.

Manage Handoff with Due Diligence Team

Optimally, the person serving as the transition team leader would serve as the due diligence team leader for a particular acquisition, and a key person or people from the due diligence team would join the transition and integration teams. In a merger this would be the responsibility of the MIO.

If the transition team leader cannot serve as the due diligence team leader, then:

1. All materials developed during due diligence are given to the transition team leader.
2. Transition team leader is fully briefed on:
   a. What analyses were and were not thoroughly completed.
   b. What was learned about the target.
   c. Any problems or issues that were identified during due diligence that would affect integration.
   d. Assumptions regarding levels and sources of synergies that were built into the valuations and purchase price.
3. The MIO or IC takes responsibility for ensuring the handoff is made.

Again, this is a critical step since many M&A activities are fragmented in organizations, especially large ones. For example, it is very likely that a corporate business development group is responsible for due diligence and an operating manager is responsible for integration. Coordination is not automatic and must be managed.

Develop an Integration Project Plan

During both the transition and integration stages, numerous activities will need to be performed to manage the integration. This requires systematic and disciplined project management. This activity should be coordinated by a support team working within the MIO or directly for the IC. As noted earlier, integration team leaders need to either have solid project management skills or get a quick course prior to beginning their work. It is essential that the transition and integration teams develop and execute project plans that detail:

1. All the analyses and activities that need to be conducted prior to closing
2. Activities that need to be executed after closing, or what some acquirers have labeled "day one" and beyond (i.e., the point at which the acquirer owns the target and can begin implementing changes)

To effectively manage all the details required to plan and execute the integration, it is essential that the transition and integration teams be provided with the following:

- Project management software
- Report templates
- Guidelines for completion of reports
- Reporting time lines
- Appropriate checklists

Project management software should be employed to develop integration plans for each team in the first weeks after the acquisition announcement is made. Each team's plan should roll up through an automated process to the MIO, in the case of a merger, and to the IC and transition team leader, in the case of multiple acquisitions, who will then manage the "critical path." This comprehensive plan will be the document that guides the implementation and monitoring of the transition and integration processes.

The plan should be reviewed and approved by the MIO, IC, and transition team leader. This plan will determine the magnitude of the overall project, the resource needs of the project, and the final project organization structure.

The progress of all teams, milestones, issues to resolve, and changes to be made will be monitored based on updates to the plan. By following a formal monitoring process, management at all levels can stay abreast of the transition-integration process. This type of monitoring allows red-flagged issues to reach management with appropriate lead time for responding successfully.

Key activities to develop project plans include:

1. Major activities to be completed
2. Time frames and milestones for completion of major activities
3. Specific responsibilities for execution of activities (departments and people)
4. Resources needed to carry out activities:
   a. People (existing and additional)
   b. Financial
   c. Timing of need
5. Pro forma and budgetary impact (recurring and incremental impact) from any proposed recommendations:
   a. Revenues
   b. Costs
   c. Capital investments
6. Contingencies and potential impact on:
   a. Employees
   b. Customers

   c. Other key stakeholders
   d. Time frames
7. Contingency plans
8. Known potential roadblocks to be dealt with and solutions for dealing with them
9. Approach for monitoring and managing the integration project plan

Table 6-6 illustrates a "high-level" project plan and time line for managing transition activities for a bank acquisition. All these activities occurred over a five-month period and were completed just prior to the closing. Table 6-7 provides a more detailed project plan for one phase of the project plan, an organizational assessment of a target. This phase was to be completed over a one-week period prior to the closing.

Table 6-8 illustrates a high-level project plan that was used to consolidate call centers. Target company centers were to be closed and consolidated into two national-scaled centers of the acquirer according to the time frame in the plan.

Project plans help ensure that the numerous activities that must be completed to integrate organizations and capture synergies are successfully managed. Project planning provides a coherent basis for organization, accountability, teamwork, communication, and ultimately control.

A FINAL NOTE

Numerous activities must be planned during the transition stage. To the extent that they can be completed prior to the closing, the greater the momentum to implement them after the closing. This requires a coherent and well-organized process, with the proper people from both an acquirer and a target or merger partners involved. It also requires that roles and responsibilities of the key people be clearly spelled out.

Table 6-6 High-Level Bank Integration Plan

ID	Task Name	Start	Finish	Resource Names	September	October	November
1	Project organization	9/3/01	9/20/01				
2	Identify transition approach	9/23/01	12/31/01				
3	Prepare for day one	9/23/01	12/31/01				
4	Manage employee retention	9/23/01	1/31/02				
5	Marketing communication strategy	9/23/01	1/15/02				
6	Bank branch optimization model	9/23/01	11/15/01				
7	Product mapping	11/1/01	1/15/02				
8	Gap analysis	12/31/01	1/31/02				
9	Systems inventory and mapping	11/1/01	1/15/02				
10	Statements/notices/reports	11/1/01	1/15/02				
11	Internal financial controls	11/1/01	1/15/02				
12	Training approach	11/1/01	1/15/02				
13	Equipment surveys	11/1/01	1/15/02				
14	Facilities surveys	9/23/01	1/15/02				
15	Early implementation opportunities	11/1/01	1/15/02				
16	Implementation/testing approach	11/1/01	1/15/02				
17	Implementation scope finalization	11/1/01	1/15/02				
18	Implementation plans	1/15/02	1/31/02				

Table 6-7 **Detailed Organizational Assessment Integration Plan**

ID	Task Name	Start	Finish	Accountable	May 20, '01	May 27, '01
1	Prepare employee retention and communication plan	5/21/01	5/25/01			
2	Create key dates document	5/21/01	5/25/01			
3	Determine teller system	5/21/01	5/25/01			
4	Establish budget time lines	5/21/01	5/25/01			
5	Identify personnel generalist for transition	5/21/01	5/25/01			
6	Identify MIO staff admin. assistant	5/21/01	5/25/01			
7	Identify staff analysts	5/21/01	5/25/01			
8	Meet with acquired bank management	5/21/01	5/25/01			
9	Name transition manager	5/21/01	5/25/01			
10	Name line executive manager	5/21/01	5/25/01			
11	Name integration team members	5/21/01	5/25/01			
12	Prepare budget templates for distribution	5/21/01	5/25/01			
13	Develop welcome letter for new employees	5/21/01	5/25/01			
14	Select physical office space for transition team	5/21/01	5/25/01			
15	Set up office equipment	5/21/01	5/25/01			
16	Set up communications	5/21/01	5/25/01			
17	Conduct project orientation and kickoff	5/21/01	5/25/01			

Table 6-8 Call Center Consolidation Time-Line

ID	Task Name	Duration	Start	Finish	Accountable	May	June	July	August
1	Dallas	24w	5/21/01	11/2/01	Jones				
2	Houston	24w	5/21/01	11/2/01	Smith				
3	Indianapolis	29w	5/21/01	12/7/01	Jenkins				
4	Kansas City	33w	5/21/01	1/4/02	Green				
5	Chicago	37w	5/21/01	2/1/02	Sloane				
6	Minneapolis	41w	5/21/01	3/1/02	Roberts				
7	Milwaukee	45w	5/21/01	3/29/02	Chavez				

7

Managing Staffing, Retention, and Redundancy

At some point in every merger or acquisition, it is inevitable that executives will have to address issues of staffing, retention, and redundancy. Invariably, there will be redundancy in areas of the organizations that overlap, and executives will have to manage the orderly departure of people from the organization. This will certainly be the case where cost synergies are being sought. Even in cases where an organization is growing through the addition of new products and services or geographic expansion, it is an excellent opportunity to examine the capabilities of people and to decide whom to retain and whom to let go. It is even more critical when executives are looking to transform a company by acquiring new capabilities.

Deciding who the best people are, developing strategies to retain them, and managing the termination of those who are not needed will be essential to building a new, more competitive company. One executive challenged me on the importance of these issues. He told me the people issues were exaggerated. He said that he would rely on attrition to eliminate redundancy. He wasn't going to worry about devising a complicated staffing process and fighting to retain people. I asked him what type of people he thought would stay and what type would leave.

In general, decisions concerning the fate of people in a merger or an acquisition are not easy to make, can be quite political, and can have a dramatic impact on everyone in an organization. Three sets of interrelated "people" decisions must be managed during the integration process, and these are addressed in the remainder of the chapter.

1. Staffing the integrated organization
2. Retaining key people
3. Managing employee redundancy

In making these decisions, two of the guiding principles discussed in Chapter 6 and highlighted below are important.

TREAT PEOPLE WITH FAIRNESS, DIGNITY, AND RESPECT

The success of the staffing process depends upon the extent to which it is perceived as fair.[1] Although people have different definitions of what fairness means, most people involved in a merger or an acquisition would agree that:

- People from both the acquirer and target or from both merger partners are given an equal opportunity to be selected for positions.
- Those who are not retained are given a reasonable opportunity to transition out of or to other parts of the organization.

Not only do these principles have a bearing on those who do not receive a position, but they also do on those who remain with the new organization. How this process is handled sends clear signals to those who remain about what the real values and culture of the new organization are—versus the espoused ones captured in executive speeches and written materials.

This point was exemplified in the merger of two major oil companies. As part of the merger, a number of redundant information technology operations in the southwest United States were to be consolidated. Decisions about whom to retain or let go were made.

Without any advanced notice, a middle-level manager from the target was met at his office by two armed guards. He was informed, for the first time, that he was no longer employed with the company. No reasons were provided. He was instructed not to touch or take anything from his office and was escorted off the premises. He was simply told that human resources would contact him with all necessary information and his personal effects would be sent to his home. Needless to say, he was devastated. He had no chance to say goodbye to friends and colleagues. The 20 years he worked for the target seemed to mean nothing, and he was humiliated. More importantly, there were 18 direct reports that watched this event take place. Within 18 months all of them had left the company. In follow-up exit interviews they indicated that on that day they knew exactly what the acquirer was all about. They did not need any fancy banners and executive speeches about the company's culture and values.

COMPETENCE

If the real objective is to build a more capable organization as a result of a merger or an acquisition, then it is essential that it be staffed with the best people possible. This is of utmost importance when the primary assets being acquired are people. Clearly it is not easy to identify who these best people are. Thus it is incumbent upon merger partners or an acquirer to develop an approach for ensuring that reasonable selection criteria and a process for choosing the best people are established.

STAFFING THE INTEGRATED ORGANIZATION

An organized systematic process for staffing is vital to the integration process, regardless of whether it involves a small acquisition or a large merger. Of all the decisions made during integration, none are more important than those that determine who will fill key positions.

In the case of a small acquisition the process may not be that complex. There may be only a few positions to name. In a large merger the process may indeed be quite complex, with thousands of positions being named, ranging from the CEO to frontline employees. In the remainder of this section I will present a basic approach that has been used successfully in both large mergers and large and small acquisitions.

In a large merger where there is overlap from the top all the way to the bottom of the organization, the process begins by naming the CEO of the combined company, with the approval of the boards of directors. This is often done by negotiation between the two CEOs or lobbying with the board. To avoid this tough choice, many merging companies have attempted the co-CEO role. I will discuss this later in the chapter. Once the CEO is named, candidates for the next level of positions are selected, usually jointly by the CEOs of both companies. It is important to name the top positions and key people as early as possible to stabilize the transition and solidify the basic organizational structure. In the Chevron-Texaco merger it involved 61 people. In the Baxter–Travenol Laboratories–American Hospital Supply it involved 100 people.

After the top positions are filled, the staffing process needs to continue until all the open or new positions in the combined organization have been named. Depending upon the nature of the integration, staffing may range from a few position changes to a complete revamping of the organization. Moreover, key people may leave the organization prior to the closing due to concerns over whether they will have a job or not, leaving unanticipated vacancies. (More will be said about retention later on.)

How positions are filled is vital. On the one hand it is important to be unbiased toward people in regard to organization of origin. On the other hand it can be problematic if the primary focus for staffing decisions is to seek balance between the two organizations. Caution should be given to the notion that balance constitutes fairness.

Some organizations attempt to provide a balance between the number of people retained from each company involved in a merger or an acquisition. Although noble, it usually does not work. When balance is more important than competence, it is unlikely that a new organization that is capable of competing will be created. It also sends a signal to the organization that competence is not the most important criterion for the future. What message does that give people? This point is driven home by Harry Stonecipher, former CEO of McDonnell Douglas. Commenting on the merger between McDonnell, Boeing, and Rockwell, he noted that:

> It's not about making everybody from McDonnell Douglas, Boeing, or Rockwell happy . . . it's about making one new Boeing company with the best people in the best place.[2]

In Chapter 4, the importance of assessing the performance, talent, competence, skills, motivation, and management style of key people during the transaction stage was discussed. The information collected then becomes a critical part of the decision making during this stage.

As the scenarios for the new organization (e.g., objectives, strategy, structure, positions, competencies, head count) are developed, it will become increasingly clear as to how many and what type of people will be needed after the deal closes. Assessments not conducted during the transaction stage must then be done during the transition stage. Again, the earlier these assessments are done, the better, since until people are named to their position, uncertainty will run rampant. Value leakage in terms of quality people leaving will become a major issue.

Typically, the staffing of lower-level positions is often not completed until late in the transition stage or even until after closing. This is the case because a thorough review of people takes time, and many of the positions cannot be detailed in advance due to lack of cooperation or the inability to discuss the organization in detail.[3] While speed is critical to a successful integration, making the right decisions may be more important. After all, such decisions affect people's lives and are the backbone of a successful organization!

Once the top spots are named and the basic organizational structure is put into place, the executives who have been assigned these positions will begin to select their staff. This process will eventually cascade down through the organization. Again, the nature of the integration will determine how extensive this effort is.

Managing the Staffing Process

Figure 7-1 presents a staffing approach that has been employed by a number of successful acquirers. The approach is similar to a general staffing approach used by many firms. What differentiates it in an M&A context is the:

- Sources of candidates considered
- Selection process utilized

Simply put, care must be taken that there is not bias in either the pool of candidates considered or the choice of candidates itself. It is very easy for executives or managers to subconsciously fall victim to bias due to friendships, or to the fact that they have worked with or know someone from their own organization better than from the target or merger partner. This is natural and is likely unless there is an articulated process to counter it.

To ensure objectivity is brought into the selection process and that a thorough pool of candidates is created, a staffing integration team should be given oversight for this effort and report directly to the MIO/IC. The team should be co-led by human resources executives and managers from both companies and interact with other integration teams whose areas are affected by selection decisions. It is important to note that the staffing integration team does not decide whom to hire. That ultimately is the responsibility of the executives and managers who will oversee the retained employee.

There are two key roles this team should play. First, as positions are identified, the staffing integration team ensures that a slate of candidates from both organizations is considered. If a viable internal candidate does not exist, external candidates should be sought. Second, the team ensures that each candidate is given "due process" in the selection decision. This means that all candidates are given serious consideration and their files reviewed. The objective is not to create a bureaucratic process but to create a systematic and fair process.

After the closing, and once the major positions in the organization are named, integration teams should be disbanded. However, there still may be numerous positions that remain unfilled. The hope is that the major positions have been taken care of and the basic organization is in place and capable of functioning. At this point the staffing process will fall in the hands of line management. With HR support, line managers should be encouraged to continue a staffing approach similar to the one outlined above. HR should also ensure that a slate and the rationale for selections are provided prior to decisions being communicated to people. To ensure fairness, one acquirer created a review and appeals board. The board reviewed every employee file to ensure that those who had been identified for one or more positions were considered. Moreover, a rationale had to be provided for people not chosen and why someone else was a better fit. The board's role was to ensure that the process was fair, not to second-guess selection decisions. Regardless of the process, it is still in the best interest of managers to retain the best people they possibly can.

The following is a brief overview of the steps in Figure 7-1:

1. Develop a position description for each position being filled. Include:
   a. Roles, responsibilities, and accountabilities.
   b. Whom they will report to.
   c. Skills, knowledge, and competencies required for the job.

2. Solicit a slate of candidates from both companies participating in the merger or acquisition for each position. Consider candidates from other functions, lines of business, and geographic areas. If no internal candidates exist, engage an external search.
3. Collect information on each candidate. Information can be secured from multiple sources (see Chapter 4 for a more comprehensive discussion). Make sure information tracks with item 1c above. The objective is to collect as much valid information as possible that will help predict a candidate's success in the proposed position. To the extent that multiple sources of information conclude the same thing about a candidate's competence, the higher the probability that an accurate judgment can be made. Certainly this must be weighed against budgetary and timing considerations.
4. Based on the above information, reduce the pool to a list of "viable candidates." The assessment can be based on the consensus of multiple decision makers. It is important that the direct manager of the position to be filled and members of the staffing integration team (or human resources after closing) participate in the decision.
5. Based on the information collected, interview candidates to fill in gaps in information and to further verify information collected. Evaluate candidates with respect to how well they exhibit the competencies required by the position. If the new position requires a geographic transfer, inquire whether the person would be willing to relocate. This can become a problem and should be verified rather than assumed. More will said about this below. In general, it is wise to make sure there are qualified backup candidates in the event the candidate rejects an offer.
6. Using all relevant information, select the candidate. Involve outside consultants if additional information or insights are needed. Once the decision has been made, document it, including the rationale. Table 7-1 presents a simple grid for capturing the selection decision-making process.
7. Before any decision is announced, make sure that:
   a. HR reviews it for Equal Employment Opportunity (EEO) analysis.
   b. Salary and benefit package is put together.
   c. Any other requisite approvals are sought.
8. Once decisions are made, be sure they are clearly communicated to the candidate, then to others as deemed necessary.
9. Once decisions are made, prepare to execute them:
   a. If the candidate has been offered a position, prepare to make a specific and attractive offer, including geographic location, salary, benefits, perks, etc., to recruit the candidate for the job.
   b. If the candidate has not been offered a position and has no role in the new organization, prepare to sever the person from the organization.

c. If the candidate has been placed on hold, prepare to provide the candidate with a temporary role and explain how the decision process will work from here. In this situation the person will be considered for reassignment into vacancies that exist.
d. If the candidate will only be retained for a defined period of time, usually to assist with the transition, explain that the person is needed for a period of time, usually to complete the transition. Prepare an incentive to motivate the person to remain throughout the transition.

As staffing decisions are made, the staffing integration team and eventually the HR organization need to continually update the actual impact of these decisions on total head count and budgets. These will then need to be tracked against forecasted budgets for each function, line of business, and geographic area to ensure they are in line with base-case financial and synergy projections. This information should be shared with the synergy capture team as well.

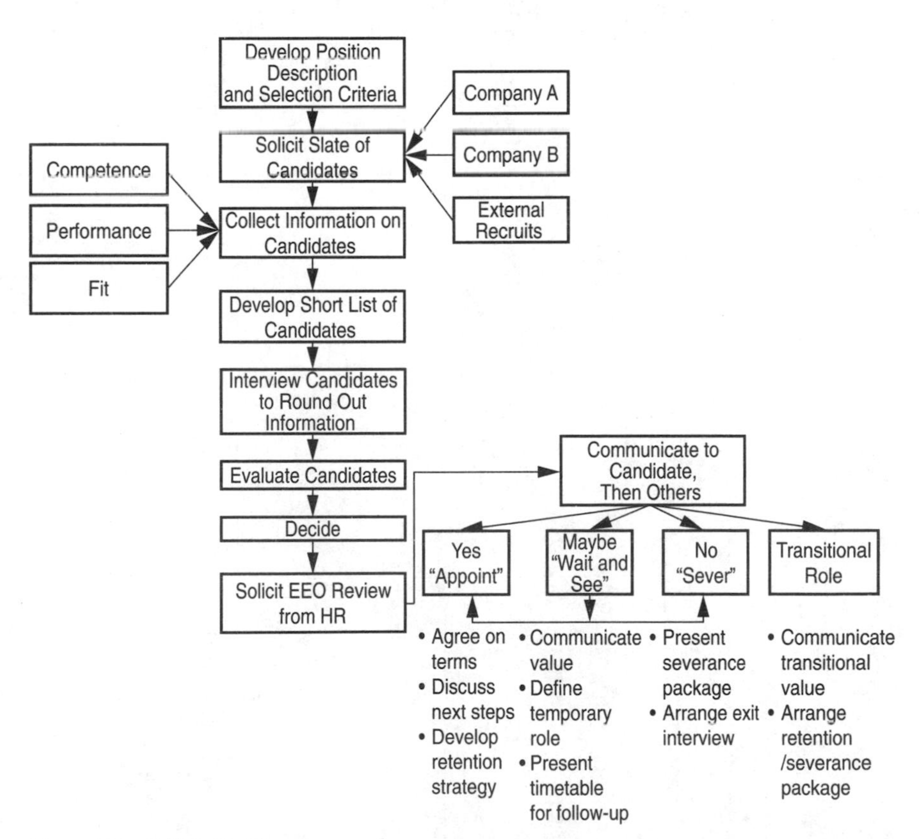

Figure 7-1 M&A Staffing Approach

Table 7-1 Selection Decision Form

Position ______________

Location ______________

Candidate (Name)	Current Position	Current Location	Predecessor Organization	Rating (Rank Order)	Willingness to Relocate and Accept the Position	Rationale for Ranking	Salary Requirements	Decision*	Action Plan

*Acceptable candidate—make an offer.
Unacceptable candidate for position but consider for another position.
Unacceptable candidate; sever from the organization.
Candidate needed during transition.

A Note on the Co-CEO

The concept of the co-CEO has become a fascination of companies seeking a "merger of equals." In an attempt to deal with egos and to send a signal that neither organization will dominate after a merger, the CEOs attempt to share power.

While nice in theory, it is extremely difficult to implement in practice. By the time executives reach the top spot, they are used to having power and have considerable ego. While the co-CEO approach may be well intentioned, the likelihood that CEOs could share the position for an extended period of time is relatively small. In fact, the *Forbes* 500 study, cited in Chapter 1, pertaining to the top 10 pitfalls in achieving synergy, notes that the clash of managerial egos and styles is the sixth most important factor leading to failure.

Based on an examination of several key mergers, it is apparent that the co-CEO is most likely to work well under a couple of conditions. The first is that it is limited to the time it takes to manage through the transition to an integrated organization. During that period it sends a signal to both organizations that neither company's employees will be treated as second-class citizens. It also provides some stability to ensure that the integration process is managed in an orderly fashion. The second is that one of the CEOs is clearly designated as the leader of the new organization, with the other on a timed retirement or severance agreement. Under these circumstances the likelihood of power battles and ego clashes is diminished. A couple of examples will help illustrate this.

The Case of Citigroup[4]

Sharing power may have been the only way to get the merger of Travelers and Citicorp done in the first place, as both companies' boards were extremely loyal to their CEOs. However, the decision to share power led to balkanization, and the two CEOs inevitably ended up fighting for territory. The ability to share power is not a typical CEO characteristic. CEOs are trained to command by individual vision. They are fond of invoking team spirit—as long as they are captains of their teams. They don't often wield equal power in major company decisions, despite public pronouncement of close consultation.

Sanford Weill

Sanford I. Weill rose to prominence in the 1960s when he started the securities firm Shearson Loeb Rhodes. After selling the firm in 1981, he bought the Commercial Credit Company, which would eventually become, after numerous acquisitions, Travelers Group, Inc.

Weill is a living legend on Wall Street. Born in a middle-class Brooklyn neighborhood, Weill rose to the top using his street smarts and flamboyant personality. In 1998, Weill was the third highest-paid CEO in the United States, receiving $167 million in compensation, largely as a result of his role in the merger. Weill earned a reputation as a tenacious cost-cutter who focuses on the short-term goals of stock prices and earnings. The acquisition-loving leader maintains a close inner circle that is among the most loyal to be found in any major corporation. He values his personal relationships and helped his son, Marc, become chief investment officer at Travelers. Weill's personality and style trickle down throughout the organization he leads and have a tremendous impact on the corporate culture of his company

In February 1998, Weill contacted Citicorp chief John Reed and presented his idea for Citigroup. The rest is history. Sanford Weill, now 67 years old, was named one of *Businessweek* magazine's top 25 managers of the year for 2000. When asked about retirement in 1998, the man who personifies corporate America replied, "I don't have any plans for retirement. That's the responsibility of our board and I enjoy what I am doing."

John Reed

Citicorp had come to reflect the personality and management style of CEO John Reed, who had led the company since 1984 and whose personality and style were manifest throughout Citicorp. The son of a U.S. businessman, he grew up in Argentina, and he was no stranger to international markets. He was reputed to be a loner who spent much time reading and thinking. Wall Street viewed Reed as a visionary, committed to long-term thinking and willing to make the investments necessary to realize his vision. Such thinking was expected at the company that created the first ATM network, and continued investments in biometric identification and Internet technology were indications of that commitment.

Reed generally was perceived as a scientific manager. Rather than developing a cadre of trusted lieutenants, as was characteristic of his counterpart at Travelers, Reed relied on memos, process, and bureaucracy to control his organization. Reed felt that the Citicorp management team was not effective in fostering an entrepreneurial spirit, perhaps, in part, a result of those tendencies.

In laying the groundwork to become CEO, Reed earned a reputation as being undiplomatic, but he performed well enough as head of the company's consumer banking division that he did become CEO. After the merger, Reed would enjoy strong connections to the merged company's board, a fact that would be important as he and Weill competed for the dominant role in the merged entity.

Reed's vision for the merger was to utilize the company's ubiquitous presence and domestic and international experience to extend Travelers' distribution channels in order to achieve cross-selling synergies. Further, he hoped that access to Travelers' strong management would help him cut costs, "cutting through the bureaucracy" and bringing greater "operational discipline" into the old Citibank organization.

The Co-CEO Structure

Many deals fail to materialize because companies are unable to resolve the question of top leadership. However, in the Citigroup merger, an approach was designed to overcome the significant egos of the respective leaders, and merger discussions proceeded. The solution was to share the responsibilities of many high-level roles via the creation of co-CEOs. The co-CEO roles of Sandy Weill and John Reed were the most significant feature of this structure.

This power-sharing approach offered several appealing advantages. As stated above, it answered the question about who would hold the number one position of the merged entity. Without this compromise, the merger would probably have never been consummated, and subsequent increases in shareholder value may have never been realized. Further, the sheer size of the integration task required the contribution of management talent from both firms. By creating co-CEO roles in the new entity, Citigroup successfully retained significant management talent during the crucial early stages of the integration.

Unfortunately many of these advantages provided only short-term benefits and in fact contributed to some problems. The co-CEO approach delayed the inevitable shakeouts and emergence of the dominant leaders throughout the company. Corporate infighting and positioning contributed to internal turmoil. Management focus was distracted from operating issues, and the integration initially proceeded at a less than ideal pace.

At the outset, the co-CEOs stated they would run Citigroup as equals. To remove the inevitable succession question, they even announced their intention to leave the company at the same time. However, most observers immediately predicted problems would soon arise. The chairmen's premerger paychecks showed a 44 percent disparity in Weill's favor. The merger was supposed to even both executives' compensations, but it would be hard for Weill to avoid treating Reed as a subordinate to whom he has given a lucrative raise. Although Weill and Reed did share a common vision for the company, their styles led to differences over execution strategies.

Self-confidence is considered by some to be the indispensable leadership characteristic, and Weill is known for abundant displays of confidence. In March 2000, Weill came to his biblical theme birthday party playing the role (complete with costume) of Moses. The choice presents some interesting analogies. Moses, who led slaves out of bondage and into nationhood, is considered one of the greatest managers of all time. It was now clear that Weill was the one to lead Citigroup to the promised land. Moses's knowledge of the Sinai Desert, developed during his years as a shepherd, enabled him to display a confidence among the wandering Israelites that secured his position of leadership.

Similarly, Weill's history of successfully meeting the challenges of large acquisitions and his resulting insider knowledge of Wall Street made him an effective and confident leader. Further, Weill exhibited the charisma and vision that inspires an organization to action. Weill tends to make decisions based on his instinct rather than through any elaborate review process.

In July 1999, in an internal memo, Weill and Reed announced the splitting of their duties and their decision to no longer make decisions jointly. Weill took over responsibility for the daily operations of the company, while Reed focused on technology and human resources initiatives. This splitting of duties foreshadowed the formal demise of the co-CEO structure. The excellent results of the company changed the dynamics of the board during 2000, giving Weill even more flexibility to do what he wants. Weill's personal attributes were undoubtedly key contributors to his eventual selection by the Citigroup board to be the sole CEO of the company.

The Case of Verizon

When GTE and Bell Atlantic decided to merge to become the largest U.S. telecommunications company, they chose to have co-CEOs lead the new company. Chuck Lee from GTE and Ivan Seidenberg from Bell Atlantic had different styles and different upbringings.

Lee went to an Ivy League school, is 61 years old, and is quite outgoing. Seidenberg, on the other hand, worked his way through night school in New York, getting a bachelor's degree and an MBA. He is 54, quiet, and soft spoken.

The relationship between the two has been described as harmonious. They get a long quite well and share adjoining offices. The lack of conflict and ability to effectively share the co-CEO role is best characterized as follows:

> Lee matter-of-factly credits the harmony mainly to an agreement that he will leave as co-chief executive in just over a year and stay as a non-executive chairman for the next two years after that. (It's an arrangement that ever-so-patient Seidenberg has down pat—during the Bell Atlantic–Nynex merger he struck a similar deal will Bell chief Raymond Smith.) Lee, who spent the last 18 years at GTE, seems content to exit with a bang. "My career's capstone is launching this company," he says.[5]

Once people have been chosen for key positions, the challenge of retaining them becomes a central focus. Failure to manage retention will mitigate all the "great" choices that were made.

RETAINING KEY PEOPLE

Just because people are offered a position in a merged or an acquired organization does not mean they will take it, especially if they are capable and mobile. And even if they do take a position, that does not mean they will stay very long and produce. Assuming they will is a big mistake, especially in the case of people who are deemed vital to the success of the merger or acquisition. These may be people who have valuable and rare skills and competencies, have connections with key constituents, or are viewed as influential leaders by many in their organization. Moreover, the cost of externally recruiting and developing a new executive, manager, or employee can be exorbitant depending upon the level. This of course assumes that a qualified external candidate even exists. As such, acquiring and merging companies must give considerable thought to retaining these people.

As an example, the importance of retention and the problems associated with defection became apparent in the merger between Harris Semiconductor and General Electric Solid State (GESS). Harris's senior management went to great pains to retain senior managers from the GESS organization. Harris was committed to balancing the top positions in the company between GESS and its own people. Harris was located in Melbourne, Florida, whereas GESS was located in Somerville, New Jersey. The new corporate headquarters would be located in Melbourne.

Harris named a GESS person to the VP of marketing position and thought he was committed to joining the new organization. Although the new VP commuted to Melbourne for a number of months, he was never on board. Unfortunately, Harris management thought he was and began building the new organization with the VP as a key part of it. It was not long before the VP left and the position had to be filled again. Clearly the defection was a blow to the new organization and created a loss of momentum and a vacuum in the marketing organization at a time when rebuilding the company's image in the marketplace was a high priority.

Why did this happen? Harris's management assumed that the VP would be thrilled to join the new company and relocate to Melbourne. The weather in Florida was clearly better than in New Jersey, and real estate dollars would go a much longer way in Florida! After all, Harris's management lived there. Why wouldn't anyone else want to? What Harris's management did not consider was that the VP had extended family, aging parents, and long-term friendships in New Jersey. He also was unsure he would fit in the new company and did not want to take the risk of relocating. He initially took the position but was never committed to it. He rented an apartment in Melbourne and commuted weekly while looking for another job in New Jersey. When asked about his plans to buy a house in Melbourne, he hedged and said he was looking. He never let on to what his intentions were, until he resigned.

This story is not dissimilar to others. In Chevron's merger with Texaco, it was decided that the new corporate headquarters would be in San Ramon, California, the home of Chevron. Texaco's headquarters in White Plains, New York, would be closed. Key people from Texaco were offered positions in San Ramon. Many Texaco people declined for many of the same reasons as the GESS VP. In the end only 14 of the top 61 positions at Chevron-Texaco have been filled with Texaco people.

Retaining people requires a sound recruiting effort similar to one that would be used with new hires, with the primary objectives being:

1. To attract people to the merged company and the proposed positions
2. To ensure they are motivated to stay and contribute
3. To ensure they adapt well to their new environment

Management can influence some of the objectives but not others. For example, willingness to relocate may not be easily influenced. Personal situations, such as elderly parents, children in school, and extended family, may preclude a person from relocating. But there are many things that can be influenced. Below are several key actions that management can take.

Significant Role

Most importantly, many people need to feel they will have a significant and meaningful role in the organization after a merger or an acquisition. Unless people have no alternatives and need the money, they will not likely take a gratuitous position. The position offered must be equal to or exceed the responsibilities and challenges that people currently have.

Mentoring and Support

The acquiring company should consider a program whereby people retained from an acquired company are given a mentor in the new company. The mentor helps them learn the ropes and adjust to the new internal work environment. More will be said about this and other approaches for assimilating new people in Chapter 8.

Fit

People will be concerned whether they will fit with the people they work with. As was illustrated in Chapter 4, fit is an important element in the selection decision. It is also important in the retention decision. A lack of fit may create an awkward situation for people and lead to their eventual departure. A study I conducted with two colleagues clearly suggests that differences in management styles between acquiring and acquired executives were significantly related to the latter's departure.[6] This suggests that if a person does not fit, then two choices are possible.

1. Do not select the person, regardless of the person's capabilities, and ensure there are backups or replacements for him or her.
2. Appreciate the person's stylistic differences and help the person feel as though he or she is a valuable member of the organization and management team.

Realistic Job Preview

All organizations and jobs have pros and cons. Typically, when people are recruited, they are often exposed to the pros, only to quickly learn about the cons. The result is unmet expectations, disillusionment, and turnover.[7] While it is understandable that an acquirer wants to put its best foot forward when selling people on the new company, that can be a mistake. If people are given a realistic preview, their expectations are likely to be more consistent with reality and their chances of adapting to the new organization much greater.

Economic Incentives

As someone once said, "People do not take jobs just for their health." Clearly people work for a variety of reasons, of which economics may be the most important one. It may be helpful to provide attractive inducements to people to take positions in a new company and continue to remain and produce. A variety of incentives can be employed, for example, compensation tied to retention for specific time periods or compensation tied to performance.

In planning a retention strategy it is important to realize that some key target people will be needed indefinitely, whereas others will only need to be retained through the transition stage. There are ways of achieving both.

Retaining Key People Indefinitely

Guarantees such as financial incentives or employment contracts may be required for key people, especially if they are being asked to relocate. A standard incentive program is difficult to develop for all people, and each person should be handled on an individual basis. Individualized attention to the retention of key people has proved successful in retention during and after the closing.

The need to tailor a program should be weighed against the need to ensure that perceived equity exists among people within an organization. Inequities between the target and the acquirer people may create conflicts if people are consolidated into the same work units. In this vein it is important to focus not only on acquired personnel but on acquiring ones as well. I have encountered numerous situations where target people were given so much attention that acquiring people felt as though they were second-class citizens.

Incentive programs should be competitive with what other organizations are offering employees of comparable position. If a program is unattractive, people may be motivated to leave, especially if the other elements discussed in this section are not taken care of and there is a strong labor market. This applies in a non-M&A context as well. Incentives to consider include salary, benefits, and other perks. Incentive programs should also provide people with the motivation to remain and produce long term and should include long-term bonus and stock option plans with long enough payout time frames and short-term restrictions to garner commitment. Clearly these will vary depending upon the level of the position being considered.

Retaining Key People through Transition

Different incentives may be required to retain those people who are needed for a limited time. The reality of most M&As is that the elimination of jobs is necessary in order to meet cost-saving goals, which may occur in either the acquirer or the target organization. However, many of the people who hold these jobs may be needed through the transition period.

For example, many acquirers realize that when integrating information systems (IS), people from a target may be needed until the conversion is completed. These people have insights into how their systems operate that are undocumented. They are needed to keep their systems operating in the short term and to provide information that will ease the conversions. Once the conversion is made, they will not be needed. This is often the case in companies such as banks that are consolidating backroom activities. Until the conversion is made, however, loss of people could be disastrous and lead to significant value leakage. There is nothing worse than a company losing its ability to process information. As noted above, CEOs of acquired or merged companies are also retained just long enough to ensure a smooth transition.

To retain people on a temporary basis, an enhanced severance package can be offered. The enhanced package provides additional benefits if people stay through a specific target date or event. If they leave before that date, they forfeit the additional benefits. Providing additional incentive not only will retain key people, but will improve their attitudes as they deal with customers.

The following are incentives that have been found to be effective by successful acquirers:

1. "Stay" packages (monetary incentives) based on staying until a specified target date or event—e.g., up to six months of additional severance for remaining until the target date. If the person leaves prior to that date, he or she forfeits the entire incentive.
2. Stock options awarded for staying for a specified time.
3. Outplacement packages to assist in job search after a specified time.

The Challenges of Relocation

Many people will not relocate in a merger or an acquisition due to the uncertainty associated with a new location. In addition to family issues that prevent people from leaving, there are also concerns about remaining in the new location if they should lose their job. Given the uncertainty in

M&As and the shakeout of positions during the first year after a deal is closed, this can become a significant issue. Provisions for dealing with this, such as specified employment contracts or severance and relocation benefits, should be considered as part of negotiating with an employee. This will likely vary by organizational level.

Economics of Relocating

Most companies have standard packages for relocating employees. These packages are quite useful in retention decisions of acquired employees and should alleviate some of the concerns people have. Packages should include:

1. Relocation expenses (e.g., moving expenses, real estate adjustments)
2. Cost-of-living adjustments to equalize living conditions
3. Relocation support (e.g., assistance in finding housing, schools)

If people are assigned to an international location, this becomes a more challenging issue.[8]

Recruiting the Family

Relocation not only affects the employees being moved, but also affects their families. It is critical to remember that an entire family needs to be recruited in the retention and relocation process. Although this may seem cumbersome, it may be pivotal in the case of a key employee.

MANAGING EMPLOYEE REDUNDANCY

It is inevitable that people will become redundant in a merger or an acquisition and not be retained. Although such decisions must be made, care should be given to how these decisions are executed. If there are redundancies, ensure they are handled firmly but compassionately. Executives want to send a signal to employees and the community that jobs are sacred and that everything reasonable will be done to ensure that no employees needlessly lose their jobs. Although few people who are being let go will be pleased with the outcome, it is possible to minimize trauma by managing the process in a compassionate way. Essentially, this can be accomplished by providing employees with sufficient support (e.g., adequate severance and outplacement) to ease their transition into another employment situation. While support can be costly, most companies would agree it is worth it. It is likely to minimize adverse reactions (e.g., discrimination lawsuits, sabotage) by those who are terminated and is also likely to maintain or enhance a company's reputation in the market. Again, it will send a strong signal to retained employees about the culture and values of the new company. Both are essential in minimizing value leakage and in creating an environment where people are willing to work hard to build the new company.

Something to Consider

Although the staffing process is designed to select the most qualified people for positions, it does not mean that those not selected are unqualified to remain in the organization. Some may qualify for other positions, or with minimal training and development may be able to do so. Further, many people who are selected for positions that require relocation may choose not to accept them and leave the organization. There needs to be an orderly process to handle these possibilities.

As an example, a major telecommunications provider created a process for managing downsizing due to mergers and acquisitions. As part of capturing cost synergies, thousands of redundant managers were to be severed. Further, a number of operations were to be relocated from San Francisco to St. Louis to take advantage of lower geographic-based operating costs. Several options had to be managed.

1. Downsizing without relocation
   a. The most qualified people were offered the same or a comparable position in their current geographic location (defined as within 50 miles).
   b. Remaining incumbents were considered for reassignment to other positions.
   c. Those who were offered and accepted downgraded positions had their salaries "red-circled" (unadjusted) for 24 months from the close of the merger.
   d. Those not offered positions were placed in a "not-selected" process.
2. Positions relocated without downsizing
   a. The most qualified people were offered a position in a new geographic location. In most cases the geographic change was due to the relocation of an operation to capture lower costs.
   b. Incumbents declining the offer were considered for positions in their current geographic area.
   c. Those not offered positions were placed in a "not-selected" process.
3. Positions relocated with downsizing
   a. Qualified incumbents in the current geographic location were offered positions first. These people were offered jobs first to minimize relocation costs and provide continuity and uninterrupted operations.
   b. Qualified incumbents from other geographic areas were then considered.
   c. Those who were offered and accepted downgraded positions had their salaries "red-circled" (unadjusted) for 24 months from the close of the merger.
   d. Those not offered positions were placed in a "not-selected" process.

The "Not Selected" Process

A clear and compassionate process was used for those who were not offered jobs. They were sent a "60-day letter." The letter explained two options they had available. They were provided an opportunity to become part of a pool of people who for 60 days could seek another position within the merged organization while remaining in their current position. They were given priority placement. Essentially, people would self-nominate and apply for a position for which they were qualified.

Positions were posted using an Intranet-based posting process. The Intranet site had a standardized resume-building process. The site became a common vehicle by which those looking to fill positions could recruit internal candidates. Several attributes of the process were notable:

1. All qualified people affected by the merger were given priority over other equally qualified people who were not affected.
2. Company-employed spouses of relocated managers were given priority over other equally qualified employees.
3. During the 60 days the company could proactively offer qualified employees a position.

The order of priority was (1) merger-affected participants, (2) relocated spouses, and (3) the general employee population.

At the end of 60 days the participants were terminated and offered severance benefits. They could also choose to leave with severance at any time prior to the 60 days. If people chose not to participate in the 60-day process, they were terminated and they were eligible to receive severance.

Severance

Severance benefits were offered as follows. No severance was provided for those who:

1. Voluntarily left the company
2. Were terminated for poor performance
3. Were offered a position at the same salary grade or equivalent and required no relocation

All others qualified for the plan.

The severance agreement provided managers with the following benefits:

1. Payment of accrued wages
2. Payment for current year's unused vacations
3. Completion of tuition payments for current courses in which they were enrolled
4. Exercise of vested stock options
5. Severance payments

6. Self-paid medical, dental, and vision care for 18 months after termination of employment under federal law (COBRA)
7. Benefits under the company's Education/Development Support program for reimbursement of up to $5000 paid out over a maximum of one year for approved courses and fees to help gain reemployment

To receive these benefits a manager had to sign a benefit plan termination and waiver agreement. The agreement specified all the obligations of both the employer and manager upon separation. This agreement is typical for many large companies.

The company also had "change in control" contractual provisions for multiple levels of management, otherwise known as golden, silver, and bronze parachutes. Generally, a change in control is defined as a beneficial change in ownership of a company's voting stock or in the composition of the company's voting stock. Changes of control usually provide enhanced benefits. Such contracts originated in the 1980s as a result of hostile takeovers. They were put in place to reduce the fear of job loss by executives and managers of acquired companies and to encourage them to look out for the interests of shareholders.

In addition to severance benefits, the company provided outplacement support to severed employees. This support was contracted to firms that specialize in this area. Such firms established contact with managers and employees as soon as they were notified of their termination. Outplacement firms provide support in resume writing, interviewing, and career counseling and assist in job searches.

Clearly this process followed the guiding principles articulated at the beginning of this chapter. People were indeed treated with fairness, dignity, and respect, and competence was the major driver of staffing decisions. The outcome was an orderly process. Those who left and those who remained did so with few adverse reactions.

What Else Can Be Done?

In addition to the severance and outplacement process, there are a number of other actions that an acquiring or merging company can do to eliminate the costs of redundancy. Many of these attempt to ease the process of involuntary job loss through either less severe or voluntary approaches. These include:

1. Work-schedule alterations:
   a. Part-time jobs
   b. Shortened workweeks
   c. Job sharing
2. Natural attrition
3. Hiring freezes
4. Early retirement incentives
5. Curtailment of promotions and transfers

6. Salary freezes and reductions
7. Temporary leaves without pay

Although these options may minimize the trauma of terminating people, they may not be sufficient to eliminate the redundancy that a merger or an acquisition can create. Certain approaches such as natural attrition and early retirement may lead to the voluntary exit of qualified people who are needed in the new organization. If severance and retirement incentives are too attractive, they may become oversubscribed and may encourage too many people to leave early. To the extent possible, an acquirer or merging company wants to influence those who stay and those who leave rather than leaving it to chance.

A FINAL NOTE

How staffing, retention, and redundancy are managed can have a profound impact on merging companies. They send clear signals to employees regarding what the company and its executives stand for. These, in turn, can have a dramatic impact on the retention and motivation of key people and thus on value preservation, synergy capture, and value creation. Ensure that they are a part of your integration process.

8

TAKING ACTION: MANAGING THE INTEGRATION STAGE

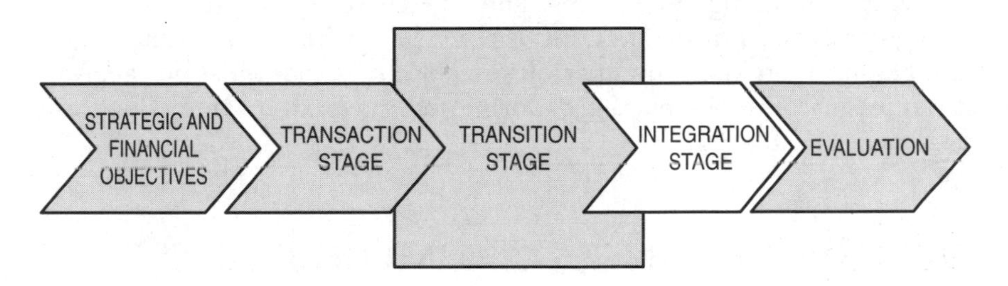

The deal has closed. The combined companies are one legal entity. Key positions have been filled, transition and integration teams have been disbanded, and the executives are ready to rebuild the new organization and work units. The theoretical exercise of planning how the companies will be integrated is over. There is clarity on what the financial and strategic objectives are and how the organizations will function. If not, these need to be completed as quickly as possible by the senior management team after the closing. If so, they need to be reaffirmed and communicated to the organization by the team.

Now the challenge is to successfully integrate the companies, preserve value, and deliver the synergies, earnings, and cashflows that were promised. It is likely that there is a cadre of people from both organizations who interacted during the transaction and transition stages. This includes senior managers, transition and integration team members, and ad hoc work-group members. They already should have had a good opportunity to learn about each other, have had cooperative experience and think well of each other. They already should have communicated this within their own respective organizations as well. In spite of this it is typical that the majority of people have likely yet to interact with counterparts from the other organization. All they have is their impressions from what they have heard, seen, and imagined.

Depending upon the nature of the deal and the synergies sought, the complexity of the integration will vary. In the case of a merger where synergies are being attempted throughout most of if not the entire organization, the integration will be quite complex and pervasive. In the case of a small acquisition where it is being integrated into an existing operation, the integration and ensuing changes will be simpler—except, of course, for those directly affected! In general, the less the synergies being sought, the less the complexity of the integration. Where there is little standardization, combination, or intervention, the less the challenges.

Success requires that executives and managers articulate clear visions, values, goals, and/or strategies for the combined organization. It also requires that they align work units and capable and motivated people from multiple organizations to drive the objectives underlying the merger or acquisition. It requires managing the integration of multiple cultures, innovating, building new teams, and in general managing a complex change process. Unfortunately, this is where many M&As fail. Where does one begin? There are a number of key objectives that must be met and activities that must be managed during the integration stage. These are presented in Table 8-1.

DEMONSTRATING A COMMITTED AND OPEN-MINDED LEADERSHIP

There is no question that the leaders of acquiring and merging companies play a vital role in the integration process. Simply put, they set the tone for the integration and set an example of how it should progress. This is not to imply that they have total control but that they set many things in motion. An excellent example of this is the role that Carlos Ghosn has played in the acquisition of Nissan by Renault. Ghosn is a highly accomplished executive who has had great success leading a number of compa-

Table 8-1 Integration Stage

Objectives
1. Complete analytical activities that were not completed prior to the closing
2. Execute actions to physically integrate the target or merger partner
3. Rebuild the organization into a stronger, more competitive entity capable of realizing financial and strategic objectives
Activities
1. Demonstrating a committed and open-minded leadership
2. Building teams and work units
3. Focusing on financial and strategic objectives
4. Remaining flexible—things change
5. Providing for capable and motivated people
6. Assimilating new people
7. Achieving cultural integration

nies and turning around Renault. He was made president and CEO of Nissan in 1999 and was charged with turning it around while successfully integrating it with Renault.

Nissan faced three main problems. It:

- Had 2.4 trillion yen (22 billion dollars) in debt
- Was unable for many years to show a profit
- Had a continuous decline in global market share since 1990

Ghosn faced a radically different culture in Japan than in either France or the United States, where many of the decisions to transform Nissan would not be embraced. He would have to work within a different culture to win support for his ideas and motivate a new organization to take on and successfully implement the challenges. Most people felt that he faced an impossible challenge.

Proving those people wrong, Ghosn skillfully got the organization and Japanese industry to focus on the issues facing Nissan and the need to turn the company around. He was tenacious in his focus on business objectives and built consensus among those around him on why these were critical for the acquisition and the companies to succeed.

Of importance, Ghosn did not attempt to utilize an ethnocentric approach to changing Nissan (he was born in Brazil, was educated in France, and worked in France and the United States prior to this challenge). As Ghosn commented:

> Cultural differences can be viewed as either a handicap or a powerful seed for something new. From the beginning, I said that I viewed cultural differences as an opportunity to innovate in achieving the pragmatic business objectives we had before us. This is risky when you say it before you even start. It's been 15 months since I arrived at Nissan. And now, six months after the start of the revival plan, I can tell you that today cultural differences are seen more as an object of cross-fertilization and innovation in the way we are doing things than as a motive for frustration or reason to disagree. This is due to one thing—the Nissan Revival Plan. When the Renault people came to Japan, the management of Nissan had from the beginning a very strong consciousness about the severity of the situation. There was no room for bickering or fighting or infinite discussions about whose method or whose process we were going to adopt.
>
> The Nissan Revival Plan came very fast and established strong objectives. It didn't leave any room for meditation on the differences about cultures. We were all mobilized and engaged in the revival of the company. What we see today is that differences in culture are being used more and more as ways of listening to

what different people can bring to the table to achieve our objectives for the future. So, it is a careful selection of best practices and best approaches. There is enormous pressure on everyone to deliver. In a way it was simple, we just established a point where everybody understood what we had to do to survive as a whole company.

Of course there are frustrations that always exist with language barriers: where you don't operate in an environment of spontaneous communication; where you have to go through a translator (you know that when you go through a translator, about 40 percent of your intended meaning is lost); where you're not sure that what you want to get across to people, on the shop floor or in meetings with customers, is actually being communicated the way you intended it to. These are what I consider small frustrations; if you accept these and other things that perhaps are part of the fact that people don't think or act the same way in France or in Japan, it is easier to deal with such things as language barriers. When you have taken the time to understand that, and when you are really motivated and mobilized by a very strong objective, then the cultural differences can become seeds for innovation as opposed to seeds for dissention.[1]

These comments and the fact that in 2001 Nissan reported its first profits in many years demonstrate the power of a committed and open-minded leader during the integration process. He did not allow cultural differences, which were significant, to become an excuse for failure, although he could have easily done so. He embraced the differences and used them. There is no doubt that the crisis at Nissan helped everyone see the need for change. However, it was still Ghosn's leadership that has made a huge difference. If not, why did it take Nissan 10 years to recover?

Ghosn attributes the success of the turnaround to:

- Focusing on the key priorities, the business goals—"And these are to create value—value in the short and midterm for our customers, our shareholders, and our employees."
- Top management's attitude and behaviors:
  - "Top management is highly visible. What we think, what we say, and what we do must be the same."
  - "We must be committed to the responsibilities we've agreed to. When we don't deliver, we have to face the consequences."
- Four dimensions of leadership behaviors:
  - Be open-minded.
  - Listen to ideas.
  - Focus on the goals.
  - Act very fast.

BUILDING TEAMS AND WORK UNITS

Once the merger or acquisition has been closed, the first order of business is to begin the process of building teams from the senior management level on down. The extensiveness of this activity will depend upon the degree of integration. In a transformational merger it may require a complete rebuilding of all teams and work units. There may be a new mix of people and an entirely new approach to the way the organization is to operate, including products, services, organizational structure, systems, and culture.

Many people will be put together who have never worked together, who are from different organizational cultures, and who bring different personal styles (see Chapter 4). In a small acquisition it may be the addition of a few people to an already functioning team. Even for those who have worked together and for the new leader it is useful to review how the team operates and should operate. To assume that people will effectively work together may be an erroneous assumption. People will be used to different ways of working and will likely be jockeying for a meaningful place on the team and in the work unit. The potential for political behavior, misunderstanding, and conflict under such a scenario is high, and the likelihood of cooperation is low, especially in the case of a complex merger.

A number of key activities should be performed to ensure that people work together and are aligned around the same financial and strategic objectives. Clearly, the alignment process must begin at the senior management level; otherwise it is not likely that managers throughout the organization will fall into alignment. If executives do not set an example for acceptable behaviors, it is not likely that those throughout the organization will consistently do so. Asking people from integrating organizations to cooperate while the senior management team battles is not likely to have the desired effect. One only needs to examine the problems that ensued at Citigroup after the merger. Senior management battled, and so did everyone else. This led to the departure of many good people who felt they did not fit in the new organization.

There are numerous ways in which to build a senior management team. Much of it depends on the style and orientation of the CEO. Some CEOs do not like "soft" team-building activities and are very task-oriented, whereas others have more patience for the "soft stuff." Some CEOs have a directive leadership style, whereas others are more involving and empowering. Regardless, it is critical that CEOs, as well as all leaders, establish ground rules by which a new team will work together and get buy-in for them. It is unlikely that everyone on a senior management team will embrace all the rules, but at a minimum the team members will need to support the rules and live with them. If they cannot, it is likely that they will not have a sustained role in the new organization.

I have worked with a number of newly formed and revitalized post-closing senior teams and have found it useful to begin by defining some basic team processes on how people will work together. Often an experienced outsider to help facilitate the management teams and to coach executives and managers can be of great value. This process is being used to build the senior management team and the ensuing management teams for the top 61 people in the Chevron-Texaco merger. Some useful topics to address as part of team building include defining:

1. What is the role of the senior management team?
2. When does the senior management team meet and for what purposes? Does it meet on a regular basis? Can any member request a meeting of the team, or is that the prerogative of the CEO? Is the team a decision-making team, or is its purpose to provide recommendations to the CEO?
3. How does the team agenda get set? Is it set by the CEO or by members of the team?
4. What is the decision-making process that will be employed by the team? Is it consensus-based? Majority vote? Does the CEO have a vote, or is he or she the final decision maker?
5. How does the team deal with differences of opinion and manage conflict? Is it through open discussion during meetings or behind closed doors?
6. What role does each person play on the team and for specific types of decisions? Does he or she have responsibility for making decisions, approving decisions, or providing resources and support?

Depending upon the CEO's leadership style and the situation, such decisions can be arrived at in a number of ways. First the CEO can just make and announce decisions. Second the CEO can involve the entire team in making them. Third the CEO can declare which decisions are his or hers and make them and which are the team's and let the team make them.

A couple of factors need to be considered when making this choice. First, most executives expect to have some input into the senior management decision-making process. In a study I conducted with two colleagues, for example, we found that executives were willing to support decisions made by the CEO only when their ideas were seriously considered, even if the decisions did not reflect their position.[2] Second, I have found that most executives can live with the approach chosen by a CEO as long as it is consistent with the expectations that have been created. In other words, if the CEO led people to believe they would be involved in decisions and were not, then they had negative reactions. A comment that an executive once shared with me summarized it best:

> I understand that it is the prerogative of the CEO to run his organization any way he wishes. However, I assume that since

> he picked me for his team he believed that I was competent and had something meaningful to contribute. Thus, at a minimum, I expect to be heard. Also, I do not have a problem if in the end the CEO makes the decisions. Again that is his prerogative. However, that is fine as long as it is consistent with the ground rules that he sets. Setting one set of expectations and playing by another just doesn't play well with me. If he needs to change the rules, fine, but just give me enough warning so I can adjust.

Once the senior team is able to operate, there are a number of issues that must form the basis of the team agenda. Some of these issues may have been worked out during the transition stage through the work of integration teams, whereas others will have to be worked out during integration. Regardless of the amount of work done during transition, some level of refinement is always needed. Issues that senior management must address or revisit include:

1. The vision and financial and strategic objectives of the merger or acquisition and the firm in general, and how that translates into organizational priorities and objectives throughout the organization
2. How the organization will be designed to support these objectives, including:
   a. Culture
   b. Activities performed
   c. Systems
   d. Business processes
   e. Operating/business models
   f. Organizational structure
   g. Measurements and rewards
   h. Positions, descriptions, and head count
   i. Operating and capital budgets
3. How the integration and change process will be managed
4. What areas are to be affected
5. What are the priorities, especially with respect to the financial and strategic objectives

Once the leadership of the merged organization is in place or some key positions have been filled in an acquisition, the process of team building needs to continue throughout the organization. Many of the team issues described above need to be cascaded through the organization. The focus of the team's agenda will change depending upon the particular area. For example, functional areas, lines of businesses, business processes, and geographic areas will focus on pursuing their objectives and strategies. However, they must be aligned with those developed by the senior management team.

Without alignment there is a risk that the financial and strategic objectives underlying the deal will not be met. The goal, however, is not to turn team building into a bureaucratic process. As long as team goals are clear and aligned and the recommendations of integration teams on consolidation and standardization are being implemented, there should be room to allow each unit some flexibility and sufficient lines of communication to make adjustments in objectives as warranted by changing situations. After all, customers, competitors, and other external elements continually change, requiring flexibility and adjustment.

The Role of Perceptual Filters in Building Teams[3]

As discussed in Chapter 4, a tool such as the Birkman Method can be of great help in the selection of people. In addition, it is also useful in helping acquirers and merger partners understand the issues involved in integrating target people into the new company and also is useful in helping them prepare for that. Armed with these insights, executives and managers can then use the information to build new merged teams or insert individuals into existing teams. The instrument can be administered to the many people who were not assessed during the transaction stage to help facilitate the development of newly created teams.

The use of an instrument such as the Birkman Method allows members of a new team to quickly learn about other members' styles and how best to deal with them. From my experience, this helps shorten the length of time it takes for people to learn about themselves and others, minimizes unnecessary conflict, and facilitates a process whereby diverse individuals can learn to work together and to address the business issues.

Let us take as an example a manufacturer of plastics that acquired a biomedical research firm to help it become the creative and visionary company it once was. The manufacturer (renamed here as Plastico), like the well-established energy companies discussed in Chapter 4, was one of the top four in the world. Competition in Europe and Asia was putting a real squeeze on its profits. The leaders of Plastico felt they had three viable options:

Option 1. They could sell off their least profitable product lines.
Option 2. They could expand further into medical prosthesis and surgical supply products (an area in which they had recent success).
Option 3. They could sell off two losing product lines and acquire a medical-related business.

They chose option 3 and bought a biomedical research company (Glower Corporation), noted for its breakthrough product ideas that created links between physics, engineering, and physiology.

The integration of Glower Corporation would involve the implementation of new structures and processes. Managers of Plastico would be asked to collaborate with team leaders from Glower Corporation to establish new ways of working. As in almost any situation, clashes can occur because people have different sets of expectations about the outcome and different assumptions about how to bring it about. When ideas or methods are really quite foreign, people frequently have an emotional reaction to the other's approach. Those reactions can then lead to stressful behaviors.

Plastico was an old-line, hard-core manufacturing company known for its style as a tightly run ship. Glower Corporation, on the other hand, was run like a freewheeling graduate research lab. It had attracted some of the brightest physicists and biologists in the country, and its culture valued individuality and cross-functional teams. These two organizations would be a test for the very best of integration thinking. It promised to be a stretch for both sides. Plastico had the capital and international infrastructure, but Glower Corporation held the key to new products and increased profitability.

Behind the human element of ingrained differences in approach is the fact that business situations consist of *structural* and *relational* elements. Structural relates to things such as departmental organization, systems, processes, finance, administration, etc. Sometimes the best designed infrastructure and control systems can go awry simply because well-intentioned leaders in different functions take different approaches in an integration project. Relational relates to how people interact with each other.

In Chapter 4, in the insurance company case with Dirk, we saw how perceptual filters play a role in organizational decision making. Here we revisit the maxim that for each party to an interaction, perception is reality. The parties get to that reality through the perceptual filters they use—their expectations and their assumptions. The degree to which there is tolerance and understanding of what each filter contributes to the whole determines the effectiveness of a new structural element (departmental configuration or process).

The specific situation we want to highlight from the integration of Glower into Plastico (renamed Mediplast for this example) was the focused and sustained effort required to meld these two disparate management teams into a unified team. There were the usual corporate change campaigns around vision, mission, goals, and the creation of a new brand led by the marketing department and the office of corporate communications. Despite these traditional efforts to communicate a "new way" at Mediplast, there were nevertheless severe clashes in personality, style, approach, and values.

The CEO of Mediplast was the former CEO of Plastico. He was a man of vision and a risk taker in a culture that had heretofore been somewhat risk averse. He knew it would take something extraordinary to break down the prejudices that the executives of each company held of the other. He believed the whole senior management team had to go through a process that was entirely new. It couldn't belong to Plastico, and it couldn't come from Glower. Something new—that grew out of the combined efforts of both—had to take the place of former conventions and styles. That meant new ways of relating to each other and a new language to create a bond among those who, at the outset of the merger, were like tourists in another's foreign territory.

In a previous company the Mediplast CEO had come to know about our executive process. He called a colleague and me in to help with the integration. We started at the top, with the combined senior management team, leading a program that set the tone and the pace for the rest of the organization. We set in place a three-month cascading team-building initiative that required people at every level in the organization to work on cross-functional teams and to learn a new way of communicating about work and about their interpersonal relationships. Everything from strategic planning, to individual performance appraisals, to watercooler conversations, was influenced by this team-building process.

It started with a 1 1/2-day retreat, which later would be replicated with every work unit. We took the new leaders of Mediplast through a series of exercises aimed first at helping them see the value of understanding their own perceptual filters and those of their colleagues. Within minutes, these exercises brought home the fact that one's own perceptual filter is not the only way of viewing a problem or situation! They were humbled and challenged. Mediplast's senior team members quickly saw how each of them gave off subtle verbal signals to others in terms of both words and body language. They further learned that by paying attention to the clues in the language a person uses to describe something, they could quickly identify the filter the other was using. Armed with that understanding and an ability to interpret "filters," they realized a growing appreciation for others' points of view (see Figure 8-1).

Not all the sailing was smooth. Early on in this retreat, we saw the warning signals of a clash between the head of operations and the head of research and development. Each had starkly different views on how the company should create new-product planning and implementation. The goal of this process was to put Mediplast in the lead against the competition for bringing new products to market.

The operations VP (former Plastico) was a bit like our friend Dirk, whom you will recall from the Healthy Life case recounted in Chapter 4. He saw things through an "operations and technical filter." As the VP of operations assessed the issues involved in designing the new-product planning and implementation process, he focused almost exclusively on the implementation aspects and paid little attention to the needs of the R&D team.

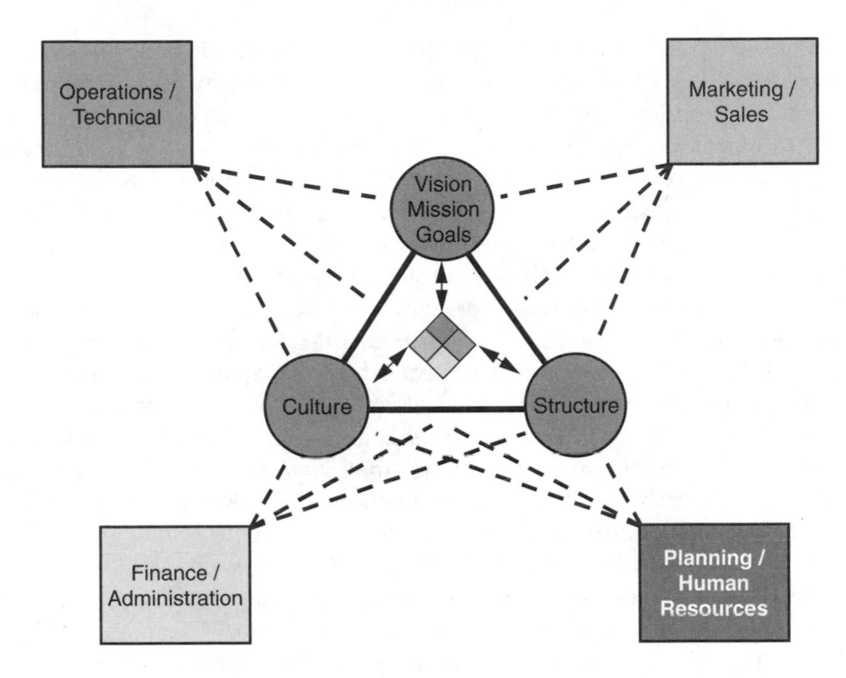

Figure 8-1 Perceptual Filters

His perceptual filter viewed issues though a prism of technology, pragmatism, and an insistence on results and having the facts at hand. He had little patience for experimenting or working the bugs out in a trial. His perception of how to get this process established was simply to "get on with it and get it done."

His R&D peer, from Glower Corporation, was a research scientist, and was known even inside Glower as the ultimate individualist. He filtered his assessment of the task through a long-range planning filter. He constantly referred to the big picture, the unreasonable hurry of those on the implementation side of the house, the complexities of having "fail-safe" products, and the lack of appreciation on the part of others for the creativity and originality of the R&D staff. He assumed that the solution would result from experimentation and then synthesis of the results. His dominant approach was strategic, experimental, and thoroughly thought-out.

The VP of R&D wanted to produce products that would meet customers' needs for utility, durability, convenience, and attractiveness. He insisted that bringing these features together couldn't happen overnight. The VP of operations wanted to get products into production in a staggered process to avoid several products hitting the assembly lines at the same time, a situation that would max out his production capacity and require overtime.

Back and forth they went. The R&D head insisted on multiple performance tests. The VP of operations knew that his bonus was contingent on reducing overtime costs. He pleaded for delivery based on staggered product development. The timing of products coming out of R&D must be precise and on schedule. The VP of R&D, whose bonus was based on reduced defects, insisted he couldn't release products until they met long-range durability tests. Sometimes this delayed the release of new products into the production cycle. The men reached a standstill.

At this point, we asked them to switch positions and describe the situation from the other's perspective. So our "do-it-now" operations and technical filter VP of operations now heard himself championing the R&D position through a long-range analytical-creative planning filter. And as difficult as it was, the VP of R&D had to package his proposal in factual, schedule-imperative ultimatums. Over lunch that day, the men kicked around ideas about what they had learned from taking an opposite problem-solving approach to their normal one. First, they discovered they had learned to appreciate, if not fully understand, an issue from the other's perspective. Next they noted that this exercise helped them become aware of the kinds of inputs on which the sales or control guys would most likely insist. They joked with each other about the predominant filter type each represented, but underneath they were keenly aware that they both held strong tendencies to operate from the premise of having their own rules and wanting others to live by those rules. Like most of us, they thought their rules were the right ones. They discovered how emotionally attached to them they were. Finally, they realized this strong attachment to *their way* of seeing a problem pushed them to just jump right in and start behaving almost automatically, as if a record needle were stuck in a groove. These were important lessons. Though neither fully realized it at the time, these insights represented colossal leaps in understanding and personal growth.

The second half of our workshop focused on the behaviors and the motivational needs of the team. We stressed two key principles. First, that when it comes to behavior, *there is no such thing as normal*. Sounds preposterous! What do you mean, "no such thing as normal"? If we go back to the lessons learned earlier from the experiences with the perceptual filters, it isn't so hard to understand that we see our own behaviors as normal. What we come to understand is that there is normal for me, for him, for her, or for "those" people. When people behave differently from us, in most cases their behavior is simply just that—different. It is usually not right or wrong. It just is.

A second principle is that the way a person behaves is not necessarily indicative of the way he or she is motivated. In other words, *there is no logical connection between the way a person behaves and the way he or she needs to be treated*. To grasp the power of this statement takes a bit of explaining and a few examples. When the meaning sinks in, it is often one of those great "ah-ha" experiences.

Let's revisit the previous example of the VPs of operations and R&D who were tussling over a product planning and implementation process. This example can be used to illustrate the way that a basic understanding of the surface behaviors and the underlying motivational needs of the other helped these two very different personalities forge a productive and congenial relationship. To explain the process of how this happened, we turn first to the 11 different personality components found in the "Strengths and Needs Report" described in Chapter 4. These components identify one's usual behavior, motivational needs, and possible stress reactions (i.e., when motivational needs are not met).

While we worked with the entire Mediplast senior team in this workshop, the CEO had privately told us that for the company changeover process to succeed, the relationship between the more traditional VP of operations and the more rebellious, scientific VP of R&D just had to work. Thus, we provide only the profiles of these two vice presidents to illustrate the process we used to help develop, first, an understanding of differences and, then, ways to work productively with those differences.

By studying the diagram in Table 8-2, which displays their profiles, we begin to see how the "needs/behavior" connection works. It is then quite obvious how team members can either thwart or foster productive contributions from their colleagues. The personality categories that follow are the same we reviewed previously in the insurance company case where Dirk was a prime candidate for CEO. Here, in the case of the two "dueling VPs," we can see at a glance, simply by how their scores align in each category, where there are similarities and differences between them. The discussion below elaborates on some of the areas that predictably could produce tension between these two and illustrates some of the lessons the two learned about each other.

Component Scores of Strengths and Needs

Recall the scoring pattern we saw with Dirk: On a scale of 1–99, scores below 50 are considered low and those above 50, high. Generally, the interpretation of scores in the range of 40–60 is dependent on the situation. Scores to the left of the slash (/) in Table 8-2 represent usual or strength behavior. Scores to the right of the slash represent motivational needs. Let's look at scoring patterns of Mediplast's two VPs to see what areas might cause stress for one or the other.

Starting with the personality component on the far left, "Esteem," which has to do with the degree of directness or subtlety in communication, we see that both men's scores to the left of the slash are in the low range, 3 and 13. This means we could expect both the VP of operations and R&D to communicate quite straightforwardly. In other words, their

Table 8-2 Strengths and Needs Report

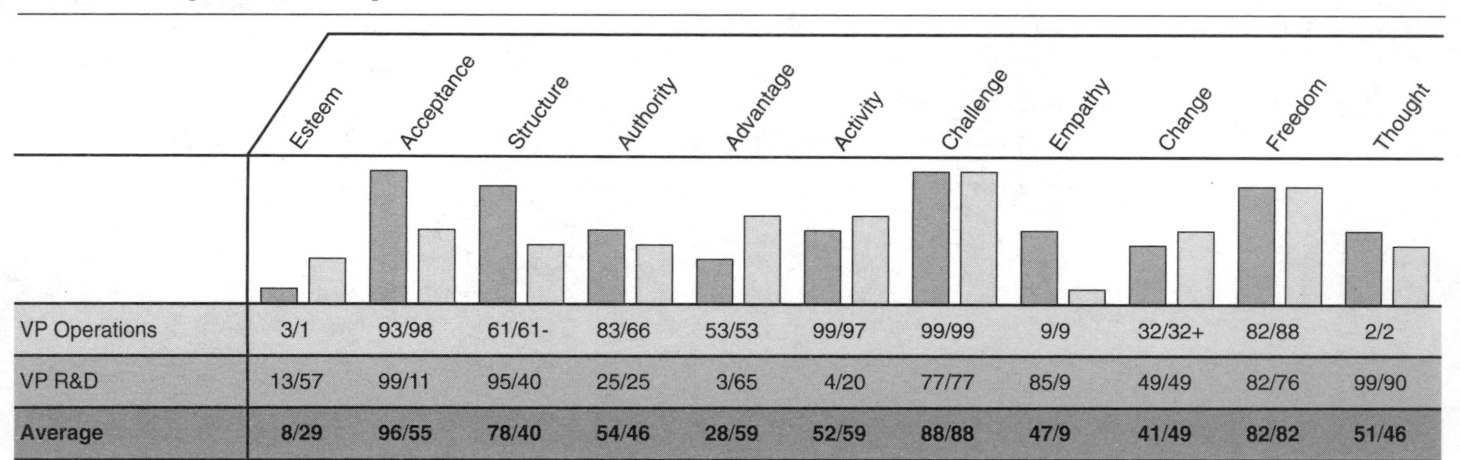

	Esteem	Acceptance	Structure	Authority	Advantage	Activity	Challenge	Empathy	Change	Freedom	Thought
VP Operations	3/1	93/98	61/61-	83/66	53/53	99/97	99/99	9/9	32/32+	82/88	2/2
VP R&D	13/57	99/11	95/40	25/25	3/65	4/20	77/77	85/9	49/49	82/76	99/90
Average	**8/29**	**96/55**	**78/40**	**54/46**	**28/59**	**52/59**	**88/88**	**47/9**	**41/49**	**82/82**	**51/46**

communication style would be pretty much the same. When we look at the scores to the right, we see there is a big jump on the needs side, from 1 to 57. A score of 1 means that the VP of operations is motivated by relationships that are very direct and frank. Given that a score of 13 means that the usual behavior of his R&D colleague is to be direct and frank, we would anticipate few conflicts. Our VP of R&D, on the other hand, will communicate in a frank and open manner only when he feels assured of the respect of the other party to the communication. If he isn't assured that his ideas are valued, he may be overly sensitive to perceived criticism, be embarrassed, or get his feelings hurt. His stress behavior would be to shut down or withhold his ideas. So right away, we have a red flag that goes up, indicating that the way the VP of operations addresses the VP of R&D will be important if they are to have a productive relationship.

Moving next to "Acceptance," or the preference for social involvement in work versus the desire to work independently or with just a small team, we see, again, common styles in "usual behavior" in that both VPs are highly sociable and tend to be skilled in meeting people easily. However, if we look at the motivational need scores to the right of the slash, we see a huge difference in needs. Our VP of operations needs the support of a team around him to stimulate his gregarious and outgoing behavior. Quite the opposite, the VP of R&D needs a great deal of time to himself, away from the social pressures of work if we expect him to be communicative and attentive. The lesson here for the VP of Operations is to give his R&D pal time to withdraw and be alone.

We can skip over the component "Structure" (which indicates how insistent one is with planning and details) because the ranges are essentially similar, and we could expect slightly similar behaviors and responses. This brings us to "Authority." Here we can see at a glance big scoring differences for each officer. The VP of operations has high scores for both usual behavior and needs, meaning that he is very directive, aggressive in thinking, and quick to take a stand; he wants the same from his environment. He needs a situation where he can direct others and where there are strictly enforced lines of authority.

The VP of R&D's behavior is quite the opposite. His style is to suggest rather than actively direct. He avoids open clashes and is outwardly pleasant and agreeable. He prefers an environment where authority is clearly defined and delegated and where he, himself, is managed through persuasion rather than being told what to do. Immediately, another and much larger red flag goes up. The VP of operations must come to realize that his pattern of dominance will not engender productive response from his colleague. If the VP of R&D is treated in an authoritarian way, he will resist that direction and have difficulty confronting that style. Between the two, there will be an issue of who is in control.

Next, we will skip over "Advantage" (which relates to competitiveness and materialism) to "Activity." This component gives us a picture of how each will use his personal energy. The VP of operations, with scores in the high 90s on both usual behavior and needs, personifies someone who is physically active, forceful, and competitive. He needs lots of things to do and opportunities to be active physically. On the other side of the ledger, we find the VP of R&D with a usual behavior score of 4, indicating he is very much a thinker and a delegator and is efficient in using his energy. He needs lots of time to reflect and to analyze, he needs the stimulation of new ideas, and he needs unhurried work conditions. Yet another gigantic red flag is raised. The tendency for the VP of operations will be to see the VP of R&D as someone who is slow and doesn't move at the pace needed for the project. R&D will see his operations counterpart as moving so quickly, he may be prone to make mistakes. Under stress, both will tend to magnify their natural tendencies.

Finally we leapfrog over "Challenge" (the way we relate to the demands of work), "Empathy" (the degree of emotion or feeling we put into or need from our day-to-day work), "Change" (the degree of focus or novelty we give to or want from work), and "Freedom" (an indicator of conventionality or indivdualism), to "Thought" (the amount of time we take or need for certain kinds of decisions). Here we find the largest red flag of all. The VP of operations has extremely low scores for usual behavior and motivational needs. A configuration of 2/2 indicates a style of making quick decisions and needing an environment that is clear and unambiguous and that provides opportunities to take immediate action. Contrast that with the 99/90 of the VP of R&D, where we have the profile of an analyst who needs to think through decisions very carefully, and we have potential for a real clash around the issue of timing.

As we explain what these and the other scores in their profiles mean, our goal is not to have either VP change himself, because this effort is not about changing who you are. It is about becoming aware of the other's needs and how a shift in behavior can motivate positive and productive work from the other. The resultant solution for Mediplast's planning and implementation process can be enriched by:

1. Both VPs facilitating communication that is direct but respectful between each other
2. Both VPs being committed to the team and by the operations VP allowing the VP of R&D to have space to think and reflect and be alone
3. The VP of R&D recognizing that speed and movement is an imperative for his colleague in operations
4. The VP of operations realizing that his style of direction will thwart the creativity of the R&D leader

Our hope is that both will learn patience and acceptance of their differences.

As we reviewed the component scores with the entire team, the senior managers had their own unique "ah-has" about themselves and their colleagues. From this point of insight, we paired up each officer with a partner the CEO had assigned to handle a "cross-functional" initiative. Along with this pairing came the charge to identify the areas where they found the greatest difference in their strengths and needs. Whether it was communication, organization, directiveness, action orientation, or decision-making style, they each chose one target at which to direct their own improvement campaign. They agreed that when one missed the other's motivational needs, the other would provide feedback in terms of what approach could have worked better.

At the Monday morning "management meetings," Mediplast's CEO would ask each officer to report on how well he or she met the designated behavior target and then what they each learned about themselves and their counterpart. The fact that the counterpart was present kept each senior manager focused on the facts. Often the reported interactions and lessons learned injected humor into the management meetings, but the overwhelming result seemed to be an increasing degree of individual humility and receptivity to others' points of view and styles.

This kind of reinforcement is expensive—to the tune of two hours per month of ten executives' time over a three-month period. Why did the CEO do it? He knew that it was not the technology or the financials that would meld these disparate companies into a unified whole, but the relationships the key officers had with one another. This would set the tone for the entire company and for interactions with customers. He felt it would be the differentiator, and he was willing to support that financially.

There were several side benefits from the team-building process. One was incorporating some new "relationship" elements into the annual 360 degree performance reviews and the bonus determinations. As the process cascaded down and was institutionalized at each level, the two very disparate organizations gradually united into one that was now very new.

Another benefit was the way officers used their knowledge and "people-reading skills" in the team-selection process. Given the heavy emphasis on cross-functional teams, an executive heading a team could use his or her self-knowledge to describe to an incoming team in both behavioral and needs terminology what behavioral outputs were desired from the new team as well as what each team member could expect to get from the team leader. Fluency with this new corporate "language" allowed team leaders to frame questions and listen to responses in a new way—a way that captured the factual as well as the emotional essence of a work situation.

Many executives and lower-level management team leaders used another element of our process to illustrate their points clearly and simply to a new team. This element was the leadership style grid, which a team leader can use to characterize the key interests, strengths, motivational needs, and stresses of each team member (see Table 8-3).

In each of four categories—interests, usual behavior, motivational needs, and stress—the initials of each team member pinpoint, in the relevant quadrant, the location of either their dominant interest, style, need, or likely stress reaction. For example, a team member who has strong interests in taking action would have his or her initials somewhere in the "Expeditors" quadrant. For interests in persuading or selling, initials would be in the "Communicators" quadrant; for planning, in the "Planners" quadrant; and for handling administrative details or systems, in the "Administrators" quadrant. The leader could easily identify where there were surfeits or deficits of strength on the grid. This could mean that for a certain project, team members might be asked to work outside their interest or most productive areas, the fallout being that it might be more difficult to motivate them to do something in which they were less interested or productive. Of course, the ideal was to put people on projects that tapped into their interests, strengths, and needs.

The grid also proved a handy way to identify stress. For example, if a team member was becoming overly domineering, a colleague would know that was typical of "Expeditors" stress behavior. One thing that helps move people out of stress is to keep them busy. A colleague could ask if it would help to have some additional things to do, or simply give the stressed person something to get done by a certain deadline. By learning what the typical stress behaviors of each quadrant were, and ways of helping the person stuck in stress move out of it, the team members contributed to both self-management and team management.

Both the grid and stress reaction scores, which are part of the components in the "Strengths and Needs Report," were used frequently by Mediplast's officers and staff to get themselves or others back on a productive track when they found their needs were not getting met. The grid gave them labels to use in describing stress behavior, and the stress-

Table 8-3 Leadership Style Grid

"Expeditors"	"Communicators"
"Administrators"	"Planners"

reactive scores from the components gave them measures of intensity and descriptions of how to deal with a specific stress situation. The newly integrated teams got pretty good at working with stress behaviors. They used examples from work situations to support the 360 degree performance review category that addressed "managing self and others."

Over the year, as we worked with Mediplast to operationalize new policies and practices, we saw many descriptions of quadrant behavior and samples of terms sprinkled throughout performance reviews. There was not a single management meeting that didn't make use of the terminology. What seemed to please Mediplast executives and staff alike was that the skills they were applying to work relationships were helping them listen better, see others' perspectives, and manage stress in their home lives as well. This resulted in no turnover among the senior managers and an effective cascading of team development throughout the new organization. It's pretty hard to put a dollar value on that side benefit.

The lesson we learned was that our "intervention" to unite two groups into a single new one was appropriate for this situation. What made it a part of the teams' nervous system was the vision of the CEO and his insistence on holding people accountable for using the lessons they learned. It is this kind of focus that differentiated this integration from so many I have seen.

While our process is useful in building cooperation among team members, the focus of a team's efforts during the integration stage is critical. Cooperation without proper focus will not result in value-creating outcomes. The next section discusses two key objectives that teams need to focus on: financial and strategic objectives.

FOCUSING ON FINANCIAL AND STRATEGIC OBJECTIVES

A recurring theme throughout this book has been the importance of financial and strategic objectives. Again, these are pivotal to the value-creation process. Nowhere is it more important than during the integration stage. It is in this stage where objectives become operational and people and teams need to focus on achieving them. Regardless of whether the deal is a small acquisition or a large merger, people's attention must be focused on these objectives. People need to be continuously reminded of their importance and the precedence they must assume during the integration stage and beyond. Failure to attend to "the business" and to deliver on these objectives will be disastrous for everyone, from the CEO to frontline employees.

Not only must broad-based objectives be set for the organization, but they must be translated into objectives that people throughout work units (e.g., functional and support areas, lines of businesses, business processes, geographic areas) can manage and control. Although higher-level objectives are important, work-unit objectives are pivotal for driving individual and team behavior.

In some cases, this process will require certain units to continue to focus on the same sets of objectives and maintain the same level. For others it will require new objectives and levels. The key is to ensure that all individual and work-unit objectives and levels of achievement are aligned with the broader objectives. Moreover, people need to be measured for these objectives and be held accountable and rewarded for achieving them. It is easy for people to take their eyes off these objectives as they become focused on the integration process itself.

REMAINING FLEXIBLE—THINGS CHANGE

Someone once told me that M&As are like marriage. No matter how well two people have planned their lives together, people and situations change and continuous adjustments have to be made. If not, the likely result is a divorce. In a merger or an acquisition it is the same. No matter how much due diligence or integration planning is done, it is almost certain that over time adjustments will have to take place. As noted in Chapters 3 and 6, due diligence and transition planning are inexact processes due to time constraints and access and availability of information. Regardless of how well they are conducted, many things will be overlooked and unanticipated.

PROVIDING FOR CAPABLE AND MOTIVATED PEOPLE

In building a merged organization it is essential that the capability and motivation of people be developed to meet the demands of the new organization. Capability is their ability to carry out a task; motivation is their desire to do so. Even though a careful process may have been used to select the most capable people for positions, it is no guarantee that people will be ready to step in and perform. This is especially the case if new systems, structures, work processes, and the like have been adopted. It will take time for people to learn and adjust to and accept the changes. As Figure 8-2 indicates, there are a number of elements that management must employ to ensure that motivation and capability are captured.

1. Once people assume positions in the new work unit, their roles and responsibilities must be clarified. Even the most motivated people will fail if they are unsure where they need to focus their energies.

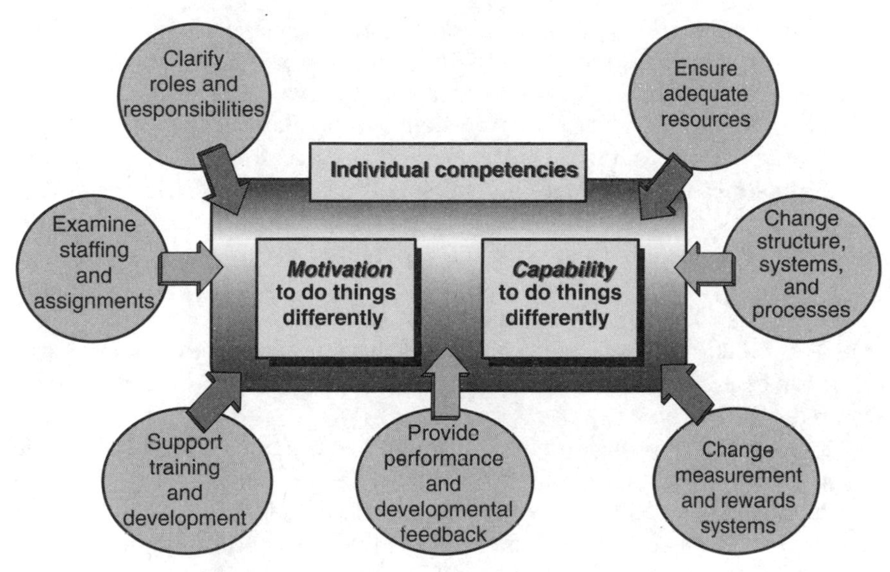

Figure 8-2 Creating Capable and Motivated People

2. Care must be taken to ensure that people are placed in the right positions. This requires matching the right person to the right job.
3. Training and development are pivotal. Highly qualified people will need training and development to meet the needs of new positions that are created, technologies that are employed, and systems and work processes that are introduced. If done properly, integration teams should identify such needs as part of their work.
4. It is important that a performance and developmental feedback process be established. Without feedback, people will not know whether they are meeting expectations or not.
5. Measurement and reward systems may be among the most powerful elements in shaping behavior. What is measured and rewarded is what people will focus on.

As an integrated example that captures all these elements, a large equipment manufacturing company used a merger as an opportunity to significantly change its after-sales service approach. Before the merger neither company did a very good job at servicing customers. A customer service integration team was created, and after careful study of best practices a new approach was developed. The team concluded that numerous aspects of the organization would have to be transformed.

1. The type of people required to staff the customer service organization would have to change. More agreeable, patient, nurturing, and technically sophisticated people would have to be hired as customer service representatives. Few people in the existing organizations qualified.

2. The people would have to be trained in a very specific protocol that helped to soothe unhappy customers and to provide technical skills to solve problems over the telephone.
3. A sophisticated information system would have to be created that would allow the representatives to access a customer's complete file to ensure that customers got personalized treatment. Moreover, the system would have to contain self-paced diagnostics that would provide all representatives with the capability to solve simple problems over the phone. This could significantly cut costs and improve customer satisfaction and retention.
4. The company would have to arrange with local service centers to provide customers with overnight repairs if problems could not be fixed over the phone.
5. Inventories of replacement equipment and logistics would have to be put in place to send customers new equipment overnight if items 3 and 4, above, did not work. Although this could increase net working capital, it was concluded, after study, that it would be more than offset by customer retention.
6. Representatives had to be empowered to make decisions to solve customers' problems without taking time to go through the hierarchy for approval. This would certainly reduce cycle times for decisions and minimize the time of people involved.
7. Representatives had to be motivated to make all of the above elements work. To that end, the performance of representatives was carefully measured and tracked, and the representatives were given incentives, recognition, and more decision-making authority based on outstanding performance.

Clearly, many organizational elements need to be aligned to ensure peoples' capabilities and motivation. Failure to achieve one element would have led to failure. What good would a motivated and well-trained person be without the proper systems? Conversely, how effective would the system be without the proper person using it and interacting with a customer?

ASSIMILATING NEW PEOPLE

In many situations, acquired people will be brought into an existing organization. Not every acquisition results in a transformation with completely new ways of doing things. For example, I worked with a major highway construction company that was growing geographically through the acquisition of small, privately held firms. The acquirer was a very well run organization that had developed best practices for its operations over a number of years and was not looking to transform itself. It was only interested in successfully acquiring and integrating new firms. With the exception of some accounting functions that were consolidated, most of the target firms' operations were geographically decentralized. Due to transportation costs, paving operations needed to be located close to where the construction work and available raw materials were located. In almost all cases, however, the targets' operations were not of the standard of the acquirer and had to go through changes.

The acquired people were pleased to have been bought by the acquirer. In fact, they knew that the acquirer sought to keep all qualified people, since the acquirer itself did not have enough people to staff the new geographic areas.

The acquirer had a reputation for being among the best companies in the industry and was known for treating its people fairly. The acquired people were receptive to the changes. After the deal was closed, the executives of the acquirer visited the targets' operations to meet with the people and to learn as much as possible about their concerns and issues regarding the acquisition. Their primary concern was whether they could successfully assimilate and succeed in the new organization. The acquirer went to great pains to ensure that would happen.

It is safe to say that acquired people who have been retained want to succeed in the new organization. The faster they can reestablish their careers and perform effectively, the better. It is therefore critical that acquiring companies create a process that quickly assimilates acquired people in an organized way.

I conducted focus groups with managers and employees of several acquired telecommunication companies that highlight this point. Many noted the importance of successful assimilation. Some of the more typical comments included:

- "I needed an orientation on company benefits, open job opportunities, access to computers, access to records and files needed to do my job."
- "I tried to get into a management position. I asked people, but no one could tell me whom to talk to."
- "I had no information about where, what, and when I was going to start my job."
- "Our managers are having trouble getting us what we need [ID cards, business cards]."
- "The acquired company has too many acronyms and nobody explained to us what they mean."
- "There was no employee orientation. I did not know where to get information or help."
- "We need someone from benefits to come talk to us."
- "We lost our four weeks of vacation and had to start from scratch."
- "We don't know how their [acquired company] systems work."
- "There was a lack of training. The computer was not accessible on day one. The hardware did not always work, and when you asked for help, you got the runaround. Reference books were not up to date."

- "HR provided us with no direction. We did not know what forms needed to be filled out. We needed guidance and did not get any help. We had to train ourselves, the hard way."

One company that has successfully assimilated acquired employees is Cisco Systems. Cisco, which has acquired more than 50 companies in a seven-year period, has created a SWAT team of 36 full-time employees that is responsible for the assimilation of acquired firms.[4] The team relies on a swift and systematic process to ensure that new employees are shepherded and adapt to the new organization.

Key to Cisco's process is the philosophy that people are the primary asset in its acquisitions; people must get integrated first, not products; and employee retention and continued motivation are critical.

After Cisco makes an acquisition, the SWAT team engages in a number of key activities. The activities described below attempt to minimize uncertainty and to provide employees with a road map for adapting quickly to Cisco.

1. Employees are provided with quick and honest communications concerning job roles and titles and changes that are planned in the acquired firm.
2. Acquired employees are immediately provided with a folder of basic information about Cisco, the phone numbers and e-mail addresses of Cisco executives, and charts comparing their benefits with those of Cisco. More importantly, afterward there are two days of follow-up question-and-answer meetings.
3. Technically, employees are provided with new photo ID cards and new business cards. E-mail and voice-mail systems are also quickly converted so that acquired employees can access Cisco systems.
4. In some deals Cisco has guaranteed that no jobs would be lost for one year without the approval of the acquired executives.
5. In some cases Cisco will increase salaries, amend expense allowances, and honor commitments to sabbaticals to keep acquired employees whole.
6. Effort is given to retain acquired entrepreneurs by giving them a role in the new organization and significant challenges and opportunities.
7. Acquired employees are given Cisco stock options. Certainly the rise in Cisco's stock price was an attractive motivator for retaining people. Unfortunately, Cisco's stock price at the time of the writing of this book has become far less attractive.

Other companies that have developed assimilation and orientation programs for new hires have used them during acquisitions. These can easily be adapted to an integration situation. Again, the purpose is to ensure that employees are quickly integrated into the new work environment and allowed to succeed.

One company developed a program that involved the human resources organization, an acquired employee's immediate manager or supervisor, and key employees within the existing work unit. The role of each is presented below:

Human Resources. Provides acquired employees through orientation meetings with a complete overview of benefits and compensation packages. This includes a clear overview of the packages and the steps needed to utilize them, as well as e-mail addresses and telephone numbers of human resources staff available to handle questions.

Manager/Supervisor. Has primary responsibility for facilitating the assimilation of acquired employees.

Key Employee Partner. Has primary responsibility of guiding an acquired employee through the orientation process.

Employee. Has ultimate responsibility for managing his or her own orientation, with the support and guidance of others.

ACHIEVING CULTURAL INTEGRATION

- "We-they"
- "We're better because. . ."
- "We bought you, therefore. . ."
- "We are superior"
- "You're second class"

These words are the "fighting words" that are at the heart of culture clash and the causes of significant conflict. They are words often heard by acquired employees. They denote a lack of respect and the feeling of siege that is likely to take place during integration. This may especially be the case when companies that have been bitter rivals in the marketplace merge. Examples of this include the mergers between Boeing and McDonnell Douglas and Lockheed and Martin Marietta.

This was driven home to me when Harris acquired General Electric Solid State (GESS). GESS in itself was the product of a previous acquisition by GE. Jack Welch, GE's CEO at the time, acquired RCA primarily to get NBC. All other parts of the RCA business, along with some of GE's businesses, were put up for sale since they did not meet Welch's goal of being either the first or second leading competitor in their markets. GESS and RCA Solid State were among them. Both organizations were on the trading block for three years before Harris bought them. Little investment was made in them during that period, and there was little attempt to carefully integrate them. Over that time the relationship between GESS and RCA was strained and conflicted. There was little cooperation. RCA was treated as an outsider. When asked to describe the integration of GESS and RCA, an RCA executive told me, "GESS's idea of synergy and integration was to take a GE lightbulb and stick it up the rear end of the Nipper." The Nipper, of course, is a famous symbol of the RCA organization. These were fighting words that did not foster a smooth integration.

During the same acquisition it was decided that the Harris name would be the new name for the corporation. Essentially, all references to GESS and RCA would eventually disappear. As part of this effort, signs on facilities, business cards, and the like would all become Harris. This was not an overly complex technical challenge. However, it was a huge cultural and psychological challenge. One day as part of this effort, a team of Harris people showed up at an RCA facility ready to change the signs. (For three years GESS never removed the RCA signs.) A Harris person requested that the sign be replaced. No problem! He also noted that there was a statue of the Nipper (that infamous dog) in the reception area and had him removed. Several hours later the employees at the location threatened to walk out of work if the statue were not returned. In fact, the Harris manager had to build the dog a house and lay the dog to rest in it to avert a crisis.

These seem like rather silly behaviors, especially from "mature adults." However, they do capture the significance of culture, history, and most importantly pride. I have found over and over again that people are proud of their companies. They are also capable and willing to change. However, these examples demonstrate that how acquirers handle things can have a profound impact on how those acquired react. The issue with the Nipper was not about the statue but about what it represented. The people at RCA felt that this Harris manager did not respect or value them. Thus, from day one there was not going to be cooperation. As someone once put it, "If we were not very good or effective, why did you buy us? What does it say about you?"

The impact of culture clash has been well documented in both research and practice.[5] Many successful acquisitions have failed because of the acquiring company's inability to manage the conflict caused by cultural differences. While such differences may vary, it is almost inevitable that two companies' cultures will never be the same. Left unattended, such conflict will almost certainly occur. Figure 8-3 depicts the four stages of culture clash.

The process innocently begins when people begin to note the differences between the two companies. This is quite normal, since such differences become apparent when employees are exposed to ways that are different from their own. The issue then becomes how such differences are handled. If unmanaged, they are likely to be magnified. As people spend more time together, they are forced to confront different ways of doing things. Such differences can become sources of conflict as people disagree on everything from how to make decisions to how to handle conflict. Conflict often escalates to the point where stereotyping and put-downs occur. Acquiring firms often adopt superiority syndromes and treat acquired people as second-class citizens.

When this occurs, acquired people typically become defensive trying to protect their pride, their ways of doing things, and their interests. The net result is that conflict rather than cooperation ensues. Promised synergies and swift integration never materialize. Shareholder value is never created. Good employees leave. Customers become frustrated and start dealing with competitors.

Although culture clash is a common by-product of integration, it can be successfully managed. Rather than conflict, cultural synergy can be created. However, it takes sound leadership, as in the case of Carlos Ghosn, and a well-managed process to do so. Figure 8-4 presents the stages of successful cultural integration. The process begins with a managed flow of information between acquiring and acquired or merging employees. The objective is to provide a constructive forum whereby the parties get "accurate" information about each other. Through such information, inaccurate perceptions are eliminated and real differences are brought to light. Rather than differences being seen as a problem, cross-fertilization is encouraged, and the best features of both cultures are highlighted. The opportunity for cultural synergy and best cultural practices is created. At this point a well-managed process for working through differences is necessary.

Cultural Mirroring: A Useful Approach

Cultural mirroring is a useful tool to help two integrated groups work through cultural differences and facilitate cooperation. Essentially, it is a

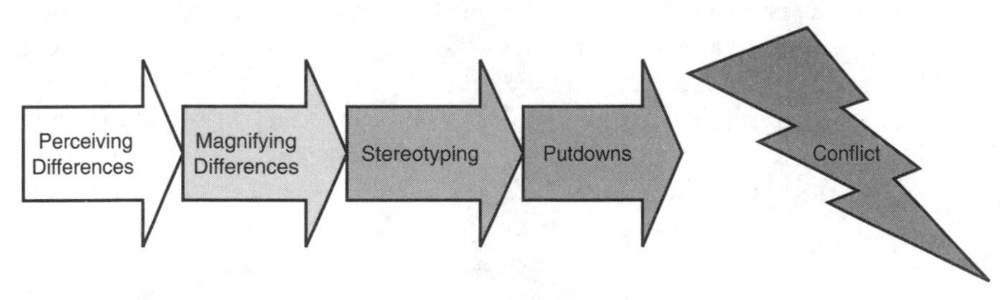

Figure 8-3 Culture Clash

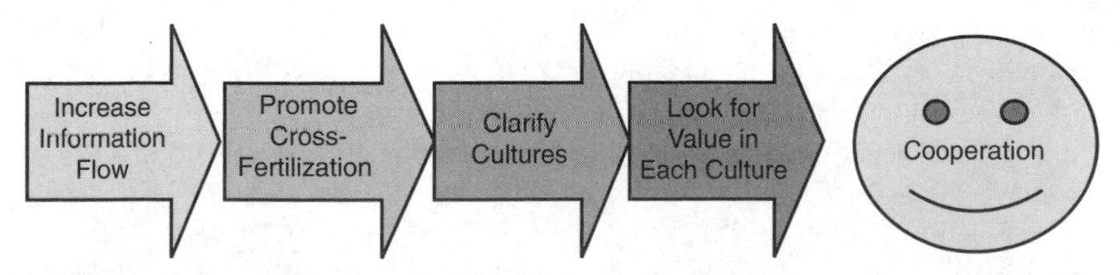

Figure 8-4 Cultural Cooperation

process whereby executives, managers, or employees from the groups are brought together as part of building a team to increase information flow, clarify cultures, and work through differences. Each of the merging groups is asked to:

- Describe your own unit's culture.
- Describe the other unit's culture.
- Describe how you think the other unit would describe your culture.

It is important to note that each group is asked to focus on its work unit's culture rather than on the organization as a whole. As noted in Chapter 3, although organizations have cultures, they may not be the same as that of a division or a functional area. Since groups (e.g., top- management team, R&D, sales) are often integrated, it is their culture that is likely to have an immediate impact on people's thinking and behaviors. Where an organization has a strong culture, it will likely pervade a group's culture.

Several methods can be employed to develop the cultural profile. First, group members can be given a definition of culture and asked to answer the questions above. Second, the group members can be given a list of cultural dimensions and asked to describe themselves and the other organization. For example, the member of a group may be asked to describe how decisions are made in their organization (e.g., centralized or decentralized). Third, the participants can be given a survey instrument that asks them to describe themselves and the other group. The last option gives them a more systematic approach to assessing similarities and differences in culture and the importance of each dimension. As an example, the participants who filled out the cultural profile survey in Chapter 3 describing their own organization were also asked to do it a second time to describe their perception of the other organization's culture. As illustrated in Table 8-4, there were some significant differences between self-descriptions and the other group's descriptions for 10 of the cultural dimensions. Clearly there were misperceptions of the other company's culture. The two groups discussed each dimension. First they clarified differences between their own self-perceptions and the other group's perception of them. This eliminated stereotypes. Second, they isolated actual differences that existed between them, which served as a basis for discussion on how to deal with the differences. More will be said about this issue later.

Based on an open-ended series of questions, the lists that follow reflect the results of the research and development organizations of two pharmaceutical companies that were merging. Prior to the closing it was anticipated that the R&D units would be merged to create a critical mass. There would be an opportunity to better focus the two organizations, eliminate redundancy, and increase collaboration. The net result would be lower product development costs (i.e., cost synergies) and a stronger pipeline of future products (i.e., intangible synergies). The senior management of

Table 8-4 Cultural Profile

	Always	Often	Elements of Both	Often	Always	
	1	2	3	4	5	
Centralized decisions		x, X		y, Y		Decentralized decisions
Fast decision making		y, Y		x, X		Slow decision making
Short-term focus		x, X,Y	y	y		Long-term focus
Individual orientation	X	x	y	Y		Team orientation
Confrontation of conflict		x, y, X		Y		Avoidance of conflict
High-risk tolerance		y	Y		x,X	Low-risk tolerance
Focus on results		x,y,X		Y		Focus on process
People held accountable	Y	x,y		X		People not held accountable
Horizontal cooperation		y,Y	X	x		Silo-oriented
High trust among people		y	Y	x,X		Highly political
Bureaucratic		x	X	y,Y		Entrepreneurial
Open and honest communications		x,X,Y		y		Guarded communications
Fast communications			x,y	X,Y		Slow communications
Direct face-to-face communications			y,X,Y	x		Indirect communications
Resistant to change		x	YX	y		Open to change

x = Acquiring firm's self-perception X = Target firm's perception
y = Target firm self-perception Y = Acquiring firm's perception of target firm

both organizations believed a priori that the cultures of the two groups were relatively similar, that there would be few problems in combining them, and that cost and intangible synergies were inevitable. Opportunities for synergies were confirmed by the R&D integration team. However, senior management's early conclusions about cultural compatibility were questioned. The integration team leaders believed that the differences were greater than anticipated. But they also believed that whatever differences existed could be worked out after the closing. This belief is quite typical of many M&As.

After the closing, preparation for integrating the groups began. To facilitate the integration, I was asked to conduct a cultural mirroring exercise to create a cooperative environment in the new R&D organization. The mirroring first began with a self- assessment as follows:

Culture: Self-Description

Company A

- Basic research/discovery mentality
- Strongly held beliefs about research freedom; passion about the role of science in improving life for people
- Emphasis on:
    - Patents
    - Publications
    - Credentials

Company B

- Search-and-develop mentality
- R&D leads toward a commercially viable endpoint rational drug design
- Emphasis on:
    - Submission
    - Results
    - Successful product in marketplace

Culture: Description of Other

Company A perceived Company B as:

- Commercially focused
- Local/parochial perspective
- Not true science
- More a development shop

Company B perceived Company A as:

- Nondirected/nonaccountable
- Global presence/international
- Not as successful overall

In addition to the self-assessments, I conducted an independent assessment of each culture utilizing interviews, company documents, and observation. The assessment yielded the following:

An Objective View of Each Company

Company A

- Keys to career progression:
  - Length of service (tenure mentality)
  - Performance
- Freedom at work to pursue academic and personal research interests as long as basic job gets done
- Research drives the business
  - Long-term focus (7–10 years)
  - Publications and patents build firm's credibility and reputation
  - Which attracts and retains top scientific talent
  - Which extends human knowledge in areas of unique interest
  - Which leads to blockbuster discoveries
- Decision making and accountability
  - Decentralized structure leads to dispersed authority and decision making
  - More difficult to determine who is accountable for what
  - Lack of clarity may encourage individual effort, entrepreneurship, and creativity (necessary in R&D environment)
- Structured by scientific discipline/geography

Company B

- Keys to career progression:
  - Performance against goals
  - Being seen as team player
- Work time very goal directed and time very focused on key priorities
- Market needs drive the business
  - Shorter-term focus (5–7 years)
  - Less patience with scientific process
  - Reliance on some basic research
  - Focus on licensing, joint ventures, co-promotion as technique to ensure new-product flow
  - Fastest way to market is the way to go, since window of opportunity is narrow
- Decision making and accountability
  - Centralized structure leads to focused authority and decision making

  - Clarity of structure, measurement, and direction
  - Accountability is clear
  - Clarity and business management orientation may meet project deadline at expense of creativity and entrepreneurship
- Structured by therapeutic category/major function

As both the objective assessment and self-perceptions indicate, the two R&D groups were not at all alike. Simply put, Company A's culture appeared to be very academic, whereas Company B's was much more applied. Could these two organizations be successfully integrated, and could synergies be created? If the two groups were left to do it on their own, the likely outcome would have been conflict. After the assessments were conducted, each group shared its perspective, as did I. The groups realized that there were many fundamental differences that would have to be worked out if they were to have a chance to successfully work together.

Whether through the use of open-ended questions or a cultural survey, the mirroring exercise creates a constructive forum for an open dialogue on discussing differences and finding a constructive way for dealing with them. Once actual differences are isolated, the key is how to reconcile them. Many experts on intergroup conflict and cooperation always point to the importance of common goals as a way of aligning the interests of separate groups. I agree! As such, it is useful to focus merging groups on the following sets of questions:

- What are the unit's major objectives, and what are the means for achieving them?
- What cultural attributes would best enable the unit to achieve its objectives and strategies?
  - What cultural attributes that neither group has should be adopted?
  - What cultural attributes that are detrimental to the unit should be eliminated?
  - What cultural attributes have no impact on the functioning of the unit but are important to each group?
- What actions should be taken to ensure that important attributes are retained, new attributes are adopted, and detrimental attributes are eliminated?
- What actions should be taken to ensure that attributes not important to the unit, but important to a group, are respected by the other group?

These questions allow the participants to focus on the future needs of the work unit rather than on their parochial interests. Through effective participation and facilitation, people can move forward and rebuild the new unit. This is not to argue that conflict has been eliminated, but that a process for effectively managing it and building cooperation has been established. In the end the test of this process will be whether the unit is successful and whether its members benefit from it.

Recently, a colleague and I conducted a study to assess the impact that cultural mirroring had on the integration of employees of two companies.[6] The research was conducted in six similar manufacturing plants of two merging companies: three from the acquiring firm and three from the acquired firm. Two plants remained independent, two were integrated and participated in the cultural mirroring process, and two were integrated but did not participate. The employees participating in this study were highly skilled. Of those participating in all phases of the study, 120 of 240 employees were from the acquired firm and 116 of 175 employees were from the acquiring firm.

The acquiring firm was a major strategic business unit (SBU) within a larger *Fortune* 500 parent company. The acquired firm was a stand-alone business that had been a competitor of the SBU prior to the acquisition. Both firms manufactured consumer products, and the acquired firm was slightly larger than the SBU in terms of sales and number of employees.

The negotiations that took place between the CEOs of the two firms were considered to be friendly, and the deal was made. Both firms felt that the acquisition was key to their competitiveness and profitability. The acquiring firm paid a premium for the acquired firm and believed that it needed to realize some operational synergies to financially justify the deal.

Neither firm was a dominant player in its industry. Although the firms competed against each other in several market segments, each firm was a leader in several of its own segments. Thus, the acquisition was somewhat complementary and provided both firms with an opportunity to expand the number of segments (i.e., customer groups and product lines) in which they participated. There were also operating synergies (e.g., operating economies of scale, reduction of redundant staff) that could be captured in manufacturing, sales, and general and administrative staff. The acquisition also improved the R&D capabilities of both firms.

A comprehensive integration plan had been developed prior to the closing. Due to premiums paid and the inherent belief that synergies needed to be secured quickly, the CEO established a very aggressive "First 100 Days Program" in which he expected significant integration would take place. However, he also felt that involvement of both firms in designing and executing the integration was critical to its success. To that end, he created an integration transition process that was staffed by key managers and employees in both organizations.

It was also agreed upon that the CEO of the acquired firm would retire shortly after the deal was completed; he would serve as a consultant until his firm was fully integrated into the acquiring firm's SBU. Prior to his departure the acquired firm's CEO, who was 63 years old, agreed to enthusiastically endorse the acquisition.

The study was begun two weeks prior to the formal announcement of the acquisition. At this time (time 1) employees in all plants participating in the study were administered an employee survey by plant personnel managers. Participation in the survey, which was not unlike ones done previously by both companies, was voluntary. The survey was administered on company time, and all results were kept confidential. The completed surveys were collected and sent directly to the researchers. Both firms' plant and personnel managers felt that employees knew that the acquisition was taking place prior to the formal announcement. Although negotiations were held in secrecy and no official announcements had been made, rumors concerning the acquisition and the name of the acquiring/acquired firm were circulating prior to the announcement.

On the day of the announcement, employees were given basic information (e.g., name, location, size, products) on the acquired/acquiring company. This information was communicated via letters to employees from their respective senior managers. No specific information concerning plants or individuals to be affected was provided. Two weeks later (time 2) the acquisition was closed. Within one week of the closing, employees were provided more specific information concerning the acquisition. Senior management of both firms, using letters and videotapes, provided employees with information concerning the strategy behind the acquisition, the vision for the new company (division), and basic plans for the integration. Employees in each plant were also told whether their plant was going to remain independent or be combined. In the two cases where the plants were to be shut down, most individuals in both firms considered these plants to be less efficient than the acquiring firm's plants. The employees were informed that attrition would primarily be used to reduce redundancy. A sufficient number of employees reaching retirement within six months had already given notice that they were leaving, avoiding a reduction in force at the time of the study. All other employees would be given an opportunity to either relocate or be considered for other jobs within the company.

Since employees' identities with their previous company were important and since both companies' products were well regarded in the marketplace, the name chosen for the new division was a hybrid of the two. A plan to change facilities' signs, stationery, and the like to reflect the new name was communicated to all employees and initiated right after the closing. Employees in the acquired company were also fully informed of and placed in the acquiring company's benefits plan with full seniority. As it turned out, the acquiring company's plan was superior to that of the acquired company. All these issues had been worked out prior to the closing by high-level integration teams and factored into the valuation models. Prior to the acquisition, both companies competed for the same employees in the marketplace.

During the next month, a first wave of employees from the acquired plants was transferred to and placed in a work unit within the acquiring plants. It was anticipated that the acquired plants would continue to operate during the ensuing three to six months while they were being shut down. Since both acquired and acquiring plants were located in the same city, no employee relocations were required. During this time no formal interventions other than information sessions for acquired employees on benefits and compensation were conducted.

One month after the closing (time 3), a second survey was administered. This survey permitted an initial assessment of the effects of the merger and combination on the work forces. One month was chosen as an appropriate period because it would provide sufficient time for the initial wave of acquired employees to be transferred to acquiring plants and for all employees to react to events.

Two days after the survey administration (time 4), an intervention to facilitate joint intercultural learning and problem solving was begun (using the cultural mirroring approach described above) at one combined plant. Finally, a third survey was administered six weeks later (time 5). This allowed for a short-term assessment of the effects of the intervention.

The results of the study indicate that those participating in the cultural mirroring process reported greater adaptability to and support for the merger than those who did not participate. Specifically, those who participated reported greater:

- Understanding of the other unit's culture
- Willingness to support the merger integration process
- Commitment to the organization
- Cooperation with those from the other organization
- Performance
- Trust in management

Although many executives, academics, and consultants continually note that culture clash can create value leakage, failure to achieve synergies, and loss of shareholder value, few present any approaches for mitigating its effects or taking advantage of cultural differences. The results of this study support mirroring as an approach that works.

Although tools such as mirroring are promising, they do not guarantee success. Executives and managers must also be prepared to deal with individuals and groups that may have their own agendas and interests in a situation. In such cases, lack of cooperation may be more the result of conflicting interests rather than learning and understanding. Failure to deal with and align them may offset any benefits that can be garnered from intercultural learning.

A FINAL NOTE

The integration stage is where synergies, earnings, and cashflow are realized. Prior stages have been nothing more than theoretical exercises to forecast what these might be. Whether they are realized or not depends heavily on the ability of executives to rebuild teams and develop capable and motivated people who are willing to drive the integration and the new organization. Failure to do so is likely to relegate a merger to the scrap heap of the many others that have failed to create value for investors.

9

EVALUATING THE ACQUISITION INTEGRATION PROCESS

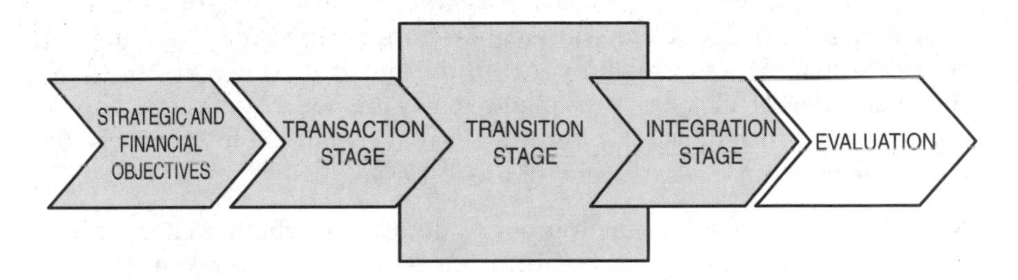

Continuous assessment and improvement are key elements in the success of a merger or an acquisition. Due to the complexity of the numerous activities to be managed during integration and the occurrence of many unanticipated events, it is easy for the process to get off track and for results not to be realized. To ensure progress requires a conscious and concerted effort to keep track of several key elements, along with answers to the following questions:

1. What impact is the integration having on key indicators of business performance? Are the synergies that were hypothesized during the valuation being realized?
2. Are the activities and milestones developed in the integration plan on target?
3. What key issues are emerging during the integration that must be dealt with?
4. What has been learned during the merger or acquisition that can be used to improve subsequent merger or acquisition integrations.

MEASURING KEY INDICATORS

The ultimate goal of a merger or acquisition is to deliver the financial results expected, namely, earnings and cashflow. However, there are a number of other measures that serve as leading indicators of financial outcomes, and they need to be measured as well. These indicators are no different from those that any well-run company would employ as a normal part of doing business.

Three levels of measurement and their interrelationship are presented in Figure 9-1. Level 1 includes financial outcomes. Level 2 consists of the component measures of these outcomes: revenues, costs, net working capital, and capital investments. And Level 3 is composed of the organizational indicators: the customers, employees, and operations that drive the components.[1]

Measurements should be taken on a regular basis to ensure that they have not declined and that forecasts are met. Measurements should be taken in all areas being integrated and in both the acquirer and target or in both merger partners. The measurements should be based on benchmarks to ensure that the changes brought by the integration are yielding the financial and strategic objectives intended and are not creating unintended side effects that might result in value leakage. When feasible, comparisons should be made in one or several of the following ways:

- First, indicators should be tracked to determine whether changes are occurring over time. It is helpful if measurements are taken prior to integration to establish a baseline. To the extent that the acquirer or seller has a history of using a key indicator, this will be easier. For

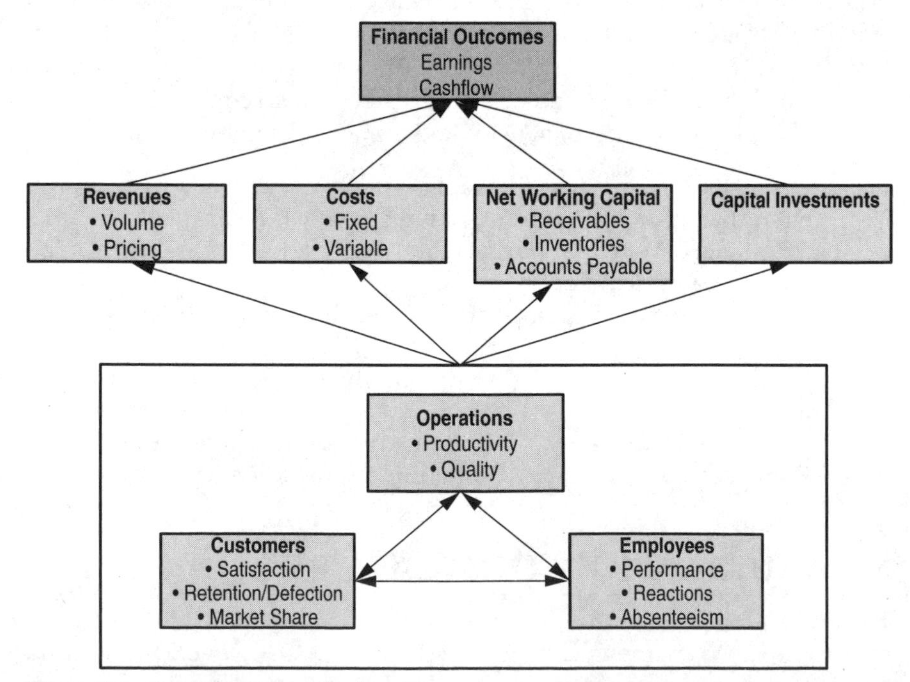

Figure 9-1 Key Indicators of Performance

example, Chapter 5 detailed a communications study a colleague and I conducted. Using premerger and postmerger measurements, we were able to establish that a communication intervention helped improve employee reactions to a merger. This was a critical determinant in the decision to continue the intervention throughout both the acquiring and acquired companies.

- Second, comparisons between similar types of units being integrated and not being integrated allow a more precise causal assessment of whether the integration is having a direct impact on an indicator. In Chapter 8, I reported a study that a colleague and I conducted to examine a cultural mirroring intervention. We employed a comparison-group methodology and were able to determine whether the intervention was impacting employee reactions or not. The results gave us the confidence to roll out the project on a larger scale, and it has worked successfully throughout the company.
- Third, comparisons against valuation forecasts and expectations help determine whether the integration is on track or not. Again, the ultimate test of the success of the deal is whether the valuation projections have been met or not.

Consistency with Financial Projections

Earnings and cashflows are the primary financial outcomes that need to be tracked since valuation models are built on them. Particular attention should be given to the components of these measures, namely, revenues, costs, investments, and net working capital. The extent to which these components are on track will determine whether value is being created or not. Further, specific attention needs to be given to tracking synergies.

A Note on Realizing Synergies

Since valuation and pricing decisions are often based on synergies, it only makes sense that such synergies be clearly documented and monitored to ensure they are realized. As I argued in Chapter 2, the better we can document synergies, the higher the probability that valuations and pricing will be accurate.

Documentation should begin during the transaction stage and be monitored through the integration stage. Not all synergies, however, will be known with precision early in the M&A process. Several, such as general and administrative overhead cost synergies, may be easy to identify; but others, such as revenues and intangibles, may not be.

Often, especially in large mergers or acquisitions, rough estimates of synergies may be made during the transaction stages, with the details to be identified by integration teams during the transition stage or found by managers during the integration stage. This is often due to the size of the transactions and the acquirer's limited time and access to complete in-depth analyses of the target.

In one merger I was involved in, it was estimated that $800 million in revenue enhancements could be accrued by cross-selling products. This estimate was based on numerous assumptions about the sales organizations, distribution channels, and customers. The challenge would be to truly find and realize the $800 million. After the deal was closed, it was discovered that some of the assumptions underlying the synergies were ill-founded, and a gap between the forecast and the reality was emerging. It turned out that the sales organization of the target was not quite as capable as the acquirer had thought, and the potential cross-selling of certain products was not as strong as was imagined. Through documentation the acquirer was able to identify certain shortfalls early. Fortunately, some unanticipated synergies were found that allowed the firm to reach the $800 million. Key to the success was the vigilant monitoring of the synergies and the growing awareness that new sources would have to be found if the $800 million was to be reached.

Prior to closing, integration teams have responsibility for finding synergies. The synergy capture team has responsibility for interacting with integration teams to continually remind them of the "numbers" they have to reach and for monitoring each synergy and the roll-up of all the synergies.

Following closing, operating managers have primary responsibility for monitoring and realizing synergies as part of their budgets, profit and loss statements, cashflow statements, and balance sheets. Ultimately these are the critical documents that will determine whether value for investors was created.

It is also useful for teams and operating managers to develop a spreadsheet to track specific synergies. It helps identify the impact of specific synergies. Table 9-1 illustrates a spreadsheet for documenting and tracking synergies, regardless of whether they are functional or support areas, lines of business, or geographic areas. The spreadsheet should be updated weekly. It should include synergies that have been validated and documented, those that are awaiting validation, and those that have been newly identified since the last tracking report. Validated synergies are those that are virtually certain. Those awaiting validation look good but need to be confirmed. New ones have just been suggested and need to be tested. Only validated synergies "can be taken to the bank." The table identifies the synergies—the net impact they have on cashflows and earnings in the first four quarters after closing and then the next four years. Earnings and cashflows are tracked since they are employed as the central elements in valuation and pricing decisions (see Chapter 2). The table also identifies possible overlaps with other areas that are performing this same exercise. It is important that synergies are not double-counted and are thus not overestimated.

Table 9-2 illustrates a spreadsheet that can be used by a synergy capture team to monitor the synergies reported by all the integration teams. The synergies are again broken down into validated, awaiting validation, and newly discovered. In conjunction with the individual-area spreadsheets, synergies can be easily monitored. For ease of use, all spreadsheets can be managed electronically and maintained on a secure Intranet site. This allows easy access to spreadsheets by those who need to access them.

Customer Reactions

Ensuring that customers are not adversely affected during the integration is an essential element in the success of a merger or an acquisition. Losing either profitable customers or a percentage of their business may have a dramatic impact on earnings and cashflows (i.e., value leakage), especially if the customer represents a large percentage of the company's revenues and profits. In most M&As the objective is either to retain or to grow the customer base. Sometimes, unprofitable customers will be deliberately pruned. Therefore it is essential that customer indicators be continually examined.

Several indicators should be employed: customer satisfaction, retention, acquisition, and market share. Satisfaction measures capture multiple dimensions (e.g., product quality and features, after-sales service, delivery speed, new-product development, price). The dimensions examined should be directly linked to the market key success factors (i.e., the criteria that customers use to decide whom to buy from). Decreases in satisfaction may be a leading indicator of customer defection, loss of market share, and thus volume loss. The impact will be lower revenues, assuming prices do not increase, and higher costs as a company needs to acquire new customers to replace the lost ones.

Retention and defection rates of customers by market segments should also be tracked. The rates are a good leading indicator of market share. These data could be examined on a weekly or monthly basis to determine if any changes and trends are occurring. Certainly the loss of a major customer should raise a red flag. Moreover, the percentage of business coming from each customer should be examined to see whether the levels are increasing, decreasing, or remaining the same. These are important measurements since many cashflow projections are based on certain assumptions about the retention and addition of customers. For example, in security monitoring, customer retention-defection rates were considered key to earnings and cashflow. Given that fixed costs were a very high percentage of the cost structure of this business, the loss of a key customer had a direct impact on both cashflow and earnings. Retention rates were measured and tracked from due diligence through integration.

Keeping track of market share and sales volume, segment by segment, is also useful. It allows a company to directly examine its competitive position within its markets. Often during mergers and acquisitions competitors

Table 9-1 Tracking Synergies by Area

Integration Team ________________ [Net cashflows (CF) and earnings (E) are reported in $ millions]

Source of Synergy	Status	Q 1 CF/E	Q 2	Q 3	Q 4	Year 1 Total	Year 2	Year 3	Year 4	Year 5	Known Overlap with Other Integration Teams
Cost savings											
1. Fixed manufacturing overhead (supervision)	Validated	$3.0/3.0									
2. Shared marketing expenses	Awaiting validation	$1.5/1.5									
Revenue increase											
1. Cross-selling product A with target's sales force	Awaiting validation	$1.7/1.7									
2. Cross-selling product B with acquirer's distributors	Awaiting validation	$2.3/2.3									
Market power improvement											
1. Raw material costs	Validated	$.9/.9									
2. Price increase	New	$.7/.7									
Intangible gains											
1. Improvement in plant operating procedures	Awaiting validation	$.4/.4									
2. Smaller inventories	Awaiting validation	$1.0/0									
Total integration team synergies		$11.5/10.5									

Table 9-2 Tracking All Synergies

Total Synergies [Net cashflows (CF) and earnings (E) are reported in $ millions]

Source of Synergy	Status	Q 1 CF/E	Q 2	Q 3	Q 4	Year 1 Total	Year 2	Year 3	Year 4	Year 5
Cost savings										
	Validated	$3.0/3.0								
	Awaiting validation	$1.5/1.5								
	New									
Revenue increase										
	Validated									
	Awaiting validation	$4.0/4.0								
	New									
Market power improvement	Validated	$.9/.9								
3. Raw material costs										
4. Price increase	Awaiting validation									
	New									
Intangible gains										
3. Improvement in plant operating procedures	Validated									
4. Smaller inventories	Awaiting validation	$1.4/0								
	New	$.7/.7								
Validated		$3.9/3.9								
Awaiting validation		$6.9/5.9								
New		$0.7/7								
Total synergies		$11.5/10.5								

attempt to disrupt the relationship between an acquirer and its customers. This happened in many markets to major banks being acquired. Smaller credit unions were mounting campaigns to dissuade retail customers from continuing a relationship with their existing bank based on the grounds that service would deteriorate throughout the integration and afterward. This implies that a company needs to do more than just maintain customer relationships. It has to make an extra effort to ensure that its business does not erode.

It would be desirable if measurements could be taken prior to an acquisition, at one point during the transition, and on an ongoing basis after integration. For the most part, preacquisition measurement will depend upon the extent to which the target's management previously conducted such assessments. Interviews with key customers, focus groups, surveys, and archival records are useful approaches for collecting customer data.

Employee Reactions

Employees can have a dramatic impact on productivity and customer satisfaction, especially in service businesses or ones in which intellectual capital is a source of value to the company. Therefore, it is important to track how employees are adapting and reacting to the acquisition. Too often this is a neglected area. Similar to the approach used to measure customer satisfaction, employee assessments made at multiple times and with the use of preexisting measures may better allow changes and trends to be spotted.

There are a number of types of reactions that could be measured, but the following are among those that I have found most important:

- *Reactions to a merger or an acquisition.* Do employees understand what is going on in the merger or acquisition and the changes that are taking place? Do they understand what is expected of them and how they can contribute to the new organization? This may have a direct bearing on employee productivity, absenteeism, turnover, and safety.
- *Satisfaction and morale.* How do employees view the new organization? Are they satisfied with various aspects of the organization and leadership (e.g., communications, compensation and benefits, involvement in decisions, recognition)? This may have a direct impact on employee turnover, absenteeism, safety, and customer relations.
- *Commitment to the new organization.* Are employees committed to the new organization? This may have a direct impact on employee turnover and willingness to put in extra effort on behalf of the organization (e.g., spend extra time on teams and task forces).
- *Willingness to support the integration.* Are employees willing to support the integration process and changes associated with it? This may have

a direct impact on the extent to which employees support changes and how successfully and quickly the integration is completed.

- *Intention to remain in the new organization.* Are employees thinking about quitting the organization? This may have a direct impact on actual voluntary turnover.
- *Employee performance and productivity*. Are employees continuing to produce? Depending upon the company and the nature of the job, numerous measures can be employed (e.g., sales per employee, patents, output per unit of time). These may have a direct impact on revenues (e.g., for the sales staff) and costs.
- *Safety*. Are employees focusing on safety, or are they focusing their attention elsewhere? This may have a direct impact on costs, absenteeism, and turnover.
- *Absenteeism and voluntary turnover.* Are employees taking time away from work or leaving the company voluntarily? This may have a direct impact on the caliber and loyalty of the remaining work force, productivity, quality, and work flow, among other elements. It will also have an impact on costs due to recruiting and hiring of new people and the time it takes for them to ascend the learning curve.

In general, these measures provide warning signs of organizational and financial problems that may emerge from the integration. They need to be monitored and responded to. Interviews with key employees, focus groups, surveys, and archival records are useful approaches for collecting employee data.[2]

Operating Measures

Operating measures should be tracked for each functional and support area, product line, and geographic area of the business. An array of measures can be employed which are idiosyncratic to the company and the area being measured. Normal operating measures (e.g., productivity, quality, safety, innovations, order-processing time, delivery time) that drive earnings and cashflows should also be continually monitored. These provide warning signals that earnings or cashflow problems are emerging. Most of this information can be gleaned from company records, to the extent that a company collects the necessary information and organizes it in a useful fashion.

Once measurements are taken, they need to be analyzed to determine if gaps are emerging. Gaps in leading indicators may provide ample time for corrective action before they have a direct impact on financial results. Gaps in financial results may leave little time and require a crisis response. Once financial results are not realized, the probability of having overpaid for an acquisition has risen dramatically. Table 9-3 presents a simple format that can be used to conduct such an assessment.

Table 9-3 Measuring Success

Key Performance Measure	Baseline Measures/ Expectations/ Benchmarks	Follow-Up Measure	Gaps	Causes	Action to Be Taken to Close Gaps	Responsibility
Financial projections						
Customer reactions						
Employee reactions						
Operating measure						

TRACKING THE INTEGRATION PROCESS

In addition to tracking key indicators, it is important to assess how the integration process is progressing and to identify and solve any emerging issues that may impinge upon it. The objective is to ensure a continuous process of learning and improvement. As such, project activities and milestones identified in Chapter 8 must be continually monitored. So too should issues that arise throughout the integration.

Managing Activities and Milestones

Project plans define both the activities to be carried out and the milestones for achieving them. Transition and integration teams need to continually monitor these to ensure that proper progress is being made. When milestones are not being met, corrective action needs to be taken. If milestones are central elements in a critical path, they may hold up the entire project execution. If this occurs, the timing of changes being implemented and forecasted earnings and cashflows could be compromised. This may result in failed synergies or value leakage. Companies such as Cisco and Bank of America have become very adept at developing and tracking project plans as part of their integration strategy. In fact, Bank of America is quite comprehensive in training its integration teams in project management.

Tracking Key Issues

It is also useful for transition or integration teams to keep track of issues created by gaps in either the key indicators or project plans. Issues will always arise regardless of how well the integration has been planned. No two deals are identical, and there are always unanticipated events. The key is how fast the acquirer identifies and responds to them.

Most successful acquirers create a formalized process of issue tracking and resolution. Simple issues may be tracked and resolved by an integration team. Complex ones may need to be elevated to the transition team or to the MIO/IC for resolution. They may involve the commitment of significant resources or be politically sensitive, requiring a higher level of authority for resolution. Each transition and integration team should formally track key issues. A few key suggestions on how to do that are as follows:

1. Transition and integration teams should meet and debrief on a periodic basis (e.g., weekly), after a major integration activity or stage in the process is completed, or when a critical issue arises. Periodic team meetings should have a portion of the agenda dedicated to identifying and resolving issues. Basic ground rules for what constitutes an issue, who can call a meeting, and what meeting format the team will employ (e.g., face-to-face, virtually) must be established by each team.

2. Team members should be encouraged to keep track of and document current integration issues that need to be resolved in the near future. Team members should also keep track of issues they have resolved and how they did so. This may help someone else who is facing the same issue. Members should also be encouraged to keep a diary noting (a) things that were done well, (b) areas of concern or things that need to be improved, and (c) recommendations on how to correct problems or improve the process for the future. More will be said about this below.

Table 9-4 presents a simple form for tracking immediate issues that can easily be posted on an Intranet. The form identifies an issue, its priority, a plan of action for resolving it, the person responsible for managing it, its date of solution, and its status.

Presented below are issues that were identified by a company (which I call AB) engaged in the roll-up of the security monitoring industry. Several small companies were being simultaneously acquired and integrated. Many backroom activities, such as monitoring were being consolidated, whereas branch (field) operations were being left geographically dispersed but standardized. As firms were being integrated, the acquirer kept track of key issues that needed to be resolved. Issues were divided into three categories: technical, political, and cultural. If they were not managed, they could significantly affect the company's operations, employees and customers, and, ultimately, financial results.

Technical Issues

1. Initial HR meeting with the branch employees is inconsistent from location to location. At some branches the discussion was too high level and did not include enough detail to reassure the very stressed acquired company employees. In other locations the meeting deteriorated into a detailed discussion of health or vacation benefits and left the acquired company employees discontent and unmotivated about AB. In other cases the meeting digressed into a micromanagement discussion about the operations of each functional area. In these cases the employees were so scared about the degree of change that was going to occur that they could not get excited about being a part of AB.
2. The initial communication to the customers is on AB letterhead, so the customers do not even open it in many cases. In other cases, the communication is sent to the wrong contact at the customer's organization. Therefore the accounts payable department does not understand why it has a bill from AB.
3. In Toronto, the initial HR packets included information about benefits that did not apply to Canada (e.g., 401K, paid medical benefit options). Also, HR requested the employees' social security number when it is illegal for an employer to request that information in Canada.

Table 9-4 Tracking Issues

Integration Team	Issue	Priority (High, Medium, Low)	Plan of Action	Responsibility	Solution Date	Status
Human Resources	Communicating benefits information	Medium				
Operations	Conversion of a product from the target's operations to the acquirer					
Information Systems	Bottleneck in generating customer invoices	High				

4. Window stickers and yard signs need to be distributed immediately to the acquired company's customers. The window stickers and yard signs are one of the most powerful and inexpensive advertising methods that support AB's branding. The XYZ branches that were acquired have large customer bases, and the task of changing all the signs is time-consuming for the local branches. This task could be handled centrally from Corporate. If not handled centrally, at least distribute the decals to the local offices of the acquired company so that they can make an effort to get the decals and signs out to the customers.
5. The branch employees need to attend another meeting with HR personnel from Corporate to better understand their benefits. Most branches were visited by HR early after the announcement of the acquisition. However, employees were still in shock at that point and were not necessarily thinking about the specifics of their new benefits. Now the branch employees need to attend a second session with HR to have the opportunity to ask the questions that were not asked at the first meeting. Many benefits and processes to receive benefits may have seemed clear to them at the initial meeting but since that time the employees have encountered problems or confusing processes. (The employees at XYZ do not have their prescription cards or their PPO books for their new benefits, and they cannot use their old benefits.) This follow-up meeting would allow the employees to get answers to questions that have come up since the acquisition. These meetings could go a long way in improving employee morale and reducing frustration.
6. AB needs an inventory, including all branches, of what has not been assimilated from the branches' perspective, from past acquisitions. Avoid distributing a survey to the branches to complete, which would just be creating work for them. The branches need someone from Corporate to visit each branch. Or the Corporate staff could do it by phone as long as the process does not require excessive time commitments from the local management. This initiative needs to be positioned properly. Corporate should emphasize that this inventory is not a "report card" on the branches, but a tool to help Corporate understand what the branches need at this point. If not positioned correctly, the branches will not accurately disclose the extent to which they have not assimilated. The branches need a project team to visit the locations that have not completed the assimilation process. The team will support the local management from various branches by:
   - Developing project plans and time lines.
   - Troubleshooting and assisting in problem solving in system conversions.
   - Developing and distributing customer communications.
   - Conducting training on AB standard procedures.
   - Conducting cultural training.

7. Employees in the branches need employee manuals and standard operations manuals for functional areas. AB may believe that this has been completed in the past, but no one out there seems to have any manuals.

Political Issues

1. On the initial conference call with XYZ to announce the acquisition, remarks were made by AB's management about the closing or sale of certain branches. This was the first that the general managers of these branches had heard of these decisions. (After further analysis, many of these branches were not actually sold or closed, but the damage was done.) This appeared to be caused by AB's corporate managers trying to establish power and control at this initial contact.
2. Staffing is a major concern right now because many general managers have two or more new locations to integrate into their facility. Everyone is aware that only one manager is needed for each department. Managers from all the companies are concerned and asking questions about staffing the management positions. Originally, Corporate told the GMs to not worry about the two new acquisitions until after the first of the year. So the managers were going to have to wait three months to find out about the status of their jobs. This problem is the result of senior management's delay in announcing organizational structure for the new organizations and markets.
3. Significant time, talent, energy, and money have been spent in short-term solutions resulting from senior management's lack of commitment to final solutions. The payroll system is one example (converting XYZ into fictitious job codes in order to meet the contractual obligation, just to convert them again when management has made a decision about the structure of the organization). Giving network connections to buildings that will not be used in the future is another. This type of duplication of work is always a strain on morale, but coupled with the current lack of communication will only increase tension among the employees.

Cultural Issues

1. Initial meeting with XYZ managers was very stiff and formal. The executive management of AB was seated at a head table, with the XYZ personnel seated in a classroom setting. The managers felt that AB management acted superior and condescending.
2. The regional managers feel it is impossible to "make plan" this year. The initial plans discussed for 1998 are more outrageous and impossible to meet. However, the regional managers go ahead and agree to the plan because they are too scared not to, even though they know they will not meet goals. Unrealistic goals and unrealistic time frames are the status quo. They do not feel comfortable in the AB environment and are uncertain about how to be successful in the AB organization.

3. False statements were made by AB managers. For example, in Texas employees were told that everyone would have a job. The general manager just found out that 40 additional employees will be fired by year-end to "make plan" for 1998. The acquired company employees are accustomed to an environment of openness and honesty and have a difficult time deciphering the messages from AB corporate office.
4. Employees want to be a part of a winning team. The initial reaction to the acquisition announcement (after the shock wears off) is excitement about being a part of a successful organization. However, this attitude soon turns to frustration because the communications from Corporate tend to focus on the negative ("You're doing it wrong," "We do not do it like that at AB," "Why have you not made your plan this quarter?" etc.). Throughout the entire assimilation, Corporate needs to emphasize the positives about AB. Regularly scheduled "morale builders" need to be organized. Recognition for effort and attitude needs to become a part of the assimilation process.
5. The "distance" between the Corporate staff and the field is disturbing. The Corporate staff jokingly refer to the field employees as "those people in the field," but the reality is that a wall exists between these two groups. This wall discourages the field from contacting Corporate staff for help in resolving issues and hinders Corporate staff from visiting the branches. The "us and them" syndrome that has been created at AB is having a negative impact on the effectiveness and efficiency of the integration process.

IMPROVING THE INTEGRATION PROCESS

It is very easy in corporations aggressively making acquisitions to reinvent the wheel many times. Typically, acquisition processes are fragmented, whereby many units and different people become involved in the process over time. This often adds to the confusion. As such, the knowledge and experience accumulated across a corporation dissipates as people who have been involved in an integration either resume their normal jobs or leave the organization. Moreover, new people, with prior acquisition experience, join a corporation. Rarely do people with experience meet to systematically debrief and share with others what they have learned.

As part of a continuous improvement process, not only should issues identified by teams be analyzed and addressed, but knowledge on how to improve the integration process should be institutionalized to improve the process for those working on future deals. Since integration begins as early as the transaction stage, the continuous improvement process should include those involved in due diligence, valuation, integration planning, and integration itself. Including people involved in different M&A activities not only will lead to improvements in specific activities but will also ensure that key interrelationships and handoffs among the activities are improved as well.

Once data are collected and analyzed, it is important that the information be shared and used to improve upon the way the acquirer manages future acquisitions. To accomplish this requires that the knowledge developed move from individuals and teams to the organization. The following are activities that successful acquirers have used to do so:

1. At the completion of the integration, a document summarizing the information contained in Table 9-5 should be prepared by each team leader and submitted to the head of the MIO or the IC. The document can be prepared in written form or shared electronically. The document should include a list of those who were involved in the process, their areas of expertise, and how they can be reached by those who are interested in following up.
2. Building on the last point in step 1 above, an electronic database containing information on all people who have been involved in integration should be created. This establishes a network of identifiable integration resources in the organization. As in step 1, be sure to capture the names of people, their integration experience, and how they can be reached.
3. The MIO, IC, or someone who has been designated as responsible for the integration process should solicit input from a variety of sources to improve or develop best-practice frameworks, guidelines, interventions, tools, etc., that are being used by the acquirer to integrate acquisitions and to document these improvements. This is especially important for companies that are serial acquirers and for large companies that may have personnel from many areas and hierarchical levels involved in the process. This may be accomplished through a variety of approaches.
   a. Enlist a team of knowledgeable people inside and outside the company to improve the integration process.
   b. Conduct an annual one- or two-day "Continuous Integration Improvement" conference for all the acquirer's (and acquired) people who have been directly involved in acquisitions. The purpose would be to bring people together to share knowledge. The conference could begin with outside experts sharing the latest ideas and methods and culminate with thematic workshops and small groups to improve specific acquisition processes.
   c. Conduct focus groups of team leaders or members.
   d. Create case studies as part of merger integration debriefings. Cases should be shared with people inside the combined organizations.
   e. Develop and circulate debriefing documents and handbooks.
   f. Develop best-practices Intranet sites.

Table 9-5 Improving the Integration Process

Integration Team	Topic	Things That Were Done Well	Things That Need to Be Improved	Recommendations and Next Steps	Accountable
Marketing	Training	• Training materials were of good quality • Product training was done well • People received solid coaching on products • Training was done on time	• Need more leadership training early • More information on culture/values and marketing strategies of the acquiring bank presented early in the training	• In future develop leadership-training program and get influential leaders to support it • Revise training program to lead with culture and ensure that all participants understand the "language" that each organization uses	
Human Resources	Employee Assimilation	• Developed an assimilation document for newly acquired employees	• Better initial training to ensure employees understand the acquirer • More two-way communications to ensure that all questions concerning assimilation are answered		

4. Individuals who might be involved in future acquisition activity should be provided with best-practices training on how to conduct integration activities. This is also an excellent opportunity for those who have previously been involved in acquisition activities to serve as trainers and to provide mentoring to those who have not.

A FINAL NOTE

It would be best if the integration process unfolded as planned in the transition stage. Unfortunately, the uncertainty of changing events and the lack of complete information to plan perfectly precludes this. That is why it is critical that executives and managers measure, track, assess, and adjust throughout the integration process. It is this flexibility that helps ensure that the strategic and financial objectives hoped for are indeed realized.

10

PERSONAL STRATEGIES FOR PROSPERING DURING THE INTEGRATION PROCESS

M&As can be challenging for those involved. The period during any M&A is surrounded by personal uncertainty that affects everyone from the CEO to frontline employees. During the transaction and transition stages there is a great deal of uncertainty since many decisions affecting people have not yet been made or implemented. As a result, people worry about whether they will have a job, and if so, what it will be and where it will be located.

For example, early on in the Chevron-Texaco merger, it was announced that $1.2 billion in recurring costs (i.e., synergies resulting in lower costs and improved earnings and cashflows) would be eliminated from the combined organizations. This translated into a proposed 7 percent cut in the combined work force, or the loss of roughly 4000 jobs. As mentioned earlier, it was also decided that Texaco's headquarters in White Plains, New York, would be shut down and that Chevron's headquarters in San Ramon, California, would remain as the headquarters for the combined companies. After a well-orchestrated selection process, some corporate staff from Texaco would be offered positions in San Ramon, whereas others would not. For those who were not retained, or did not want to relocate, severance packages would be provided.

This example is typical of many mergers and acquisitions where synergies are sought. They can be very disruptive for those involved. Given that M&As are a common part of the business landscape affecting millions of people each year, it is essential that executives, managers, and employees prepare themselves to prosper, rather than suffer, during these times. The remainder of this chapter gives insights for doing so, all of which are derived from the tens of thousands of merged and acquired people I have been involved with and the ideas of others who have written on this topic.

PSYCHOLOGICAL PREPARATION

The Serenity Prayer

God grant me the serenity
to accept the things
I cannot change,
courage to change
the things I can
and the wisdom
to know the difference.

Reinhold Niebuhr

These powerful words of wisdom are at the heart of psychological preparation for M&As, and other changes you may face during organizational transformations. Many changes are outside of your control—circumstances that you cannot influence. As such, it is essential that you understand what you can and cannot control and focus on the former. I like to use the term *sphere of influence* to describe people's area of control. (At the end of the day, the only things you can really control are your own thoughts and behaviors.) You may be able to influence others, if you are lucky, but rarely do you control other people.[1] It is the thoughts you have and the behaviors you engage in that will ultimately determine how you deal with the events of a merger or acquisition—whether you prosper or whether you are victimized by them.

Get Comfortable with Uncertainty and Change

The first step in psychological preparation is to realize that M&As are pervasive and that they can easily happen to your organization. Second is to realize that M&As result in change for many people. As noted in Chapter 5, people go through a variety of stages in coping with change. Only one stage, acceptance, is constructive and allows people to move on with their lives. The other stages, while often part of the process, delay effective coping and action.

The bottom line is for you to become comfortable with changes and transitions and to prepare for them. Part of becoming comfortable is to view change as an opportunity rather than a threat. For it to be an opportunity, however, requires that you know how to take advantage of the opportunity and that you are not vulnerable to the events taking place.

Create Options for Yourself

An essential element in preparation is to create options, which minimize your dependence on an organization and on a particular situation. When someone has no options and is dependent, he or she becomes vulnerable. When vulnerable and dependent, coping with uncertainty becomes more difficult. The result is more stress and decreased happiness. So here are some suggestions to create options.

Continually Think about and Create Career Options

Often the greatest limitation is an unwillingness to consider and create options, because you are either afraid or unwilling to change. Many people have more options than they think.

Do Not Become Institutionally Dependent

It is important to realize that you can and should be able to work in another organization. In fact, the evidence suggests that most people will have worked for seven companies before they retire.

Maintain External Visibility—Maintain Contacts

Maintaining a network of contacts inside and outside an organization is critical. Contacts provide a valuable source of options for people wanting or needing to make changes. Make sure that you cultivate your network and provide help to others within it when they need it. This strategy will pay off when you need help.

Maintain Marketability—Return Recruiters' Calls

Recruiters are a valuable source of job options. However, they only benefit if they place a person in a new job. Although they do not expect everyone they call to make a change, they will maintain contact with you if they believe there is some chance they can market you. So return the calls and keep an open mind.

Avoid Overspecialization—Develop Marketable Skills

Be careful of the types of assignment that you take on in a company. The more able you are to develop skills, competencies, and experiences that are of value to other companies, the better able you are to have external options. Of interest is that a number of companies encourage and support the idea that it is important to make people employable, whether it be with their current company or another one.

Maintain Credibility and Reputation

Your personal reputation is one of the most valuable assets you have today, and it can have a dramatic impact on your relationship with others whom you may need to rely on. This includes not only your skills and competencies but your reputation for trustworthiness and integrity. The following example nicely illustrates this.

An executive I worked with told me a story about a person he volunteered with on a charitable fund-raising campaign. The person had made a serious commitment to raising funds. As such, the charity and the executive came to depend on this person. At the beginning of the fund-raising effort the person made a solid contribution. As the campaign progressed, his involvement seemed to diminish. He started missing a number of key meetings and often did not return phone calls. Further, he did not live up to his fund-raising commitments. The executive suspected that work or family obligations were an issue. But not even a phone call to explain!

A year later the person went to interview for a job. He had recently lost his job as part of a merger. Ironically, the person he interviewed with was the executive. During the interview the executive asked him what had happened during the fund-raising campaign. The person told him how corporate and family pressures took over his life and how sorry he was. The executive, while sympathetic and understanding, did not offer him a job.

Learn How to Find a Job

It is amazing how many people do not know how to find a job, perhaps because they have not had to in many years. Worse yet, they do not think they will have to in the future. They feel quite secure and believe that it is an act of disloyalty to their company. What they do not realize, however, is that it is an act of loyalty to their families and themselves. Whether you change jobs or not, it is good to know you have the capability to do so.

As part of the options—creating process, learn how to find jobs, prepare a resume, and take an interview. These are not difficult things to learn how to do. Numerous books and courses are available on such topics. In fact, a number of companies provide their employees with such resources. Many companies will provide these as part of relocation programs during mergers, acquisitions, and restructuring. If your company does not, make sure you learn on your own.

Keep Your Bags Packed

This metaphor addresses your psychology rather than your luggage. Simply put, do not have such a deep psychological commitment to your company and job that you feel you cannot leave it. I do not want to encourage you to "job hop" or to perform poorly but to ensure that you have a healthy psychological detachment from your company. This means that if an opportunity comes along that's better for you, and/or your family, allow yourself the freedom to entertain and possibly act on it. Again, you should not be afraid to entertain and exercise options. And companies should not be afraid of people doing so. Leaders should create a work environment that motivates people to stay and produce.

Diversify Your Self-Identity

There is an old saying that we should all pay a great deal of attention to:

"Don't put all your eggs in one basket."

This saying clearly points to the importance of diversification of risk. As important as it is to diversify your investment portfolio, it is just as important for you to diversify your self-identity. Investment advisers preach diversification, so that if one investment goes bad, the entire portfolio does not become worthless. Unfortunately, people do not always see the wisdom of this advice, especially when the one investment they have made is doing quite well. Just witness the euphoria surrounding the run-up of e-commerce stocks in the late 1990s. While the stocks were going well, diversification looked like a poor strategy. Unfortunately, things can change with the downtick of a stock. Witness the number of people who lost a fortune when e-commerce stocks took a beating at the beginning of the new millennium.

Well, the story is quite the same for self-identity. Many people have tied their self-identity to only one thing, often their career and their company. They have everything vested in this one "investment." While the company is doing well and their careers are moving along, everything is just fine. But if there is a merger or acquisition that changes things, the potential impact on their self-identity is severe. Consider the following story.

During the early 1990s I was involved in integrating the merger of two oil companies. I had come to know a senior-level financial executive in the company that ostensibly was being bought. The executive had worked for his company for 25 years. He was quite dedicated and gave the company his total commitment. In fact, he often worked seven days a week and traveled extensively on behalf of the company. During this time his career blossomed and he was compensated quite well for it. Unfortunately, his personal life did not do so well. The extended time away deteriorated his relationship with his wife and two daughters. This led to a divorce and subsequent alienation with his daughters.

The executive seemed to have coped with the events of his life until it was announced that his services were no longer required. He was "made redundant." One day he showed up in my office to share the news with me. It was a rainy day. He was in a suit and tie. Strangely though, he was wearing sunglasses. Shortly after we began our conversation he started to cry. He removed his sunglasses. His eyes were red, indicative of a long bout of crying. After he regained his composure, he became angry. After so many years and so many personal sacrifices, how could the company do this to him! As he was sitting there, I noticed that he was still wearing the company's lapel pin.

Several years later I ran into him only to find a lost soul who had yet to find much happiness. He had nothing to look forward to and was still devastated.

Although this is an extreme example, it does illustrate how lack of diversification is dangerous, especially in a rapidly and constantly changing world. This is not to argue that work is a small or unimportant part of life. On the contrary, it is a major element that is critical to our psychological and financial well-being. Moreover, it is a part of our life that demands significant time and energy if we are to do it right. However, it is not the only thing in our lives. Given the amount of change facing corporations and people today, overinvolvement with an organization can leave people too vulnerable to the events that bring change. When such events happen, it is valuable for people to have other elements in their lives that they can draw satisfaction and happiness from, other things that will allow them to deal with events and to move on. What those other things are is for each person to decide. So ask yourself: "Have I put all my eggs in one basket?"

FINANCIAL PREPARATION

Americans are notorious for not saving. Perhaps this helps explain the strong economy we witnessed during the late 1990s. The spending afforded people a certain lifestyle. For some it was a period of luxury, whereas for others it allowed them to survive.

Unfortunately, the lack of savings and other investments has created a situation where people do not have a cushion that minimizes their financial vulnerability in the event of a job loss. For many, this has not been a problem because of the economic growth and low unemployment that had, until recently, characterized the U.S. economy. It is amazing how many people have forgotten about the corporate restructuring of the 1980s or are ignoring the financial challenges that a number of companies in early 2001 are facing. More and more we are hearing about job loss due to M&As and to cost cutting as revenue growth and earnings have slowed.

Without a cushion, people are less able to withstand job loss. Thus, it is essential for people to have a "cushion" to reduce their vulnerability to changes. It provides a twofold benefit. First, it minimizes the financial crisis of a job loss. Second, it is easier for people to change jobs in a merger or acquisition if they are not happy with their new situation; e.g., they do not like the new culture or their new boss. If nothing else, at worst, they will have added money for their retirement!

It is beyond the scope of this chapter to provide advice on financial strategies. However, numerous books and courses are easily available that address these. A personal commitment to face this issue and start a process of investment is the most critical step.

AVOID THE RUMOR MILL

As noted in Chapter 5, people need to make sense out of the world they live in. In the absence of information, they will use the rumor mill and their imaginations to do so. Too much imagination and reliance on rumors can be dangerous. Often the information is negative and exaggerated. The rumors distract you and often mislead you. Estimates indicate that the rumor mill is accurate 50 percent of the time. The problem is that it is virtually impossible to distinguish the accurate from the inaccurate information. So it is best to seek information from your manager or to do your own research to understand the events taking place. In the absence of information, continue to focus on doing your work and creating and preparing to execute other options. Try to be patient, although it may not be easy to do so. Not only will this minimize your dependence, but it will allow you to control your own destiny. Both create a positive psychology.

DIAGNOSE THE SITUATION

When rumors or a formal announcement of a merger or acquisition hits, don't panic and overreact. However, don't underreact either. It is a good time to assess your personal situation and prepare to respond. As noted throughout this chapter, preparation will give you the capability and the wherewithal to act. It will give you some control over your situation. Now is the time to assess your situation to determine the likelihood that you will be affected, and if so, how.

Your assessment should focus on two issues: the buyer and your current situation. Assessment of the buyer will help you understand what the buyer's motives are in acquiring your company and how the buyer has handled previous mergers and acquisitions. Assessment of your situation will help you understand your personal vulnerability.

Assessing the Buyer

The Internet has made it very easy to gather information on a company, especially if it is a highly visible company or its stock is publicly traded. There is significant information to be had based on Securities and Exchange Commission filings, analysts' reports, and articles in business publications and national and local newspapers. Not only is general information on the company available, but so too is information on previous and current mergers and acquisitions. Such information addresses issues such as how an acquirer has handled or plans to handle staffing decisions and reductions in force, severance, conflicts between acquirers and targets, culture clashes, and sources of synergies, among many others. Pay particular attention to where operations are likely to be located, the staffing decision process to be used, policies on geographic transfers, severance packages, and compensation and benefits packages.

As an example, a large part of the assessment of the hospital management corporation provided in Appendix 3-1 was conducted through Internet searches. I was amazed at how much information was available in local newspapers in areas where the company operated. With a little bit of time, you will be able to learn a lot.

Assessing Your Situation

Once you understand more about the acquirer, and perhaps the merger itself, you will be able to begin to size up your personal situation. Some key questions that will help you understand your vulnerability include:

- *Is my position tied to key executives in my current company?* You may be vulnerable if your position is dependent upon a particular executive who is not retained after the deal is done. Conversely, you may be in a strong position if the executive has been named to a key postclosing position. For example, when SBC bought Ameritech, it retained the president of the Ameritech Directories business. Due to its success, the Ameritech organization's business model would likely survive.
- *Am I in a line versus staff position?* Staff positions are almost always vulnerable in M&As. One of the easiest sources of cost reductions is the elimination of redundant staff, especially at the corporate level.
- *Am I in a corporate or division position?* It is important to understand the acquirer's philosophy concerning centralization and decentralization. For example, in the merger between Sandoz and Ciba Geigy to form Novartis, Sandoz had a decentralized organization and philosophy concerning staff, whereas Ciba Geigy had a centralized organization and philosophy. The message was clear. Corporate staff would be eliminated, with positions that remain being located in the divisions. This left many Ciba Geigy corporate people vulnerable, especially those who could not or did not want to move.
- *Am I in a position that is redundant with that of the acquirer?* Beyond staff positions, certain jobs may be rendered redundant as manufacturing operations, sales organization, and R&D laboratories are combined to reduce costs and improve productivity.
- *Am I in a specialized position?* I will never forget a comment made to me by an employee of a target company who gleefully noted: " I did my homework on the acquirer and they have no one in their organization that does what I do." Unfortunately, this person did not realize that the acquirer did not place any value on what the person did and had moved way beyond the capabilities of that person's position. Understanding what are important capabilities in the acquirer's business model is crucial.

- *Do I have weak or outdated skills and competencies?* In today's environment this is the greatest source of vulnerability. Many acquirers will make a reasonable attempt to staff the new organization with the best talent they can find, regardless of company of origin. With relatively low unemployment, retaining the best talent is key to competitive success and profitability. As noted in Chapter 4, many companies attempt to examine personal competencies in addition to past performance in making staffing decisions. Those who are out of date are likely to be most vulnerable. In some instances, people who are outdated may be retained for a period of time just to provide continuity during the transition period. In fact, they may be offered attractive severance packages if they stay through the transition.

CREATING, CHOOSING, AND EXECUTING YOUR OPTION

Once you have assessed your situation, you need to consider what your options are likely to be. You can either do this early or wait until the acquisition unfolds. The earlier you prepare, the more time you will have to execute. For example, one 53-year-old merged executive told me that he saw the handwriting on the wall, even before the actual closing. The companies were waiting on antitrust clearances and shareholder approval. In the end, he realized that his company was being acquired. The acquirer had announced that the target's headquarters were to be closed and those who were asked to stay would be transferred to the acquirer's headquarters located on the other side of the country. Although he had a chance to stay, he decided that he needed to create other options for himself.

Fortunately, he was prudent throughout his career and saved and invested enough to withstand a loss of income for a sustained period of time. Thus he had the ability to be patient and look for an opportunity that he might enjoy. He quietly contacted executive search firms to identify new employment opportunities. He entertained thoughts of starting a new company—something he had never considered before. The idea rather excited him. He did not wait for a decision to be made about his career and then wonder what he might do. He started the ball rolling early.

Further, he did not panic and overreact. He decided to delay his decision until he "knew the score." He wanted to see how his options materialized before he made a choice. But he knew he was in control because he had some choices. Although he could afford to do so, he clearly was not ready for retirement.

In general, a merger or acquisition will present you with three broad situations. (1) You will be invited to join the new organization and you will choose to stay. (2) You will be offered a position but choose not to stay. (3) You will be let go. How you handle these situations will impact your psychological and financial health and your reputation. This section presents three personal scenarios and strategies for dealing with them: staying and prospering, exiting voluntarily, and exiting involuntarily.

Staying and Prospering

If you are invited to remain and you decide to stay with the combined organization, it is wise to adopt a positive attitude. Joining, but grumbling, not only will make you unhappy, but will eventually wear down those around you. Someone once gave me some good advice concerning this issue: "If you are going to be in the game, then play it well and succeed in it. If you do not like the game, then get out of it and move on to another game." I have found this to be sound advice that is applicable to a merger situation. Given that advice, below are some key strategies that will help you succeed in the game.

Stay Focused on Work and Be a Producer

Staying focused on work has several key benefits. First, it helps you avoid being caught up in all the angst that often surrounds a merger. Second, it sends the right signal to management that you want to be part of the new organization and are ready to make a contribution. Actions speak louder than words.

Do Not Take Sides—Weigh Politics Carefully

It is often not clear during the early stages of a merger who has won and who has lost. I have witnessed many people who have allied themselves with specific executives in a merged organization, thinking that it would help them advance their careers. Unfortunately, the staffing of merged organizations takes some time to shake out. During the first year following the closing there is often a shift in leadership as people who have taken key leadership positions have changed. Some decide after a period of time that they really don't fit. Some never intended to stay in the first place. They stayed long enough to reap certain severance benefits. Trying to figure out who the winners and losers are and aligning with them can be lethal. It is best to commit to performing and trying to stay as neutral as possible for as long as possible.

Get on board the New Culture

As noted earlier, join the new game as quickly as possible and attempt to learn how it operates and what it takes to succeed within it. Sometimes managers will assist you in this effort, whereas other times you will have to figure it out for yourself.

Avoid the Rumor Mill

Since we all need to make sense of what is going on around us, it is tempting to seek information through the rumor mill. This is especially the case when uncertainty has been prolonged and there has not been much information from management. As noted previously, however, the rumor mill is filled with a glut of inaccurate information that is often negative and exaggerated. It is more likely to worry you than to provide you with useful information. It is best to seek information from your immediate manager and to rely on trusted sources of information that you have had experience with before. In many cases you will just have to be patient and deal with the uncertainty since answers to questions may not yet be known.

Continue to Assess Management—Actual and Symbolic Communication

Someone once said that talk is cheap. During mergers and acquisitions, many statements are often made by management. Some are true and some are not. It is important that you focus on management's actions as well as words. When you see inconsistencies, pay attention to the actions. They are a more accurate reflection of what is going on. Also, watch changes in actions over time. What was intended at the beginning of the merger may not be what is realized later. Situations change, and initial commitments cannot be kept. More than once a well-intentioned manager made a statement that "nobody would lose their job due to the merger." Unfortunately, the manager could not keep that promise over time. As information and actions evolve, you will get a better feel for your situation and whether you want to remain in the organization.

Make It Known You Want to Stay

One of the challenges of selecting people in a merging organization is knowing who will take and keep a job if offered it. Sometimes offers are not made because it is assumed that the person is not interested. As such, another, perhaps less qualified, candidate is offered the position. Thus, it is in your interest to let your manager know that you are interested in a career in the new organization.

Don't Become Paralyzed—Continue to Evaluate Internal and External Job Opportunities

Never become too comfortable. Always be prepared to make a change if it is necessary. Although it is not always easy, there are many opportunities that can greatly improve your situation. You may not like a job you took in the new company. If that's the case, examine opportunities in different areas of the company, or look on the outside. In today's environment there are plenty of opportunities for qualified and motivated people.

Keep Your Resume Updated

That says it all. It always pays to keep your resume updated. You never know when you will need it.

Prepare for and Embrace Change—Stay Flexible

It is clear to most of us that the pace of change in the world we live in is accelerating. It is doubtful that organizations and jobs will stay constant.

Moreover, it will require us to make rapid changes. Flexibility is a good attribute for people to have during these times. In a merger, in particular, there will be a lot of change after the closing. No matter how good the due diligence and integration planning processes were, there is still much learning that will take place between the merging firms. It is inevitable that opportunities and threats were not completely understood prior to the closing. There will be unanticipated synergies and some that were exaggerated. There will be key executives who agreed to stay indefinitely, only to leave after six months. The net result is that things will continue to change, and they will have a direct impact on you. Failure to be flexible and make needed adjustments can lead to many frustrations and poor adaptation.

Seek Social Support

A merger or an acquisition, just like any other major event, can be quite overwhelming. As such, it is easy to lose perspective and experience negative feelings. Sometimes sharing our ideas and feelings allows us to vent and blow off steam. Sometimes it helps us put things back in perspective. All of us lose perspective at times, especially when we are caught up in an emotionally demanding and traumatic situation. After all, the worst that is at stake in most organizations is just a job.

Most people tell me how important it is to have others to talk with about what is happening to them. What is also interesting is that they almost always note that such people are not from their work environment. It is very difficult to reveal your true feelings to colleagues. Although we may have excellent relationships with colleagues, organizations are still political environments. It is best to talk to people whom you trust and who have no vested interest in your work situation. These should be people whose only interest is your well-being.

Exiting Voluntarily

Although you have been given the option to stay you may not choose to. There could be many reasons why. These may include the need to move to a new geographic location, changes in the nature of your job, the culture being adopted by the merged organization, and the like. Moreover, after remaining in the new organization for a period of time, you may decide that things have not turned out the way you anticipated. Perhaps commitments or promises made by the management of the merged organization have not been kept. Before making and executing the decision to leave, there are some things to consider.

Seek Professional Outplacement Help

If you choose to leave voluntarily, it is likely that the company will not provide you with professional outplacement help. Essentially you will be on your own. If you have worked for your company for a long time, you may not be comfortable or conversant with finding a new job. Certainly, there are numerous books and minicourses on how to prepare for and find a new job. As well, there are numerous employment and search firms that can help you. These resources will help you prepare a resume, prepare for interviews, and conduct an orderly and productive job search. Much of this today is done on the Internet. It is a wise person who takes advantage of resources!

Examine Severance Packages Closely

Many companies have severance packages available for people who have not been retained due to elimination of redundant positions. Furthermore, if people have been offered a job more than a certain distance from their current one (e.g., 50 miles) or a job not equivalent to their current level of responsibilities, they may qualify for a severance package. Although such packages vary by company, most take into account length of service and position in the current organization. A little patience may pay off and provide you with an attractive nest egg that can give you some time to decide what you want to do. The key here is not to overreact. Often people become impatient and leave their organization quickly, only to miss an attractive opportunity.

Quietly Conduct a Job Search—Don't Showboat

If you decide you want to leave, search for a job and do so quietly. There is no need to make a show of it or to destabilize those around you. Some people need to make a show to demonstrate to everyone how fortunate and "valuable" they are. There is no need to rub it in. Not only does it bother other people, but it will often damage your reputation. You never know whether you will want to come back to the organization, or encounter these people in other situations where you need their support—e.g., a letter of recommendation.

Don't Threaten to Quit Unless You Are Prepared to Do So

It is important to realize that at some point all of us are replaceable in our jobs. Testing that limit may not be such a good idea. I once had a colleague who overestimated his value to the organization. He thought he was undervalued and underpaid and decided to leverage our manager for a raise. So he undertook a poorly thought-out strategy. He went to the manager and told her that he was looking at another job that paid significantly more than the current one he had. After some thought she told him, "You would be crazy not to take the other job." End of negotiation! Unfortunately, he did not really want the other job and was not prepared to leave. But he only had a weak alternative and thus was not in a real position to negotiate. He wound up leaving and has not been happy in his new job. Ultimatums often do not work on sophisticated people. If you do use them, then you better be sure of your value and have a viable alternative to a negotiated solution.

Consider Internal and External Opportunities

Frequently in mergers there are opportunities to transfer to other divisions or operations if the one you are in is not working out. Thus be sure to explore both internal and external opportunities. Most companies will provide job postings of such opportunities and create formal processes for seeing them. Today, jobs are often posted on a company's Intranet.

Time Personal Finances and Your Job Search
Do not overreact. You may regret it. As someone once said, "Timing is everything in life." So is leaving an organization. Be sure that you have enough financial resources to buffer the income loss from leaving your job. While your work situation may seem unbearable, significant financial problems are likely to be worse. That is why waiting for a severance package may be useful. In general it is easier to find a job while you have a job. For one thing, you do not have to explain why you are currently unemployed. For another, having an income allows you to be more patient in deciding what you want to do next. As your income dwindles and your financial needs become more challenging, your choices in jobs diminish.

Examine Transition Benefits (COBRA)
In addition to income, benefits are also an important issue to consider. Federal law requires a company to allow employees who have exited an organization to participate in a company's health plan at the group rate up to 18 months after they have resigned. While this is a huge discount over going it alone, the individuals must pay both their normal contribution and what the company used to pay for them.

Don't Be Negative about Your Past Employer in Job Interviews
The worse thing people can do when interviewing for a new job is complain about their previous employer. It clearly suggests that if and when you leave your new employer, you are likely to do the same thing. What company in its right mind would like that? Second, there are always two sides to a story. Thus whose fault is it that there was a problem? Why leave questions about whether you or your employer was the problem? The best thing is to communicate that you are looking for a new or better opportunity and to be prepared to explain what that opportunity is. Focusing on moving forward tells a new employer that you are part of solutions rather than problems.

Seek Social Support
As noted in the last section, seek social support to help you see things in a clear light. It is particularly important in this situation. Typically, people are more negative about their current job than a new one. This is because they are much more familiar with their current situation and see all the "holes." Most new jobs look brighter than they really are. Moreover, prospective employers do not always provide a completely realistic job preview. Perhaps if they did, fewer people would be interested! It is thus important to seek others who are likely to be more objective and challenge you to think more realistically about your assumptions and the pros and cons of each alternative. This should improve both your comfort level and the probability that you are making the right choice.

Exiting Involuntarily

The final situation is one in which you may not have a choice. You have not been retained by the merging or acquiring firm. Although this can be difficult for you to cope with, it is not the end of the world. In fact, for some it may be the beginning of a new life. It may be the impetus that you need to make changes that you have not been willing, or able, to make in the past. Regardless, it will be challenging and will require adjustments on your part. Here are some things to consider.

Maintain Self-Esteem, Learn, and Move On

In addition to potential economic challenges, not being retained can be a blow to your ego. Nobody likes being rejected. However, one has to move on. Of course, people deal with transitions differently. Some people pass through different stages before they successfully accept what has happened and move on. Some people take longer to do so. Regardless, the only way to manage in such a situation is for you to maintain your self-esteem and to plan and execute alternatives.

Even in seemingly hopeless situations the human spirit is strong enough to find a way to survive and even prosper. Since you cannot change the past, the only way to gain from it is to learn from it, and to use what you have learned to move forward. Thus, although you need to move forward and keep your head high, it is important to ask a fundamental question: Why was I not retained? Was it because I did not have the competencies and skills required in the new organization? If so, how can I ensure I stay current in my next job? Was it because I did not manage my politics carefully? If so, perhaps I may be a bit less naïve in the future. Was it because I was unwilling to take a different job or relocate? If so, perhaps I need to examine my future willingness to change or the flexibility of my personal and family situation. Regardless of the reason, it is important to learn and not repeat mistakes. As someone once told me, "No matter how difficult the situation and negative the outcomes, there is always something positive that can be gained from it, a lesson."

Don't Become Hostile—It's Over

Coming to the point of acceptance is critical. As noted in Chapter 5, many people become angry when faced with a traumatic event. If you do, be careful. The work environment is a poor place to demonstrate such anger. Ranting, raving, and complaining accomplishes absolutely nothing positive. Often, all you do is burn bridges with other people whom you might run across or need in the future. They may be the sources of future jobs, letters of recommendations, and the like. If you are angry, work it out elsewhere, and do so constructively. The key is to accept that a decision has been made, it is final, and all you can do is move on.

Learn about In-House Transfers

Even though your position may have been eliminated in a merger, there may be job opportunities in other departments or divisions of the companies. As noted in Chapter 7, many companies will post such jobs and give priority to existing employees. However, priority will usually be given to those who have the competencies and skills needed in those jobs. So before you conclude that the only opportunities are on the outside, learn about internal opportunities.

Learn about Outplacement Opportunities

As mentioned earlier, often companies will provide outplacement support for people not being retained due to redundancy. The source of such information is usually the human resources department, but do not hesitate to ask your direct manager. He or she may be in the loop. Outplacement support will vary by company and often by your level in the organization. Such support may include resume writing, assistance with interviewing skills, and job postings. Some companies will even outsource outplacement, at their expense, to a specialist firm. If you have not sought work in a number of years and are not sure how to do so, take advantage of this opportunity. Also, there are many Internet-based services that you can use to post your resume.

Learn about Severance (Salary and Benefits)

As with outplacement, companies typically offer severance packages for redundant employees. Such packages will vary by the number of years of employment with the company and with position. However, the benefits often cap at some maximum value. Although a variety of formulas are used to determine severance benefits, typically redundant employees are given their monthly salary times the number of years of service. Some companies cap the benefit at two years' salary. That is not a bad buffer to provide time to regain employment. Again, as noted previously, it is useful not to overreact early during a merger and leave. You may miss a valuable opportunity.

Seek Professional Psychological Counseling

If you are having problems dealing with the situation and are unable to cope, it may be useful to seek psychological help. There is a point where all of us have difficulty dealing with situations, and friends are not skillful in helping us. Seeking professional help is often stigmatized in our society as a sign of weakness or inadequacy. This may especially be the case for men, who have often been raised to be "tough." Actually seeking help is a sign of strength. Strong people can admit that they have a problem and realize they can't handle it by themselves. Even "normal" people lose perspective and are unable to help themselves. Professionals can guide you in understanding the causes of your problems and feelings and help you explore and choose alternatives that can solve them. If you do not know of any sources of help, you can seek advice from your company's human resources professional, your doctor, the American Psychiatric Association, or the American Psychological Association.

Counseling may also provide you with an opportunity to explore what you are truly interested in and what you may be best at doing. There are numerous tests psychologists and counselors use to help people explore their interests and capabilities. They are easy to take and usually not very expensive.

Focus on Finding a New Job (Prepare to Wait)
Solving problems is among the best ways for you to deal with stress, disappointment, and trauma. Seeking a job is an excellent way for you to solve the problem of job loss. With that said, however, you must be realistic. Many people who have lost their job on Friday hit the pavement on Monday seeking work. They have decided to accept their fate and move on with enthusiasm and energy. This is clearly commendable. However, when they do not find a job by the end of the week, they become depressed. Why? Because they have unrealistic expectations of how long it might take to find work and did not realize that many things were outside of their control. The nature of the job you are looking for, the economic environment, your work experience, and the geographic market you are focused on may greatly impact the length of your search. Fortunately, throughout the 1990s and the year 2000, the economy was sound, unemployment relatively low, and the need for skilled people high. These all made the job search much easier and shorter. However, the environment changes, as it did in the year 2001. The bottom line: Be realistic, but be deliberate.

Seek Social Support
Once again, social support remains a critical element in moving forward. Support networks can help you put things into perspective. They can also provide a sounding board as you explore and evaluate new job opportunities. A dispassionate view during this time can help you uncover your own assumptions to ensure that you do not take a position hastily. Often, people are not realistic about new jobs, especially when they feel desperate. Nor do interviewers always tell people all the gory details. Also, people, in their eagerness, often overestimate the positives.

A FINAL THOUGHT

Whether you prosper during a merger or an acquisition is a function of whether you are prepared to deal with it. Prepare now! Create options and do not be afraid to execute them when the time is ripe. Doing so will minimize your dependence upon events that are outside your control. And doing so may open your life to things you never imagined you could or would do. Be among the survivors, not the victims.

ENDNOTES

Chapter 1

[1] Information regarding the merger of Daimler-Benz and Chrysler from Daimler-Benz AG, Investor Relations, 7056 Stuttgart, Germany.

[2] Taken from From the Chairman, *GTE Together*, Vol. 17, Fall/Winter 1998.

[3] For the sake of brevity, hereafter I will use *mergers* and *acquisitions* interchangeably. I recognize that from a statutory perspective the nature of the transaction of the two forms may vary. I will distinguish between the two when necessary.

[4] See Thomson Financial Securities Data, 2001.

[5] There are numerous studies that have examined the relationship between M&As and a variety of measures of performance. Since there are too many studies to review here I suggest you read the following sources for an overview: A. R. Lajoux, *The Art of M&A Integration*, New York: McGraw-Hill, 1998; D. M. Schweiger and J. P. Walsh, "Mergers and acquisitions: An interdisciplinary view," in K. M. Rowland and G. R. Ferris (Eds.), *Research in Personnel and Human Resource Management*, Vol. 8, Greenwich, CT: JAI Press, 1990, pp. 41–107; and M. A. Hitt, J. S. Harrison, R. D. Ireland, *Mergers and Acquisitions: A Guide for Creating Value for Shareholders*, New York: Oxford University Press, 2001.

[6] The ideas in this section were originally developed by E. N. Csiszar and D. M. Schweiger, "An integrative framework for creating value through acquisition," in H. E. Glass and B. N. Craven (Eds.), *Handbook of Business Strategy,* New York: Warren, Gorham & Lamont, 1994, pp. 93–115.

[7] A continuing stream of research by practitioners and academics points to the importance of integration in M&A value creation. These include several studies by major consulting firms such as Coopers and Lybrand, Mercer Management Consulting, A. T. Kearney, and Hewitt Associates, which are reported in J. R. Carleton, "Cultural due diligence," *Training*, November 1997, pp. 67–75; and J. S. Lublin and B. O'Brien, "When dis-

parate firms merge, cultures often collide," *The Wall Street Journal*, February 1997. A study of *Forbes* 500 executives on why synergies are not realized cites 5 organizational issues as among the top 10 (study reported in Towers Perrin internal document). A comprehensive review of academic research identifying integration as an important element in M&A value creation is presented in D. M. Schweiger and J. P. Walsh, "Mergers and acquisitions: An interdisciplinary view," in K. M. Rowland and G. R. Ferris (Eds.), *Research in Personnel and Human Resource Management*, Vol. 8, Greenwich, CT: JAI Press, 1990, pp. 41–107; and D. M. Schweiger and P. Goulet, "Integrating acquisitions: An international research review," in C. Cooper and A. Gregory (Eds.), *Advances in Mergers and Acquisitions*, Vol. I, Greenwich, CT: JAI/Elsevier Press, 2000, pp. 61–91. Also see S. Chatterjee, M. Lubatkin, D. M. Schweiger, and Y. Weber, "Cultural differences and shareholder value: Explaining the variability in the performance of related merger," *Strategic Management Journal*, Vol. 13, 1992, pp. 319–334.

[8] M&A agreements can be structured with such clauses to protect the acquirer against certain liabilities. Insurance policies and escrowed funds can also be employed. However, it is most prudent if the acquirers do their analyses and identify key issues a priori and understand the risks they are assuming. Relying on indemnification often requires a civil lawsuit, of which the results can be quite uncertain.

[9] D. Rankine, *A Practical Guide to Acquisitions*, Chichester, UK: Wiley, 1998.

[10] See, for example, J. P. Kotter, *Leading Change*, Boston: Harvard Business School Press, 1996.

Chapter 2

[1] For example, see R. F. Brunner, K. M. Eades, R. S. Harris, and R. C. Higgins, "Best practices in estimating the cost of capital: Survey and synthesis," *Financial Practice and Education*, Vol. 8, 1998, pp. 13–28, who found that 89 percent of the firms they studied used DCF or a similar approach. It is important to note that increasingly firms are relying on a real-options approach to valuation (T. A. Luehrman, "Investment opportunities as real options: Getting started on the numbers," *Harvard Business Review*, Vol. 76, No. 4, 1998, pp. 51–67).

[2] The total value includes both the equity and debt portion of the firm's capital structure. To determine the equity portion of the firm, the debt is subtracted from the total valuation.

[3] T. Copeland, T. Koller, and J. Murrin, *Valuation: Measuring and Managing the Value of Companies*, New York: Wiley, 1995.

[4] Although beyond the scope of this book, it is important to note that there is much debate concerning the use of terminal values and which approach is best. As such, the value of a firm can vary greatly depending upon which approach (e.g., P/E multiple, perpetuity value) is chosen (see E. L. Morris, "Why acquirers may need to rethink terminal values," *Mergers & Acquisitions*, July/August 1996, pp. 24–29). Further the weighted-average cost of capital can also greatly affect valuation and can vary depending upon the percentage of debt and equity used to finance an acquisition.

[5] In practice, a number of pro forma statements would be developed reflecting different assumptions about sales growth and costs and net working capital as a percentage of sales. For the sake of brevity, only one stand-alone forecast is presented. The purpose of this example is to illustrate the impact of proposed synergies rather than a full treatment of valuation.

[6] M. L. Sirower, *The Synergy Trap*, New York: The Free Press, 1997.

[7] R. G. Eccles, K. L. Lanes, and T. C. Wilson, "Are you paying too much for that acquisition?" *Harvard Business Review*, Vol. 77, No. 4, 1999, pp. 136–146.

[8] This has been clearly documented in research by D. B. Jemison and S. B. Sitkin, "Acquisitions: The process can be the problem," *Harvard Business Review*, Vol. 64, 1986, pp. 107–116.

[9] With that said, it is also important to recognize that it is not always easy to identify and quantify all synergies prior to closing. Unless you can identify enough, however, the risks of doing a deal may become quite significant.

[10] Hilton Hotels Corporation *Annual Report*, 2000.

[11] For a more detailed treatment of the concept of integration and how others have defined it, see D. M. Schweiger and P. Goulet, "Integrating acquisitions: An international research review," in C. Cooper and A. Gregory (Eds.), *Advances in Mergers and Acquisitions*, Vol. I, Greenwich, CT: JAI/Elsevier Press, 2000, pp. 61–91.

[12] Return on net assets and return on capital employed are identical.

Chapter 3

[1] For excellent sources of information, see S. Foster Reed and A. Reed Lajoux, *The Art of M&A: A Merger Acquisition Buyout Guide*, Burr Ridge, IL: Irwin, 1995.

[2] D. B. Jemison and S. B. Sitkin, "Acquisitions: The process can be the problem," *Harvard Business Review*, Vol. 64, 1986, pp. 107–116.

[3] P. Very and D. M. Schweiger, "Creating value through mergers and acquisitions: Key challenges and solutions in domestic and international deals," *Journal of World Business*, Vol. 36, 2001, pp. 11–31.

[4] For an excellent discussion of culture see E. Schein, *Organizational Culture and Leadership: A Dynamic View*, San Francisco: Jossey-Bass, 1985.

[5] See J. P. Kotter and J. L. Heskett, *Corporate Culture and Performance*, New York: The Free Press, 1992.

[6] The importance of cultural differences has been documented in a study of 350 European mergers and acquisitions. The study found a strong correlation between cultural differences and the success of the integration (D. Rankine, *A Practical Guide to Acquisitions*, Chichester, UK: Wiley, 1998). As noted earlier, a study of *Forbes* 500 executives found cultural differences to be the number one pitfall in achieving synergies. A study that several of my colleagues and I conducted compared the cultures as reflected in the top-management teams of 35 acquiring and acquired firms. We examined the impact that cultural differences would have on the stock performance of the acquiring firms. Comparing the performance prior to and after the deal was closed, and controlling for normal fluctuations in the stock market itself, we found that there was a strong negative relationship between cultural differences and stock price. In fact it explained over 30 percent of the variation in stock price! Simply put, the greater the difference, the worse the performance (S. Chatterjee, M. Lubatkin, D. M. Schweiger, and Y. Weber, "Cultural differences and shareholder value: Explaining the variability in the performance of related merger," *Strategic Management Journal*, Vol. 13, 1992, pp. 319–334).

[7] Many approaches and tools are available for assessing culture. Unfortunately, there is little standardization among them. Rarely, do they capture the same dimensions. Thus, the results are not always comparable, making analyses of differences difficult if not impossible. In a merger and acquisition it is best to attempt to use the same or comparable instruments.

[8] Numerous studies have addressed the impact of both national and organizational cultures on M&As. For a thorough review of these studies, see D. M. Schweiger and P. Goulet, "Integrating acquisitions: An international research review," in C. Cooper and A. Gregory (Eds.), *Advances in Mergers and Acquisitions*, Vol. I, Greenwich, CT: JAI/Elsevier Press, 2000, pp. 61–91.

[9] My colleagues and I have studied the impact of these particular dimensions on various aspects of integration. Using a survey instrument, we found that these dimensions were significantly related to postacquisition stock price (S. Chatterjee, M. Lubatkin, D. M. Schweiger, and Y. Weber, "Cultural differences and shareholder value: Explaining the variability in the performance of related merger," *Strategic Management Journal*, Vol. 13,

1992, pp. 319–342.) and executive turnover (M. Lubatkin, D. M. Schweiger, and Y. Weber, "Top management turnover in related M&A's: An additional test of the theory of relative standing," *Journal of Management*, Vol. 25, 1999, pp. 55–68). These studies provide some evidence of the validity of the dimensions and the survey instrument.

[10] A mulitvariate analysis of variance (MANOVA) was conducted across all the dimensions to test whether there was a general cultural difference between the firms. Afterward an individual analysis of variances (ANOVA) for each dimension was conducted between the groups to determine which dimensions were significant. Where significant, the results indicated that the differences between the organizations were greater than the differences within each organization.

Chapter 4

[1] The importance of assessing key people has been documented in a study of 350 European mergers and acquisitions. The study found a strong correlation between the extent of due diligence concerning management and key people and the success of the merger or acquisition (D. Rankine, *A Practical Guide to Acquisitions*, Chichester, UK: Wiley, 1998).

[2] As with cultural assessment, the acquirer's human resource group may have already performed these analyses for the acquirer's organization. To the extent possible, such analyses can be used for the target, or the existing methodology can be applied to the target.

[3] I would like to thank Victoria Emerson, who contributed many of the ideas and materials in this section. She has considerable consulting experience using the Birkman and has worked with me on a number of mergers and acquisitions such as the ones described in this chapter. I would also like to thank Birkman International for their permission to utilize the Birkman Method in this section.

Chapter 5

[1] The digital dilemma, *The Economist*, July 22, 2000, pp. 67–68.

[2] See D. M. Schweiger and A. S. DeNisi, "Communication with employees following a merger: A longitudinal field experiment," *Academy of Management Journal*, Vol. 34, No. 1, 1991, pp. 110–135.

[3] For an excellent discussion of this issue, see T. J. Larkin and S. Larkin, *Communicating Change: Winning Employee Support for New Business Goals*, New York: McGraw-Hill, 1994.

[4] Since multiple companies were being acquired simultaneously, multiple transition teams were created. Each team was responsible for each

acquisition. Due to limited staff and the sizes of the acquisitions, several people served on multiple transition teams. The transition communication leader interacted with the leader of each transition team to ensure each acquisition was receiving effective communications.

[5] E. Kubler-Ross, *On Death and Dying*, New York: Macmillan, 1969.

[6] Clearly, many physical illnesses produce the same reaction, and people should see a medical doctor before concluding it is a psychological problem.

[7] See N. K. Schlossberg, "Taking the mystery out of change," *Psychology Today*, 1987.

Chapter 6

[1] The material presented here is adapted from *GTE Together*, Vol. 17, Fall/Winter 1998.

[2] This material is presented in Robert J. Kramer, *Post-Merger Organization Handbook*, The Conference Board, Research Report 1241-99-RR.

[3] This material is presented in Kramer, *Post-Merger Organization Handbook.*

[4] For an excellent discussion of the transnational organization, see C. A. Bartlett and S. Ghoshal, *Managing across Borders: The Transnational Solution*, Boston: Harvard Business School Press, 1998.

[5] "Building a new Boeing," *The Economist*, August 12, 2000, pp. 61–62.

[6] M. Murray and P. Beckett, "Recipe for a deal: Do it fast," *The Wall Street Journal*, August 10, 1999, pp. B1, B4.

[7] PriceWaterhouseCoopers, "A survey of mergers and acquisitions," 1997.

[8] R. Olie, "Shades of culture and institutions in international mergers," *Organization Studies*, Vol. 15, No. 3, 1994, pp. 381–405.

[9] A. Mayo and T. Hadaway, "Cultural adaptation—the ICL-Nokia-Data merger 1991–92," *Journal of Management Development*, Vol. 13, No. 2, 1994, pp. 59–71.

[10] T. J. Gerpott, "Successful integration of R&D functions after acquisitions: An exploratory empirical study," *R&D Management*, Vol. 25, No. 2, 1995, pp. 161–178.

[11] F. Leroy and B. Ramanantsoa, "The cognitive and behavioural dimensions of organizational learning in a merger: An empirical study," *Journal of Management Studies*, Vol. 34, No. 6, 1997, pp. 871–894.

Chapter 7

[1] Numerous studies point to the importance of fairness in human resources decision making and its impact on people's reactions. For a detailed treatment of this issue, see M. A. Konovsky and J. Brockner, "Managing victim and survivor layoff reactions: A procedural justice perspective," in R. Cropanzano (Ed.), *Justice in the Workplace: Approaching Justice in Human Resource Management*, Hillsdale, NJ: Lawrence Erlbaum, 1993, pp. 113–153; E. A. Lind and T. Tyler, *The Social Psychology of Procedural Justice*, New York: Plenum Press, 1988; and J. Greenberg, "The social side of fairness: Interpersonal and informational classes of organizational justice," in R. Cropanzano (Ed.), *Justice in the Workplace: Approaching Justice in Human Resources Management*, pp. 79–103.

[2] "Building a new Boeing," *The Economist*, August 12, 2000, pp. 61–62.

[3] For example, antitrust guidelines prevent direct competitors that are merging to discuss information that might lead to possible collusion. This may include information on products, costs, pricing, etc. Without knowledge of how these are to be dealt with, it may be impossible to specify all the organizational positions and the number and type of people required.

[4] I would like to thank my graduate students Carolina Jaramillo, Glenn McGuffen, and Joe Pearson for their work in helping to develop this section. Several excellent sources were used in their analysis. These include "The top 25 managers," *Businessweek*, January 8, 2000; "Citicorp-Travelers merger: Troubled times ahead?" Reuters, April 8, 1998; "Citigroup: Is this marriage working?" *Businessweek Online*, 1999; and "Alone at the top: How John Reed lost the reigns of Citigroup to his co-chairman," *The Wall Street Journal*, April 14, 2000.

[5] From Scott Wooley, "The new Ma Bell," *Forbes*, April 16, 2001, p. 70.

[6] M. Lubatkin, D. M. Schweiger, and Y. Weber, "Top management turnover in related M&As: An additional test of the theory of relative standing," *Journal of Management*, Vol. 25, 1999, pp. 55–68.

[7] There is a long line of research in industrial and organizational psychology to support this conclusion.

[8] For an excellent source of information on facilitating expatriate assignments see S. Lomax *Best Practices for Managers and Expatriates*, New York: Wiley, 2001.

Chapter 8

[1] V. Emerson, "An interview with Carlos Ghosn, president of Nissan Motors, Ltd," and industry leader of the year (*Automotive News*, 2000), *Journal of World Business*, Vol. 36, No. 1, 2001, pp. 3–10.

[2] A. Korsgaard, D. M. Schweiger, and H. Sapienza, "The role of procedural justice in building commitment, attachment, and trust in strategic decision-making teams,"*Academy of Management Journal*, Vol. 38, 1995, pp. 60–84.

[3] I would like to thank Victoria Emerson, who contributed many of the ideas and materials in this section. She has considerable consulting experience using the Birkman and has worked with me on a number of mergers and acquisitions. The case presented in this section is one such example. I would also like to thank Birkman International for their permission to utilize the Birkman Method in this section.

[4] This section is drawn from the work of D. Bunnell, *Making the Cisco Connection*, New York: Wiley, 2000, and S. Thurm, "Under Cisco's system, mergers usually work: That defies the odds," *The Wall Street Journal*, March 1, 2000, pp. A1, A13.

[5] A number of excellent theoretical and research articles and books have examined both corporate and national cultural differences on mergers and acquisitions. A few of them are S. Cartwright and C. L. Cooper, *Managing Mergers, Acquisitions and Strategic Alliances: Integrating People and Cultures*, Oxford: Butterworth-Heinemann, 1996; R. Greenwood, C. R. Hinings, and J. Brown, "Merging professional service firms," *Organization Science*, Vol. 5, No. 2, 1994, pp. 239–257; M. R. Lubatkin, R. Calori, P. Very, and J. Veiga, "Managing mergers across borders: A two-nation exploration of a nationally bound administrative heritage, *Organization Science*, Vol. 9, No. 6, 1998, pp. 670-684; M.L. Marks and P.H. Mirvis, *Joining Forces*, San Francisco: Jossey-Bass, 1998; A. Mayo and T. Hadaway, "Cultural adaptation—the ICL-Nokia-Data merger 1991-92," *Journal of Management Development*, Vol. 13, No. 2, 1994, pp. 59-71; P. Morosini, S. Shane, and H. Singh,"National cultural distance and cross-border acquisition performance," *Journal of International Business Studies*, Vol. 29, No.1, 1998, pp. 137-158; A. Nahavandi and A.R. Malekzedah, "Acculturation in mergers and acquisitions," *Academy of Management Review*, Vol. 13, 1988, pp. 79-90; R. Olie, "Shades of culture and institutions in international mergers," *Organization Studies*, Vol. 15, No. 3, 1994, pp. 381–405; A. L. Sales and P. H. Mirvis, "When cultures collide: Issues in acquisition," in J. R. Kimberly and R. E. Quinn (Eds.), *Managing Organizational Transitions*, Homewood, IL: Irwin, 1985, pp. 107–133; P. M. Very, M. Lubatkin, and R. Calori, "A cross-national assessment of acculturative stress in recent European mergers," *International Studies of Management & Organizations*, Vol. 26, No. 1, 1996, pp. 59–86; and Y. Weber, O. Shenkar, and A. Raveh, "National and corporate cultural fit in mergers/acquisitions: An exploratory study," *Management Science*, Vol. 42, No. 8, 1996, pp. 1215–1227.

[6] D. M. Schweiger and P. Goulet, "Facilitating cultural learning during an acquisition: A longitudinal field experiment," unpublished paper, 2001.

Chapter 9

[1] For an excellent overview of integrated measurement, see Robert S. Kaplan and David P. Norton, *The Balanced Scorecard*, Boston: Harvard Business School Press, 1996.

[2] For many of the measures noted, there are well-validated survey instruments and interview and focus group protocols available. I have used a number of them successfully in both research and consulting.

Chapter 10

[1] Unless, of course, we resort to psychological or physical threats. Such control, however, requires the constant presence of the threat and is not a very useful way of managing an organization.

INDEX

Note: Locators in **bold** indicate tables and charts; company names in "quotes" indicate pseudonyms.

About the Author

David M. Schweiger, Ph.D., is the Buck Mickel/Fluor Daniel Professor at the Moore School of Business at the University of South Carolina, adjunct professor at EM Lyon in France, and president of the strategic management consulting firm Schweiger and Associates. He has assisted executives of numerous companies in successfully managing the M&A integration process. The coauthor of *Strategic Management Skills,* Dr. Schweiger is the international strategic management editor of *Journal of World Business.* His work has been widely published in professional journals, including *Strategic Management Journal, Academy of Management Journal, Human Resource Planning,* and *Organizational Dynamics.*